MW00988065

Theodicy

Theodicy

Essays on
the Goodness of God
the Freedom of Man and
the Origin of Evil

G. W. LEIBNIZ

Edited with an Introduction
by Austin Farrer, Fellow of Trinity College, Oxford

Translated by E. M. Huggard from C. J. Gerhardt's Edition
of the Collected Philosophical Works, 1875-90

Open ❖ Court
La Salle, Illinois   61301

OPEN COURT and the above logo are registered in the U.S. Patent &
Trademark Office.

Published 1985 by Open Court Publishing Company, Peru, Illinois 61354.
This edition first published 1951 by Routledge & Kegan Paul Limited,
London.
Second printing 1988
Third printing 1990
Fourth printing 1993

Printed and bound in the United States of America.

Library of Congress Cataloging in Publication Data

Leibniz, Gottfried Wilhelm, Freiherr von, 1646–1716.
    Theodicy: essays on the goodness of God, the
freedom of man, and the origin of evil.

    Translation of: Essais de théodicée.
    Includes index.
    1. Theodicy—Early works to 1800. I. Title.
B2590.E5   1985   231'.8   85-8833
ISBN 0-87548-437-9

CONTENTS

APPENDICES

EDITOR'S
INTRODUCTION

I

LEIBNIZ was above all things a metaphysician. That does not mean that his head was in the clouds, or that the particular sciences lacked interest for him. Not at all—he felt a lively concern for theological debate, he was a mathematician of the first rank, he made original contributions to physics, he gave a realistic attention to moral psychology. But he was incapable of looking at the objects of any special enquiry without seeing them as aspects or parts of one intelligible universe. He strove constantly after system, and the instrument on which his effort relied was the speculative reason. He embodied in an extreme form the spirit of his age. Nothing could be less like the spirit of ours. To many people now alive metaphysics means a body of wild and meaningless assertions resting on spurious argument. A professor of metaphysics may nowadays be held to deal handsomely with the duties of his chair if he is prepared to handle metaphysical statements at all, though it be only for the purpose of getting rid of them, by showing them up as confused forms of something else. A chair in metaphysical philosophy becomes analogous to a chair in tropical diseases : what is taught from it is not the propagation but the cure.

Confidence in metaphysical construction has ebbed and flowed through philosophical history; periods of speculation have been followed by periods of criticism. The tide will flow again, but it has not turned yet, and such metaphysicians as survive scarcely venture further than to argue a case for the possibility of their art. It would be an embarrassing task to open an approach to Leibnitian metaphysics from the present metaphysical position, if there is a present position. If we want an agreed starting-point, it will have to be historical.

The historical importance of Leibniz's ideas is anyhow unmistakable. If metaphysical thinking is nonsensical, its empire over the human imagination must still be confessed; if it is as chimerical a science as alchemy, it is no less fertile in by-products of importance. And if we are to consider Leibniz historically, we cannot do better than take up his *Theodicy*, for two reasons. It was the only one of his main philosophical works to be published in his lifetime, so that it was a principal means of his direct influence; the Leibniz his own age knew was the Leibniz of the *Theodicy*. Then in the second place, the *Theodicy* itself is peculiarly rich in historical material. It reflects the world of men and books which Leibniz knew; it expresses the theological setting of metaphysical speculation which still predominated in the first years of the eighteenth century.

Leibniz is remembered for his philosophy; he was not a professional philosopher. He was offered academic chairs, but he declined them. He was a gentleman, a person of means, librarian to a reigning prince, and frequently employed in state affairs of trust and importance. The librarian might at any moment become the political secretary, and offer his own contributions to policy. Leibniz was for the greater part of his active life the learned and confidential servant of the House of Brunswick; when the Duke had nothing better to do with him, he set him to research into ducal history. If Leibniz had a profession in literature, it was history rather than philosophy. He was even more closely bound to the interests of his prince than John Locke was to those of the Prince of Orange. The Houses of Orange and of Brunswick were on the same side in the principal contest which divided Europe, the battle between Louis XIV and his enemies. It was a turning-point of the struggle when the Prince of Orange supplanted Louis's Stuart friends on the English throne. It was a continuation of the same movement, when Leibniz's master, George I, succeeded to the same throne, and frustrated the restoration of the Stuart heir. Locke returned to England in the wake of the Prince of Orange, and became the representative thinker of the régime. Leibniz wished to come to the English court of George I, but was unkindly ordered to attend to the duties of his librarianship. So he remained in Hanover. He was then an old man, and before the tide of favour had turned, he died.

Posterity has reckoned Locke and Leibniz the heads of rival sects, but politically they were on the same side. As against Louis's political absolutism and enforced religious uniformity, both championed religious toleration and the freedom of the mind. Their theological liberalism was political prudence; it was not necessarily for that reason the less personally sincere. They had too much wisdom to meet bigotry with bigotry, or set Protestant intolerance against Catholic absolutism. But they had too much sympathy with the spirit of Europe to react into free thinking or to make a frontal attack on revealed truth. They took their stand on a fundamental Christian theism, the common religion of all good men; they repudiated the negative enormities of Hobbes and Spinoza.

The Christian was to hold a position covered by three lines of defences. The base line was to be the substance of Christian theism and of Christian morals, and it was to be held by the forces of sheer reason, without aid from scriptural revelation. The middle line was laid down by the general sense of Scripture, and the defence of it was this. 'Scriptural doctrine is reconcilable with the findings of sheer reason, but it goes beyond them. We believe the Scriptures, because they are authenticated by marks of supernatural intervention in the circumstances of their origin. We believe them, but reason controls our interpretation of them.' There remained the most forward and the most hazardous line: the special positions which a Church, a sect, or an individual might found upon the scriptural revelation. A prudent man would not hold his advance positions in the same force or defend them with the same obstinacy as either of the lines behind them. He could argue for them, but he could not require assent to them.

One cannot help feeling, indeed, the readiness of these writers to fall back, not only from the front line to the middle line, but from the middle line itself to the base line. Leibniz, for example, writes with perfect seriousness and decency about the Christian scheme of redemption, but it hardly looks like being for him a crucial deliverance from perdition. It is not the intervention of Mercy, by which alone He possesses himself of us : it is one of the ways in which supreme Benevolence carries out a cosmic policy ; and God's benevolence is known by pure reason, and apart from Christian revelation. In one politically important particular the theological attitude of Leibniz differed from that of Locke. Both stood for toleration and for the minimizing of the differences between the sects. This was a serious enough matter in England, but it was an even more serious matter in Germany. For Germany was divided between Catholics and Protestants ; effective toleration must embrace them both. English toleration might indulge a harmless Catholic minority, while rejecting the Catholic régime as the embodiment of intolerance. But this was not practical politics on the Continent ; you must tolerate Catholicism on an equal footing, and come to terms with Catholic régimes. Leibniz was not going to damn the Pope with true Protestant fervour. It was his consistent aim to show that his theological principles were as serviceable to Catholic thinkers as to the doctors of his own church. On some points, indeed, he found his most solid support from Catholics ; in other places there are hints of a joint Catholic-Lutheran front against Calvinism. But on the whole Leibniz's writings suggest that the important decisions cut across all the Churches, and not between them.

Leibniz was impelled to a compromise with 'popery', not only by the religious divisions of Germany, but (at one stage) by the political weakness of the German Protestant States. At the point of Louis XIV's highest success, the Protestant princes had no hope but in Catholic Austria, and Austria was distracted by Turkish pressure in the rear. Leibniz hoped to relieve the situation by preaching a crusade. Could not the Christian princes sink their differences and unite against the infidel? And could not the Christian alliance be cemented by theological agreement? Hence Leibniz's famous negotiation with Bossuet for a basis of Catholic-Lutheran concord. It was plainly destined to fail ; and it was bound to recoil upon its author. How could he be a true Protestant who treated the differences with the Catholics as non-essentials? How could he have touched pitch and taken no defilement? Leibniz was generally admired, but he was not widely trusted. As a mere politician, he may be judged to have over-reached himself.

It has been the object of the preceding paragraphs to show that

Leibniz the politician and Leibniz the theologian were one and the same person; not at all to suggest that his rational theology was just political expediency. We may apply to him a parody of his own doctrine, the pre-established harmony between nature and grace. Everything happens as though Leibniz were a liberal politician, and his theology expressed his politics. Yes, but equally, everything happens as though Leibniz were a philosophical theologian, and his politics expressed his theology. His appreciation of Catholic speculation was natural and sincere; his dogmatic ancestry is to be looked for in Thomism and Catholic humanism as much as anywhere. Above all, he had himself a liberal and generous mind. It gave him pleasure to appreciate good wherever he could see it, and to discover a soul of truth in every opinion.

From the moment when Leibniz became aware of himself as an independent thinker, he was the man of a doctrine. Sometimes he called it 'my principles', sometimes 'the new system', sometimes 'pre-established harmony'. It could be quite briefly expressed; he was always ready to oblige his friends with a summary statement, either in a letter or an enclosed memorandum, and several such have come down to us. The doctrine may have been in Leibniz's view simple, but it was applicable to every department of human speculation or enquiry. It provided a new alphabet of philosophical ideas, and everything in heaven and earth could be expressed in it; not only could be, but ought to be, and Leibniz showed tireless energy in working out restatements of standing problems.

As a man with an idea, with a philosophical nostrum, Leibniz may be compared to Bishop Berkeley. There was never any more doubt that Leibniz was a Leibnitian than that Berkeley was a Berkeleian. But there is no comparison between the two men in the width of their range. About many things Berkeley never took the trouble to Berkeleianize. To take the most surprising instance of his neglect—he assured the world that his whole doctrine pointed to, and hung upon, theology. But what sort of a theology? He scarcely took the first steps in the formulation of it. He preferred to keep on defending and explaining his *esse est percipi*. With Leibniz it is wholly different; he carries his new torch into every corner, to illuminate the dark questions.

The wide applicability of pre-established harmony might come home to its inventor as a rich surprise. The reflective historian will find it less surprising, for he will suspect that the applications were in view from the start. What was Leibniz thinking of when the new principle flashed upon him? What was he *not* thinking of? He had a many-sided mind. If the origins of the principle were complex, little wonder that its applications were manifold. Every expositor of Leibniz who does not wish to be endlessly tedious must concentrate attention on one aspect of Leibniz's principle, and one source of its origin. We will here give an account of the matter which, we trust, will go most directly to the heart of it, but we will make no claims to sufficient interpretation of Leibniz's thought-processes.

Leibniz, then, like all the philosophers of the seventeenth century, was reforming scholasticism in the light of a new physical science. The science was mathematical in its form, mechanistical in its doctrine, and unanswerable in its evidence—it got results. But it was metaphysically intractable, and the doctrines of infinite and finite substance which it generated furnish a gallery of metaphysical grotesques; unless we are to except Leibniz; his system is, if nothing else, a miracle of ingenuity, and there are moments when we are in danger of believing it.

It is a natural mistake for the student of seventeenth-century thought to underestimate the tenacity of scholastic Aristotelianism. Descartes, we all know, was reared in it, but then Descartes overthrew it; and he had done his work and died by the time that Leibniz was of an age to philosophize at all. We expect to see Leibniz starting on his shoulders and climbing on from there. We are disappointed. Leibniz himself tells us that he was raised in the scholastic teaching. His acquaintance with Descartes's opinions was second-hand, and they were retailed to him only that they might be derided. He agreed, like an amiable youth, with his preceptors.

The next phase of his development gave him a direct knowledge of Cartesian writings, and of other modern books beside, such as those of the atomist Gassendi. He was delighted with what he read, because of its fertility in the field of physics and mathematics; and for a short time he was an enthusiastic modern. But presently he became dissatisfied. The new systems did not go far enough, they were still scientifically inadequate. At the same time they went too far, and carried metaphysical paradox beyond the limits of human credulity.

There is no mystery about Leibniz's scientific objections to the new philosophers. If he condemned them here, it was on the basis of scientific thought and observation. Descartes's formulation of the laws of motion could, for example, be refuted by physical experiment; and if his general view of physical nature was bound up with it, then so much the worse for the Cartesian philosophy. But whence came Leibniz's more strictly metaphysical objections? Where had he learned that standard of metaphysical adequacy which showed up the inadequacy of the new metaphysicians? His own disciples might be satisfied to reply, that he learnt it from Reason herself; but the answer will not pass with us. Leibniz reasoned, indeed, but he did not reason from nowhere, nor would he have got anywhere if he had. His conception of metaphysical reason was what his early scholastic training had made it.

There are certain absurd opinions which we are sure we have been taught, although, when put to it, we find it hard to name the teacher. Among them is something of this sort. 'Leibniz was a scholarly and sympathetic thinker. He had more sense of history than his contemporaries, and he was instinctively eclectic. He believed he could learn something from each of his great predecessors. We see him reaching back to cull a notion from Plato or from Aristotle; he even found something of use in the scholastics. In particular, he picked out the Aristotelian "entelechy" to stop a gap in the philosophy of his own age.' What this form of statement ignores is that Leibniz *was* a scholastic: a scholastic endeavouring, like Descartes before him, to revolutionize scholasticism. The word 'entelechy' was, indeed, a piece of antiquity which Leibniz revived, but the thing for which it stood was the most familiar of current scholastic conceptions. 'Entelechy' means active principle of wholeness or completion in an individual thing. Scholasticism was content to talk about it under the name of 'substantial form' or 'formal cause'. But the scholastic interpretation of the idea was hopelessly discredited by the new science, and the scholastic terms shared the discredit of scholastic doctrine. Leibniz wanted a term with a more general sound. 'There is an X', he wanted to say, 'which scholasticism has defined as substantial form, but I am going to give a new definition of it.' Entelechy was a useful name for X, the more so as it had the authority of Aristotle, the master of scholasticism.

Under the name of entelechy Leibniz was upholding the soul of scholastic doctrine, while retrenching the limbs and outward flourishes. The doctrine of substantial form which he learnt in his youth had had *something* in it; he could not settle down in the principles of Descartes or of Gassendi, because both ignored this vital *something*. Since the requirements of a new science would not allow a return to sheer scholasticism, it was necessary to find a fresh philosophy, in which entelechy and mechanism might be accommodated side by side.

If one had asked any 'modern' of the seventeenth century to name the 'ancient' doctrine he most abominated, he would most likely have replied, 'Substantial form'. Let us recall what was rejected under this name, and why.

The medieval account of physical nature had been dominated by what we may call common-sense biology. Biology, indeed, is the science of the living, and the medievals were no more inclined than we are to endow all physical bodies with life. What they did do was to take living bodies as typical, and to treat other bodies as imperfectly analogous to them. Such an approach was *a priori* reasonable enough. For we may be expected to know best the physical being closest to our own; and we, at any rate, are alive. Why not argue from the better known to the less known, from the nearer to the more remote, interpreting other things by the formula of our own being, and allowing whatever discount is necessary for their degree of unlikeness to us?

Common-sense biology reasons as follows. In a living body there is a certain pattern of organized parts, a certain rhythm of successive motions, and a certain range of characteristic activities. The pattern, the sheer anatomy, is basic; but it cannot long continue to exist (outside a refrigerator) without accompanying vital rhythms in heart, respiration and digestion. Nor do these perform their parts without the intermittent support of variable but still characteristic activities: dogs not only breathe and digest, they run about, hunt their food, look for mates, bark at cats, and so on. The anatomical pattern, the vital rhythm, and the characteristic acts together express dogginess; they reveal the specific form of the dog. They *reveal* it; exactly what the specific form *consisted in* was the subject of much medieval speculation. It need not concern us here.

Taking the form of the species for granted, common-sense biology proceeds to ask how it comes to be in a given instance, say in the dog Toby. Before this dog was born or thought of, his form or species was displayed in each of his parents. And now it looks as though the form of dog had detached itself from them through the generative act, and set up anew on its own account. How does it do that? By getting hold of some materials in which to express itself. At first it takes them from the body of the mother, afterwards it collects them from a wider environment, and what the dog eats becomes the dog.

What, then, is the relation of the assimilated materials to the dog-form which assimilates them? Before assimilation, they have their own form. Before the dog eats the leg of mutton, it has the form given to it by its place in the body of a sheep. What happens to the mutton? Is it without remainder transubstantiated from sheep into dog? It loses all its distinctively sheep-like character-istics, but there may be some more basically material character-istics which it preserves. They underlay the structure of the mutton, and they continue to underlie the structure of the dog's flesh which supplants it. Whatever these characteristics may be, let us call them common material characteristics, and let us say that they belong to or compose a common material nature.

The common material nature has its own way of existing, and perhaps its own principles of physical action. We may suppose that we know much or that we know little about it. This one thing at least we know, that it is capable of becoming alternatively either mutton or dog's flesh. It is not essential to it to be mutton, or mutton it would always be; nor dog's flesh, or it would always be dog's flesh. It is capable of becoming either, according as it is captured by one or other system of formal organization. So the voters who are to go to the polls are, by their common nature, Englishmen; they are essentially neither Socialist curs nor Con-servative sheep, but intrinsically capable of becoming either, if they become captured by either system of party organization.

According to this way of thinking, there is a certain *looseness* about the relation of the common material nature to the higher forms of organization capable of capturing it. Considered in itself alone, it is perhaps to be seen as governed by absolutely deter-mined laws of its own. It is heavy, then it will fall unless ob-structed; it is solid, then it will resist intrusions. But considered as material for organization by higher forms, it is indeterminate. It acts in one sort of way under the persuasion of the sheep-form, and in another sort of way under the persuasion of the dog-form, and we cannot tell how it will act until we know which form is going to capture it. No amount of study bestowed on the common material nature will enable us to judge how it will behave under the persuasion of the higher organizing form. The only way to discover that is to examine the higher form itself.

Every form, then, will really be the object of a distinct science. The form of the sheep and the form of the dog have much in common, but that merely happens to be so; we cannot depend upon it, or risk inferences from sheep to dog: we must examine each in itself; we shall really need a science of probatology about sheep, and cynology about dogs. Again, the common material nature has its own principles of being and action, so it will need a science of itself, which we may call hylology. Each of these sciences is mistress in her own province; but how many there are, and how puzzlingly they overlap! So long as we remain within the province of a single science, we may be able to think rigorously, everything will be 'tight'. But as soon as we consider border-issues between one province and another, farewell to exactitude: everything will be 'loose'. We can think out hylology till we are blue in the face, but we shall never discover anything about the entry of material elements into higher organizations, or how they behave when they get there. We may form perfect definitions and descriptions of the form of the dog as such, and still derive no rules for telling what elements of matter will enter into the body of a given dog or how they will be placed when they do. All we can be sure of is, that the dog-form will keep itself going in, and by means of, the material it embodies—unless the dog dies. But what happens to the matter in the body of the dog is 'accidental' to the nature of the matter; and the use of this matter, rather than of some other equally suitable, is accidental to the nature of the dog.

No account of material events can dispense with accidental relations altogether. We must at least recognize that there are accidental relations between particular things. Accident in the sense of brute fact had to be acknowledged even by the tidiest and most dogmatic atomism of the last century. That atomism must allow it to be accidental, in this sense, that the space surrounding any given atom was occupied by other atoms in a given manner. It belonged neither to the nature of space to be occupied by just those atoms in just those places, nor to the nature of the atoms to be distributed just like that over space; and so in a certain sense the environment of any atom was an accidental environment. That is, the particular arrangement of the environment was accidental. The nature of the environment was not accidental at all. It was proper to the nature of the atom to be in interaction with other atoms over a spatial field, and it never encountered in the fellow-denizens of space any other nature but its own. It was not subject to the accident of meeting strange natures, nor of becoming suddenly subject to strange or unequal laws of interaction. All interactions, being with its own kind, were reciprocal and obedient to a single set of calculable laws.

But the medieval philosophy had asserted accidental relations between distinct sorts of *natures*, the form of living dog and the form of dead matter, for example. No one could know *a priori* what effect an accidental relation would produce, and all accidental relations between different pairs of natures were different: at the most there was analogy between them. Every different nature had to be separately observed, and when you had observed them all, you could still simply write an inventory of them, you could not hope to rationalize your body of knowledge. Let us narrow the field and consider what this doctrine allows us to know about the wood of a certain kind of tree. We shall begin by observing the impressions it makes on our several senses, and we shall attribute to it a substantial form such as naturally to give rise to these impressions, without, perhaps, being so rash as to claim a knowledge of what this substantial form is. Still we do not know what its capacities of physical action and passion may be. We shall find them out by observing it in relation to different 'natures'. It turns out to be combustible by fire, resistant to water, tractable to the carpenter's tools, intractable to his digestive organs, harmless to ostriches, nourishing to wood-beetles. Each of these capacities of the wood is distinct; we cannot relate them intelligibly to one another, nor deduce them from the assumed fundamental 'woodiness'.

We can now see why 'substantial forms' were the *bêtes noires* of the seventeenth-century philosophers. It was because they turned nature into an unmanageable jungle, in which trees, bushes, and parasites of a thousand kinds wildly interlaced. There was nothing for it, if science was to proceed, but to clear the ground and replant with spruce in rows: to postulate a single uniform nature, of which there should be a single science. Now neither probatology

nor cynology could hope to be universal—the world is not all
sheep nor all dog: it would have to be hylology; for the world is,
in its spatial aspect, all material. Let us say, then, that there is one
uniform material nature of things, and that everything else consists in the arrangements of the basic material nature; as the show
of towers and mountains in the sunset results simply from an
arrangement of vapours. And let us suppose that the interactions of
the parts of matter are all like those which we can observe in dead
manipulable bodies—in mechanism, in fact. Such was the postulate of the new philosophers, and it yielded them results.

It yielded them results, and that was highly gratifying. But
what, meanwhile, had happened to those palpable facts of common experience from which the whole philosophy of substantial
forms had taken its rise? Is the wholeness of a living thing the
mere resultant of the orderly operations of its parts? Is a bee no
more essentially one than a swarm is? Is the life of a living animal
indistinguishable from the rhythm of a going watch, except in
degree of complication and subtlety of contrivance? And if an
animal's body, say my own, is simply an agglomerate of minute
interacting material units, and its wholeness is merely accidental
and apparent, how is my conscious mind to be adjusted to it?
For my consciousness appears to identify itself with that whole
vital pattern which used to be called the substantial form. We
are now told that the pattern is nothing real or active, but the
mere accidental resultant of distinct interacting forces: it does no
work, it exercises no influence or control, it *is* nothing. How then
can it be the vehicle and instrument of my conscious soul? It
cannot. Then is my soul homeless? Or is it to be identified with
the activity and fortunes of a single atomic constituent of my
body, a single cog in the animal clockwork? If so, how irrational!
For the soul does not experience itself as the soul of one minute
part, but as the soul of the body.

Such questions rose thick and fast in the minds of the seventeenth-century philosophers. It will cause us no great surprise that
Leibniz should have quickly felt that the Formal Principle of
Aristotle and of the Scholastic philosophy must be by hook
or by crook reintroduced—not as the detested *substantial form*,
but under a name by which it might hope to smell more sweet,
entelechy.

Nothing so tellingly revealed the difficulties of the new philosophy in dealing with living bodies as the insufficiency of the solutions Descartes had proposed. He had boldly declared the unity of animal life to be purely mechanical, and denied that brutes had souls at all, or any sensation. He had to admit soul in man, but he still denied the substantial unity of the human body. It was put together like a watch, it was many things, not one: if Descartes had lived in our time, he would have been delighted to compare it with a telephone system, the nerves taking the place of the wires, and being so arranged that all currents of 'animal spirit' flowing in them converged upon a single unit, a gland at the base of the brain. In this unit, or in the convergence of all the motions upon it, the 'unity' of the body virtually consisted; and the soul was incarnate, not in the plurality of members (for how could it, being one, indwell many things?), but in the single gland.

Even so, the relation between the soul and the gland was absolutely unintelligible, as Descartes disarmingly confessed. Incarnation was all very well in the old philosophy: those who had allowed the interaction of disparate natures throughout the physical world need find no particular difficulty about the special case of it provided by incarnation. Why should not a form of conscious life so interact with what would otherwise be dead matter as to 'indwell' it? But the very principle of the new philosophy disallowed the interaction of disparate natures, because such an interaction did not allow of exact formulation, it was a 'loose' and not a 'tight' relation.

From a purely practical point of view the much derided pineal gland theory would serve. If we could be content to view Descartes as a man who wanted to make the world safe for physical science, then there would be a good deal to be said for his doctrine. In the old philosophy exact science had been frustrated by the hypothesis of loose relations all over the field of nature. Descartes had cleared them from as much of the field as science was then in a position to investigate; he allowed only one such relation to subsist, the one which experience appeared unmistakably to force upon us—that between our own mind and its bodily vehicle. He had exorcized the spirits from the rest of nature; and though there was a spirit here which could not be exorcized, the philosophic conjurer had nevertheless confined it and its unaccountable pranks within a minutely narrow magic circle: all mind could do was to turn the one tiny switch at the centre of its animal telephone system. It could create no energy—it could merely redirect the currents actually flowing. Practically this might do, but speculatively it was most disturbing. For if the 'loose relation' had to be admitted in one instance, it was admitted in principle; and one could not get rid of the suspicion that it would turn up elsewhere, and that the banishment of it from every other field represented a convenient pragmatic postulate rather than a solid metaphysical truth. Moreover, the correlation of the unitary soul with the unitary gland might do justice to a mechanistical philosophy, but it did not do justice to the soul's own consciousness of itself. The soul's consciousness is the 'idea' or 'representation' of the life of the whole body, certainly not of the life of the pineal gland nor, as the unreflective nowadays would say, of the brain. I am not conscious in, or of, my brain except when I have a headache; consciousness is in my eyes and finger-tips and so on. It is physically true, no doubt, that consciousness in and of my finger-tips is not possible without the functioning of my brain; but that is a poor reason for locating the consciousness in the brain. The filament of the electric bulb will not be incandescent apart from the functioning of the dynamo; but that is a poor reason for saying that the incandescence is in the dynamo.

Certainly the area of representation in our mind is not simply equivalent to the area of our body. But in so far as the confines of mental representation part company with the confines of the body, it is not that they may contract and fall back upon the pineal gland, but that they may expand and advance over the surrounding world. The mind does not represent its own body merely, it represents the world in so far as the world affects that body or is physically reproduced in it. The mind has no observable natural relation to the pineal gland. It has only two natural relations: to its body as a whole and to its effective environment. What Descartes had really done was to pretend that the soul was related to the pineal gland as it is in fact related to its whole body; and then that it was related to the bodily members as in fact it is related to outer environment. The members became an inner environment, known only in so far as they affected the pineal gland; just as the outer environment in its turn was to be known only in so far as it affected the members.

This doctrine of a double environment was wholly artificial. It was forced on Descartes by the requirements of mechanistical science: if the members were simply a plurality of things, they must really be parts of environment; the body which the soul indwelt must be *a* body; presumably, then, the pineal gland. An untenable compromise, surely, between admitting and denying the reality of the soul's incarnation.

What, then, was to be done? Descartes's rivals and successors attempted several solutions, which it would be too long to examine here. They dissatisfied Leibniz and they have certainly no less dissatisfied posterity. It will be enough for us here to consider what Leibniz did. He admitted, to begin with, the psychological fact. The unity of consciousness is the representation of a plurality— the plurality of the members, and through them the plurality of the world. Here, surely, was the very principle the new philosophy needed for the reconciliation of substantial unity with mechanical plurality of parts. For it is directly evident to us that consciousness focuses the plurality of environing things in a unity of representation. This is no philosophical theory, it is a simple fact. Our body, then, as a physical system is a mechanical plurality; as focused in consciousness it is a unity of 'idea'.

Very well: but we have not got far yet. For the old difficulty still remains—it is purely arbitrary, after all, that a unitary consciousness should be attached to, and represent, a mechanical collection of things which happen to interact in a sort of pattern. If there is a consciousness attached to human bodies, then why not to systems of clockwork? If the body is *represented* as unity, it must surely be because it *is* unity, as the old philosophy had held. But how can we reintroduce unity into the body without reintroducing substantial form, and destroying the mechanistical plurality which the new science demanded?

It is at this point that Leibniz produces the speculative postulate of his system. Why not reverse the relation, and make the members represent the mind as the mind represents the members? For then the unity of person represented in the mind will become something actual in the members also.

Representation appears to common sense to be a one-way sort of traffic. If my mind represents my bodily members, something happens to my mind, for it becomes a representation of such members in such a state; but nothing happens to the members by their being so represented in the mind. The mental representation obeys the bodily facts; the bodily facts do not obey the mental representation. It seems nonsense to say that my members obey my mind *because* they are mirrored in it. And yet my members do obey my mind, or at least common sense supposes so. Sometimes my mind, instead of representing the state my members are in, represents a state which it intends that they shall be in, for example, that my hand should go through the motion of writing these words. And my hand obeys; its action becomes the moving diagram of my thought, my thought is represented or expressed in the manual act. Here the relation of mind and members appears to be reversed: instead of its representing them, they represent it. With this representation it is the opposite of what it was with the other. By the members' being represented in the mind, something happened to the mind, and nothing to the members; by the mind's being represented in the members something happens to the members and nothing to the mind.

Why should not we take this seriously? Why not allow that there is two-way traffic—by one relation the mind represents the members, by another the members represent the mind? But then again, how can we take it seriously? For representation, in the required sense, is a mental act; brute matter can represent nothing, only mind can represent. And the members are brute matter. But are they? How do we know that? By brute matter we understand extended lumps of stuff, interacting with one another mechanically, as do, for example, two cogs in a piece of clockwork. But this is a large-scale view. The cogs are themselves composed of interrelated parts and those parts of others, and so on *ad infinitum*. Who knows what the ultimate constituents really are? The 'modern' philosophers, certainly, have proposed no hypothesis about them which even looks like making sense. They have supposed that the apparently inert lumps, the cogs, are composed of parts themselves equally inert, and that by subdivision we shall still reach nothing but the inert. But this supposition is in flat contradiction with what physical theory demands. We have to allow the reality of *force* in physics. Now the force which large-scale bodies display may easily be the block-effect of activity in their minute real constituents. If not, where does it come from? Let it be supposed, then, that these minute real constituents are active because they are alive, because they are minds; for indeed we have no notion of activity other than the perception we have of our own. We have no notion of it except as something mental. On the hypothesis that the constituents of active body are also mental, this limitation in our conception of activity need cause us neither sorrow nor surprise.

The mind-units which make up body will not of course be developed and fully conscious minds like yours or mine, and it is only for want of a better word that we call them minds at all. They will be mere unselfconscious representations of their physical environment, as it might be seen from the physical point to which they belong by a human mind paying no attention at all to its own seeing. How many of these rudimentary 'minds' will there be in my body? As many as you like—as many as it is possible there should be—say an infinite number and have done with it.

We may now observe how this hypothesis introduces real formal unity without prejudicing mechanical plurality. Each of the mind-units in my body is itself and substantially distinct. But since each, in its own way and according to its own position, represents the superior and more developed mind which I call 'me', they will order themselves according to a common form. The order is real, not accidental: it is like the order of troops on a parade-ground. Each man is a distinct active unit, but each is really expressing by his action the mind of the officer in command. He is expressing no less his relation to the other men in the ranks—to obey the officer is to keep in step with them. So the metaphysical units of the body, being all minds, represent one another as well as the dominant mind: one another co-ordinately, the dominant mind subordinately.

But if the metaphysically real units of the body are of the nature of mind, then *the* mind is a mind among minds, a spirit-atom among spirit-atoms. What then constitutes its superiority or dominance, and makes it a mind *par excellence*? Well, what constitutes the officer an officer? Two things: a more developed mentality and the fact of being obeyed. In military life these two factors are not always perfectly proportioned to one another, but in the order of Leibniz's universe they are. A fuller power to represent the universe is necessarily combined with dominance over an organized troop of members; for the mind knows the universe only in so far as the universe is expressed in its body.

That is what the *finitude* of the mind means. Only an infinite mind appreciates the whole plurality of things in themselves; a finite mind perceives them in so far as mirrored in the physical being of an organized body of members. The more adequate the mirror, the more adequate the representation: the more highly organized the body, the more developed the mind.

The developed mind has an elaborate body; but the least developed mind has still some body, or it would lack any mirror whatever through which to represent the world. This means, in effect, that Leibniz's system is not an unmitigated spiritual atomism. For though the spiritual atoms, or monads, are the ultimate constituents out of which nature is composed, they stand composed together from the beginning in a minimal order which cannot be broken up. Each monad, if it is to be anything at all, must be a continuing finite representation of the universe, and to be that it must have a body, that is to say, it must have other monads in a permanent relation of mutual correspondence with it. And if you said to Leibniz, 'But surely any physical body can be broken up, and this must mean the dissolution of the organic relation between its monadical constituents,' he would take refuge in the infinitesimal. The wonders revealed by that new miracle, the microscope, suggested what the intrinsic divisibility of space itself suggests—whatever organization is broken up, there will still be a minute organization within each of the fragments which remains unbroken—and so *ad infinitum*. You will never come down to loose monads, monads out of all organization. You will never disembody the monads, and so remove their representative power; you will only reduce their bodies and so impoverish their representative power. In this sense no animal dies and no animal is generated. Death is the reduction and generation the enrichment of some existing monad's body; and, by being that, is the enrichment or the reduction of the monad's mental life.

'But,' our common sense protests, 'it is too great a strain on our credulity to make the real nature of things so utterly different from what sense and science make of them. If the real universe is what you say it is, why do our minds represent it to us as they do?' The philosopher's answer is, 'Because they *represent* it. According to the truth of things, each monad is simply its own mental life, its own world-view, its own thoughts and desires. To know things as they are would be simultaneously to live over, as though from within and by a miracle of sympathy, the biographies of an infinite number of distinct monads. This is absolutely impossible. Our senses represent the coexistent families of monads *in the gross*, and therefore conventionally; what is in fact the mutual representation of monads in ordered systems, is represented as the mechanical interaction of spatially extended and material parts.' This does not mean that science is overthrown. The physical world-view is in terms of the convention of representation, but it is not, for all that, illusory. It can, ideally, be made as true as it is capable of being. There is no reason whatever for confusing the 'well-grounded seemings' of the apparent physical world with the fantastic seemings of dream and hallucination.

So far the argument seems to draw whatever cogency it has from the simplicity and naturalness of the notion of representation. The nature of idea, it is assumed, is to represent plurality in a unified view. If idea did not represent, it would not be idea. And since there *is* idea (for our minds at least exist and are made up of idea) there is representation. It belongs to idea to represent, and since the whole world has now been interpreted as a system of mutually representing ideations, or ideators, it might seem that all their mutual relations are perfectly natural, a harmony of agreement which could not be other than it is. But if so, why does Leibniz keep saying that the harmony is *pre-established*, by special and infinitely elaborate divine decrees?

Leibniz himself says that the very nature of representation excludes interaction. By representing environment a mind does not do anything to environment, that is plain. But it is no less plain that environment does nothing to it, either. The act of representing is simply the act of the mind; it represents *in view of* environment, of course, but not under the causal influence of environment. Representation is a business carried on by the mind on its own account, and in virtue of its innate power to represent.

Very well; but does this consideration really drive us into theology? Is not Leibniz the victim of a familiar fallacy, that of incompletely stated alternatives? '*Either* finite beings interact *or else* they do not directly condition one another. Monads do not interact, therefore they do not directly condition one another. How then explain the actual conformity of their mutual representation, without recourse to divine fore-ordaining?' It seems sufficient to introduce a further alternative in the first line of the argument, and we are rid of the theology. Things may condition the action of a further thing, without acting upon it. It acts of itself, but it acts in view of what they are. We are tempted to conclude that Leibniz has introduced the *Deus ex machina* with the fatal facility of his age. 'Where a little further meditation on the characters in the play would furnish a natural *dénouement*, he swings divine intervention on to the scene by wires from the ceiling. It is easy for us to reconstruct for him the end of the piece without recourse to stage-machines.'

Is it? No, I fear it is not. There is really no avoiding the pre-established harmony. And so we shall discover, if we pursue our train of reflexion a little further. It is natural, we were saying, than an idea should represent an environment; indeed, it *is* the representation of one. Given no environment to represent, it would be empty, a mere capacity for representation. Then every idea or ideator, taken merely in itself, *is* an empty capacity. But of what is the environment of each made up? According to the Leibnitian theory, of further ideas or ideators: of empty capacities, therefore. Then no idea will either be anything in itself, or find anything in its neighbours to represent. An unhappy predicament, like that of a literary clique in which all the members are adepts at discussing one another's ideas—only that unfortunately none of them are provided with any; or like the shaky economics of the fabled Irish village where they all lived by taking in one another's washing.

It is useless, then, to conceive representations as simply coming into existence in response to environment, and modelling them-selves on environment. They must all mutually reflect environ-ment or they would not be representations; but they must also exist as themselves and in their own right or there would be no en-vironment for them mutually to represent. Since the world is in-finitely various, each representor must have its own distinct character or nature, as our minds have: that is to say, it must represent in its own individual way; and all these endlessly various representations must be so constituted as to form a mutually reflecting harmony. Considered as a representation, each monadical existence simply reflects the universe after its own manner. But considered as something to be represented by the others, it is a self-existent mental life, or world of ideas. Now when we are considering the fact of representation, that which is to be represented comes first and the representation follows upon it.

Thus in considering the Leibnitian universe, we must begin with the monads as self-existent mental lives, or worlds of ideas; their representation of one another comes second. Nothing surely, then, but omnipotent creative wisdom could have pre-established between so many distinct given mental worlds that harmony which constitutes their mutual representation.

Our common-sense pluralistic thinking escapes from the need of the pre-established harmony by distinguishing what we are from what we do. Let the world be made up of a plurality of agents in a 'loose' order, with room to manœuvre and to adjust themselves to one another. Then, by good luck or good management, through friction and disaster, by trial and error, by accident or invention, they may work out for themselves a harmony of *action*. There is no need for divine preordaining here. But on Leibniz's view what the monads do is to represent, and what they are is representation; there is no ultimate distinction between what they are and what they do: all that they do belongs to what· they are. The whole system of action in each monad, which fits with such infinite complexity the system of action in each other monad, is precisely the existence of that monad, and apart from it the monad is not. The monads do not *achieve* a harmony, they *are* a harmony, and therefore they are pre-established in harmony.

Leibniz denied that he invoked God to intervene in nature, or that there was anything arbitrary or artificial about his physical theology. He was simply analysing nature and finding it to be a system of mutual representation; he was analysing mutual representation and finding it to be of its nature intrinsically pre-established, and therefore God-dependent. He was not adding anything to mutual representation, he was just showing what it necessarily contained or implied. At least he was doing nothing worse than recognized scholastic practice. Scholastic Aristotelianism explained all natural causality as response to stimulus, and then had to postulate a stimulus which stimulated without being stimulated, and this was God. Apart from this supreme and first stimulus nothing would in fact be moving. The Aristotelians claimed simply to be analysing the nature of physical motion as they perceived it, and to find the necessity of perpetually applied divine stimulation implicit in it. No violence was thereby done to the system of physical motion nor was anything brought in from without to patch it up; it was simply found to be of its own nature God-dependent.

It seems as though the reproachful description '*Deus ex machina*' should be reserved for more arbitrary expedients than Aristotle's or Leibniz's, say for the occasionalist theory. Occasionalism appeared to introduce God that he might make physical matter do what it had no natural tendency to do, viz. to obey the volitions of finite mind. Ideas, on the other hand, have a natural tendency to represent one another, for to be an idea is to be a representation; God is not introduced by Leibniz to make them correspond, he is introduced to work a system in which they shall correspond. This may not be *Deus-ex-machina philosophy*, but it is *physical theology*; that is to say, it treats divine action as one factor among the factors which together constitute the working of the natural system. And this appears to be perhaps unscientific, certainly blasphemous: God's action cannot be a factor among factors; the Creator works through and in all creaturely action equally; we can never say 'This is the creature, and that is God' of distinguishable causalities in the natural world. The creature is, in its creaturely action, self-sufficient: but because a creature, insufficient to itself throughout, and sustained by its Creator both in existence and in action.

The only acceptable argument for theism is that which corresponds to the religious consciousness, and builds upon the insufficiency of finite existence throughout, because it is finite. All arguments to God's existence from a particular gap in our account of the world of finites are to be rejected. They do not indicate God, they indicate the failure of our power to analyse the world-order. When Leibniz discovered that his system of mutual representations needed to be pre-established, he ought to have seen that he had come up a cul-de-sac and backed out; he ought not to have said, 'With the help of God I will leap over the wall.'

If we condemn Leibniz for writing physical theology, we condemn not him but his age. No contemporary practice was any better, and much of it a good deal worse, as Leibniz liked somewhat complacently to point out. And because he comes to theology through physical theology, that does not mean that all his theology was physical theology and as such to be written off. On the contrary, Leibniz is led to wrestle with many problems which beset any philosophical theism of the Christian type. This is particularly so in the *Theodicy*, as its many citations of theologians suggest. His discussions never lack ingenuity, and the system of creation and providence in which they result has much of that luminous serenity which colours the best works of the Age of Reason.

Every theistic philosopher is bound, with whatever cautions, to conceive God by the analogy of the human mind. When Leibniz declares the harmony of monads to be pre-established by God, he is invoking the image of intelligent human pre-arrangement. Nor is he content simply to leave it at that: he endeavours as well as he may to conceive the sort of act by which God pre-arranges; and this involves the detailed adaptation for theological purposes of Leibnitian doctrine about the human mind.

The human mind, as we have seen, is the mind predominant in a certain system of 'minds', viz. in those which constitute the members of the human body. If we call it predominant, we mean that its system of ideas is more developed than theirs, so that there are more points in which each of them conforms to it than in which it conforms to any one of them. The conception of a divine pre-establishing mind will be analogous. It will be the conception of a mind *absolutely* dominant, to whose ideas, that is to say, the whole system simply corresponds, without any reciprocating correspondence on his side. In a certain sense this is to make God the 'Mind of the World'; and yet the associations of the phrase are misleading. It suggests that the world is an organism or body in which the divine mind is incarnate, and on which he relies for his representations. But that is nonsense; the world is not *a* body, nor is it organic to God. Absolute dominance involves absolute transcendence: if everything in the world without remainder simply obeys the divine thoughts, that is only another way of saying that the world is the creature of God; the whole system is pre-established by him who is absolute Being and perfectly independent of the world.

Of createdness, or pre-establishedness, there is no more to be said: we can think of it as nothing but the pure or absolute case of subjection to dominant mind. It is no use asking further *how* God's thoughts are obeyed in the existence and action of things. What we can and must enquire into further, is the nature of the divine thoughts which are thus obeyed. They must be understood to be volitions or decrees. There are indeed two ways in which things obey the divine thought, and correspondingly two sorts of divine thoughts that they obey. In so far as created things conform to the mere universal principles of reason, they obey a reasonableness which is an inherent characteristic of the divine mind itself. If God wills the existence of any creature, that creature's existence must observe the limits prescribed by eternal reason: it cannot, for example, both have and lack a certain characteristic in the same sense and at the same time; nor can it contain two parts and two parts which are not also countable as one part and three parts. Finite things, if they exist at all, must thus conform to the reasonableness of the divine nature, but what the divine reasonableness thus prescribes is highly general: we can deduce from it only certain laws which any finite things must obey, we can never deduce from it which finite things there are to be, nor indeed that there are to be any. Finite things are particular and individual: each of them might have been other than it is or, to speak more properly, instead of any one of them there might have existed something else; it was, according to the mere principles of eternal reason, equally possible. But if so, the whole universe, being made up of things each of which might be otherwise, might as a whole be otherwise. Therefore the divine thoughts which it obeys by existing have the nature of *choices* or *decrees*.

What material does the finite mind supply for an analogical picture of the infinite mind making choices or decrees? If we use such language of God, we are using language which has its first and natural application to ourselves. We all of us choose, and those of us who are in authority make decrees. What is to choose? It involves a real freedom in the mind. A finite mind, let us remember, is nothing but a self-operating succession of perceptions, ideas, or representations. With regard to some of our ideas we have no freedom, those, for example, which represent to us our body. We think of them as constituting our given substance. They are sheer datum for us, and so are those reflexions of our environment which they mediate to us. They make up a closely packed and confused mass; they persevere in their being with an obstinate innate force, the spiritual counterpart of the force which we have to recognize in things as physically interpreted. Being real spiritual force, it is quasi-voluntary, and indeed do we not love our own existence and, in a sense, will it in all its necessary circumstances? But if we can be said to will to be ourselves and to enact with native force what our body and its environment makes us, we are merely willing to conform to the conditions of our existence; we are making no choice. When, however, we think freely or perform deliberate acts, there is not only force but choice in our activity. Choice between what? Between alternative possibilities arising out of our situation. And choice in virtue of what? In virtue of the appeal exercised by one alternative as seemingly better.

Can we adapt our scheme of choice to the description of God's creative decrees? We will take the second point in it first: our choice is in virtue of the appeal of the seeming best. Surely the only corrective necessary in applying this to God is the omission of the word 'seeming'. His choice is in virtue of the appeal of the simply best. The other point causes more trouble. We choose between possibilities which arise for us out of our situation in the system of the existing world. But as the world does not exist before God's creative choices, he is in no world-situation, and no alternative possibilities can arise out of it, between which he should have to choose. But if God does not choose between intrinsic possibilities of some kind, his choice becomes something absolutely meaningless to us—it is not a choice at all, it is an arbitrary and unintelligible *fiat*.

Leibniz's solution is this: what are mere possibilities of thought for us are possibilities of action for God. For a human subject, possibilities of action are limited to what arises out of his actual situation, but possibilities for thought are not so limited. I can conceive a world different in many respects from this world, in which, for example, vegetables should be gifted with thought and speech; but I can do nothing towards bringing it about. My imaginary world is practically impossible but speculatively possible, in the sense that it contradicts no single principle of necessary and immutable reason. I, indeed, can explore only a very little way into the region of sheer speculative possibility; God does not explore it, he simply possesses it all: the whole region of the possible is but a part of the content of his infinite mind. So among all possible creatures he chooses the best and creates it.

But the whole realm of the possible is an actual infinity of ideas. Out of the consideration of an infinity of ideas, how can God arrive at a choice? Why not? His mind is not, of course, discursive; he does not successively turn over the leaves of an infinite book of sample worlds, for then he would never come to the end of it. Embracing infinite possibility in the single act of his mind, he settles his will with intuitive immediacy upon the best. The inferior, the monstrous, the absurd is not a wilderness through which he painfully threads his way, it is that from which he immediately turns; his wisdom is his elimination of it.

But in so applying the scheme of choice to God's act, have we not invalidated its application to our own? For if God has chosen the whole form and fabric of the world, he has chosen everything in it, including the choices we shall make. And if our choices have already been chosen for us by God, it would seem to follow that they are not real open choices on our part at all, but are predetermined. And if they are pre-determined, it would seem that they are not really even choices, for a determined choice is not a choice. But if we do not ourselves exercise real choice in any degree, then we have no clue to what any choice would be: and if so, we have no power of conceiving divine choice, either; and so the whole argument cuts its own throat.

There are two possible lines of escape from this predicament. One is to define human choice in such a sense that it allows of predetermination without ceasing to be choice; and this is Leibniz's method, and it can be studied at length in the *Theodicy*. He certainly makes the very best he can of it, and it hardly seems that any of those contemporaries whose views he criticizes was in a position to answer him. The alternative method is to make the most of the negative element involved in all theology. After all, we do not positively or adequately understand the nature of infinite creative will. Perhaps it is precisely the transcendent glory of divine freedom to be able to work infallibly through free instruments. But so mystical a paradox is not the sort of thing we can expect to appeal to a late-seventeenth-century philosopher.

One criticism of Leibniz's argument we cannot refrain from making. He allows himself too easy a triumph when he says that the only alternative to a choice determined by a prevailing inclination towards one proposal is a choice of mere caprice. There is a sort of choice Leibniz never so much as considers and which appears at least to fall quite outside his categories, and that is the sort of choice exercised in artistic creativity. In such choice we freely feel after the shaping of a scheme, we do not arbitrate simply between shaped and given possible schemes. And perhaps some such element enters into all our choices, since our life is to some extent freely designed by ourselves. If so, our minds are even more akin to the divine mind than Leibniz realized. For the sort of choice we are now referring to seems to be an intuitive turning away from an infinite, or at least indefinite, range of less attractive possibility. And such is the nature of the divine creative choice. The consequence of such a line of speculation would be, that the divine mind designs more through us, and less simply for us, than Leibniz allowed: the 'harmony' into which we enter would be no longer simply 'pre-established'. Leibniz, in fact, could have nothing to do with such a suggestion, and he would have found it easy to be ironical about it if his contemporaries had proposed it.

II

Leibniz wrote two books; a considerable number of articles in learned periodicals; and an enormous number of unpublished notes, papers and letters, preserved in the archives of the Electors of Hanover not because of the philosophical significance of some of them, but because of the political importance of most of them. From among this great mass various excerpts of philosophical interest have been made by successive editors of Leibniz's works. It may be that the most profound understanding of his mind is to be derived from some of these pieces, but if we wish to consider the public history of Leibniz, we may set them aside.

Of the two books, one was published, and the other never was. The *New Essays* remained in Leibniz's desk, the *Theodicy* saw the light. And so, to his own and the succeeding generation, Leibniz was known as the author of the *Theodicy*.

The articles in journals form the immediate background to the two books. In 1696 Leibniz heard that a French translation of Locke's *Essay concerning Human Understanding* was being prepared at Amsterdam. He wrote some polite comments on Locke's great work, and published them. He also sent them to Locke, hoping that Locke would write a reply, and that Leibniz's reflexions and Locke's reply might be appended to the projected French translation. But Locke set Leibniz's comments aside. Leibniz, not to be defeated, set to work upon the *New Essays*, in which the whole substance of Locke's book is systematically discussed in dialogue. The *New Essays* were written in 1703. But meanwhile a painful dispute had broken out between Leibniz and the disciples of Locke and Newton, in which the English, and perhaps Newton himself, were much to blame, and Leibniz thought it impolitic to publish his book. It was not issued until long after his death, in the middle of the century.

The discussion with Locke was a failure: Locke would not play, and the book in which the whole controversy was to be systematized never appeared. The discussion with Bayle, on the other hand, was a model of what a discussion should be. Bayle played up tirelessly, and was never embarrassingly profound; he provided just the sort of objections most useful for drawing forth illuminating expositions; he was as good as a fictitious character in a philosophical dialogue. And the book in which the controversy was systematized duly appeared with great éclat.

Here is the history of the controversy. In 1695 Leibniz was forty-nine years old. He had just emerged from a period of close employment under his prince's commands, and he thought fit to try his metaphysical principles upon the polite world and see what would come of it. He therefore published an article in the *Journal des Savants* under the title: 'New System of Nature and of the Communication of Substances, as well as of the Union between Soul and Body'. In the same year Foucher published an article in the *Journal* controverting Leibniz; and in the next year Leibniz replied with an 'Explanation'. A second explanation in the same year appeared in Basnage's *Histoire des Ouvrages des Savants*, in answer to reflexions by the editor. M. Pierre Bayle had all these articles before him when he inserted a note on Leibniz's doctrine in his article on 'Rorarius', in the first edition of his *Historical and Critical Dictionary*. The point of connexion between Rorarius and Leibniz was no more than this, that both held views about the souls of beasts.

Pierre Bayle was the son of a Calvinist pastor, early converted to Catholicism, but recovered to his old faith after a short time. He held academic employments in Switzerland and Holland; he promoted and edited the *Nouvelles de la République des Lettres*, and he produced that extraordinary work the *Historical and Critical Dictionary*. The notices it contains of authors and thinkers are little more than pegs upon which Bayle could hang his philosophical reflexions. He could write an intelligent discussion on any opinion; what he could not do was to reconcile the points of view from which he felt impelled to write upon this author and that. His was not a systematic mind. So far as he had a philosophical opinion, he was a Cartesian; in theology he was an orthodox Calvinist. He could not reconcile his theology with his Cartesianism and he did not try to. He made a merit of the oppositions of faith to reason and reason to itself, so that he could throw himself upon a meritorious and voluntary faith.

There is nothing original in this position. It was characteristic of decadent scholasticism, it squared with Luther's exaggerations about the impotence of reason in fallen man, and Pascal had given his own highly personal twist to it. Bayle has been hailed as a forerunner of Voltairean scepticism. It would be truer to say that a Voltairean sceptic could read Bayle's discussions in his own sense and for his own purposes if he wished. But Bayle was not a sceptic. It is hard to say what he was; his whole position as between faith and reason is hopelessly confused. He was a scholar, a wit, and a philosophical sparring-partner of so perfectly convenient a kind that if we had not evidence of his historical reality, we might have suspected Leibniz of inventing him.

In the first edition of his *Dictionary*, under the article 'Rorarius', Bayle gave a very fair account of Leibniz's doctrine concerning the souls of animals, as it could be collected from his article in the *Journal des Savants*, 27 June 1695. He then proceeded to comment upon it in the following terms:

'There are some things in Mr. Leibniz's hypothesis that are liable to some difficulties, though they show the great extent of his genius. He will have it, for example, that the soul of a dog acts independently of outward bodies; that *it stands upon its own bottom, by a perfect* spontaneity *with respect to itself, and yet with a perfect* conformity *to outward things.* . . . That *its internal perceptions arise from its original constitution, that is to say, the representative constitution (capable of expressing beings outside itself in relation to its organs) which was bestowed upon it from the time of its creation, and makes its individual character* (*Journal des Savants*, 4 July 1695). From whence it results that it would feel hunger and thirst at such and such an hour, though there were not any one body in the universe, and *though nothing should exist but God and that soul.* He has explained (*Histoire des Ouvrages des Savants*, Feb. 1696) his thought by the example of two pendulums that should perfectly agree: that is, he supposes that according to the particular laws which put the soul upon action, it must feel hunger at such an hour; and that according to the particular laws which direct the motion of matter, the body which is united to that soul must be modified at that same hour as it is modified when the soul is hungry. I will forbear preferring this system to that of occasional causes till the learned author has perfected it. I cannot apprehend the connexion of internal and spontaneous actions which would have this effect, that the soul of a dog would feel pain immediately after having felt joy, though it were alone in the universe. I understand why a dog passes immediately from pleasure to pain when, being very hungry and eating a piece of bread, he is suddenly struck with a cudgel. But I cannot apprehend that his soul should be so framed that at the very moment of his being beaten he should feel pain though he were not beaten, and though he should continue to eat bread without any trouble or hindrance. Nor do I see how the spontaneity of that soul should be consistent with the sense of pain, and in general with any unpleasing perceptions.

'Besides, the reason why this learned man does not like the Cartesian system seems to me to be a false supposition; for it cannot be said that the system of occasional causes brings in God acting by a miracle (ibid.), *Deum ex machina*, in the mutual dependency of the body and soul: for since God does only intervene according to general laws, he cannot be said to act in an extraordinary manner. Does the internal and active virtue communicated to the forms of bodies according to M. Leibniz know the train of actions which it is to produce? By no means; for we know by experience that we are ignorant whether we shall have such and such perceptions in an hour's time. It were therefore necessary that the forms should be directed by some internal principle in the production of their acts. But this would be *Deus ex machina*, as much as in the system of occasional causes. In fine, as he supposes with great reason that all souls are simple and indivisible, it cannot be apprehended how they can be compared with a pendulum, that is, how by their original constitution they can diversify their operations by using the spontaneous activity bestowed upon them by their Creator. It may clearly be conceived that a simple being will always act in a uniform manner, if no external cause hinders it. If it were composed of several pieces, as a machine, it would act different ways, because the peculiar activity of each piece might change every moment the progress of others; but how will you find in a simple substance the cause of a change of operation?'

Leibniz published a reply to Bayle in the *Histoire des Ouvrages des Savants* for July 1698. As in all his references to Bayle, he is studiously polite and repays compliment for compliment. The following are perhaps the principal points of his answer.

1. On the example of the dog:

(*a*) How should it of itself change its sentiment, since everything left to itself continues in the state in which it is? Because the state may be a state of *change*, as in a moving body which, unless hindered, continues to move. And such is the nature of simple substances—they continue to evolve steadily.

(*b*) Would it really feel as though beaten if it were not beaten, since Leibniz says that the action of every substance takes place as though nothing existed but God and itself? Leibniz replies that his remark refers to the causality behind an action, not to the reasons for it. The spontaneous action of the dog, which leads to the feeling of pain, is only decreed to be what it is, for the reason that the dog is part of a world of mutually reflecting substances, a world which also includes the cudgel.

(*c*) Why should the dog ever be displeased *spontaneously*? Leibniz distinguishes the spontaneous from the voluntary: many things occur in the mind, of itself, but not chosen by it.

2. On Cartesianism and miracle:

Cartesianism in the form of occasionalism *does* involve miracle, for though God is said by it to act according to laws in conforming body and mind to one another, he thereby causes them to act beyond their natural capacities.

3. On the problem, how can the simple act otherwise than uniformly?

Leibniz distinguishes: some uniform action is monotonous, but some is not. A point moves uniformly in describing a parabola, for it constantly fulfils the formula of the curve. But it does not move monotonously, for the curve constantly varies. Such is the uniformity of the action of simple substances.

Bayle read this reply, and was pleased but not satisfied with it. In the second edition of the dictionary, under the same article 'Rorarius', he added the following note:

'I declare first of all that I am very glad I have proposed some small difficulties against the system of that great philosopher, since they have occasioned some answers whereby that subject has been made clearer to me, and which have given me a more distinct notion of what is most to be admired in it. I look now upon that new system as an important conquest, which enlarges the bounds of philosophy. We had only two hypotheses, that of the Schools and that of the Cartesians: the one was a *way of influence* of the body upon the soul and of the soul upon the body; the other was a *way of assistance* or occasional causality. But here is a new acquisition, a new hypothesis, which may be called, as Fr. Lami styles it, a *way of pre-established harmony*. We are beholden for it to M. Leibniz, and it is impossible to conceive anything that gives us a nobler idea of the power and wisdom of the Author of all things. This, together with the advantage of setting aside all notions of a miraculous conduct, would engage me to prefer this new system to that of the Cartesians, if I could conceive any possibility in the *way of pre-established harmony*.

'I desire the reader to take notice that though I confess that this way removes all notions of a miraculous conduct, yet I do not retract what I have said formerly, that the system of occasional causes does not bring in God acting miraculously. (See M. Leibniz's article in *Histoire des Ouvrages des Savants*, July 1698.) I am as much persuaded as ever I was that an action cannot be said to be miraculous, unless God produces it as an exception to the general laws; and that everything of which he is immediately the author according to those laws is distinct from a miracle properly so called. But being willing to cut off from this dispute as many things as I possibly can, I consent it should be said that the surest way of removing all notions that include a miracle is to suppose that all created substances are actively the immediate causes of the effects of nature. I will therefore lay aside what I might reply to that part of M. Leibniz's answer.

'I will also omit all objections which are not more contrary to his opinion than to that of some other philosophers. I will not therefore propose the difficulties that may be raised against the supposition that a creature can receive from God the power of moving itself. They are strong and almost unanswerable, but M. Leibniz's system does not lie more open to them than that of the Aristotelians; nay, I do not know whether the Cartesians would presume to say that God cannot communicate to our souls a power of acting. If they say so, how can they own that Adam sinned?

And if they dare not say so they weaken the arguments whereby they endeavour to prove that matter is not capable of any activity. Nor do I believe that it is more difficult for M. Leibniz than for the Cartesians or other philosophers, to free himself from the objection of a fatal mechanism which destroys human liberty. Wherefore, waiving this, I shall only speak of what is peculiar to the system of the *pre-established harmony*.

'I. My first observation shall be, that it raises the power and wisdom of the divine art above everything that can be conceived. Fancy to yourself a ship which, without having any sense or knowledge, and without being directed by any created or uncreated being, has the power of moving itself so seasonably as to have always the wind favourable, to avoid currents and rocks, to cast anchor where it ought to be done, and to retire into a harbour precisely when it is necessary. Suppose such a ship sails in that manner for several years successively, being always turned and situated as it ought to be, according to the several changes of the air and the different situations of seas and lands; you will acknowledge that God, notwithstanding his infinite power, cannot communicate such a faculty to a ship; or rather you will say that the nature of a ship is not capable of receiving it from God. And yet what M. Leibniz supposes about the machine of a human body is more admirable and more surprising than all this. Let us apply his system concerning the union of the soul with the body to the person of Julius Caesar.

'II. We must say according to this system that the body of Julius Caesar did so exercise its moving faculty that from its birth to its death it went through continual changes which did most exactly answer the perpetual changes of a certain soul which it did not know and which made no impression on it. We must say that the rule according to which that faculty of Caesar's body performed such actions was such, that he would have gone to the Senate upon such a day and at such an hour, that he would have spoken there such and such words, etc., though God had willed to annihilate his soul the next day after it was created. We must say that this moving power did change and modify itself exactly according to the volubility of the thoughts of that ambitious man, and that it was affected precisely in a certain manner rather than in another, because the soul of Caesar passed from a certain thought to another. Can a blind power modify itself so exactly

39

by virtue of an impression communicated thirty or forty years before and never renewed since, but left to itself, without ever knowing what it is to do? Is not this much more incomprehensible than the navigation I spoke of in the foregoing paragraph?

'III. The difficulty will be greater still, if it be considered that the human machine contains an almost infinite number of organs, and that it is continually exposed to the shock of the bodies that surround it,* and which by an innumerable variety of shakings produce in it a thousand sorts of modifications. How is it possible to conceive that this *pre-established harmony* should never be disordered, but go on still during the longest life of a man, notwithstanding the infinite varieties of the reciprocal action of so many organs upon one another, which are surrounded on all sides with infinite corpuscles, sometimes hot and sometimes cold, sometimes dry and sometimes moist, and always acting, and pricking the nerves a thousand different ways? Suppose that the multiplicity of organs and of external agents be a necessary instrument of the almost infinite variety of changes in a human body: will that variety have the exactness here required? Will it never disturb the correspondence of those changes with the changes of the soul? This seems to be altogether impossible.

'IV. It is in vain to have recourse to the power of God, in order to maintain that brutes are mere machines; it is in vain to say that God was able to make machines so artfully contrived that the voice of a man, the reflected light of an object, etc., will strike them exactly where it is necessary, that they may move in a given manner. This supposition is rejected by everybody except some Cartesians; and no Cartesian would admit it if it were to be extended to man; that is, if anyone were to assert that God was able to form such bodies as would mechanically do whatever we see other men do. By denying this we do not pretend to limit the power and knowledge of God: we only mean that the nature of things does not permit that the faculties imparted to a creature should not be necessarily confined within certain bounds. The

---

* 'According to M. Leibniz what is active in every substance ought to be reduced to a true unity. Since therefore the body of every man is composed of several substances, each of them ought to have a principle of action really distinct from the principle of each of the others. He will have the action of every principle to be spontaneous. Now this must vary the effects *ad infinitum*, and confound them. For the impression of the neighbouring bodies must needs put some constraint upon the natural spontaneity of every one of them.'

actions of creatures must be necessarily proportioned to their essential state, and performed according to the character belonging to each machine; for according to the maxim of the philosophers, whatever is received is proportionate to the capacity of the subject that receives it. We may therefore reject M. Leibniz's hypothesis as being impossible, since it is liable to greater difficulties than that of the Cartesians, which makes beasts to be mere machines. It puts a perpetual harmony between two beings, which do not act one upon another; whereas if servants were mere machines, and should punctually obey their masters' command, it could not be said that they do it without a real action of their masters upon them; for their masters would speak words and make signs which would really shake and move the organs of the servants.

'V. Now let us consider the soul of Julius Caesar, and we shall find the thing more impossible still. That soul was in the world without being exposed to the influence of any spirit. The power it received from God was the only principle of the actions it produced at every moment: and if those actions were different one from another, it was not because some of them were produced by the united influence of some springs which did not contribute to the production of others, for the soul of man is simple, indivisible and immaterial. M. Leibniz owns it; and if he did not acknowledge it, but if, on the contrary, he should suppose with most philosophers and some of the most excellent metaphysicians of our age (Mr. Locke, for instance) that a compound of several material parts placed and disposed in a certain manner, is capable of thinking, his hypothesis would appear to be on that very ground absolutely impossible, and I could refute it several other ways; which I need not mention since he acknowledges the immateriality of our soul and builds upon it.

'Let us return to the soul of Julius Caesar, and call it an immaterial automaton (M. Leibniz's own phrase), and compare it with an atom of Epicurus; I mean an atom surrounded with a vacuum on all sides, and which will never meet any other atom. This is a very just comparison: for this atom, on the one hand, has a natural power of moving itself and exerts it without any assistance, and without being retarded or hindered by anything: and, on the other hand, the soul of Caesar is a spirit which has received the faculty of producing thoughts, and exerts it without the influence of any other spirit or of any body. It is neither assisted nor thwarted by anything whatsoever. If you consult the common notions and the ideas of order, you will find that this atom can never stop, and that having been in motion in the foregoing moment, it will continue in it at the present moment and in all the moments that shall follow, and that it will always move in the same manner. This is the consequence of an axiom approved by M. Leibniz: *since a thing does always remain in the same state wherein it happens to be, unless it receives some alteration from some other thing . . . we conclude,* says he, *not only that a body which is at rest will always be at rest, but that a body in motion will always keep that motion or change, that is, the same swiftness and the same direction, unless something happens to hinder it.* (M. Leibniz, ibid.)

'Everyone clearly sees that this atom, whether it moves by an innate power, as Democritus and Epicurus would have it, or by a power received from the Creator, will always move in the same line equally and after a uniform manner, without ever turning or going back. Epicurus was laughed at, when he invented the motion of declination; it was a needless supposition, which he wanted in order to get out of the labyrinth of a fatal necessity; and he could give no reason for this new part of his system. It was inconsistent with the clearest notions of our minds: for it is evident that an atom which describes a straight line for the space of two days cannot turn away at the beginning of a third, unless it meets with some obstacle, or has a mind all of a sudden to go out of its road, or contains some spring which begins to play at that very moment. The first of these reasons cannot be admitted in a vacuum. The second is impossible, since an atom has not the faculty of thinking. And the third is likewise impossible in a corpuscle that is a perfect unity. I must make some use of all this.

'VI. Caesar's soul is a being to which unity belongs in a strict sense. The faculty of producing thoughts is a property of its nature (so M. Leibniz), which it has received from God, both as to possession and exercise. If the first thought it produces is a sense of pleasure, there is no reason why the second should not likewise be a sense of pleasure; for when the total cause of an effect remains the same, the effect cannot be altered. Now this soul, at the second moment of its existence, does not receive a new faculty of thinking; it only preserves the faculty it had at the first moment, and it is as independent of the concourse of any other cause at the second moment as it was at the first. It must therefore produce again at the second moment the same thought it had produced just before. If it be objected that it ought to be in a state of change, and that it would not be in such a state, in the case that I have supposed; I answer that its change will be like the change of the atom; for an atom which continually moves in the same line acquires a new situation at every moment, but it is like the preceding situation. A soul may therefore continue in its state of change, if it does but produce a new thought like the preceding.

'But suppose it to be not confined within such narrow bounds; it must be granted at least that its going from one thought to another implies some reason of affinity. If I suppose that in a certain moment the soul of Caesar sees a tree with leaves and blossoms, I can conceive that it does immediately desire to see one that has only leaves, and then one that has only blossoms, and that it will thus successively produce several images arising from one another; but one cannot conceive the odd change of thoughts, which have no affinity with, but are even contrary to, one another, and which are so common in men's souls. One cannot apprehend how God could place in the soul of Julius Caesar the principle of what I am going to say. He was without doubt pricked with a pin more than once, when he was sucking; and therefore according to M. Leibniz's hypothesis which I am here considering, his soul must have produced in itself a sense of pain immediately after the pleasant sensations of the sweetness of the milk, which it had enjoyed for the space of two or three minutes. By what springs was it determined to interrupt its pleasures and to give itself all of a sudden a sense of pain, without receiving any intimation of preparing itself to change, and without any new alteration in its substance? If you run over the life of that Roman emperor, every page will afford you matter for a stronger objection than this is.

'VII. The thing would be less incomprehensible if it were supposed that the soul of man is not one spirit but rather a multitude of spirits, each of which has its functions, that begin and end precisely as the changes made in a human body require. By virtue of this supposition it should be said that something analogous to a great number of wheels and springs, or of matters that ferment, disposed according to the changes of our machine, awakens or lulls asleep for a certain time the action of each of those spirits. But then the soul of man would be no longer a single substance but an *ens per aggregationem*, a collection and heap of substances just like all material beings. We are here in quest of a single being, which produces in itself sometimes joy, sometimes pain, etc., and not of many beings, one of which produces hope, another despair, etc.

'In these observations I have merely cleared and unfolded those which M. Leibniz has done me the honour to examine: and now I shall make some reflexions upon his answers.

'VIII. He says (ibid., p. 332) that *the law of the change which happens in the substance of the animal transports him from pleasure to pain at the very moment that a solution of continuity is made in his body; because the law of the indivisible substance of that animal is to represent what is done in his body as we experience it, and even to represent in some manner, and with respect to that body, whatever is done in the world.* These words are a very good explication of the grounds of this system; they are, as it were, the unfolding and key of it; but at the same time they are the very things at which the objections of those who take this system to be impossible are levelled. The law M. Leibniz speaks of supposes a decree of God, and shows wherein this system agrees with that of occasional causes. Those two systems agree in this point, that there are laws according to which the soul of man is *to represent what is done in the body of man, as we experience it.* But they disagree as to the manner of executing those laws. The Cartesians say that God executes them; M. Leibniz will have it, that the soul itself does it; which appears to me impossible, because the soul has not the necessary instruments for such an execution. Now however infinite the power and knowledge of God be, he cannot perform with a machine deprived of a certain piece, what requires the concourse of such a piece. He must supply that defect; but then the effect would be produced by him and not by the machine. I shall show that the soul has not the instruments requisite for the divine law we speak of, and in order to do it I shall make use of a comparison.

'Fancy to yourself an animal created by God and designed to sing continually. It will always sing, that is most certain; but if God designs him a certain tablature, he must necessarily either put it before his eyes or imprint it upon his memory or dispose his muscles in such a manner that according to the laws of mechanism one certain note will always come after another, agreeably to the order of the tablature. Without this one cannot apprehend that the animal can always follow the whole set of the notes appointed him by God. Let us apply this to man's soul. M. Leibniz will have it that it has received not only the power of producing thoughts continually, but also the faculty of following always a certain set of thoughts, which answers the continual changes that happen in the machine of the body. This set of thoughts is like the tablature prescribed to the singing animal above mentioned. Can the soul change its perceptions or modifications at every moment according to such a set of thoughts, without knowing the series of the notes, and actually thinking upon them? But experience teaches us that it knows nothing of it. Were it not at least necessary that in default of such a knowledge, there should be in the soul a set of particular instruments, each of which would be a necessary cause of such and such a thought? Must they not be so placed and disposed as to operate precisely one after another, according to the correspondence *pre-established* between the changes of the body and the thoughts of the soul? but it is most certain that an immaterial simple and indivisible substance cannot be made up of such an innumerable multitude of particular instruments placed one before another, according to the order of the tablature in question. It is not therefore possible that a human soul should execute that law.

'M. Leibniz supposes that the soul does not distinctly know its future perceptions, *but that it perceives them confusedly,* and that *there are in each substance traces of whatever hath happened, or shall happen to it: but that an infinite multitude of perceptions hinders us from distinguishing them. The present state of each substance is a natural consequence of its preceding state. The soul, though never so simple, has always a sentiment composed of several perceptions at one time: which answers our end as well as though it were composed of pieces, like a machine. For each foregoing perception has an influence on those that follow agreeably to a law of order, which is in perceptions as well as in motions. . . . The perceptions that are together in one and the same soul at the same time, including an infinite multitude of little and indistinguishable sentiments that are to be unfolded, we need not wonder at the infinite variety of what is to result from it in time. This is only a consequence of the representative nature of the soul, which is, to express what happens and what will happen in its body, by the connexion and correspondence of all the parts of the world.* I have but little to say in answer to this: I shall only observe that this supposition when sufficiently cleared is the right way of solving all the difficulties. M. Leibniz, through the penetration of his great genius, has very well conceived the extent and strength of this objection, and what remedy ought to be applied to the main inconveniency. I do not doubt but that he will smooth the rough parts of his system, and teach us some excellent things about the nature of spirits. Nobody can travel more usefully or more safely than he in the intellectual world. I hope that his curious explanations will remove all the impossibilities which I have hitherto found in his system, and that he will solidly remove my difficulties, as well as those of Father Lami. And these hopes made me say before, without designing to pass a compliment upon that learned man, that his system ought to be looked upon as an important conquest.

'He will not be much embarrassed by this, viz. that whereas according to the supposition of the Cartesians there is but one general law for the union of spirits and bodies, he will have it that God gives a particular law to each spirit; from whence it seems to result that the primitive constitution of each spirit is specifically different from all others. Do not the Thomists say, that there are as many species as individuals in angelic nature?'

Leibniz acknowledged Bayle's note in a further reply, which is written as though for publication. It was communicated to Bayle, but it was not in fact published. It is dated 1702. It may be found in the standard collections of Leibniz's philosophical works. It reads almost like a sketch for the *Theodicy*.

The principal point developed by Leibniz is the richness of content which, according to him, is to be found in each 'simple substance'. Its simplicity is more like the infinitely rich simplicity of the divine Being, than like the simplicity of the atom of Epicurus, with which Bayle had chosen to compare it. It contains a condensation in confused idea of the whole universe: and its essence is from the first defined by the part it is to play in the total harmony.

As to the musical score ('tablature of notes') which the individual soul plays from, in order to perform its ordained part in the universal harmony, this 'score' is to be found in the confused or implicit ideas at any moment present, from which an omniscient observer could always deduce what is to happen next. To the objection 'But the created soul is not an omniscient observer, and if it cannot read the score, the score is useless to it', Leibniz replies by affirming that much spontaneous action arises from subjective and yet unperceived reasons, as we are all perfectly aware, once we attend to the relevant facts. All he claims to be doing is to generalize this observation. All events whatsoever arise from the 'interpretation of the score' by monads, but very little of this 'interpretation' is in the least conscious.

Leibniz passes from the remarks about his own doctrine under the article 'Rorarius' to other articles of Bayle's dictionary, and touches the question of the origin of evil, and other matters which receive their fuller treatment in the *Theodicy*.

In the same year Leibniz wrote a very friendly letter to Bayle himself, offering further explanations of disputed points. He concluded it with a paragraph of some personal interest, comparing himself the historian-philosopher with Bayle the philosophic lexicographer, and revealing by the way his attitude to philosophy, science and history:

'We have good reason to admire, Sir, the way in which your striking reflexions on the deepest questions of philosophy remain unhindered by your boundless researches into matters of fact. I too am not always able to excuse myself from discussions of the sort, and have even been obliged to descend to questions of genealogy, which would be still more trifling, were it not that the interests of States frequently depend upon them. I have worked much on the history of Germany in so far as it bears upon these countries, a study which has furnished me with some observations belonging to general history. So I have learnt not to neglect the knowledge of sheer facts. But if the choice were open to me, I should prefer natural history to political, and the customs and laws God has established in nature, to what is observed among mankind.'

Leibniz now conceived the idea of putting together all the passages in Bayle's works which interested him, and writing a systematic answer to them. Before he had leisure to finish the task, Bayle died. The work nevertheless appeared in 1710 as the Essays in *Theodicy*.

PREFACE

IT HAS ever been seen that men in general have resorted to outward forms for the expression of their religion: sound piety, that is to say, light and virtue, has never been the portion of the many. One should not wonder at this, nothing is so much in accord with human weakness. We are impressed by what is outward, while the inner essence of things requires consideration of such a kind as few persons are fitted to give. As true piety consists in principles and practice, the outward forms of religion imitate these, and are of two kinds: the one kind consists in ceremonial practices, and the other in the formularies of·belief. Ceremonies resemble virtuous actions, and formularies are like shadows of the truth and approach, more or less, the true light. All these outward forms would be commendable if those who invented them had rendered them appropriate to maintain and to express that which they imitate—if religious ceremonies, ecclesiastical discipline, the rules of communities, human laws were always like a hedge round the divine law, to withdraw us from any approach to vice, to inure us to the good and to make us familiar with virtue. That was the aim of Moses and of other good lawgivers, of the wise men who founded religious orders, and above all of Jesus Christ, divine founder of the purest and most enlightened religion. It is just the same with the formularies of belief: they would be valid provided there were nothing in them inconsistent with truth unto salvation, even though the full truth concerned were not there. But it happens only too often that religion is choked in ceremonial, and that the divine light is obscured by the opinions of men.

The pagans, who inhabited the earth before Christianity was founded, had only one kind of outward form: they had ceremonies in their worship, but they had no articles of faith and had never dreamed of drawing up formularies for their dogmatic theology. They knew not whether their gods were real persons or symbols of the forces of Nature, as the sun, the planets, the elements. Their mysteries consisted not in difficult dogmas but in certain secret observances, whence the profane, namely those who were not initiated, were excluded. These observances were very often ridiculous and absurd, and it was necessary to conceal them in order to guard them against contempt. The pagans had their superstitions: they boasted of miracles, everything with them was full of oracles, auguries, portents, divinations; the priests invented signs of the anger or of the goodness of the gods, whose interpreters they claimed to be. This tended to sway minds through fear and hope concerning human events; but the great future of another life was scarce envisaged; one did not trouble to impart to men true notions of God and of the soul.

Of all ancient peoples, it appears that the Hebrews alone had public dogmas for their religion. Abraham and Moses established the belief in one God, source of all good, author of all things. The Hebrews speak of him in a manner worthy of the Supreme Substance; and one wonders at seeing the inhabitants of one small region of the earth more enlightened than the rest of the human race. Peradventure the wise men of other nations have sometimes said the same, but they have not had the good fortune to find a sufficient following and to convert the dogma into law. Nevertheless Moses had not inserted in his laws the doctrine of the immortality of souls: it was consistent with his ideas, it was taught by oral tradition; but it was not proclaimed for popular acceptance until Jesus Christ lifted the veil, and, without having force in his hand, taught with all the force of a lawgiver that immortal souls pass into another life, wherein they shall receive the wages of their deeds. Moses had already expressed the beautiful conceptions of the greatness and the goodness of God, whereto many civilized peoples to-day assent; but Jesus Christ demonstrated fully the results of these ideas, proclaiming that divine goodness and justice are shown forth to perfection in God's designs for the souls of men.

I refrain from considering here the other points of the Christian doctrine, and I will show only how Jesus Christ brought about the conversion of natural religion into law, and gained for it the authority of a public dogma. He alone did that which so many philosophers had endeavoured in vain to do; and Christians having at last gained the upper hand in the Roman Empire, the master of the greater part of the known earth, the religion of the wise men became that of the nations. Later also Mahomet showed no divergence from the great dogmas of natural theology: his followers spread them abroad even among the most remote races of Asia and of Africa, whither Christianity had not been carried; and they abolished in many countries heathen superstitions which were contrary to the true doctrine of the unity of God and the immortality of souls.

It is clear that Jesus Christ, completing what Moses had begun, wished that the Divinity should be the object not only of our fear and veneration but also of our love and devotion. Thus he made men happy by anticipation, and gave them here on earth a foretaste of future felicity. For there is nothing so agreeable as loving that which is worthy of love. Love is that mental state which makes us take pleasure in the perfections of the object of our love, and there is nothing more perfect than God, nor any greater delight than in him. To love him it suffices to contemplate his perfections, a thing easy indeed, because we find the ideas of these within ourselves. The perfections of God are those of our souls, but he possesses them in boundless measure; he is an Ocean, whereof to us only drops have been granted; there is in us some power, some knowledge, some goodness, but in God they are all in their entirety. Order, proportions, harmony delight us; painting and music are samples of these: God is all order; he always keeps truth of proportions, he makes universal harmony; all beauty is an effusion of his rays.

It follows manifestly that true piety and even true felicity consist in the love of God, but a love so enlightened that its fervour is attended by insight. This kind of love begets that pleasure in good actions which gives relief to virtue, and, relating all to God as to the centre, transports the human to the divine. For in doing one's duty, in obeying reason, one carries out the orders of Supreme Reason. One directs all one's intentions to the common good, which is no other than the glory of God. Thus one finds that there is no greater individual interest than to espouse that of the community, and one gains satisfaction for oneself by taking pleasure in the acquisition of true benefits for men. Whether one succeeds therein or not, one is content with what comes to pass, being once resigned to the will of God and knowing that what he wills is best. But before he declares his will by the event one endeavours to find it out by doing that which appears most in accord with his commands. When we are in this state of mind, we are not disheartened by ill success, we regret only our faults; and the ungrateful ways of men cause no relaxation in the exercise of our kindly disposition. Our charity is humble and full of moderation, it presumes not to domineer; attentive alike to our own faults and to the talents of others, we are inclined to criticize our own actions and to excuse and vindicate those of others. We must work out our own perfection and do wrong to no man. There is no piety where there is not charity; and without being kindly and beneficent one cannot show sincere religion.

Good disposition, favourable upbringing, association with pious and virtuous persons may contribute much towards such a propitious condition for our souls; but most securely are they grounded therein by good principles. I have already said that insight must be joined to fervour, that the perfecting of our understanding must accomplish the perfecting of our will. The practices of virtue, as well as those of vice, may be the effect of a mere habit, one may acquire a taste for them; but when virtue is reasonable, when it is related to God, who is the supreme reason of things, it is founded on knowledge. One cannot love God without knowing his perfections, and this knowledge contains the principles of true piety. The purpose of religion should be to imprint these principles upon our souls: but in some strange way it has happened all too often that men, that teachers of religion have strayed far from this purpose. Contrary to the intention of our divine Master, devotion has been reduced to ceremonies and doctrine has been cumbered with formulae. All too often these ceremonies have not been well fitted to maintain the exercise of virtue, and the formulae sometimes have not been lucid. Can one believe it? Some Christians have imagined that they could be devout without loving their neighbour, and pious without loving God; or else people have thought that they could love their neighbour without serving him and could love God without knowing him. Many centuries have passed without recognition of this defect by the people at large; and there are still great traces of the reign of darkness. There are divers persons who speak much of piety, of devotion, of religion, who are even busied with the teaching of such things, and who yet prove to be by no means versed in the divine perfections. They ill understand the goodness and the justice of the Sovereign of the universe; they imagine a God who deserves neither to be imitated nor to be loved. This indeed seemed to me dangerous in its effect, since it is of serious moment that the very source of piety should be preserved from infection. The old errors of those who arraigned the Divinity or who made thereof an evil principle have been renewed sometimes in our own days: people have pleaded the irresistible power of God when it was a question rather of presenting his supreme goodness; and they have assumed a despotic power when they should rather have conceived of a power ordered by the most perfect wisdom. I have observed that these opinions, apt to do harm, rested especially on confused notions which had been formed concerning freedom, necessity and destiny; and I have taken up my pen more than once on such an occasion to give explanations on these important matters. But finally I have been compelled to gather up my thoughts on all these connected questions, and to impart them to the public. It is this that I have undertaken in the Essays which I offer here, on the Goodness of God, the Freedom of Man, and the Origin of Evil.

There are two famous labyrinths where our reason very often goes astray: one concerns the great question of the Free and the Necessary, above all in the production and the origin of Evil; the other consists in the discussion of continuity and of the indivisibles which appear to be the elements thereof, and where the consideration of the infinite must enter in. The first perplexes almost all the human race, the other exercises philosophers only. I shall have perchance at another time an opportunity to declare myself on the second, and to point out that, for lack of a true conception of the nature of substance and matter, people have taken up false positions leading to insurmountable difficulties, difficulties which should properly be applied to the overthrow of these very positions. But if the knowledge of continuity is important for speculative enquiry, that of necessity is none the less so for practical application; and it, together with the questions therewith connected, to wit, the freedom of man and the justice of God, forms the object of this treatise.

Men have been perplexed in well-nigh every age by a sophism which the ancients called the 'Lazy Reason', because it tended towards doing nothing, or at least towards being careful for nothing and only following inclination for the pleasure of the moment. For, they said, if the future is necessary, that which must happen will happen, whatever I may do. Now the future (so they said) is necessary, whether because the Divinity foresees everything, and even pre-establishes it by the control of all things in the universe; or because everything happens of necessity, through the concatenation of causes; or finally, through the very nature of truth, which is determinate in the assertions that can be made on future events, as it is in all assertions, since the assertion must always be true or false in itself, even though we know not always which it is. And all these reasons for determination which appear different converge finally like lines upon one and the same centre; for there is a truth in the future event which is predetermined by the causes, and God pre-establishes it in establishing the causes.

The false conception of necessity, being applied in practice, has given rise to what I call *Fatum Mahometanum*, fate after the Turkish fashion, because it is said of the Turks that they do not shun danger or even abandon places infected with plague, owing to their use of such reasoning as that just recorded. For what is called *Fatum Stoicum* was not so black as it is painted: it did not divert men from the care of their affairs, but it tended to give them tranquillity in regard to events, through the consideration of necessity, which renders our anxieties and our vexations needless. In which respect these philosophers were not far removed from the teaching of our Lord, who deprecates these anxieties in regard to the morrow, comparing them with the needless trouble a man would give himself in labouring to increase his stature.

It is true that the teachings of the Stoics (and perhaps also of some famous philosophers of our time), confining themselves to this alleged necessity, can only impart a forced patience; whereas our Lord inspires thoughts more sublime, and even instructs us in the means of gaining contentment by assuring us that since God, being altogether good and wise, has care for everything, even so far as not to neglect one hair of our head, our confidence in him ought to be entire. And thus we should see, if we were capable of understanding him, that it is not even possible to wish for anything better (as much in general as for ourselves) than what he does. It is as if one said to men: Do your duty and be content with that which shall come of it, not only because you cannot resist divine providence, or the nature of things (which may suffice for tranquillity, but not for contentment), but also because you have to do with a good master. And that is what may be called *Fatum Christianum*.

Nevertheless it happens that most men, and even Christians, introduce into their dealings some mixture of fate after the Turkish fashion, although they do not sufficiently acknowledge it. It is true that they are not inactive or negligent when obvious perils or great and manifest hopes present themselves; for they will not fail to abandon a house that is about to fall and to turn aside from a precipice they see in their path; and they will burrow in the earth to dig up a treasure half uncovered, without waiting for fate to finish dislodging it. But when the good or the evil is remote and uncertain and the remedy painful or little to our taste, the lazy reason seems to us to be valid. For example, when it is a question of preserving one's health and even one's life by good diet, people to whom one gives advice thereupon very often answer that our days are numbered and that it avails nothing to try to struggle against that which God destines for us. But these same persons run to even the most absurd remedies when the evil they had neglected draws near. One reasons in somewhat the same way when the question for consideration is somewhat thorny, as for instance when one asks oneself, *quod vitae sectabor iter?* what profession one must choose; when it is a question of a marriage being arranged, of a war being undertaken, of a battle being fought; for in these cases many will be inclined to evade the difficulty of consideration and abandon themselves to fate or to inclination, as if reason should not be employed except in easy cases. One will then all too often reason in the Turkish fashion (although this way is wrongly termed trusting in providence, a thing that in reality occurs only when one has done one's duty) and one will employ the lazy reason, derived from the idea of inevitable fate, to relieve oneself of the need to reason properly.

One will thus overlook the fact that if this argument contrary to the practice of reason were valid, it would always hold good, whether the consideration were easy or not. This laziness is to some extent the source of the superstitious practices of fortune-tellers, which meet with just such credulity as men show towards the philosopher's stone, because they would fain have short cuts to the attainment of happiness without trouble.

I do not speak here of those who throw themselves upon fortune because they have been happy before, as if there were something permanent therein. Their argument from the past to the future has just as slight a foundation as the principles of astrology and of other kinds of divination. They overlook the fact that there is usually an ebb and flow in fortune, *una marea*, as Italians playing basset are wont to call it. With regard to this they make their own particular observations, which I would, nevertheless, counsel none to trust too much. Yet this confidence that people have in their fortune serves often to give courage to men, and above all to soldiers, and causes them to have indeed that good fortune they ascribe to themselves. Even so do predictions often cause that to happen which has been foretold, as it is supposed that the opinion the Mahometans hold on fate makes them resolute. Thus even errors have their use at times, but generally as providing a remedy for other errors: and truth is unquestionably better.

But it is taking an unfair advantage of this alleged necessity of fate to employ it in excuse for our vices and our libertinism. I have often heard it said by smart young persons, who wished to play the freethinker, that it is useless to preach virtue, to censure vice, to create hopes of reward and fears of punishment, since it may be said of the book of destiny, that what is written is written, and that our behaviour can change nothing therein. Thus, they would say, it were best to follow one's inclination, dwelling only upon such things as may content us in the present. They did not reflect upon the strange consequences of this argument, which would prove too much, since it would prove (for instance) that one should take a pleasant beverage even though one knows it is poisoned. For the same reason (if it were valid) I could say: if it is written in the records of the Parcae that poison will kill me now or will do me harm, this will happen even though I were not to take this beverage; and if this is not written, it will not happen even though I should take this same beverage; consequently I shall be able to follow with impunity my inclination to take what is pleasing, however injurious it may be; the result of which reasoning is an obvious absurdity. This objection disconcerted them a little, but they always reverted to their argument, phrased in different ways, until they were brought to understand where the fault of the sophism lies. It is untrue that the event happens whatever one may do: it will happen because one does what leads thereto; and if the event is written beforehand, the cause that will make it happen is written also. Thus the connexion of effects and causes, so far from establishing the doctrine of a necessity detrimental to conduct, serves to overthrow it.

Yet, without having evil intentions inclined towards libertinism, one may envisage differently the strange consequences of an inevitable necessity, considering that it would destroy the freedom of the will, so essential to the morality of action: for justice and injustice, praise and blame, punishment and reward cannot attach to necessary actions, and nobody will be under obligation to do the impossible or to abstain from doing what is absolutely necessary. Without any intention of abusing this consideration in order to favour irregularity, one will nevertheless not escape embarrassment sometimes, when it comes to a question of judging the actions of others, or rather of answering objections, amongst which there are some even concerned with the actions of God, whereof I will speak presently. And as an insuperable necessity would open the door to impiety, whether through the impunity one could thence infer or the hopelessness of any attempt to resist a torrent that sweeps everything along with it, it is important to note the different degrees of necessity, and to show that there are some which cannot do harm, as there are others which cannot be admitted without giving rise to evil consequences.

Some go even further: not content with using the pretext of necessity to prove that virtue and vice do neither good nor ill, they have the hardihood to make the Divinity accessary to their licentious way of life, and they imitate the pagans of old, who ascribed to the gods the cause of their crimes, as if a divinity drove them to do evil. The philosophy of Christians, which recognizes better than that of the ancients the dependence of things upon the first Author and his co-operation with all the actions of creatures, appears to have increased this difficulty. Some able men in our own time have gone so far as to deny all action to creatures, and M. Bayle, who tended a little towards this extraordinary opinion, made use of it to restore the lapsed dogma of the two principles, or two gods, the one good, the other evil, as if this dogma were a better solution to the difficulties over the origin of evil. Yet again he acknowledges that it is an indefensible opinion and that the oneness of the Principle is incontestably founded on *a priori* reasons; but he wishes to infer that our Reason is confounded and cannot meet her own objections, and that one should disregard them and hold fast the revealed dogmas, which teach us the existence of one God altogether good, altogether powerful and altogether wise. But many readers, convinced of the irrefutable nature of his objections and believing them to be at least as strong as the proofs for the truth of religion, would draw dangerous conclusions.

Even though there were no co-operation by God in evil actions, one could not help finding difficulty in the fact that he foresees them and that, being able to prevent them through his omnipotence, he yet permits them. This is why some philosophers and even some theologians have rather chosen to deny to God any knowledge of the detail of things and, above all, of future events, than to admit what they believed repellent to his goodness. The Socinians and Conrad Vorstius lean towards that side; and Thomas Bonartes, an English Jesuit disguised under a pseudonym but exceedingly learned, who wrote a book *De Concordia Scientiae cum Fide*, of which I will speak later, appears to hint at this also.

They are doubtless much mistaken; but others are not less so who, convinced that nothing comes to pass save by the will and the power of God, ascribe to him intentions and actions so unworthy of the greatest and the best of all beings that one would say these authors have indeed renounced the dogma which recognizes God's justice and goodness. They thought that, being supreme Master of the universe, he could without any detriment to his holiness cause sins to be committed, simply at his will and pleasure, or in order that he might have the pleasure of punishing; and even that he could take pleasure in eternally afflicting innocent people without doing any injustice, because no one has the right or the power to control his actions. Some even have gone so far as to say that God acts thus indeed; and on the plea that we are as nothing in comparison with him, they liken us to earthworms which men crush without heeding as they walk, or in general to animals that are not of our species and which we do not scruple to ill-treat.

I believe that many persons otherwise of good intentions are misled by these ideas, because they have not sufficient knowledge of their consequences. They do not see that, properly speaking, God's justice is thus overthrown. For what idea shall we form of such a justice as has only will for its rule, that is to say, where the will is not guided by the rules of good and even tends directly towards evil? Unless it be the idea contained in that tyrannical definition by Thrasymachus in Plato, which designated as *just* that which pleases the stronger. Such indeed is the position taken up, albeit unwittingly, by those who rest all obligation upon constraint, and in consequence take power as the gauge of right. But one will soon abandon maxims so strange and so unfit to make men good and charitable through the imitation of God. For one will reflect that a God who would take pleasure in the misfortune of others cannot be distinguished from the evil principle of the Manichaeans, assuming that this principle had become sole master of the universe; and that in consequence one must attribute to the true God sentiments that render him worthy to be called the good Principle.

Happily these extravagant dogmas scarce obtain any longer among theologians. Nevertheless some astute persons, who are pleased to make difficulties, revive them: they seek to increase our perplexity by uniting the controversies aroused by Christian theology to the disputes of philosophy. Philosophers have considered the questions of necessity, of freedom and of the origin of evil; theologians have added thereto those of original sin, of grace and of predestination. The original corruption of the human race, coming from the first sin, appears to us to have imposed a natural necessity to sin without the succour of divine grace: but necessity being incompatible with punishment, it will be inferred that a sufficient grace ought to have been given to all men; which does not seem to be in conformity with experience.

But the difficulty is great, above all, in relation to God's dispositions for the salvation of men. There are few saved or chosen; therefore the choice of many is not God's decreed will. And since it is admitted that those whom he has chosen deserve it no more than the rest, and are not even fundamentally less evil, the goodness which they have coming only from the gift of God, the difficulty is increased. Where is, then, his justice (people will say), or at the least, where is his goodness? Partiality, or respect of persons, goes against justice, and he who without cause sets bounds to his goodness cannot have it in sufficient measure. It is true that those who are not chosen are lost by their own fault: they lack good will or living faith; but it rested with God alone to grant it them. We know that besides inward grace there are usually outward circumstances which distinguish men, and that training, conversation, example often correct or corrupt natural disposition. Now that God should call forth circumstances favourable to some and abandon others to experiences which contribute to their misfortune, will not that give us cause for astonishment? And it is not enough (so it seems) to say with some that inward grace is universal and equal for all. For these same authors are obliged to resort to the exclamations of St. Paul, and to say: 'O the depth!' when they consider how men are distinguished by what we may call outward graces, that is, by graces appearing in the diversity of circumstances which God calls forth, whereof men are not the masters, and which have nevertheless so great an influence upon all that concerns their salvation.

Nor will it help us to say with St. Augustine that, all men being involved in the damnation caused by the sin of Adam, God might have left them all in their misery; and that thus his goodness alone induces him to deliver some of them. For not only is it strange that the sin of another should condemn anyone, but there still remains the question why God does not deliver all—why he delivers the lesser number and why some in preference to others. He is in truth their master, but he is a good and just master; his power is absolute, but his wisdom permits not that he exercise that power in an arbitrary and despotic way, which would be tyrannous indeed.

Moreover, the fall of the first man having happened only with God's permission, and God having resolved to permit it only when once he had considered its consequences, which are the corruption of the mass of the human race and the choice of a small number of elect, with the abandonment of all the rest, it is useless to conceal the difficulty by limiting one's view to the mass already corrupt. One must, in spite of oneself, go back to the knowledge of the consequences of the first sin, preceding the decree whereby God permitted it, and whereby he permitted simultaneously that the damned should be involved in the mass of perdition and should not be delivered: for God and the sage make no resolve without considering its consequences.

I hope to remove all these difficulties. I will point out that absolute necessity, which is called also logical and metaphysical and sometimes geometrical, and which would alone be formidable in this connexion, does not exist in free actions, and that thus freedom is exempt not only from constraint but also from real necessity. I will show that God himself, although he always chooses the best, does not act by an absolute necessity, and that the laws of nature laid down by God, founded upon the fitness of things, keep the mean between geometrical truths, absolutely necessary, and arbitrary decrees; which M. Bayle and other modern philosophers have not sufficiently understood. Further I will show that there is an indifference in freedom, because there is no absolute necessity for one course or the other; but yet that there is never an indifference of perfect equipoise. And I will demonstrate that there is in free actions a perfect spontaneity beyond all that has been conceived hitherto. Finally I will make it plain that the hypothetical and the moral necessity which subsist in free actions are open to no objection, and that the 'Lazy Reason' is a pure sophism.

Likewise concerning the origin of evil in its relation to God, I offer a vindication of his perfections that shall extol not less his holiness, his justice and his goodness than his greatness, his power and his independence. I show how it is possible for everything to depend upon God, for him to co-operate in all the actions of creatures, even, if you will, to create these creatures continually, and nevertheless not to be the author of sin. Here also it is demonstrated how the privative nature of evil should be understood. Much more than that, I explain how evil has a source other than the will of God, and that one is right therefore to say of moral evil that God wills it not, but simply permits it. Most important of all, however, I show that it has been possible for God to permit sin and misery, and even to co-operate therein and promote it, without detriment to his holiness and his supreme goodness: although, generally speaking, he could have avoided all these evils.

Concerning grace and predestination, I justify the most debatable assertions, as for instance: that we are converted only through the prevenient grace of God and that we cannot do good except with his aid; that God wills the salvation of all men and that he condemns only those whose will is evil; that he gives to all a sufficient grace provided they wish to use it; that, Jesus Christ being the source and the centre of election, God destined the elect for salvation, because he foresaw that they would cling with a lively faith to the doctrine of Jesus Christ. Yet it is true that this reason for election is not the final reason, and that this very prevision is still a consequence of God's anterior decree. Faith likewise is a gift of God, who has predestinated the faith of the elect, for reasons lying in a superior decree which dispenses grace and circumstance in accordance with God's supreme wisdom.

Now, as one of the most gifted men of our time, whose eloquence was as great as his acumen and who gave great proofs of his vast erudition, had applied himself with a strange predilection to call attention to all the difficulties on this subject which I have just touched in general, I found a fine field for exercise in considering the question with him in detail. I acknowledge that M. Bayle (for it is easy to see that I speak of him) has on his side all the advantages except that of the root of the matter, but I hope that truth (which he acknowledges himself to be on our side) by its very plainness, and provided it be fittingly set forth, will prevail over all the ornaments of eloquence and erudition. My hope for success therein is all the greater because it is the cause of God I plead, and because one of the maxims here upheld states that God's help is never lacking for those that lack not good will. The author of this discourse believes that he has given proof of this good will in the attention he has brought to bear upon this subject. He has meditated upon it since his youth; he has conferred with some of the foremost men of the time; and he has schooled himself by the reading of good authors. And the success which God has given him (according to the opinion of sundry competent judges) in certain other profound meditations, of which some have much influence on this subject, gives him peradventure some right to claim the attention of readers who love truth and are fitted to search after it.

The author had, moreover, particular and weighty reasons inducing him to take pen in hand for discussion of this subject. Conversations which he had concerning the same with literary and court personages, in Germany and in France, and especially with one of the greatest and most accomplished of princesses, have repeatedly prompted him to this course. He had had the honour of expressing his opinions to this Princess upon divers passages of the admirable *Dictionary* of M. Bayle, wherein religion and reason appear as adversaries, and where M. Bayle wishes to silence reason after having made it speak too loud: which he calls the triumph of faith. The present author declared there and then that he was of a different opinion, but that he was nevertheless well pleased that a man of such great genius had brought about an occasion for going deeply into these subjects, subjects as important as they are difficult. He admitted having examined them also for some long time already, and having sometimes been minded to publish upon this matter some reflexions whose chief aim should be such knowledge of God as is needed to awaken piety and to foster virtue. This Princess exhorted and urged him to carry out his long-cherished intention, and some friends added their persuasions. He was all the more tempted to accede to their requests since he had reason to hope that in the sequel to his investigation M. Bayle's genius would greatly aid him to give the subject such illumination as it might receive with his support. But divers obstacles intervened, and the death of the incomparable Queen was not the least. It happened, however, that M. Bayle was attacked by excellent men who set themselves to examine the same subject; he answered them fully and always ingeniously. I followed their dispute, and was even on the point of being involved therein. This is how it came about.

I had published a new system, which seemed well adapted to explain the union of the soul and the body: it met with considerable applause even from those who were not in agreement with it, and certain competent persons testified that they had already been of my opinion, without having reached so distinct an explanation, before they saw what I had written on the matter. M. Bayle examined it in his *Historical and Critical Dictionary*, article 'Rorarius'. He thought that my expositions were worthy of further development; he drew attention to their usefulness in various connexions, and he laid stress upon what might still cause difficulty. I could not but reply in a suitable way to expressions so civil and to reflexions so instructive as his. In order to turn them to greater account, I published some elucidations in the *Histoire des Ouvrages des Savants*, July 1698. M. Bayle replied to them in the second edition of his *Dictionary*. I sent him a rejoinder which has not yet been published; I know not whether he ever made a further reply.

Meanwhile it happened that M. le Clerc had inserted in his *Select Library* an extract from the *Intellectual System* of the late Mr. Cudworth, and had explained therein certain 'plastic natures' which this admirable author applied to the formation of animals. M. Bayle believed (see the continuation of *Divers Thoughts on the Comet*, ch. 21, art. 11) that, these natures being without cognition, in establishing them one weakened the argument which proves, through the marvellous formation of things, that the universe must have an intelligent Cause. M. le Clerc replied (4th art. of the 5th vol. of his *Select Library*) that these natures required to be directed by divine wisdom. M. Bayle insisted (7th article of the *Histoire des Ouvrages des Savants*, August 1704) that direction alone was not sufficient for a cause devoid of cognition, unless one took the cause to be a mere instrument of God, in which case direction would be needless. My system was touched upon in passing; and that gave me an opportunity to send a short essay to the illustrious author of the *Histoire des Ouvrages des Savants*, which he inserted in the month of May 1705, art. 9. In this I endeavoured to make clear that in reality mechanism is sufficient to produce the organic bodies of animals, without any need of other plastic natures, provided there be added thereto the *preformation* already completely organic in the seeds of the bodies that come into existence, contained in those of the bodies whence they spring, right back to the primary seeds. This could only proceed from the Author of things, infinitely powerful and infinitely wise, who, creating all in the beginning in due order, had *pre-established* there all order and artifice that was to be. There is no chaos in the inward nature of things, and there is organism everywhere in a matter whose disposition proceeds from God. More and more of it would come to light if we pressed closer our examination of the anatomy of bodies; and we should continue to observe it even if we could go on to infinity, like Nature, and make subdivision as continuous in our knowledge as Nature has made it in fact.

In order to explain this marvel of the formation of animals, I made use of a Pre-established Harmony, that is to say, of the same means I had used to explain another marvel, namely the correspondence of soul with body, wherein I proved the uniformity and the fecundity of the principles I had employed. It seems that this reminded M. Bayle of my system of accounting for this correspondence, which he had examined formerly. He declared (in chapter 180 of his *Reply to the Questions of a Provincial*, vol. III, p. 1253) that he did not believe God could give to matter or to any other cause the faculty of becoming organic without communicating to it the idea and the knowledge of organic nature. Also he was not yet disposed to believe that God, with all his power over Nature and with all the foreknowledge which he has of the contingencies that may arrive, could have so disposed things that by the laws of mechanics alone a vessel (for instance) should go to its port of destination without being steered during its passage by some intelligent guide. I was surprised to see that limits were placed on the power of God, without the adduction of any proof and without indication that there was any contradiction to be feared on the side of the object or any imperfection on God's side. Whereas I had shown before in my Rejoinder that even men often produce through automata something like the movements that come from reason, and that even a finite mind (but one far above ours) could accomplish what M. Bayle thinks impossible to the Divinity. Moreover, as God orders all things at once beforehand, the accuracy of the path of this vessel would be no more strange than that of a fuse passing along a cord in fireworks, since the whole disposition of things preserves a perfect harmony between them by means of their influence one upon the other.

This declaration of M. Bayle pledged me to an answer. I therefore purposed to point out to him, that unless it be said that God forms organic bodies himself by a perpetual miracle, or that he has entrusted this care to intelligences whose power and knowledge are almost divine, we must hold the opinion that God *preformed* things in such sort that new organisms are only a mechanical consequence of a preceding organic constitution. Even so do butterflies come out of silkworms, an instance where M. Swammerdam has shown that there is nothing but development. And I would have added that nothing is better qualified than the preformation of plants and of animals to confirm my System of Preestablished Harmony between the soul and the body. For in this the body is prompted by its original constitution to carry out with the help of external things all that it does in accordance with the will of the soul. So the seeds by their original constitution carry out naturally the intentions of God, by an artifice greater still than that which causes our body to perform everything in conformity with our will. And since M. Bayle himself deems with reason that there is more artifice in the organism of animals than in the most beautiful poem in the world or in the most admirable invention whereof the human mind is capable, it follows that my system of the connexion between the body and the soul is as intelligible as the general opinion on the formation of animals. For this opinion (which appears to me true) states in effect that the wisdom of God has so made Nature that it is competent in virtue of its laws to form animals; I explain this opinion and throw more light upon the possibility of it through the system of preformation. Whereafter there will be no cause for surprise that God has so made the body that by virtue of its own laws it can carry out the intentions of the reasoning soul: for all that the reasoning soul can demand of the body is less difficult than the organization which God has demanded of the seeds. M. Bayle says (*Reply to the Questions of a Provincial*, ch. 182, p. 1294) that it is only very recently there have been people who have understood that the formation of living bodies cannot be a natural process. This he could say also (in accordance with his principles) of the communication between the soul and the body, since God effects this whole communication in the system of occasional causes to which this author subscribes. But I admit the supernatural here only in the beginning of things, in respect of the first formation of animals or in respect of the original constitution of pre-established harmony between the soul and the body. Once that has come to pass, I hold that the formation of animals and the relation between the soul and the body are something as natural now as the other most ordinary operations of Nature. A close parallel is afforded by people's ordinary thinking about the instinct and the marvellous behaviour of brutes. One recognizes reason there not in the brutes but in him who created them. I am, then, of the general opinion in this respect; but I hope that my explanation will have added clearness and lucidity, and even a more ample range, to that opinion.

Now when preparing to justify my system in face of the new difficulties of M. Bayle, I purposed at the same time to communicate to him the ideas which I had had for some time already, on the difficulties put forward by him in opposition to those who endeavour to reconcile reason with faith in regard to the existence of evil. Indeed, there are perhaps few persons who have toiled more than I in this matter. Hardly had I gained some tolerable understanding of Latin writings when I had an opportunity of turning over books in a library. I flitted from book to book, and since subjects for meditation pleased me as much as histories and fables, I was charmed by the work of Laurentius Valla against Boethius and by that of Luther against Erasmus, although I was well aware that they had need of some mitigation. I did not omit books of controversy, and amongst other writings of this nature the records of the Montbéliard Conversation, which had revived the dispute, appeared to me instructive. Nor did I neglect the teachings of our theologians: and the study of their opponents, far from disturbing me, served to strengthen me in the moderate opinions of the Churches of the Augsburg Confession. I had opportunity on my journeys to confer with some excellent men of different parties, for instance with Bishop Peter von Wallenburg, Suffragan of Mainz, with Herr Johann Ludwig Fabricius, premier theologian of Heidelberg, and finally with the celebrated M. Arnauld. To him I even tendered a Latin Dialogue of my own composition upon this subject, about the year 1673, wherein already I laid it down that God, having chosen the most perfect of all possible worlds, had been prompted by his wisdom to permit the evil which was bound up with it, but which still did not prevent this world from being, all things considered, the best that could be chosen. I have also since read many and various good authors on these subjects, and I have endeavoured to make progress in the knowledge that seems to me proper for banishing all that could have obscured the idea of supreme perfection which must be acknowledged in God. I have not neglected to examine the most rigorous authors, who have extended furthest the doctrine of the necessity of things, as for instance Hobbes and Spinoza, of whom the former advocated this absolute necessity not only in his *Physical Elements* and elsewhere, but also in a special book against Bishop Bramhall. And Spinoza insists more or less (like an ancient Peripatetic philosopher named Strato) that all has come from the first cause or from primitive Nature by a blind and geometrical necessity, with complete absence of capacity for choice, for goodness and for understanding in this first source of things.

I have found the means, so it seems to me, of demonstrating the contrary in a way that gives one a clear insight into the inward essence of the matter. For having made new discoveries on the nature of active force and the laws of motion, I have shown that they have no geometrical necessity, as Spinoza appears to have believed they had. Neither, as I have made plain, are they purely arbitrary, even though this be the opinion of M. Bayle and of some modern philosophers: but they are dependent upon the fitness of things as I have already pointed out above, or upon that which I call the 'principle of the best'. Moreover one recognizes therein, as in every other thing, the marks of the first substance, whose productions bear the stamp of a supreme wisdom and make the most perfect of harmonies. I have shown also that this harmony connects both the future with the past and the present with the absent. The first kind of connexion unites times, and the other places. This second connexion is displayed in the union of the soul with the body, and in general in the communication of true substances with one another and with material phenomena. But the first takes place in the preformation of organic bodies, or rather of all bodies, since there is organism everywhere, although all masses do not compose organic bodies. So a pond may very well be full of fish or of other organic bodies, although it is not itself an animal or organic body, but only a mass that contains them. Thus I had endeavoured to build upon such foundations, established in a conclusive manner, a complete body of the main articles of knowledge that reason pure and simple can impart to us, a body whereof all the parts were properly connected and capable of meeting the most important difficulties of the ancients and the moderns. I had also in consequence formed for myself a certain system concerning the freedom of man and the co-operation of God. This system appeared to me to be such as would in no wise offend reason and faith; and I desired to submit it to the scrutiny of M. Bayle, as well as of those who are in controversy with him. Now he has departed from us, and such a loss is no small one, a writer whose learning and acumen few have equalled. But since the subject is under consideration and men of talent are still occupied with it, while the public also follows it attentively, I take this to be a fitting moment for the publication of certain of my ideas.

It will perhaps be well to add the observation, before finishing this preface, that in denying the physical influence of the soul upon the body or of the body upon the soul, that is, an influence causing the one to disturb the laws of the other, I by no means deny the union of the one with the other which forms of them a suppositum; but this union is something metaphysical, which changes nothing in the phenomena. This is what I have already said in reply to the objection raised against me, in the *Mémoires de Trévoux*, by the Reverend Father de Tournemine, whose wit and learning are of no ordinary mould. And for this reason one may say also in a metaphysical sense that the soul acts upon the body and the body upon the soul. Moreover, it is true that the soul is the Entelechy or the active principle, whereas the corporeal alone or the mere material contains only the passive. Consequently the principle of action is in the soul, as I have explained more than once in the *Leipzig Journal*. More especially does this appear in my answer to the late Herr Sturm, philosopher and mathematician of Altorf, where I have even demonstrated that, if bodies contained only the passive, their different conditions would be indistinguishable. Also I take this opportunity to say that, having heard of some objections made by the gifted author of the book on *Self-knowledge*, in that same book, to my System of Pre-established Harmony, I sent a reply to Paris, showing that he has attributed to me opinions I am far from holding. On another matter recently I met with like treatment at the hands of an anonymous Doctor of the Sorbonne. And these misconceptions would have become plain to the reader at the outset if my own words, which were being taken in evidence, had been quoted.

This tendency of men to make mistakes in presenting the opinions of others leads me to observe also, that when I said somewhere that man helps himself in conversion through the succour of grace, I mean only that he derives advantage from it through the cessation of the resistance overcome, but without any co-operation on his part: just as there is no co-operation in ice when it is broken. For conversion is purely the work of God's grace, wherein man co-operates only by resisting it; but human resistance is more or less great according to the persons and the occasions. Circumstances also contribute more or less to our attention and to the motions that arise in the soul; and the co-operation of all these things, together with the strength of the impression and the condition of the will, determines the operation of grace, although not rendering it necessary. I have expounded sufficiently elsewhere that in relation to matters of salvation unregenerate man is to be considered as dead; and I greatly approve the manner wherein the theologians of the Augsburg Confession declare themselves on this subject. Yet this corruption of unregenerate man is, it must be added, no hindrance to his possession of true moral virtues and his performance of good actions in his civic life, actions which spring from a good principle, without any evil intention and without mixture of actual sin. Wherein I hope I shall be forgiven, if I have dared to diverge from the opinion of St. Augustine: he was doubtless a great man, of admirable intelligence, but inclined sometimes, as it seems, to exaggerate things, above all in the heat of his controversies. I greatly esteem some persons who profess to be disciples of St. Augustine, amongst others the Reverend Father Quênel, a worthy successor of the great Arnauld in the pursuit of controversies that have embroiled them with the most famous of Societies. But I have found that usually in disputes between people of conspicuous merit (of whom there are doubtless some here in both parties) there is right on both sides, although in different points, and it is rather in the matter of defence than attack, although the natural malevolence of the human heart generally renders attack more agreeable to the reader than defence. I hope that the Reverend Father Ptolemei, who does his Society credit and is occupied in filling the gaps left by the famous Bellarmine, will give us, concerning all of that, some explanations worthy of his acumen and his knowledge, and I even dare to add, his moderation. And one must believe that among the theologians of the Augsburg Confession there will arise some new Chemnitz or some new Callixtus; even as one is justified in thinking that men like Usserius or Daillé will again appear among the Reformed, and that all will work more and more to remove the misconceptions wherewith this matter is charged. For the rest I shall be well pleased that those who shall wish to examine it closely read the objections with the answers I have given thereto, formulated in the small treatise I have placed at the end of the work by way of summary. I have endeavoured to forestall some new objections. I have explained, for instance, why I have taken the antecedent and consequent will as preliminary and final, after the example of Thomas, of Scotus and others; how it is possible that there be incomparably more good in the glory of all the saved than there is evil in the misery of all the damned, despite that there are more of the latter; how, in saying that evil has been permitted as a *conditio sine qua non* of good, I mean not according to the principle of necessity, but according to the principle of the fitness of things. Furthermore I show that the predetermination I admit is such as always to predispose, but never to necessitate, and that God will not refuse the requisite new light to those who have made a good use of that which they had. Other elucidations besides I have endeavoured to give on some difficulties which have been put before me of late. I have, moreover, followed the advice of some friends who thought it fitting that I should add two appendices: the one treats of the controversy carried on between Mr. Hobbes and Bishop Bramhall touching Freedom and Necessity, the other of the learned work on *The Origin of Evil*, published a short time ago in England.

Finally I have endeavoured in all things to consider edification: and if I have conceded something to curiosity, it is because I thought it necessary to relieve a subject whose seriousness may cause discouragement. It is with that in view that I have introduced into this dissertation the pleasing chimera of a certain astronomical theology, having no ground for apprehension that it will ensnare anyone and deeming that to tell it and refute it is the same thing. Fiction for fiction, instead of imagining that the planets were suns, one might conceive that they were masses melted in the sun and thrown out, and that would destroy the foundation of this hypothetical theology. The ancient error of the two principles, which the Orientals distinguished by the names Oromasdes and Arimanius, caused me to explain a conjecture on the primitive history of peoples. It appears indeed probable that these were the names of two great contemporary princes, the one monarch of a part of upper Asia, where there have since been others of this name, the other king of the Scythian Celts who made incursions into the states of the former, and who was also named amongst the divinities of Germania. It seems, indeed, that Zoroaster used the names of these princes as symbols of the invisible powers which their exploits made them resemble in the ideas of Asiatics. Yet elsewhere, according to the accounts of Arab authors, who in this might well be better informed than the Greeks, it appears from detailed records of ancient oriental history, that this Zerdust or Zoroaster, whom they make contemporary with the great Darius, did not look upon these two principles as completely primitive and independent, but as dependent upon one supreme and single principle. They relate that he believed, in conformity with the cosmogony of Moses, that God, who is without an equal, created all and separated the light from the darkness; that the light conformed with his original design, but that the darkness came as a consequence, even as the shadow follows the body, and that this is nothing but privation. Such a thesis would clear this ancient author of the errors the Greeks imputed to him. His great learning caused the Orientals to compare him with the Mercury or Hermes of the Egyptians and Greeks; just as the northern peoples compared their Wodan or Odin to this same Mercury. That is why Mercredi (Wednesday), or the day of Mercury, was called Wodansdag by the northern peoples, but day of Zerdust by the Asiatics, since it is named Zarschamba or Dsearschambe by the Turks and the Persians, Zerda by the Hungarians from the north-east, and Sreda by the Slavs from the heart of Great Russia, as far as the Wends of the Luneburg region, the Slavs having learnt the name also from the Orientals. These observations will perhaps not be displeasing to the curious. And I flatter myself that the small dialogue ending the Essays written to oppose M. Bayle will give some satisfaction to those who are well pleased to see difficult but important truths set forth in an easy and familiar way. I have written in a foreign language at the risk of making many errors in it, because that language has been recently used by others in treating of my subject, and because it is more generally read by those whom one would wish to benefit by this small work. It is to be hoped that the language errors will be pardoned: they are to be attributed not only to the printer and the copyist, but also to the haste of the author, who has been much distracted from his task. If, moreover, any error has crept into the ideas expressed, the author will be the first to correct it, once he has been better informed: he has given elsewhere such indications of his love of truth that he hopes this declaration will not be regarded as merely an empty phrase.

PRELIMINARY DISSERTATION
ON THE CONFORMITY OF
FAITH WITH REASON

1. I BEGIN with the preliminary question of the *conformity of faith with reason*, and the use of philosophy in theology, because it has much influence on the main subject of my treatise, and because M. Bayle introduces it everywhere. I assume that two truths cannot contradict each other; that the object of faith is the truth God has revealed in an extraordinary way; and that reason is the linking together of truths, but especially (when it is compared with faith) of those whereto the human mind can attain naturally without being aided by the light of faith. This definition of reason (that is to say of strict and true reason) has surprised some persons accustomed to inveigh against reason taken in a vague sense. They gave me the answer that they had never heard of any such explanation of it: the truth is that they have never conferred with people who expressed themselves clearly on these subjects. They have confessed to me, nevertheless, that one could not find fault with reason, understood in the sense which I gave to it. It is in the same sense that sometimes reason is contrasted with experience. Reason, since it consists in the linking together of truths, is entitled to connect also those wherewith experience has furnished it, in order thence to draw mixed conclusions; but reason pure and simple, as distinct from experience, only has to do with truths independent of the senses. And one may compare faith with experience, since faith (in

respect of the motives that give it justification) depends upon the experience of those who have seen the miracles whereon revelation is founded, and upon the trustworthy tradition which has handed them down to us, whether through the Scriptures or by the account of those who have preserved them. It is rather as we rely upon the experience of those who have seen China and on the credibility of their account when we give credence to the wonders that are told us of that distant country. Yet I would also take into account the inward motion of the Holy Spirit, who takes possession of souls and persuades them and prompts them to good, that is, to faith and to charity, without always having need of motives.

2. Now the truths of reason are of two kinds: the one kind is ot those called the 'Eternal Verities', which are altogether necessary, so that the opposite implies contradiction. Such are the truths whose necessity is logical, metaphysical or geometrical, which one cannot deny without being led into absurdities. There are others which may be called *positive*, because they are the laws which it has pleased God to give to Nature, or because they depend upon those. We learn them either by experience, that is, *a posteriori*, or by reason and *a priori*, that is, by considerations of the fitness of things which have caused their choice. This fitness of things has also its rules and reasons, but it is the free choice of God, and not a geometrical necessity, which causes preference for what is fitting and brings it into existence. Thus one may say that physical necessity is founded on moral necessity, that is, on the wise one's choice which is worthy of his wisdom; and that both of these ought to be distinguished from geometrical necessity. It is this physical necessity that makes order in Nature and lies in the rules of motion and in some other general laws which it pleased God to lay down for things when he gave them being. It is therefore true that God gave such laws not without reason, for he chooses nothing from caprice and as though by chance or in pure indifference; but the general reasons of good and of order, which have prompted him to the choice, may be overcome in some cases by stronger reasons of a superior order.

3. Thus it is made clear that God can exempt creatures from the laws he has prescribed for them, and produce in them that which their nature does not bear by performing a miracle. When they have risen to perfections and faculties nobler than those whereto they can by their nature attain, the Schoolmen call this

74

faculty an 'Obediential Power', that is to say, a power which the thing acquires by obeying the command of him who can give that which the thing has not. The Schoolmen, however, usually give instances of this power which to me appear impossible: they maintain, for example, that God can give the creature the faculty to create. It may be that there are miracles which God performs through the ministry of angels, where the laws of Nature are not violated, any more than when men assist Nature by art, the skill of angels differing from ours only by degree of perfection. Nevertheless it still remains true that the laws of Nature are subject to be dispensed from by the Law-giver; whereas the eternal verities, as for instance those of geometry, admit no dispensation, and faith cannot contradict them. Thus it is that there cannot be any invincible objection to truth. For if it is a question of proof which is founded upon principles or incontestable facts and formed by a linking together of eternal verities, the conclusion is certain and essential, and that which is contrary to it must be false; otherwise two contradictories might be true at the same time. If the objection is not conclusive, it can only form a probable argument, which has no force against faith, since it is agreed that the Mysteries of religion are contrary to appearances. Now M. Bayle declares, in his posthumous Reply to M. le Clerc, that he does not claim that there are demonstrations contrary to the truths of faith: and as a result all these insuperable difficulties, these so-called wars between reason and faith, vanish away.

> *Hi motus animorum atque haec discrimina tanta,*
> *Pulveris exigui jactu compressa quiescunt.*

4. Protestant theologians as well as those of the Roman confession admit the maxims which I have just laid down, when they handle the matter with attention; and all that is said against reason has no force save against a kind of counterfeit reason, corrupted and deluded by false appearances. It is the same with our notions of the justice and the goodness of God, which are spoken of sometimes as if we had neither any idea nor any definition of their nature. But in that case we should have no ground for ascribing these attributes to him, or lauding him for them. His goodness and his justice as well as his wisdom differ from ours only because they are infinitely more perfect. Thus the simple notions, the necessary truths and the conclusive results of philosophy

cannot be contrary to revelation. And when some philosophical maxims are rejected in theology, the reason is that they are considered to have only a physical or moral necessity, which speaks only of that which takes place usually, and is consequently founded on appearances, but which may be withheld if God so pleases.

5. It seems, according to what I have just said, that there is often some confusion in the expressions of those who set at variance philosophy and theology, or faith and reason: they confuse the terms 'explain', 'comprehend', 'prove', 'uphold'. And I find that M. Bayle, shrewd as he is, is not always free from this confusion. Mysteries may be *explained* sufficiently to justify belief in them; but one cannot *comprehend* them, nor give understanding of how they come to pass. Thus even in natural philosophy we explain up to a certain point sundry perceptible qualities, but in an imperfect manner, for we do not comprehend them. Nor is it possible for us, either, to prove Mysteries by reason; for all that which can be proved *a priori*, or by pure reason, can be comprehended. All that remains for us then, after having believed in the Mysteries by reason of the proofs of the truth of religion (which are called 'motives of credibility') is to be able to *uphold* them against objections. Without that our belief in them would have no firm foundation; for all that which can be refuted in a sound and conclusive manner cannot but be false. And such proofs of the truth of religion as can give only a *moral certainty* would be balanced and even outweighed by such objections as would give an *absolute certainty*, provided they were convincing and altogether conclusive. This little might suffice me to remove the difficulties concerning the use of reason and philosophy in relation to religion if one had not to deal all too often with prejudiced persons. But as the subject is important and it has fallen into a state of confusion, it will be well to take it in greater detail.

6. The question of the *conformity of faith with reason* has always been a great problem. In the primitive Church the ablest Christian authors adapted themselves to the ideas of the Platonists, which were the most acceptable to them, and were at that time most generally in favour. Little by little Aristotle took the place of Plato, when the taste for systems began to prevail, and when theology itself became more systematic, owing to the decisions of the General Councils, which provided precise and positive formularies. St. Augustine, Boethius and Cassiodorus in the West, and

St. John of Damascus in the East contributed most towards reducing theology to scientific form, not to mention Bede, Alcuin, St. Anselm and some other theologians versed in philosophy. Finally came the Schoolmen. The leisure of the cloisters giving full scope for speculation, which was assisted by Aristotle's philosophy translated from the Arabic, there was formed at last a compound of theology and philosophy wherein most of the questions arose from the trouble that was taken to reconcile faith with reason. But this had not met with the full success hoped for, because theology had been much corrupted by the unhappiness of the times, by ignorance and obstinacy. Moreover, philosophy, in addition to its own faults, which were very great, found itself burdened with those of theology, which in its turn was suffering from association with a philosophy that was very obscure and very imperfect. One must confess, notwithstanding, with the incomparable Grotius, that there is sometimes gold hidden under the rubbish of the monks' barbarous Latin. I have therefore ofttimes wished that a man of talent, whose office had necessitated his learning the language of the Schoolmen, had chosen to extract thence whatever is of worth, and that another Petau or Thomasius had done in respect of the Schoolmen what these two learned men have done in respect of the Fathers. It would be a very curious work, and very important for ecclesiastical history, and it would continue the History of Dogmas up to the time of the Revival of Letters (owing to which the aspect of things has changed) and even beyond that point. For sundry dogmas, such as those of physical predetermination, of mediate knowledge, philosophical sin, objective precisions, and many other dogmas in speculative theology and even in the practical theology of cases of conscience, came into currency even after the Council of Trent.

7. A little before these changes, and before the great schism in the West that still endures, there was in Italy a sect of philosophers which disputed this conformity of faith with reason which I maintain. They were dubbed 'Averroists' because they were adherents of a famous Arab author, who was called the Commentator by pre-eminence, and who appeared to be the one of all his race that penetrated furthest into Aristotle's meaning. This Commentator, extending what Greek expositors had already taught, maintained that according to Aristotle, and even according to reason (and at that time the two were considered almost identical)

there was no case for the immortality of the soul. Here is his reasoning. The human kind is eternal, according to Aristotle, therefore if individual souls die not, one must resort to the metempsychosis rejected by that philosopher. Or, if there are always new souls, one must admit the infinity of these souls existing from all eternity; but actual infinity is impossible, according to the doctrine of the same Aristotle. Therefore it is a necessary conclusion that the souls, that is, the forms of organic bodies, must perish with the bodies, or at least this must happen to the passive understanding that belongs to each one individually. Thus there will only remain the active understanding common to all men, which according to Aristotle comes from outside, and which must work wheresoever the organs are suitably disposed; even as the wind produces a kind of music when it is blown into properly adjusted organ pipes.

8. Nothing could have been weaker than this would-be proof. It is not true that Aristotle refuted metempsychosis, or that he proved the eternity of the human kind; and after all, it is quite untrue that an actual infinity is impossible. Yet this proof passed as irresistible amongst Aristotelians, and induced in them the belief that there was a certain sublunary intelligence and that our active intellect was produced by participation in it. But others who adhered less to Aristotle went so far as to advocate a universal soul forming the ocean of all individual souls, and believed this universal soul alone capable of subsisting, whilst individual souls are born and die. According to this opinion the souls of animals are born by being separated like drops from their ocean, when they find a body which they can animate; and they die by being reunited to the ocean of souls when the body is destroyed, as streams are lost in the sea. Many even went so far as to believe that God is that universal soul, although others thought that this soul was subordinate and created. This bad doctrine is very ancient and apt to dazzle the common herd. It is expressed in these beautiful lines of Vergil (*Aen.*, VI, v. 724):

> *Principio coelum ac terram camposque liquentes,*
> *Lucentemque globum Lunae Titaniaque astra,*
> *Spiritus intus alit, totamque infusa per artus*
> *Mens agitat molem, et magno se corpore miscet.*
> *Inde hominum pecudumque genus vitaeque volantum.*

And again elsewhere (*Georg.*, IV, v. 221):

> *Deum namque ire per omnes*
> *Terrasque tractusque maris caelumque profundum:*
> *Hinc pecudes, armenta, viros, gęnus omne ferarum,*
> *Quemque sibi tenues nascentem arcessere vitas.*
> *Scilicet huc reddi deinde ac resoluta referri.*

9. Plato's Soul of the World has been taken in this sense by some, but there is more indication that the Stoics succumbed to that universal soul which swallows all the rest. Those who are of this opinion might be called 'Monopsychites', since according to them there is in reality only one soul that subsists. M. Bernier observes that this is an opinion almost universally accepted amongst scholars in Persia and in the States of the Grand Mogul; it appears even that it has gained a footing with the Cabalists and with the mystics. A certain German of Swabian birth, converted to Judaism some years ago, who taught under the name Moses Germanus, having adopted the dogmas of Spinoza, believed that Spinoza revived the ancient Cabala of the Hebrews. And a learned man who confuted this proselyte Jew appears to be of the same opinion. It is known that Spinoza recognizes only substance in the world, whereof individual souls are but transient modifications. Valentin Weigel, Pastor of Zschopau in Saxony, a man of wit, even of excessive wit, although people would have it that he was a visionary, was perhaps to some extent of that opinion; as was also a man known as Johann Angelus Silesius, author of certain quite pleasing little devotional verses in German, in the form of epigrams, which have just been reprinted. In general, the mystics' doctrine of deification was liable to such a sinister interpretation. Gerson already has written opposing Ruysbroek, a mystical writer, whose intention was evidently good and whose expressions are excusable. But it would be better to write in a manner that has no need of excuses: although I confess that ofttimes expressions which are extravagant, and as it were poetical, have greater force to move and to persuade than correct forms of statement.

10. The annihilation of all that belongs to us in our own right, carried to great lengths by the Quietists, might equally well be veiled irreligion in certain minds, as is related, for example, concerning the Quietism of Foë, originator of a great Chinese sect.

After having preached his religion for forty years, when he felt death was approaching, he declared to his disciples that he had hidden the truth from them under the veil of metaphors, and that all reduced itself to Nothingness, which he said was the first source of all things. That was still worse, so it would seem, than the opinion of the Averroists. Both of these doctrines are indefensible and even extravagant; nevertheless some moderns have made no difficulty about adopting this one and universal Soul that engulfs the rest. It has met with only too much applause amongst the so-called freethinkers, and M. de Preissac, a soldier and man of wit, who dabbled in philosophy, at one time aired it publicly in his discourses. The System of Pre-established Harmony is the one best qualified to cure this evil. For it shows that there are of necessity substances which are simple and without extension, scattered throughout all Nature; that these substances must subsist independently of every other except God; and that they are never wholly separated from organic body. Those who believe that souls capable of feeling but incapable of reason are mortal, or who maintain that none but reasoning souls can have feeling, offer a handle to the Monopsychites. For it will ever be difficult to persuade men that beasts feel nothing; and once the admission has been made that that which is capable of feeling can die, it is difficult to found upon reason a proof of the immortality of our souls.

11. I have made this short digression because it appeared to me seasonable at a time when there is only too much tendency to overthrow natural religion to its very foundations. I return then to the Averroists, who were persuaded that their dogma was proved conclusively in accordance with reason. As a result they declared that man's soul is, according to philosophy, mortal, while they protested their acquiescence in Christian theology, which declares the soul's immortality. But this distinction was held suspect, and this divorce between faith and reason was vehemently rejected by the prelates and the doctors of that time, and condemned in the last Lateran Council under Leo X. On that occasion also, scholars were urged to work for the removal of the difficulties that appeared to set theology and philosophy at variance. The doctrine of their incompatibility continued to hold its ground *incognito*. Pomponazzi was suspected of it, although he declared himself otherwise; and that very sect of the Averroists survived as a school. It is thought

that Caesar Cremoninus, a philosopher famous in his time, was one of its mainstays. Andreas Cisalpinus, a physician (and an author of merit who came nearest after Michael Servetus to the discovery of the circulation of the blood), was accused by Nicolas Taurel (in a book entitled *Alpes Caesae*) of belonging to these antireligious Peripatetics. Traces of this doctrine are found also in the *Circulus Pisanus Claudii Berigardi*, an author of French nationality who migrated to Italy and taught philosophy at Pisa: but especially the writings and the letters of Gabriel Naudé, as well as the *Naudaeana*, show that Averroism still lived on when this learned physician was in Italy. Corpuscular philosophy, introduced shortly after, appears to have extinguished this excessively Peripatetic sect, or perhaps to have been intermixed with its teaching. It may be indeed that there have been Atomists who would be inclined to teach dogmas like those of the Averroists, if circumstances so permitted: but this abuse cannot harm such good as there is in Corpuscular philosophy, which can very well be combined with all that is sound in Plato and in Aristotle, and bring them both into harmony with true theology.

12. The Reformers, and especially Luther, as I have already observed, spoke sometimes as if they rejected philosophy, and deemed it inimical to faith. But, properly speaking, Luther understood by philosophy only that which is in conformity with the ordinary course of Nature, or perhaps even philosophy as it was taught in the schools. Thus for example he says that it is impossible in philosophy, that is, in the order of Nature, that the word be made flesh; and he goes so far as to maintain that what is true in natural philosophy might be false in ethics. Aristotle was the object of his anger; and so far back as the year 1516 he contemplated the purging of philosophy, when he perhaps had as yet no thoughts of reforming the Church. But at last he curbed his vehemence and in the *Apology for the Augsburg Confession* allowed a favourable mention of Aristotle and his *Ethics*. Melanchthon, a man of sound and moderate ideas, made little systems from the several parts of philosophy, adapted to the truths of revelation and useful in civic life, which deserve to be read even now. After him, Pierre de la Ramée entered the lists. His philosophy was much in favour: the sect of the Ramists was powerful in Germany, gaining many adherents among the Protestants, and even concerning itself with theology, until the revival of Corpuscular philosophy, which

caused that of Ramée to fall into oblivion and weakened the authority of the Peripatetics.

13. Meanwhile sundry Protestant theologians, deviating as far as they could from Scholastic philosophy, which prevailed in the opposite party, went so far as to despise philosophy itself, which to them was suspect. The controversy blazed up finally owing to the rancour of Daniel Hoffmann. He was an able theologian, who had previously gained a reputation at the Conference of Quedlinburg, when Tilemann Heshusius and he had supported Duke Julius of Brunswick in his refusal to accept the Formula of Concord. For some reason or other Dr. Hoffmann flew into a passion with philosophy, instead of being content to find fault with the wrong uses made thereof by philosophers. He was, however, aiming at the famous Caselius, a man esteemed by the princes and scholars of his time; and Henry Julius, Duke of Brunswick (son of Julius, founder of the University), having taken the trouble himself to investigate the matter, condemned the theologian. There have been some small disputes of the kind since, but it has always been found that they were misunderstandings. Paul Slevogt, a famous Professor at Jena in Thuringia, whose still extant treatises prove how well versed he was in Scholastic philosophy, as also in Hebrew literature, had published in his youth under the title of *Pervigilium* a little book 'de dissidio Theologi et Philosophi in utriusque principiis fundato', bearing on the question whether God is accidentally the cause of sin. But it was easy to see that his aim was to demonstrate that theologians sometimes misuse philosophical terms.

14. To come now to the events of my own time, I remember that when in 1666 Louis Meyer, a physician of Amsterdam, published anonymously the book entitled *Philosophia Scripturae Interpres* (by many persons wrongly attributed to Spinoza, his friend) the theologians of Holland bestirred themselves, and their written attacks upon this book gave rise to great disputes among them. Divers of them held the opinion that the Cartesians, in confuting the anonymous philosopher, had conceded too much to philosophy. Jean de Labadie (before he had seceded from the Reformed Church, his pretext being some abuses which he said had crept into public observance and which he considered intolerable) attacked the book by Herr von Wollzogen, and called it pernicious. On the other hand Herr Vogelsang, Herr van der Weye and some

other anti-Cocceïans also assailed the same book with much acrimony. But the accused won his case in a Synod. Afterwards in Holland people spoke of 'rational' and 'non-rational' theologians, a party distinction often mentioned by M. Bayle, who finally declared himself against the former. But there is no indication that any precise rules have yet been defined which the rival parties accept or reject with regard to the use of reason in the interpretation of Holy Scripture.

15. A like dispute has threatened of late to disturb the peace in the Churches of the Augsburg Confession. Some Masters of Arts in the University of Leipzig gave private lessons at their homes, to students who sought them out in order to learn what is called 'Sacra Philologia', according to the practice of this university and of some others where this kind of study is not restricted to the Faculty of Theology. These masters pressed the study of the Holy Scriptures and the practice of piety further than their fellows had been wont to do. It is alleged that they had carried certain things to excess, and aroused suspicions of certain doctrinal innovations. This caused them to be dubbed 'Pietists', as though they were a new sect; and this name is one which has since caused a great stir in Germany. It has been applied somehow or other to those whom one suspected, or pretended to suspect, of fanaticism, or even of hypocrisy, concealed under some semblance of reform. Now some of the students attending these masters had become conspicuous for behaviour which gave general offence, and amongst other things for their scorn of philosophy, even, so it was said, burning their notebooks. In consequence the belief arose that their masters rejected philosophy: but they justified themselves very well; nor could they be convicted either of this error or of the heresies that were being imputed to them.

16. The question of the use of philosophy in theology was debated much amongst Christians, and difficulty was experienced over settling the limits of its use when it came to detailed consideration. The Mysteries of the Trinity, of the Incarnation and of the Holy Communion gave most occasion for dispute. The new Photinians, disputing the first two Mysteries, made use of certain philosophic maxims which Andreas Kessler, a theologian of the Augsburg Confession, summarized in the various treatises that he published on the parts of the Socinian philosophy. But as to their metaphysics, one might instruct oneself better therein by reading

the work of Christopher Stegmann the Socinian. It is not yet in print; but I saw it in my youth and it has been recently again in my hands.

17. Calovius and Scherzer, authors well versed in Scholastic philosophy, and sundry other able theologians answered the Socinians at great length, and often with success: for they would not content themselves with the general and somewhat cavalier answers that were commonly used against that sect. The drift of such answers was: that their maxims were good in philosophy and not in theology; that it was the fault of heterogeneousness called μετάβασις εἰς ἄλλο γένος to apply those maxims to a matter transcending reason; and that philosophy should be treated as a servant and not a mistress in relation to theology, according to the title of the book by a Scot named Robert Baronius, *Philosophia Theologiae ancillans*. In fine, philosophy was a Hagar beside Sara and must be driven from the house with her Ishmael when she was refractory. There is something good in these answers: but one might abuse them, and set natural truths and truths of revelation at variance. Scholars therefore applied themselves to distinguishing between what is necessary and indispensable in natural or philosophic truths and that which is not so.

18. The two Protestant parties are tolerably in agreement when it is a question of making war on the Socinians; and as the philosophy of these sectaries is not of the most exact, in most cases the attack succeeded in reducing it. But the Protestants themselves had dissensions on the matter of the Eucharistic Sacrament. A section of those who are called Reformed (namely those who on that point follow rather Zwingli than Calvin) seemed to reduce the participation in the body of Jesus Christ in the Holy Communion to a mere figurative representation, employing the maxim of the philosophers which states that a body can only be in one place at a time. Contrariwise the Evangelicals (who name themselves thus in a particular sense to distinguish themselves from the Reformed), being more attached to the literal sense of Scripture, opined with Luther that this participation was real, and that here there lay a supernatural Mystery. They reject, in truth, the dogma of Transubstantiation, which they believe to be without foundation in the Text; neither do they approve that of Consubstantiation or of Impanation, which one could only impute to them if one were ill-informed on their opinion. For they admit no inclusion of the body

of Jesus Christ in the bread, nor do they even require any union of the one with the other: but they demand at least a concomitance, so that these two substances be received both at the same time. They believe that the ordinary sense of the words of Jesus Christ on an occasion so important as that which concerned the expression of his last wishes ought to be preserved. Thus in order to show that this sense is free from all absurdity which could make it repugnant to us, they maintain that the philosophic maxim restricting the existence of, and partaking in, bodies to one place alone is simply a consequence of the ordinary course of Nature. They make that no obstacle to the presence, in the ordinary sense of the word, of the body of our Saviour in such form as may be in keeping with the most glorified body. They do not resort to a vague diffusion of ubiquity, which would disperse the body and leave it nowhere in particular; nor do they admit the multiple-reduplication theory of some Schoolmen, as if to say one and the same body could be at the same time seated here and standing elsewhere. In fine, they so express themselves that many consider the opinion of Calvin, authorized by sundry confessions of faith from the Churches that have accepted his teaching, to be not so far removed from the Augsburg Confession as one might think: for he affirmed a partaking in the substance. The divergence rests perhaps only upon the fact that Calvin demands true faith in addition to the oral reception of the symbols, and consequently excludes the unworthy.

19. Thence we see that the dogma of real and substantial participation can be supported (without resorting to the strange opinions of some Schoolmen) by a properly understood analogy between *immediate operation* and *presence*. Many philosophers have deemed that, even in the order of Nature, a body may operate from a distance immediately on many remote bodies at the same time. So do they believe, all the more, that nothing can prevent divine Omnipotence from causing one body to be present in many bodies together, since the transition from immediate operation to presence is but slight, the one perhaps depending upon the other. It is true that modern philosophers for some time now have denied the immediate natural operation of one body upon another remote from it, and I confess that I am of their opinion. Meanwhile remote operation has just been revived in England by the admirable Mr. Newton, who maintains that it is the nature of

bodies to be attracted and gravitate one towards another, in proportion to the mass of each one, and the rays of attraction it receives. Accordingly the famous Mr. Locke, in his answer to Bishop Stillingfleet, declares that having seen Mr. Newton's book he retracts what he himself said, following the opinion of the moderns, in his *Essay concerning Human Understanding*, to wit, that a body cannot operate immediately upon another except by touching it upon its surface and driving it by its motion. He acknowledges that God can put properties into matter which cause it to operate from a distance. Thus the theologians of the Augsburg Confession claim that God may ordain not only that a body operate immediately on divers bodies remote from one another, but that it even exist in their neighbourhood and be received by them in a way with which distances of place and dimensions of space have nothing to do. Although this effect transcends the forces of Nature, they do not think it possible to show that it surpasses the power of the Author of Nature. For him it is easy to annul the laws that he has given or to dispense with them as seems good to him, in the same way as he was able to make iron float upon water and to stay the operation of fire upon the human body.

20. I found in comparing the *Rationale Theologicum* of Nicolaus Vedelius with the refutation by Johann Musaeus that these two authors, of whom one died while a Professor at Franecker after having taught at Geneva and the other finally became the foremost theologian at Jena, are more or less in agreement on the principal rules for the use of reason, but that it is in the application of these rules they disagree. For they both agree that revelation cannot be contrary to the truths whose necessity is called by philosophers 'logical' or 'metaphysical', that is to say, whose opposite implies contradiction. They both admit also that revelation will be able to combat maxims whose necessity is called 'physical' and is founded only upon the laws that the will of God has prescribed for Nature. Thus the question whether the presence of one and the same body in divers places is possible in the supernatural order only touches the application of the rule; and in order to decide this question conclusively by reason, one must needs explain exactly wherein the essence of body consists. Even the Reformed disagree thereon amongst themselves; the Cartesians confine it to extension, but their adversaries oppose that; and I think I have even observed that Gisbertus Voëtius, a famous

theologian of Utrecht, doubted the alleged impossibility of plurality of locations.

21. Furthermore, although the two Protestant parties agree that one must distinguish these two necessities which I have just indicated, namely metaphysical necessity and physical necessity, and that the first excludes exceptions even in the case of Mysteries, they are not yet sufficiently agreed upon the rules of interpretation, which serve to determine in what cases it is permitted to desert the letter of Scripture when one is not certain that it is contrary to strictly universal truths. It is agreed that there are cases where one must reject a literal interpretation that is not absolutely impossible, when it is otherwise unsuitable. For instance, all commentators agree that when our Lord said that Herod was a fox he meant it metaphorically; and one must accept that, unless one imagine with some fanatics that for the time the words of our Lord lasted Herod was actually changed into a fox. But it is not the same with the texts on which Mysteries are founded, where the theologians of the Augsburg Confession deem that one must keep to the literal sense. Since, moreover, this discussion belongs to the art of interpretation and not to that which is the proper sphere of logic, we will not here enter thereon, especially as it has nothing in common with the disputes that have arisen recently upon the conformity of faith with reason.

22. Theologians of all parties, I believe (fanatics alone excepted), agree at least that no article of faith must imply contradiction or contravene proofs as exact as those of mathematics, where the opposite of the conclusion can be reduced *ad absurdum*, that is, to contradiction. St. Athanasius with good reason made sport of the preposterous ideas of some writers of his time, who maintained that God had suffered without any suffering. '*Passus est impassibiliter. O ludicram doctrinam aedificantem simul et demolientem!*' It follows thence that certain writers have been too ready to grant that the Holy Trinity is contrary to that great principle which states that two things which are the same as a third are also the same as each other: that is to say, if A is the same as B, and if C is the same as B, then A and C must also be the same as each other. For this principle is a direct consequence of that of contradiction, and forms the basis of all logic; and if it ceases, we can no longer reason with certainty. Thus when one says that the Father is God, that the Son is God and that the Holy Spirit is God, and that

nevertheless there is only one God, although these three Persons differ from one another, one must consider that this word *God* has not the same sense at the beginning as at the end of this statement. Indeed it signifies now the Divine Substance and now a Person of the Godhead. In general, one must take care never to abandon the necessary and eternal truths for the sake of upholding Mysteries, lest the enemies of religion seize upon such an occasion for decrying both religion and Mysteries.

23. The distinction which is generally drawn between that which is *above* reason and that which is *against* reason is tolerably in accord with the distinction which has just been made between the two kinds of necessity. For what is contrary to reason is contrary to the absolutely certain and inevitable truths; and what is above reason is in opposition only to what one is wont to experience or to understand. That is why I am surprised that there are people of intelligence who dispute this distinction, and that M. Bayle should be of this number. The distinction is assuredly very well founded. A truth is above reason when our mind (or even every created mind) cannot comprehend it. Such is, as it seems to me, the Holy Trinity; such are the miracles reserved for God alone, as for instance Creation; such is the choice of the order of the universe, which depends upon universal harmony, and upon the clear knowledge of an infinity of things at once. But a truth can never be contrary to reason, and once a dogma has been disputed and refuted by reason, instead of its being incomprehensible, one may say that nothing is easier to understand, nor more obvious, than its absurdity. For I observed at the beginning that by REASON here I do not mean the opinions and discourses of men, nor even the habit they have formed of judging things according to the usual course of Nature, but rather the inviolable linking together of truths.

24. I must come now to the great question which M. Bayle brought up recently, to wit, whether a truth, and especially a truth of faith, can prove to be subject to irrefutable objections. This excellent author appears to answer with a bold affirmative: he quotes theologians of repute in his party, and even in the Church of Rome, who appear to say the same as he affirms; and he cites philosophers who have believed that there are even philosophical truths whose champions cannot answer the objections that are brought up against them. He believes that the theological

doctrine of predestination is of this nature, and in philosophy that of the composition of the *Continuum*. These are, indeed, the two labyrinths which have ever exercised theologians and philosophers. Libertus Fromondus, a theologian of Louvain (a great friend of Jansenius, whose posthumous book entitled *Augustinus* he in fact published), who also wrote a book entitled explicitly *Labyrinthus de Compositione Continui*, experienced in full measure the difficulties inherent in both doctrines; and the renowned Ochino admirably presented what he calls 'the labyrinths of predestination'.

25. But these writers have not denied the possibility of finding thread in the labyrinth; they have recognized the difficulty, but they have surely not turned difficulty into sheer impossibility. As for me, I confess that I cannot agree with those who maintain that a truth can admit of irrefutable objections: for is an *objection* anything but an argument whose conclusion contradicts our thesis? And is not an irrefutable argument a *demonstration*? And how can one know the certainty of demonstrations except by examining the argument in detail, the form and the matter, in order to see if the form is good, and then if each premiss is either admitted or proved by another argument of like force, until one is able to make do with admitted premisses alone? Now if there is such an objection against our thesis we must say that the falsity of this thesis is demonstrated, and that it is impossible for us to have reasons sufficient to prove it; otherwise two contradictories would be true at once. One must always yield to proofs, whether they be proposed in positive form or advanced in the shape of objections. And it is wrong and fruitless to try to weaken opponents' proofs, under the pretext that they are only objections, since the opponent can play the same game and can reverse the denominations, exalting his arguments by naming them 'proofs' and sinking ours under the blighting title of 'objections'.

26. It is another question whether we are always obliged to examine the objections we may have to face, and to retain some doubt in respect of our own opinion, or what is called *formido oppositi*, until this examination has been made. I would venture to say no, for otherwise one would never attain to certainty and our conclusion would be always provisional. I believe that able geometricians will scarce be troubled by the objections of Joseph Scaliger against Archimedes, or by those of Mr. Hobbes against

Euclid; but that is because they have fully understood and are sure of the proofs. Nevertheless it is sometimes well to show oneself ready to examine certain objections. On the one hand it may serve to rescue people from their error, while on the other we ourselves may profit by it; for specious fallacies often contain some useful solution and bring about the removal of considerable difficulties. That is why I have always liked ingenious objections made against my own opinions, and I have never examined them without profit: witness those which M. Bayle formerly made against my System of Pre-established Harmony, not to mention those which M. Arnauld, M. l'Abbé Foucher and Father Lami, O.S.B., made to me on the same subject. But to return to the principal question, I conclude from reasons I have just set forth that when an objection is put forward against some truth, it is always possible to answer it satisfactorily.

27. It may be also that M. Bayle does not mean 'insoluble objections' in the sense that I have just explained. I observe that he varies, at least in his expressions: for in his posthumous Reply to M. le Clerc he does not admit that one can bring demonstrations against the truths of faith. It appears therefore that he takes the objections to be insoluble only in respect of our present degree of enlightenment; and in this Reply, p. 35, he even does not despair of the possibility that one day a solution hitherto unknown may be found by someone. Concerning that more will be said later. I hold an opinion, however, that will perchance cause surprise, namely that this solution has been discovered entire, and is not even particularly difficult. Indeed a mediocre intelligence capable of sufficient care, and using correctly the rules of common logic, is in a position to answer the most embarrassing objection made against truth, when the objection is only taken from reason, and when it is claimed to be a 'demonstration'. Whatever scorn the generality of moderns have to-day for the logic of Aristotle, one must acknowledge that it teaches infallible ways of resisting error in these conjunctures. For one has only to examine the argument according to the rules and it will always be possible to see whether it is lacking in form or whether there are premisses such as are not yet proved by a good argument.

28. It is quite another matter when there is only a question of *probabilities*, for the art of judging from probable reasons is not yet well established; so that our logic in this connexion is still very

imperfect, and to this very day we have little beyond the art of judging from demonstrations. But this art is sufficient here: for when it is a question of opposing reason to an article of our faith, one is not disturbed by objections that only attain probability. Everyone agrees that appearances are against Mysteries, and that they are by no means probable when regarded only from the standpoint of reason; but it suffices that they have in them nothing of absurdity. Thus demonstrations are required if they are to be refuted.

29. And doubtless we are so to understand it when Holy Scripture warns us that the wisdom of God is foolishness before men, and when St. Paul observed that the Gospel of Jesus Christ is foolishness unto the Greeks, as well as unto the Jews a stumbling-block. For, after all, one truth cannot contradict another, and the light of reason is no less a gift of God than that of revelation. Also it is a matter of no difficulty among theologians who are expert in their profession, that the motives of credibility justify, once for all, the authority of Holy Scripture before the tribunal of reason, so that reason in consequence gives way before it, as before a new light, and sacrifices thereto all its probabilities. It is more or less as if a new president sent by the prince must show his letters patent in the assembly where he is afterwards to preside. That is the tendency of sundry good books that we have on the truth of religion, such as those of Augustinus Steuchus, of Du Plessis-Mornay or of Grotius: for the true religion must needs have marks that the false religions have not, else would Zoroaster, Brahma, Somonacodom and Mahomet be as worthy of belief as Moses and Jesus Christ. Nevertheless divine faith itself, when it is kindled in the soul, is something more than an opinion, and depends not upon the occasions or the motives that have given it birth; it advances beyond the intellect, and takes possession of the will and of the heart, to make us act with zeal and joyfully as the law of God commands. Then we have no further need to think of reasons or to pause over the difficulties of argument which the mind may anticipate.

30. Thus what we have just said of human reason, which is extolled and decried by turns, and often without rule or measure, may show our lack of exactitude and how much we are accessary to our own errors. Nothing would be so easy to terminate as these disputes on the rights of faith and of reason if men would make use

of the commonest rules of logic and reason with even a modicum of attention. Instead of that, they become involved in oblique and ambiguous phrases, which give them a fine field for declamation, to make the most of their wit and their learning. It would seem, indeed, that they have no wish to see the naked truth, peradventure because they fear that it may be more disagreeable than error: for they know not the beauty of the Author of all things, who is the source of truth.

31. This negligence is a general defect of humanity, and one not to be laid to the charge of any particular person. *Abundamus dulcibus vitiis*, as Quintilian said of the style of Seneca, and we take pleasure in going astray. Exactitude incommodes us and rules we regard as puerilities. Thus it is that common logic (although it is more or less sufficient for the examination of arguments that tend towards certainty) is relegated to schoolboys; and there is not even a thought for a kind of logic which should determine the balance between probabilities, and would be so necessary in deliberations of importance. So true is it that our mistakes for the most part come from scorn or lack of the art of thinking: for nothing is more imperfect than our logic when we pass beyond necessary arguments. The most excellent philosophers of our time, such as the authors of *The Art of Thinking*, of *The Search for Truth* and of the *Essay concerning Human Understanding*, have been very far from indicating to us the true means fitted to assist the faculty whose business it is to make us weigh the probabilities of the true and the false: not to mention the art of discovery, in which success is still more difficult of attainment, and whereof we have nothing beyond very imperfect samples in mathematics.

32. One thing which might have contributed most towards M. Bayle's belief that the difficulties of reason in opposition to faith cannot be obviated is that he seems to demand that God be justified in some such manner as that commonly used for pleading the cause of a man accused before his judge. But he has not remembered that in the tribunals of men, which cannot always penetrate to the truth, one is often compelled to be guided by signs and probabilities, and above all by presumptions or prejudices; whereas it is agreed, as we have already observed, that Mysteries are not probable. For instance, M. Bayle will not have it that one can justify the goodness of God in the permission of sin, because probability would be against a man that should happen to be in

circumstances comparable in our eyes to this permission. God foresees that Eve will be deceived by the serpent if he places her in the circumstances wherein she later found herself; and nevertheless he placed her there. Now if a father or a guardian did the same in regard to his child or his ward, if a friend did so in regard to a young person whose behaviour was his concern, the judge would not be satisfied by the excuses of an advocate who said that the man only permitted the evil, without doing it or willing it : he would rather take this permission as a sign of ill intention, and would regard it as a sin of omission, which would render the one convicted thereof accessary in another's sin of commission.

33. But it must be borne in mind that when one has foreseen the evil and has not prevented it although it seems as if one could have done so with ease, and one has even done things that have facilitated it, it does not follow on that account *necessarily* that one is accessary thereto. It is only a very strong presumption, such as commonly replaces truth in human affairs, but which would be destroyed by an exact consideration of the facts, supposing we were capable of that in relation to God. For amongst lawyers that is called 'presumption' which must provisionally pass for truth in case the contrary is not proved; and it says more than 'conjecture', although the *Dictionary* of the Academy has not sifted the difference. Now there is every reason to conclude unquestionably that one would find through this consideration, if only it were attainable, that reasons most just, and stronger than those which appear contrary to them, have compelled the All-Wise to permit the evil, and even to do things which have facilitated it. Of this some instances will be given later.

34. It is none too easy, I confess, for a father, a guardian, a friend to have such reasons in the case under consideration. Yet the thing is not absolutely impossible, and a skilled writer of fiction might perchance find an extraordinary case that would even justify a man in the circumstances I have just indicated. But in reference to God there is no need to suppose or to establish particular reasons such as may have induced him to permit the evil; general reasons suffice. One knows that he takes care of the whole universe, whereof all the parts are connected; and one must thence infer that he has had innumerable considerations whose result made him deem it inadvisable to prevent certain evils.

35. It should even be concluded that there must have been

great or rather invincible reasons which prompted the divine Wisdom to the permission of the evil that surprises us, from the mere fact that this permission has occurred: for nothing can come from God that is not altogether consistent with goodness, justice and holiness. Thus we can judge by the event (or *a posteriori*) that the permission was indispensable, although it be not possible for us to show this (*a priori*) by the detailed reasons that God can have had therefor; as it is not necessary either that we show this to justify him. M. Bayle himself aptly says concerning that (*Reply to the Questions of a Provincial*, vol. III, ch. 165, p. 1067): Sin made its way into the world; God therefore was able to permit it without detriment to his perfections; *ab actu ad potentiam valet consequentia.* In God this conclusion holds good: he did this, therefore he did it well. It is not, then, that we have no notion of justice in general fit to be applied also to God's justice; nor is it that God's justice has other rules than the justice known of men, but that the case in question is quite different from those which are common among men. Universal right is the same for God and for men; but the question of fact is quite different in their case and his.

36. We may even assume or pretend (as I have already observed) that there is something similar among men to this circumstance in God's actions. A man might give such great and strong proofs of his virtue and his holiness that all the most apparent reasons one could put forward against him to charge him with an alleged crime, for instance a larceny or murder, would deserve to be rejected as the calumnies of false witnesses or as an extraordinary play of chance which sometimes throws suspicion on the most innocent. Thus in a case where every other would run the risk of being condemned or put to the torture (according to the laws of the country), this man would be absolved by his judges unanimously. Now in this case, which indeed is rare, but which is not impossible, one might say in a sense (*sano sensu*) that there is a conflict between reason and faith, and that the rules of law are other in respect of this person than they are in respect of the remainder of mankind. But that, when explained, will signify only that appearances of reason here give way before the faith that is due to the word and the integrity of this great and holy man, and that he is privileged above other men; not indeed as if there were one law for others and another for him, nor as if one had no understanding of what justice is in relation to him. It is rather

because the rules of universal justice do not find here the application that they receive elsewhere, or because they favour him instead of accusing him, since there are in this personage qualities so admirable, that by virtue of a good logic of probabilities one should place more faith in his word than in that of many others.

37. Since it is permitted here to imagine possible cases, may one not suppose this incomparable man to be the Adept or the Possessor of

> *'that blessed Stone*
> *Able to enrich all earthly Kings alone'*

and that he spends every day prodigious sums in order to feed and to rescue from distress countless numbers of poor men? Be there never so many witnesses or appearances of every kind tending to prove that this great benefactor of the human race has just committed some larceny, is it not true that the whole earth would make mock of the accusation, however specious it might be? Now God is infinitely above the goodness and the power of this man, and consequently there are no reasons at all, however apparent they be, that can hold good against faith, that is, against the assurance or the confidence in God wherewith we can and ought to say that God has done all things well. The objections are therefore not insoluble. They only involve prejudices and probabilities, which are, however, overthrown by reasons incomparably stronger. One must not say either that what we call *justice* is nothing in relation to God, that he is the absolute Master of all things even to the point of being able to condemn the innocent without violating his justice, or finally that justice is something arbitrary where he is concerned. Those are rash and dangerous expressions, whereunto some have been led astray to the discredit of the attributes of God. For if such were the case there would be no reason for praising his goodness and his justice: rather would it be as if the most wicked spirit, the Prince of evil genii, the evil principle of the Manichaeans, were the sole master of the universe, just as I observed before. What means would there be of distinguishing the true God from the false God of Zoroaster if all things depended upon the caprice of an arbitrary power and there were neither rule nor consideration for anything whatever?

38. It is therefore more than evident that nothing compels us to commit ourselves to a doctrine so strange, since it suffices to say

that we have not enough knowledge of the facts when there is a question of answering probabilities which appear to throw doubt upon the justice and the goodness of God, and which would vanish away if the facts were well known to us. We need neither renounce reason in order to listen to faith nor blind ourselves in order to see clearly, as Queen Christine used to say: it is enough to reject ordinary appearances when they are contrary to Mysteries; and this is not contrary to reason, since even in natural things we are very often undeceived about appearances either by experience or by superior reasons. All that has been set down here in advance, only with the object of showing more plainly wherein the fault of the objections and the abuse of reason consists in the present case, where the claim is made that reason has greatest force against faith: we shall come afterwards to a more exact discussion of that which concerns the origin of evil and the permission of sin with its consequences.

39. For now, it will be well to continue our examination of the important question of the use of reason in theology, and to make reflexions upon what M. Bayle has said thereon in divers passages of his works. As he paid particular attention in his *Historical and Critical Dictionary* to expounding the objections of the Manichaeans and those of the Pyrrhonians, and as this procedure had been criticized by some persons zealous for religion, he placed a dissertation at the end of the second edition of this *Dictionary*, which aimed at showing, by examples, by authorities and by reasons, the innocence and usefulness of his course of action. I am persuaded (as I have said above) that the specious objections one can urge against truth are very useful, and that they serve to confirm and to illumine it, giving opportunity to intelligent persons to find new openings or to turn the old to better account. But M. Bayle seeks therein a usefulness quite the reverse of this: it would be that of displaying the power of faith by showing that the truths it teaches cannot sustain the attacks of reason and that it nevertheless holds its own in the heart of the faithful. M. Nicole seems to call that 'the triumph of God's authority over human reason', in the words of his quoted by M. Bayle in the third volume of his *Reply to the Questions of a Provincial* (ch. 177, p. 120). But since reason is a gift of God, even as faith is, contention between them would cause God to contend against God; and if the objections of reason against any article of faith are insoluble, then it must be said that

this alleged article will be false and not revealed: this will be a chimera of the human mind, and the triumph of this faith will be capable of comparison with bonfires lighted after a defeat. Such is the doctrine of the damnation of unbaptized children, which M. Nicole would have us assume to be a consequence of original sin; such would be the eternal damnation of adults lacking the light that is necessary for the attainment of salvation.

40. Yet everyone need not enter into theological discussions; and persons whose condition allows not of exact researches should be content with instruction on faith, without being disturbed by the objections; and if some exceeding great difficulty should happen to strike them, it is permitted to them to avert the mind from it, offering to God a sacrifice of their curiosity: for when one is assured of a truth one has no need to listen to the objections. As there are many people whose faith is rather small and shallow to withstand such dangerous tests, I think one must not present them with that which might be poisonous for them; or, if one cannot hide from them what is only too public, the antidote must be added to it; that is to say, one must try to add the answer to the objection, certainly not withhold it as unobtainable.

41. The passages from the excellent theologians who speak of this triumph of faith can and should receive a meaning appropriate to the principles I have just affirmed. There appear in some objects of faith two great qualities capable of making it triumph over reason, the one is *incomprehensibility*, the other is *the lack of probability*. But one must beware of adding thereto the third quality whereof M. Bayle speaks, and of saying that what one believes is *indefensible*: for that would be to cause reason in its turn to triumph in a manner that would destroy faith. Incomprehensibility does not prevent us from believing even natural truths. For instance (as I have already pointed out) we do not comprehend the nature of odours and savours, and yet we are persuaded, by a kind of faith which we owe to the evidence of the senses, that these perceptible qualities are founded upon the nature of things and that they are not illusions.

42. There are also things contrary to appearances, which we admit when they are sufficiently verified. There is a little romance of Spanish origin, whose title states that one must not always believe what one sees. What was there more specious than the lie of the false Martin Guerre, who was acknowledged as the true

Martin by the true Martin's wife and relatives, and caused the judges and the relatives to waver for a long time even after the arrival of the other? Nevertheless the truth was known in the end. It is the same with faith. I have already observed that all one can oppose to the goodness and the justice of God is nothing but appearances, which would be strong against a man, but which are nullified when they are applied to God and when they are weighed against the proofs that assure us of the infinite perfection of his attributes. Thus faith triumphs over false reasons by means of sound and superior reasons that have made us embrace it; but it would not triumph if the contrary opinion had for it reasons as strong as or even stronger than those which form the foundation of faith, that is, if there were invincible and conclusive objections against faith.

43. It is well also to observe here that what M. Bayle calls a 'triumph of faith' is in part a triumph of demonstrative reason against apparent and deceptive reasons which are improperly set against the demonstrations. For it must be taken into consideration that the objections of the Manichaeans are hardly less contrary to natural theology than to revealed theology. And supposing one surrendered to them Holy Scripture, original sin, the grace of God in Jesus Christ, the pains of hell and the other articles of our religion, one would not even so be delivered from their objections: for one cannot deny that there is in the world physical evil (that is, suffering) and moral evil (that is, crime) and even that physical evil is not always distributed here on earth according to the proportion of moral evil, as it seems that justice demands. There remains, then, this question of natural theology, how a sole Principle, all-good, all-wise and all-powerful, has been able to admit evil, and especially to permit sin, and how it could resolve to make the wicked often happy and the good unhappy?

44. Now we have no need of revealed faith to know that there is such a sole Principle of all things, entirely good and wise. Reason teaches us this by infallible proofs; and in consequence all the objections taken from the course of things, in which we observe imperfections, are only based on false appearances. For, if we were capable of understanding the universal harmony, we should see that what we are tempted to find fault with is connected with the plan most worthy of being chosen; in a word, we *should see*, and should not *believe* only, that what God has done is the best. I call

'seeing' here what one knows *a priori* by the causes; and 'believing' what one only judges by the effects, even though the one be as certainly known as the other. And one can apply here too the saying of St. Paul (2 Cor. v. 7), that we walk by *faith* and not by *sight*. For the infinite wisdom of God being known to us, we conclude that the evils we experience had to be permitted, and this we conclude from the effect or *a posteriori*, that is to say, because they exist. It is what M. Bayle acknowledges; and he ought to content himself with that, and not claim that one must put an end to the false appearances which are contrary thereto. It is as if one asked that there should be no more dreams or optical illusions.

45. And it is not to be doubted that this faith and this confidence in God, who gives us insight into his infinite goodness and prepares us for his love, in spite of the appearances of harshness that may repel us, are an admirable exercise for the virtues of Christian theology, when the divine grace in Jesus Christ arouses these motions within us. That is what Luther aptly observed in opposition to Erasmus, saying that it is love in the highest degree to love him who to flesh and blood appears so unlovable, so harsh toward the unfortunate and so ready to condemn, and to condemn for evils in which he appears to be the cause or accessary, at least in the eyes of those who allow themselves to be dazzled by false reasons. One may therefore say that the triumph of true reason illumined by divine grace is at the same time the triumph of faith and love.

46. M. Bayle appears to have taken the matter quite otherwise: he declares himself against reason, when he might have been content to censure its abuse. He quotes the words of Cotta in Cicero, where he goes so far as to say that if reason were a gift of the gods providence would be to blame for having given it, since it tends to our harm. M. Bayle also thinks that human reason is a source of destruction and not of edification (*Historical and Critical Dictionary*, p. 2026, col. 2), that it is a runner who knows not where to stop, and who, like another Penelope, herself destroys her own work.

Destruit, aedificat, mutat quadrata rotundis.

(*Reply to the Questions of a Provincial*, vol. III, p. 725). But he takes pains especially to pile up many authorities one upon the other, in order to show that theologians of all parties reject the use of reason just as he does, and that they call attention to such gleams of reason as oppose religion only that they may sacrifice them to faith by a mere repudiation, answering nothing but the conclusion of the argument that is brought against them. He begins with the New Testament. Jesus Christ was content to say: 'Follow Me' (Luke v. 27; ix. 59). The Apostles said: 'Believe, and thou shalt be saved' (Acts xvi. 3). St. Paul acknowledges that his 'doctrine is obscure' (1 Cor. xiii. 12), that 'one can comprehend nothing therein' unless God impart a spiritual discernment, and without that it only passes for foolishness (1 Cor. ii. 14). He exhorts the faithful 'to beware of philosophy' (Col. ii. 8) and to avoid disputations in that science, which had caused many persons to lose faith.

47. As for the Fathers of the Church, M. Bayle refers us to the collection of passages from them against the use of philosophy and of reason which M. de Launoy made (*De Varia Aristotelis Fortuna*, cap. 2) and especially to the passages from St. Augustine collected by M. Arnauld (against Mallet), which state: that the judgements of God are inscrutable; that they are not any the less just for that they are unknown to us; that it is a deep abyss, which one cannot fathom without running the risk of falling down the precipice; that one cannot without temerity try to elucidate that which God willed to keep hidden; that his will cannot but be just; that many men, having tried to explain this incomprehensible depth, have fallen into vain imaginations and opinions full of error and bewilderment.

48. The Schoolmen have spoken in like manner. M. Bayle quotes a beautiful passage from Cardinal Cajetan (Part 1, *Summ.*, qu. 22, art. 4) to this effect: 'Our mind', he says, 'rests not upon the evidence of known truth but upon the impenetrable depth of hidden truth. And as St. Gregory says: He who believes touching the Divinity only that which he can gauge with his mind belittles the idea of God. Yet I do not surmise that it is necessary to deny any of the things which we know, or which we see as appertaining to the immutability, the actuality, the certainty, the universality, etc., of God: but I think that there is here some secret, either in regard to the relation which exists between God and the event, or in respect of what connects the event itself with his prevision. Thus, reflecting that the understanding of our soul is the eye of the owl, I find the soul's repose only in ignorance. For it is better both for the Catholic Faith and for Philosophic Faith to confess our blindness, than to affirm as evident what does not afford our mind the contentment which self-evidence gives. I do not accuse of

presumption, on that account, all the learned men who stammer-
ingly have endeavoured to suggest, as far as in them lay, the im-
mobility and the sovereign and eternal efficacy of the understanding, of the will and of the power of God, through the infallibility
of divine election and divine relation to all events. Nothing of all
that interferes with my surmise that there is some depth which is
hidden from us.' This passage of Cajetan is all the more notable
since he was an author competent to reach the heart of the matter.

49. Luther's book against Erasmus is full of vigorous comments
hostile to those who desire to submit revealed truths to the
tribunal of our reason. Calvin often speaks in the same tone,
against the inquisitive daring of those who seek to penetrate into
the counsels of God. He declares in his treatise on predestination
that God had just causes for damning some men, but causes unknown to us. Finally M. Bayle quotes sundry modern writers who
have spoken to the same effect (*Reply to the Questions of a Provincial*,
ch. 161 *et seq.*).

50. But all these expressions and innumerable others like them
do not prove that the objections opposed to faith are so insoluble
as M. Bayle supposes. It is true that the counsels of God are inscrutable, but there is no invincible objection which tends to the
conclusion that they are unjust. What appears injustice on the part
of God, and foolishness in our faith, only appears so. The famous
passage of Tertullian (*De Carne Christi*), 'mortuus est Dei filius,
credibile est, quia ineptum est; et sepultus revixit, certum est,
quia impossibile', is a sally that can only be meant to concern
appearances of absurdity. There are others like them in Luther's
book on *Freewill in Bondage*, as when he says (ch. 174): 'Si placet
tibi Deus indignos coronans, non debet displicere immeritos
damnans.' Which being reduced to more temperate phrasing,
means: If you approve that God give eternal glory to those who
are not better than the rest, you should not disapprove that he
abandon those who are not worse than the rest. And to judge that
he speaks only of appearances of injustice, one only has to weigh
these words of the same author taken from the same book: 'In all
the rest', he says, 'we recognize in God a supreme majesty; there
is only justice that we dare to question: and we will not believe
provisionally [tantisper] that he is just, albeit he has promised us
that the time shall come when his glory being revealed all men
shall see clearly that he has been and that he is just.'

51. It will be found also that when the Fathers entered into a discussion they did not simply reject reason. And, in disputations with the pagans, they endeavour usually to show how paganism is contrary to reason, and how the Christian religion has the better of it on that side also. Origen showed Celsus how reasonable Christianity is and why, notwithstanding, the majority of Christians should believe without examination. Celsus had jeered at the behaviour of Christians, 'who, willing', he said, 'neither to listen to your reasons nor to give you any for what they believe, are content to say to you: Examine not, only believe, or: Your faith will save you; and they hold this as a maxim, that the wisdom of the world is an evil.'

52. Origen gives the answer of a wise man, and in conformity with the principles we have established in the matter. For reason, far from being contrary to Christianity, serves as a foundation for this religion, and will bring about its acceptance by those who can achieve the examination of it. But, as few people are capable of this, the heavenly gift of plain faith tending towards good suffices for men in general. 'If it were possible', he says, 'for all men, neglecting the affairs of life, to apply themselves to study and meditation, one need seek no other way to make them accept the Christian religion. For, to say nothing likely to offend anyone' (he insinuates that the pagan religion is absurd, but he will not say so explicitly), 'there will be found therein no less exactitude than elsewhere, whether in the discussion of its dogmas, or in the elucidation of the enigmatical expressions of its prophets, or in the interpretation of the parables of its gospels and of countless other things happening or ordained symbolically. But since neither the necessities of life nor the infirmities of men permit of this application to study, save for a very small number of persons, what means could one find more qualified to benefit everyone else in the world than those Jesus Christ wished to be used for the conversion of the nations? And I would fain ask with regard to the great number of those who believe, and who thereby have withdrawn themselves from the quagmire of vices wherein before they were plunged, which would be the better: to have thus changed one's morals and reformed one's life, believing without examination that there are punishments for sin and rewards for good actions; or to have waited for one's conversion until one not only believed but had examined with care the foundations of these dogmas? It is certain

that, were this method to be followed, few indeed would reach that point whither they are led by their plain and simple faith, but the majority would remain in their corruption.'

53. M. Bayle (in his explanation concerning the objections of the Manichaeans, placed at the end of the second edition of the *Dictionary*) takes those words where Origen points out that religion can stand the test of having her dogmas discussed, as if it were not meant in relation to philosophy, but only in relation to the accuracy wherewith the authority and the true meaning of Holy Scripture is established. But there is nothing to indicate this restriction. Origen wrote against a philosopher whom such a restriction would not have suited. And it appears that this Father wished to point out that among Christians there was no less exactitude than among the Stoics and some other philosophers, who established their doctrine as much by reason as by authorities, as, for example, Chrysippus did, who found his philosophy even in the symbols of pagan antiquity.

54. Celsus brings up still another objection to the Christians, in the same place. 'If they withdraw', he says, 'regularly into their "Examine not, only believe", they must tell me at least what are the things they wish me to believe.' Therein he is doubtless right, and that tells against those who would say that God is good and just, and who yet would maintain that we have no notion of goodness and of justice when we attribute these perfections to him. But one must not always demand what I call 'adequate notions', involving nothing that is not explained, since even perceptible qualities, like heat, light, sweetness, cannot give us such notions. Thus we agreed that Mysteries should receive an explanation, but this explanation is imperfect. It suffices for us to have some analogical understanding of a Mystery such as the Trinity and the Incarnation, to the end that in accepting them we pronounce not words altogether devoid of meaning: but it is not necessary that the explanation go as far as we would wish, that is, to the extent of comprehension and to the *how*.

55. It appears strange therefore that M. Bayle rejects the tribunal of *common notions* (in the third volume of his *Reply to the Questions of a Provincial*, pp. 1062 and 1140) as if one should not consult the idea of goodness in answering the Manichaeans; whereas he had declared himself quite differently in his *Dictionary*. Of necessity there must be agreement upon the meaning of *good*

and *bad*, amongst those who are in dispute over the question whether there is only one principle, altogether good, or whether there are two, the one good and the other bad. We understand something by union when we are told of the union of one body with another or of a substance with its accident, of a subject with its adjunct, of the place with the moving body, of the act with the potency; we also mean something when we speak of the union of the soul with the body to make thereof one single person. For albeit I do not hold that the soul changes the laws of the body, or that the body changes the laws of the soul, and I have introduced the Pre-established Harmony to avoid this derangement, I nevertheless admit a true union between the soul and the body, which makes thereof a suppositum. This union belongs to the metaphysical, whereas a union of influence would belong to the physical. But when we speak of the union of the Word of God with human nature we should be content with an analogical knowledge, such as the comparison of the union of the soul with the body is capable of giving us. We should, moreover, be content to say that the Incarnation is the closest union that can exist between the Creator and the creature; and further we should not want to go.

56. It is the same with the other Mysteries, where moderate minds will ever find an explanation sufficient for belief, but never such as would be necessary for understanding. A certain *what it is* ($\tau\acute{\iota}\ \acute{\epsilon}\sigma\tau\iota$) is enough for us, but the *how* ($\pi\hat{\omega}s$) is beyond us, and is not necessary for us. One may say concerning the explanations of Mysteries which are given out here and there, what the Queen of Sweden inscribed upon a medal concerning the crown she had abandoned, 'Non mi bisogna, e non mi basta.' Nor have we any need either (as I have already observed) to prove the Mysteries *a priori*, or to give a reason for them; it suffices us *that the thing is thus* ($\tau\grave{o}\ \acute{o}\tau\iota$) even though we know not the *why* ($\tau\grave{o}\ \delta\iota\acute{o}\tau\iota$), which God has reserved for himself. These lines, written on that theme by Joseph Scaliger, are beautiful and renowned:

Ne curiosus quaere causas omnium,
Quaecumque libris vis Prophetarum indidit
Afflata caelo, plena veraci Deo:
Nec operta sacri supparo silentii
Irrumpere aude, sed pudenter praeteri.

Nescire velle, quae Magister optimus
Docere non vult, erudita inscitia est.

M. Bayle, who quotes them (*Reply to the Questions of a Provincial*, vol. III, p. 1055), holds the likely opinion that Scaliger made them upon the disputes between Arminius and Gomarus. I think M. Bayle repeated them from memory, for he put *sacrata* instead of *afflata*. But it is apparently the printer's fault that *prudenter* stands in place of *pudenter* (that is, modestly) which the metre requires.

57. Nothing can be more judicious than the warning these lines contain; and M. Bayle is right in saying (p. 729) that those who claim that the behaviour of God with respect to sin and the consequences of sin contains nothing but what they can account for, deliver themselves up to the mercy of their adversary. But he is not right in combining here two very different things, 'to account for a thing', and 'to uphold it against objections'; as he does when he presently adds: 'They are obliged to follow him [their adversary] everywhere whither he shall wish to lead them, and it would be to retire ignominiously and ask for quarter, if they were to admit that our intelligence is too weak to remove completely all the objections advanced by a philosopher.'

58. It seems here that, according to M. Bayle, 'accounting for' comes short of 'answering objections', since he threatens one who should undertake the first with the resulting obligation to pass on to the second. But it is quite the opposite: he who maintains a thesis (the *respondens*) is not bound to account for it, but he is bound to meet the objections of an opponent. A defendant in law is not bound (as a general rule) to prove his right or to produce his title to possession; but he is obliged to reply to the arguments of the plaintiff. I have marvelled many times that a writer so precise and so shrewd as M. Bayle so often here confuses things where so much difference exists as between these three acts of reason: to comprehend, to prove, and to answer objections; as if when it is a question of the use of reason in theology one term were as good as another. Thus he says in his posthumous Conversations, p. 73: 'There is no principle which M. Bayle has more often inculcated than this, that the incomprehensibility of a dogma and the insolubility of the objections that oppose it provide no legitimate reason for rejecting it.' This is true as regards the incomprehensibility, but it is not the same with the insolubility. And it is indeed

just as if one said that an invincible reason against a thesis was not a legitimate reason for rejecting it. For what other legitimate reason for rejecting an opinion can one find, if an invincible opposing argument is not such an one? And what means shall one have thereafter of demonstrating the falsity, and even the absurdity, of any opinion?

59. It is well to observe also that he who proves a thing *a priori* accounts for it through the efficient cause; and whosoever can thus account for it in a precise and adequate manner is also in a position to comprehend the thing. Therefore it was that the Scholastic theologians had already censured Raymond Lully for having undertaken to demonstrate the Trinity by philosophy. This so-called demonstration is to be found in his *Works*; and Bartholo-maeus Keckermann, a writer renowned in the Reformed party, having made an attempt of just the same kind upon the same Mystery, has been no less censured for it by some modern theologians. Therefore censure will fall upon those who shall wish to account for this Mystery and make it comprehensible, but praise will be given to those who shall toil to uphold it against the objections of adversaries.

60. I have said already that theologians usually distinguish between what is above reason and what is against reason. They place *above* reason that which one cannot comprehend and which one cannot account for. But *against* reason will be all opinion that is opposed by invincible reasons, or the contrary of which can be proved in a precise and sound manner. They avow, therefore, that the Mysteries are above reason, but they do not admit that they are contrary to it. The English author of a book which is ingenious, but has met with disapproval, entitled *Christianity not Mysterious*, wished to combat this distinction; but it does not seem to me that he has at all weakened it. M. Bayle also is not quite satisfied with this accepted distinction. This is what he says on the matter (vol. III of the *Reply to the Questions of a Provincial*, ch. 158). Firstly (p. 998) he distinguishes, together with M. Saurin, between these two theses: the one, *all the dogmas of Christianity are in conformity with reason;* the other, *human reason knows that they are in conformity with reason.* He affirms the first and denies the second. I am of the same opinion, if in saying 'that a dogma conforms to reason' one means that it is possible to account for it or to explain its *how* by reason; for God could doubtless do so, and we cannot. But I think that one

must affirm both theses if by 'knowing that a dogma conforms to reason' one means that we can demonstrate, if need be, that there is no contradiction between this dogma and reason, repudiating the objections of those who maintain that this dogma is an absurdity.

61. M. Bayle explains himself here in a manner not at all convincing. He acknowledges fully that our Mysteries are in accordance with the supreme and universal reason that is in the divine understanding, or with reason in general; yet he denies that they are in accordance with that part of reason which man employs to judge things. But this portion of reason which we possess is a gift of God, and consists in the natural light that has remained with us in the midst of corruption; thus it is in accordance with the whole, and it differs from that which is in God only as a drop of water differs from the ocean or rather as the finite from the infinite. Therefore Mysteries may transcend it, but they cannot be contrary to it. One cannot be contrary to one part without being contrary to the whole. That which contradicts a proposition of Euclid is contrary to the *Elements* of Euclid. That which in us is contrary to the Mysteries is not reason nor is it the natural light or the linking together of truths; it is corruption, or error, or prejudice, or darkness.

62. M. Bayle (p. 1002) is not satisfied with the opinion of Josua Stegman and of M. Turretin, Protestant theologians who teach that the Mysteries are contrary only to corrupt reason. He asks, mockingly, whether by right reason is meant perchance that of an orthodox theologian and by corrupt reason that of an heretic; and he urges the objection that the evidence of the Mystery of the Trinity was no greater in the soul of Luther than in the soul of Socinius. But as M. Descartes has well observed, good sense is distributed to all: thus one must believe that both the orthodox and heretics are endowed therewith. Right reason is a linking together of truths, corrupt reason is mixed with prejudices and passions. And in order to discriminate between the two, one need but proceed in good order, admit no thesis without proof, and admit no proof unless it be in proper form, according to the commonest rules of logic. One needs neither any other criterion nor other arbitrator in questions of reason. It is only through lack of this consideration that a handle has been given to the sceptics, and that even in theology François Véron and some others, who

exacerbated the dispute with the Protestants, even to the point of dishonesty, plunged headlong into scepticism in order to prove the necessity of accepting an infallible external judge. Their course meets with no approval from the most expert, even in their own party: Calixtus and Daillé derided it as it deserved, and Bellarmine argued quite otherwise.

63. Now let us come to what M. Bayle says (p. 999) on the distinction we are concerned with. 'It seems to me', he says, 'that an ambiguity has crept into the celebrated distinction drawn between things that are above reason and things that are against reason. The Mysteries of the Gospel are above reason, so it is usually said, but they are not contrary to reason. I think that the same sense is not given to the word reason in the first part of this axiom as in the second: by the first is understood rather the reason of man, or reason *in concreto* and by the second reason in general, or reason *in abstracto*. For supposing that it is understood always as reason in general or the supreme reason, the universal reason that is in God, it is equally true that the Mysteries of the Gospels are not above reason and that they are not against reason. But if in both parts of the axiom human reason is meant, I do not clearly see the soundness of the distinction: for the most orthodox confess that we know not how our Mysteries can conform to the maxims of philosophy. It seems to us, therefore, that they are not in conformity with our reason. Now that which appears to us not to be in conformity with our reason appears contrary to our reason, just as that which appears to us not in conformity with truth appears contrary to truth. Thus why should not one say, equally, that the Mysteries are against our feeble reason, and that they are above our feeble reason?' I answer, as I have done already, that 'reason' here is the linking together of the truths that we know by the light of nature, and in this sense the axiom is true and without any ambiguity. The Mysteries transcend our reason, since they contain truths that are not comprised in this sequence; but they are not contrary to our reason, and they do not contradict any of the truths whereto this sequence can lead us. Accordingly there is no question here of the universal reason that is in God, but of our reason. As for the question whether we know the Mysteries to conform with our reason, I answer that at least we never know of any non-conformity or any opposition between the Mysteries and reason. Moreover, we can always abolish such alleged

opposition, and so, if this can be called reconciling or harmonizing faith with reason, or recognizing the conformity between them, it must be said that we can recognize this conformity and this harmony. But if the conformity consists in a reasonable explanation of the *how*, we cannot recognize it.

64. M. Bayle makes one more ingenious objection, which he draws from the example of the sense of sight. 'When a square tower', he says, 'from a distance appears to us round, our eyes testify very clearly not only that they perceive nothing square in this tower, but also that they discover there a round shape, incompatible with the square shape. One may therefore say that the truth which is the square shape is not only above, but even against, the witness of our feeble sight.' It must be admitted that this observation is correct, and although it be true that the appearance of roundness comes simply from the effacement of the angles, which distance causes to disappear, it is true, notwithstanding, that the round and the square are opposites. Therefore my answer to this objection is that the representation of the senses, even when they do all that in them lies, is often contrary to the truth; but it is not the same with the faculty of reasoning, when it does its duty, since a strictly reasoned argument is nothing but a linking together of truths. And as for the sense of sight in particular, it is well to consider that there are yet other false appearances which come not from the 'feebleness of our eyes' nor from the loss of visibility brought about by distance, but from the very *nature of vision*, however perfect it be. It is thus, for instance, that the circle seen sideways is changed into that kind of oval which among geometricians is known as an ellipse, and sometimes even into a parabola or a hyperbola, or actually into a straight line, witness the ring of Saturn.

65. The *external* senses, properly speaking, do not deceive us. It is our inner sense which often makes us go too fast. That occurs also in brute beasts, as when a dog barks at his reflexion in the mirror: for beasts have *consecutions* of perception which resemble reasoning, and which occur also in the inner sense of men, when their actions have only an empirical quality. But beasts do nothing which compels us to believe that they have what deserves to be properly called a *reasoning* sense, as I have shown elsewhere. Now when the understanding uses and follows the false decision of the inner sense (as when the famous Galileo thought that Saturn had

two handles) it is deceived by the judgement it makes upon the effect of appearances, and it infers from them more than they imply. For the appearances of the senses do not promise us absolutely the truth of things, any more than dreams do. It is we who deceive ourselves by the use we make of them, that is, by our consecutions. Indeed we allow ourselves to be deluded by probable arguments, and we are inclined to think that phenomena such as we have found linked together often are so always. Thus, as it happens usually that that which appears without angles has none, we readily believe it to be always thus. Such an error is pardonable, and sometimes inevitable, when it is necessary to act promptly and choose that which appearances recommend; but when we have the leisure and the time to collect our thoughts, we are in fault if we take for certain that which is not so. It is therefore true that appearances are often contrary to truth, but our reasoning never is when it proceeds strictly in accordance with the rules of the art of reasoning. If by *reason* one meant generally the faculty of reasoning whether well or ill, I confess that it might deceive us, and does indeed deceive us, and the appearances of our understanding are often as deceptive as those of the senses: but here it is a question of the linking together of truths and of objections in due form, and in this sense it is impossible for reason to deceive us.

66. Thus it may be seen from all I have just said that M. Bayle carries too far *the being above reason*, as if it included the insoluble nature of objections: for according to him (*Reply to the Questions of a Provincial*, vol. III, ch. 130, p. 651) 'once a dogma is above reason, philosophy can neither explain it nor comprehend it, nor meet the difficulties that are urged against it'. I agree with regard to comprehension, but I have already shown that the Mysteries receive a necessary verbal explanation, to the end that the terms employed be not *sine mente soni*, words signifying nothing. I have shown also that it is necessary for one to be capable of answering the objections, and that otherwise one must needs reject the thesis.

67. He adduces the authority of theologians, who appear to recognize the insoluble nature of the objections against the Mysteries. Luther is one of the chief of these; but I have already replied, in § 12, to the passage where he seems to say that philosophy contradicts theology. There is another passage (*De Servo Arbitrio*, ch. 246) where he says that the apparent injustice of

God is proved by arguments taken from the adversity of good people and the prosperity of the wicked, an argument irresistible both for all reason and for natural intelligence ('Argumentis talibus traducta, quibus nulla ratio aut lumen naturae potest resistere'). But soon afterwards he shows that he means it only of those who know nothing of the life to come, since he adds that an expression in the Gospel dissipates this difficulty, teaching us that there is another life, where that which has not been punished and rewarded in this life shall receive its due. The objection is then far from being insuperable, and even without the aid of the Gospel one could bethink oneself of this answer. There is also quoted (*Reply*, vol. III, p. 652) a passage from Martin Chemnitz, criticized by Vedelius and defended by Johann Musaeus, where this famous theologian seems to say clearly that there are truths in the word of God which are not only above reason but also against reason. But this passage must be taken as referring only to the principles of reason that are in accordance with the order of Nature, as Musaeus also interprets it.

68. It is true nevertheless that M. Bayle finds some authorities who are more favourable to him, M. Descartes being one of the chief. This great man says positively (Part I of his *Principles*, art. 41) 'that we shall have not the slightest trouble in ridding ourselves of the difficulty' (which one may have in harmonizing the freedom of our will with the order of the eternal providence of God) 'if we observe that our thought is finite, and that the Knowledge and the Omnipotence of God, whereby he has not only known from all eternity all that which is or which can be, but also has willed it, is infinite. We have therefore quite enough intelligence to recognize clearly and distinctly that this knowledge and this power are in God; but we have not enough so to comprehend their scope that we can know how they leave the actions of men entirely free and undetermined. Yet the Power and the Knowledge of God must not prevent us from believing that we have a free will; for we should be wrong to doubt of that whereof we are inwardly conscious, and which we know by experience to be within us, simply because we do not comprehend some other thing which we know to be incomprehensible in its nature.'

69. This passage from M. Descartes, followed by his adherents (who rarely think of doubting what he asserts), has always appeared strange to me. Not content with saying that, as for him,

he sees no way of reconciling the two dogmas, he puts the whole human race, and even all rational creatures, in the same case. Yet could he have been unaware that there is no possibility of an insuperable objection against truth? For such an objection could only be a necessary linking together of other truths whose result would be contrary to the truth that one maintains; and consequently there would be contradiction between the truths, which would be an utter absurdity. Moreover, albeit our mind is finite and cannot comprehend the infinite, of the infinite nevertheless it has proofs whose strength or weakness it comprehends; why then should it not have the same comprehension in regard to the objections? And since the power and the wisdom of God are infinite and comprehend everything, there is no pretext for doubting their scope. Further, M. Descartes demands a freedom which is not needed, by his insistence that the actions of the will of man are altogether undetermined, a thing which never happens. Finally, M. Bayle himself maintains that this experience or this inward sense of our independence, upon which M. Descartes founds the proof of our freedom, does not prove it: for from the fact that we are not conscious of the causes whereon we depend, it does not follow, according to M. Bayle, that we are independent. But that is something we will speak of in its proper place.

70. It seems that M. Descartes confesses also, in a passage of his *Principles*, that it is impossible to find an answer to the difficulties on the division of matter to infinity, which he nevertheless recognizes as actual. Arriaga and other Schoolmen make wellnigh the same confession: but if they took the trouble to give to the objections the form these ought to have, they would see that there are faults in the reasoning, and sometimes false assumptions which cause confusion. Here is an example. A man of parts one day brought up to me an objection in the following form: Let the straight line BA be cut in two equal parts at the point C, and the part CA at the point D, and the part DA at the point E, and so on to infinity; all the halves, BC, CD, DE, etc., together make the whole BA; therefore there must be a last half, since the straight line BA finishes at A. But this last half is absurd: for since it is a line, it will be possible again to cut it in two. Therefore division to infinity cannot be admitted. But I pointed out to him that one is not justified in the inference that there must be a last half, although there be a last point A, for this last point belongs to all

the halves of its side. And my friend acknowledged it himself when he endeavoured to prove this deduction by a formal argument; on the contrary, just because the division goes on to infinity, there is no last half. And although the straight line AB be finite, it does not follow that the process of dividing it has any final end. The same confusion arises with the series of numbers going on to infinity. One imagines a final end, a number that is infinite, or infinitely small; but that is all simple fiction. Every number is finite and specific; every line is so likewise, and the infinite or infinitely small signify only magnitudes that one may take as great or as small as one wishes, to show that an error is smaller than that which has been specified, that is to say, that there is no error; or else by the infinitely small is meant the state of a magnitude at its vanishing point or its beginning, conceived after the pattern of magnitudes already actualized.

71. It will, however, be well to consider the argument that M. Bayle puts forward to show that one cannot refute the objections which reason opposes to the Mysteries. It is in his comment on the Manichaeans (p. 3140 of the second edition of his *Dictionary*). 'It is enough for me', he says, 'that it be unanimously acknowledged that the Mysteries of the Gospel are above reason. For thence comes the necessary conclusion that it is impossible to settle the difficulties raised by the philosophers, and in consequence that a dispute where only the light of Nature is followed will always end unfavourably for the theologians, and that they will see themselves forced to give way and to take refuge in the canon of the supernatural light.' I am surprised that M. Bayle speaks in such general terms, since he has acknowledged himself that the light of Nature is against the Manichaeans, and for the oneness of the Principle, and that the goodness of God is proved incontrovertibly by reason. Yet this is how he continues:

72. 'It is evident that reason can never attain to that which is above it. Now if it could supply answers to the objections which are opposed to the dogma of the Trinity and that of hypostatic union, it would attain to those two Mysteries, it would have them in subjection and submit them to the strictest examination by comparison with its first principles, or with the aphorisms that spring from common notions, and proceed until finally it had drawn the conclusion that they are in accordance with natural light. It would therefore do what exceeds its powers, it would soar

above its confines, and that is a formal contradiction. One must therefore say that it cannot provide answers to its own objections, and that thus they remain victorious, so long as one does not have recourse to the authority of God and to the necessity of subjugating one's understanding to the obedience of faith.' I do not find that there is any force in this reasoning. We can attain to that which is above us not by penetrating it but by maintaining it; as we can attain to the sky by sight, and not by touch. Nor is it necessary that, in order to answer the objections which are made against the Mysteries, one should have them in subjection to oneself, and submit them to examination by comparison with the first principles that spring from common notions. For if he who answers the objections had to go so far, he who proposes the objections needs must do it first. It is the part of the objection to open up the subject, and it is enough for him who answers to say Yes or No. He is not obliged to counter with a distinction: it will do, in case of need, if he denies the universality of some proposition in the objection or criticizes its form, and one may do both these things without penetrating beyond the objection. When someone offers me a proof which he maintains is invincible, I can keep silence while I compel him merely to prove in due form all the enunciations that he brings forward, and such as appear to me in the slightest degree doubtful. For the purpose of doubting only, I need not at all probe to the heart of the matter; on the contrary, the more ignorant I am the more shall I be justified in doubting. M. Bayle continues thus:

73. 'Let us endeavour to clarify that. If some doctrines are above reason they are beyond its reach, it cannot attain to them; if it cannot attain to them, it cannot comprehend them.' (He could have begun here with the 'comprehend', saying that reason cannot comprehend that which is above it.) 'If it cannot comprehend them, it can find in them no idea' (*Non valet consequentia*: for, to 'comprehend' something, it is not enough that one have some ideas thereof; one must have all the ideas of everything that goes to make it up, and all these ideas must be clear, distinct, *adequate*. There are a thousand objects in Nature in which we understand something, but which we do not therefore necessarily comprehend. We have some ideas on the rays of light, we demonstrate upon them up to a certain point; but there ever remains something which makes us confess that we do not yet comprehend the whole

nature of light.) 'nor any principle such as may give rise to a solution;' (Why should not evident principles be found mingled with obscure and confused knowledge?) 'and consequently the objections that reason has made will remain unanswered;' (By no means; the difficulty is rather on the side of the opposer. It is for him to seek an evident principle such as may give rise to some objection; and the more obscure the subject, the more trouble he will have in finding such a principle. Moreover, when he has found it he will have still more trouble in demonstrating an opposition between the principle and the Mystery: for, if it happened that the Mystery was evidently contrary to an evident principle, it would not be an obscure Mystery, it would be a manifest absurdity.) 'or what is the same thing, answer will be made with some distinction as obscure as the very thesis that will have been attacked.' (One can do without distinctions, if need be, by denying either some premiss or some conclusion; and when one is doubtful of the meaning of some term used by the opposer one may demand of him its definition. Thus the defender has no need to incommode himself when it is a question of answering an adversary who claims that he is offering us an invincible proof. But even supposing that the defender, perchance being kindly disposed, or for the sake of brevity, or because he feels himself strong enough, should himself vouchsafe to show the ambiguity concealed in the objection, and to remove it by making some distinction, this distinction need not of necessity lead to anything clearer than the first thesis, since the defender is not obliged to elucidate the Mystery itself.)

74. 'Now it is certain', so M. Bayle continues, 'that an objection which is founded on distinct notions remains equally victorious, whether you give to it no answer, or you make an answer where none can comprehend anything. Can the contest be equal between a man who alleges in objection to you that which you and he very clearly conceive, and you, who can only defend yourself by answers wherein neither of you understands anything?' (It is not enough that the objection be founded on quite distinct notions, it is necessary also that one apply it in contradiction of the thesis. And when I answer someone by denying some premiss, in order to compel him to prove it, or some conclusion, to compel him to put it in good form, it cannot be said that I answer nothing or that I answer nothing intelligible. For as it is the doubtful

premiss of the adversary that I deny, my denial will be as intelligible as his affirmation. Finally, when I am so obliging as to explain myself by means of some distinction, it suffices that the terms I employ have some meaning, as in the Mystery itself. Thus something in my answer will be comprehended: but one need not of necessity comprehend all that it involves; otherwise one would comprehend the Mystery also.)

75. M. Bayle continues thus: 'Every philosophical dispute assumes that the disputant parties agree on certain definitions' (This would be desirable, but usually it is only in the dispute itself that one reaches such a point, if the necessity arises.) 'and that they admit the rules of Syllogisms, and the signs for the recognition of bad arguments. After that everything lies in the investigation as to whether a thesis conforms mediately or immediately to the principles one is agreed upon' (which is done by means of the syllogisms of him who makes objections); 'whether the premisses of a proof' (advanced by the opposer) 'are true; whether the conclusion is properly drawn; whether a four-term Syllogism has been employed; whether some aphorism of the chapter *de oppositis* or *de sophisticis elenchis*, etc., has not been violated.' (It is enough, putting it briefly, to deny some premiss or some conclusion, or finally to explain or get explained some ambiguous term.) 'One comes off victorious either by showing that the subject of dispute has no connexion with the principles which had been agreed upon' (that is to say, by showing that the objection proves nothing, and then the defender wins the case), 'or by reducing the defender to absurdity' (when all the premisses and all the conclusions are well proved). 'Now one can reduce him to that point either by showing him that the conclusions of his thesis are "yes" and "no" at once, or by constraining him to say only intelligible things in answer.' (This last embarrassment he can always avoid, because he has no need to advance new theses.) 'The aim in disputes of this kind is to throw light upon obscurities and to arrive at self-evidence.' (It is the aim of the opposer, for he wishes to demonstrate that the Mystery is false; but this cannot here be the aim of the defender, for in admitting Mystery he agrees that one cannot demonstrate it.) 'This leads to the opinion that during the course of the proceedings victory sides more or less with the defender or with the opposer, according to whether there is more or less clarity in the propositions of the one than in the

propositions of the other.' (That is speaking as if the defender and the opposer were equally unprotected; but the defender is like a besieged commander, covered by his defence works, and it is for the attacker to destroy them. The defender has no need here of self-evidence, and he seeks it not: but it is for the opposer to find it against him, and to break through with his batteries in order that the defender may be no longer protected.)

76. 'Finally, it is judged that victory goes against him whose answers are such that one comprehends nothing in them,' (It is a very equivocal sign of victory: for then one must needs ask the audience if they comprehend anything in what has been said, and often their opinions would be divided. The order of formal disputes is to proceed by arguments in due form and to answer them by denying or making a distinction.) 'and who confesses that they are incomprehensible.' (It is permitted to him who maintains the truth of a Mystery to confess that this mystery is incomprehensible; and if this confession were sufficient for declaring him vanquished there would be no need of objection. It will be possible for a truth to be incomprehensible, but never so far as to justify the statement that one comprehends nothing at all therein. It would be in that case what the ancient Schools called *Scindapsus* or *Blityri* (Clem. Alex., *Stromateis*, 8), that is, words devoid of meaning.) 'He is condemned thenceforth by the rules for awarding victory; and even when he cannot be pursued in the mist wherewith he has covered himself, and which forms a kind of abyss between him and his antagonists, he is believed to be utterly defeated, and is compared to an army which, having lost the battle, steals away from the pursuit of the victor only under cover of night.' (Matching allegory with allegory, I will say that the defender is not vanquished so long as he remains protected by his entrenchments; and if he risks some sortie beyond his need, it is permitted to him to withdraw within his fort, without being open to blame for that.)

77. I was especially at pains to analyse this long passage where M. Bayle has put down his strongest and most skilfully reasoned statements in support of his opinion: and I hope that I have shown clearly how this excellent man has been misled. That happens all too easily to the ablest and shrewdest persons when they give free rein to their wit without exercising the patience necessary for delving down to the very foundations of their systems. The details

we have entered into here will serve as answer to some other arguments upon the subject which are dispersed through the works of M. Bayle, as for instance when he says in his *Reply to the Questions of a Provincial* (vol. III, ch. 133, p. 685): 'To prove that one has brought reason and religion into harmony one must show not only that one has philosophic maxims favourable to our faith, but also that the particular maxims cast up against us as not being consistent with our Catechism are in reality consistent with it in a clearly conceived way.' I do not see that one has need of all that, unless one aspire to press reasoning as far as the *how* of the Mystery. When one is content to uphold its truth, without attempting to render it comprehensible, one has no need to resort to philosophic maxims, general or particular, for the proof; and when another brings up some philosophic maxims against us, it is not for us to prove clearly and distinctly that these maxims are consistent with our dogma, but it is for our opponent to prove that they are contrary thereto.

78. M. Bayle continues thus in the same passage: 'For this result we need an answer as clearly evident as the objection.' I have already shown that it is obtained when one denies the premisses, but that for the rest it is not necessary for him who maintains the truth of the Mystery always to advance evident propositions, since the principal thesis concerning the Mystery itself is not evident. He adds further: 'If we must make reply and rejoinder, we must never rest in our positions, nor claim that we have accomplished our design, so long as our opponent shall make answer with things as evident as our reasons can be.' But it is not for the defender to adduce reasons; it is enough for him to answer those of his opponent.

79. Finally the author draws the conclusion: 'If it were claimed that, on making an evident objection, a man has to be satisfied with an answer which we can only state as a thing possible though incomprehensible to us, that would be unfair.' He repeats this in the posthumous Dialogues, against M. Jacquelot, p. 69. I am not of this opinion. If the objection were completely evident, it would triumph, and the thesis would be overthrown. But when the objection is only founded on appearances or on instances of the most frequent occurrence, and when he who makes it desires to draw from it a universal and certain conclusion, he who upholds the Mystery may answer with the instance of a bare possibility.

For such an instance suffices to show that what one wished to infer from the premisses, is neither certain nor general; and it suffices for him who upholds the Mystery to maintain that it is possible, without having to maintain that it is probable. For, as I have often said, it is agreed that the Mysteries are against appearances. He who upholds the Mystery need not even adduce such an instance; and should he adduce it, it were indeed a work of supererogation, or else an instrument of greater confusion to the adversary.

80. There are passages of M. Bayle in the posthumous reply that he made to M. Jacquelot which seem to me still worthy of scrutiny. 'M. Bayle' (according to pp. 36, 37) 'constantly asserts in his *Dictionary*, whenever the subject allows, that our reason is more capable of refuting and destroying than of proving and building; that there is scarcely any philosophical or theological matter in respect of which it does not create great difficulties. Thus', he says, 'if one desired to follow it in a disputatious spirit, as far as it can go, one would often be reduced to a state of troublesome perplexity; and in fine, there are doctrines certainly true, which it disputes with insoluble objections.' I think that what is said here in reproach of reason is to its advantage. When it overthrows some thesis, it builds up the opposing thesis. And when it seems to be overthrowing the two opposing theses at the same time, it is then that it promises us something profound, provided that we follow it *as far as it can go*, not in a disputatious spirit but with an ardent desire to search out and discover the truth, which will always be recompensed with a great measure of success.

81. M. Bayle continues: 'that one must then ridicule these objections, recognizing the narrow bounds of the human mind.' And I think, on the other hand, that one must recognize the signs of the force of the human mind, which causes it to penetrate into the heart of things. These are new openings and, as it were, rays of the dawn which promises us a greater light: I mean in philosophical subjects or those of natural theology. But when these objections are made against revealed faith it is enough that one be able to repel them, provided that one do so in a submissive and zealous spirit, with intent to sustain and exalt the glory of God. And when we succeed in respect of his justice, we shall likewise be impressed by his greatness and charmed by his goodness, which will show themselves through the clouds of a seeming reason that is

deceived by outward appearances, in proportion as the mind is elevated by true reason to that which to us is invisible, but none the less sure.

82. 'Thus' (to continue with M. Bayle) 'reason will be compelled to lay down its arms, and to subjugate itself to the obedience of the faith, which it can and ought to do, in virtue of some of its most incontestable maxims. Thus also in renouncing some of its other maxims it acts nevertheless in accordance with that which it is, that is to say, in reason.' But one must know 'that such maxims of reason as must be renounced in this case are only those which make us judge by appearances or according to the ordinary course of things.' This reason enjoins upon us even in philosophical subjects, when there are invincible proofs to the contrary. It is thus that, being made confident by demonstrations of the goodness and the justice of God, we disregard the appearances of harshness and injustice which we see in this small portion of his Kingdom that is exposed to our gaze. Hitherto we have been illumined by the *light of Nature* and by that of *grace*, but not yet by that of *glory*. Here on earth we see apparent injustice, and we believe and even know the truth of the hidden justice of God; but we shall.see that justice when at last the Sun of Justice shall show himself as he is.

83. It is certain that M. Bayle can only be understood as meaning those ostensible maxims which must give way before the eternal verities; for he acknowledges that reason is not in reality contrary to faith. In these posthumous Dialogues he complains (p. 73, against M. Jacquelot) of being accused of the belief that our Mysteries are in reality against reason, and (p. 9, against M. le Clerc) of the assertion made that he who acknowledges that a doctrine is exposed to irrefutable objections acknowledges also by a necessary consequence the falsity of this doctrine. Nevertheless one would be justified in the assertion if the irrefutability were more than an outward appearance.

84. It may be, therefore, that having long contended thus against M. Bayle on the matter of the use of reason I shall find after all that his opinions were not fundamentally so remote from mine as his expressions, which have provided matter for our considerations, have led one to believe. It is true that frequently he appears to deny absolutely that one can ever answer the objections of reason against faith, and that he asserts the necessity of comprehending, in order to achieve such an end, how the Mystery comes

to be or exists. Yet there are passages where he becomes milder, and contents himself with saying that the answers to these objections are unknown to him. Here is a very precise passage, taken from the excursus on the Manichaeans, which is found at the end of the second edition of his *Dictionary*: 'For the greater satisfaction of the most punctilious readers, I desire to declare here' (he says, p. 3148) 'that wherever the statement is to be met with in my *Dictionary* that such and such arguments are irrefutable I do not wish it to be taken that they are so in actuality. I mean naught else than that they appear to me irrefutable. That is of no consequence: each one will be able to imagine, if he pleases, that if I deem thus of a matter it is owing to my lack of acumen.' I do not imagine such a thing; his great acumen is too well known to me: but I think that, after having applied his whole mind to magnifying the objections, he had not enough attention left over for the purpose of answering them.

85. M. Bayle confesses, moreover, in his posthumous work against M. le Clerc, that the objections against faith have not the force of proofs. It is therefore *ad hominem* only, or rather *ad homines*, that is, in relation to the existing state of the human race, that he deems these objections irrefutable and the subject unexplainable. There is even a passage where he implies that he despairs not of the possibility that the answer or the explanation may be found, and even in our time. For here is what he says in his posthumous Reply to M. le Clerc (p. 35): 'M. Bayle dared to hope that his toil would put on their mettle some of those great men of genius who create new systems, and that they could discover a solution hitherto unknown.' It seems that by this 'solution' he means such an explanation of Mystery as would penetrate to the *how*: but that is not necessary for replying to the objections.

86. Many have undertaken to render this *how* comprehensible, and to prove the possibility of Mysteries. A certain writer named Thomas Bonartes Nordtanus Anglus, in his *Concordia Scientiae cum Fide*, claimed to do so. This work seemed to me ingenious and learned, but crabbed and involved, and it even contains indefensible opinions. I learned from the *Apologia Cyriacorum* of the Dominican Father Vincent Baron that that book was censured in Rome, that the author was a Jesuit, and that he suffered for having published it. The Reverend Father des Bosses, who now teaches Theology in the Jesuit College of Hildesheim, and who has

combined rare erudition with great acumen, which he displays in philosophy and theology, has informed me that the real name of Bonartes was Thomas Barton, and that after leaving the Society he retired to Ireland, where the manner of his death brought about a favourable verdict on his last opinions. I pity the men of talent who bring trouble upon themselves by their toil and their zeal. Something of like nature happened in time past to Pierre Abélard, to Gilbert de la Porrée, to John Wyclif, and in our day to the Englishman Thomas Albius, as well as to some others who plunged too far into the explanation of the Mysteries.

87. St. Augustine, however (as well as M. Bayle), does not despair of the possibility that the desired solution may be found upon earth; but this Father believes it to be reserved for some holy man illumined by a peculiar grace: 'Est aliqua causa fortassis occultior, quae melioribus sanctioribusque reservatur, illius gratia potius quam meritis illorum' (in *De Genesi ad Literam*, lib. 11, c. 4). Luther reserves the knowledge of the Mystery of Election for the academy of heaven (lib. *De Servo Arbitrio*, c. 174): 'Illic [Deus] gratiam et misericordiam spargit in indignos, hic iram et severitatem spargit in immeritos; utrobique nimius et iniquus apud homines, sed justus et verax apud se ipsum. Nam quomodo hoc justum sit ut indignos coronet, incomprehensibile est modo, videbimus autem, cum illuc venerimus, ubi jam non credetur, sed revelata facie videbitur. Ita quomodo hoc justum sit, ut immeritos damnet, incomprehensibile est modo, creditur tamen, donec revelabitur filius hominis.' It is to be hoped that M. Bayle now finds himself surrounded by that light which is lacking to us here below, since there is reason to suppose that he was not lacking in good will.

VIRGIL
Candidus insueti miratur limen Olympi,
Sub pedibusque videt nubes et sidera Daphnis.

LUCAN
. . . Illic postquam se lumine vero
Implevit, stellasque vagas miratur et astra
Fixa polis, vidit quanta sub nocte jaceret
Nostra dies.

ESSAYS

ON THE JUSTICE OF GOD

AND THE FREEDOM OF MAN

IN THE ORIGIN OF EVIL

PART ONE

1. HAVING so settled the rights of faith and of reason as rather to place reason at the service of faith than in opposition to it, we shall see how they exercise these rights to support and harmonize what the light of nature and the light of revelation teach us of God and of man in relation to evil. The *difficulties* are distinguishable into two classes. The one kind springs from man's freedom, which appears incompatible with the divine nature; and nevertheless freedom is deemed necessary, in order that man may be deemed guilty and open to punishment. The other kind concerns the conduct of God, and seems to make him participate too much in the existence of evil, even though man be free and participate also therein. And this conduct appears contrary to the goodness, the holiness and the justice of God, since God co-operates in evil as well physical as moral, and co-operates in each of them both morally and physically; and since it seems that these evils are manifested in the order of nature as well as in that of grace, and in the future and eternal life as well as, nay, more than, in this transitory life.

2. To present these difficulties in brief, it must be observed that freedom is opposed, to all appearance, by determination or certainty of any kind whatever; and nevertheless the common dogma of our philosophers states that the truth of contingent futurities is

determined. The foreknowledge of God renders all the future certain and determined, but his providence and his foreordinance, whereon foreknowledge itself appears founded, do much more: for God is not as a man, able to look upon events with unconcern and to suspend his judgement, since nothing exists save as a result of the decrees of his will and through the action of his power. And even though one leave out of account the co-operation of God, all is perfectly connected in the order of things, since nothing can come to pass unless there be a cause so disposed as to produce the effect, this taking place no less in voluntary than in all other actions. According to which it appears that man is compelled to do the good and evil that he does, and in consequence that he deserves therefor neither recompense nor chastisement: thus is the morality of actions destroyed and all justice, divine and human, shaken.

3. But even though one should grant to man this freedom wherewith he arrays himself to his own hurt, the conduct of God could not but provide matter for a criticism supported by the presumptuous ignorance of men, who would wish to exculpate themselves wholly or in part at the expense of God. It is objected that all the reality and what is termed the substance of the act in sin itself is a production of God, since all creatures and all their actions derive from him that reality they have. Whence one could infer not only that he is the physical cause of sin, but also that he is its moral cause, since he acts with perfect freedom and does nothing without a complete knowledge of the thing and the consequences that it may have. Nor is it enough to say that God has made for himself a law to co-operate with the wills or resolutions of man, whether we express ourselves in terms of the common opinion or in terms of the system of occasional causes. Not only will it be found strange that he should have made such a law for himself, of whose results he was not ignorant, but the principal difficulty is that it seems the evil will itself cannot exist without co-operation, and even without some predetermination, on his part, which contributes towards begetting this will in man or in some other rational creature. For an action is not, for being evil, the less dependent on God. Whence one will come at last to the conclusion that God does all, the good and the evil, indifferently; unless one pretend with the Manichaeans that there are two principles, the one good and the other evil. Moreover, according to the general

opinion of theologians and philosophers, conservation being a perpetual creation, it will be said that man is perpetually created corrupt and erring. There are, furthermore, modern Cartesians who claim that God is the sole agent, of whom created beings are only the purely passive organs; and M. Bayle builds not a little upon that idea.

4. But even granting that God should co-operate in actions only with a general co-operation, or even not at all, at least in those that are bad, it suffices, so it is said, to inculpate him and to render him the moral cause that nothing comes to pass without his permission. To say nothing of the fall of the angels, he knows all that which will come to pass, if, having created man, he places him in such and such circumstances; and he places him there notwithstanding. Man is exposed to a temptation to which it is known that he will succumb, thereby causing an infinitude of frightful evils, by which the whole human race will be infected and brought as it were into a necessity of sinning, a state which is named 'original sin'. Thus the world will be brought into a strange confusion, by this means death and diseases being introduced, with a thousand other misfortunes and miseries that in general afflict the good and the bad; wickedness will even hold sway and virtue will be oppressed on earth, so that it will scarce appear that a providence governs affairs. But it is much worse when one considers the life to come, since but a small number of men will be saved and since all the rest will perish eternally. Furthermore these men destined for salvation will have been withdrawn from the corrupt mass through an unreasoning election, whether it be said that God in choosing them has had regard to their future actions, to their faith or to their works, or one claim that he has been pleased to give them these good qualities and these actions because he has predestined them to salvation. For though it be said in the most lenient system that God wished to save all men, and though in the other systems commonly accepted it be granted, that he has made his Son take human nature upon him to expiate their sins, so that all they who shall believe in him with a lively and final faith shall be saved, it still remains true that this lively faith is a gift of God; that we are dead to all good works; that even our will itself must be aroused by a prevenient grace, and that God gives us the power to will and to do. And whether that be done through a grace efficacious of itself, that is to say, through a divine inward motion

which wholly determines our will to the good that it does; or whether there be only a sufficient grace, but such as does not fail to attain its end, and to become efficacious in the inward and outward circumstances wherein the man is and has been placed by God: one must return to the same conclusion that God is the final reason of salvation, of grace, of faith and of election in Jesus Christ. And be the election the cause or the result of God's design to give faith, it still remains true that he gives faith or salvation to whom he pleases, without any discernible reason for his choice, which falls upon but few men.

5. So it is a terrible judgement that God, giving his only Son for the whole human race and being the sole author and master of the salvation of men, yet saves so few of them and abandons all others to the devil his enemy, who torments them eternally and makes them curse their Creator, though they have all been created to diffuse and show forth his goodness, his justice and his other perfections. And this outcome inspires all the more horror, as the sole cause why all these men are wretched to all eternity is God's having exposed their parents to a temptation that he knew they would not resist; as this sin is inherent and imputed to men before their will has participated in it; as this hereditary vice impels their will to commit actual sins; and as countless men, in childhood or maturity, that have never heard or have not heard enough of Jesus Christ, Saviour of the human race, die before receiving the necessary succour for their withdrawal from this abyss of sin. These men too are condemned to be for ever rebellious against God and plunged in the most horrible miseries, with the wickedest of all creatures, though in essence they have not been more wicked than others, and several among them have perchance been less guilty than some of that little number of elect, who were saved by a grace without reason, and who thereby enjoy an eternal felicity which they had not deserved. Such in brief are the difficulties touched upon by sundry persons; but M. Bayle was one who insisted on them the most, as will appear subsequently when we examine his passages. I think that now I have recorded the main essence of these difficulties: but I have deemed it fitting to refrain from some expressions and exaggerations which might have caused offence, while not rendering the objections any stronger.

6. Let us now turn the medal and let us also point out what can be said in answer to those objections; and here a course of

explanation through fuller dissertation will be necessary: for many difficulties can be opened up in few words, but for their discussion one must dilate upon them. Our end is to banish from men the false ideas that represent God to them as an absolute prince employing a despotic power, unfitted to be loved and unworthy of being loved. These notions are the more evil in relation to God inasmuch as the essence of piety is not only to fear him but also to love him above all things: and that cannot come about unless there be knowledge of his perfections capable of arousing the love which he deserves, and which makes the felicity of those that love him. Feeling ourselves animated by a zeal such as cannot fail to please him, we have cause to hope that he will enlighten us, and that he will himself aid us in the execution of a project undertaken for his glory and for the good of men. A cause so good gives confidence: if there are plausible appearances against us there are proofs on our side, and I would dare to say to an adversary:

Aspice, quam mage sit nostrum penetrabile telum.

7. *God is the first reason of things*: for such things as are bounded, as all that which we see and experience, are contingent and have nothing in them to render their existence necessary, it being plain that time, space and matter, united and uniform in themselves and indifferent to everything, might have received entirely other motions and shapes, and in another order. Therefore one must seek the reason for the existence of the world, which is the whole assemblage of *contingent* things, and seek it in the substance which carries with it the reason for its existence, and which in consequence is *necessary* and eternal. Moreover, this cause must be intelligent: for this existing world being contingent and an infinity of other worlds being equally possible, and holding, so to say, equal claim to existence with it, the cause of the world must needs have had regard or reference to all these possible worlds in order to fix upon one of them. This regard or relation of an existent substance to simple possibilities can be nothing other than the *understanding* which has the ideas of them, while to fix upon one of them can be nothing other than the act of the *will* which chooses. It is the *power* of this substance that renders its will efficacious. Power relates to *being*, wisdom or understanding to *truth*, and will to *good*. And this intelligent cause ought to be infinite in all ways, and absolutely perfect in *power*, in *wisdom* and in *goodness*, since it

relates to all that which is possible. Furthermore, since all is connected together, there is no ground for admitting more than *one*. Its understanding is the source of *essences*, and its will is the origin of *existences*. There in few words is the proof of one only God with his perfections, and through him of the origin of things.

8. Now this supreme wisdom, united to a goodness that is no less infinite, cannot but have chosen the best. For as a lesser evil is a kind of good, even so a lesser good is a kind of evil if it stands in the way of a greater good; and there would be something to correct in the actions of God if it were possible to do better. As in mathematics, when there is no maximum nor minimum, in short nothing distinguished, everything is done equally, or when that is not possible nothing at all is done: so it may be said likewise in respect of perfect wisdom, which is no less orderly than mathematics, that if there were not the best (*optimum*) among all possible worlds, God would not have produced any. I call 'World' the whole succession and the whole agglomeration of all existent things, lest it be said that several worlds could have existed in different times and different places. For they must needs be reckoned all together as one world or, if you will, as one Universe. And even though one should fill all times and all places, it still remains true that one might have filled them in innumerable ways, and that there is an infinitude of possible worlds among which God must needs have chosen the best, since he does nothing without acting in accordance with supreme reason.

9. Some adversary not being able to answer this argument will perchance answer the conclusion by a counter-argument, saying that the world could have been without sin and without sufferings; but I deny that then it would have been *better*. For it must be known that all things are *connected* in each one of the possible worlds: the universe, whatever it may be, is all of one piece, like an ocean: the least movement extends its effect there to any distance whatsoever, even though this effect become less perceptible in proportion to the distance. Therein God has ordered all things beforehand once for all, having foreseen prayers, good and bad actions, and all the rest; and each thing *as an idea* has contributed, before its existence, to the resolution that has been made upon the existence of all things; so that nothing can be changed in the universe (any more than in a number) save its essence or, if you will, save its *numerical individuality*. Thus, if the smallest evil

that comes to pass in the world were missing in it, it would no longer be this world; which, with nothing omitted and all allowance made, was found the best by the Creator who chose it.

10. It is true that one may imagine possible worlds without sin and without unhappiness, and one could make some like Utopian or Sevarambian romances: but these same worlds again would be very inferior to ours in goodness. I cannot show you this in detail. For can I know and can I present infinities to you and compare them together? But you must judge with me *ab effectu*, since God has chosen this world as it is. We know, moreover, that often an evil brings forth a good whereto one would not have attained without that evil. Often indeed two evils have made one great good:

Et si fata volunt, bina venena juvant.

Even so two liquids sometimes produce a solid, witness the spirit of wine and spirit of urine mixed by Van Helmont; or so do two cold and dark bodies produce a great fire, witness an acid solution and an aromatic oil combined by Herr Hoffmann. A general makes sometimes a fortunate mistake which brings about the winning of a great battle; and do they not sing on the eve of Easter, in the churches of the Roman rite:

O certe necessarium Adae peccatum, quòd Christi morte deletum est!
O felix culpa, quae talem ac tantum meruit habere Redemptorem!

11. The illustrious prelates of the Gallican church who wrote to Pope Innocent XII against Cardinal Sfondrati's book on predestination, being of the principles of St. Augustine, have said things well fitted to elucidate this great point. The cardinal appears to prefer even to the Kingdom of Heaven the state of children dying without baptism, because sin is the greatest of evils, and they have died innocent of all actual sin. More will be said of that below. The prelates have observed that this opinion is ill founded. The apostle, they say (Rom. iii. 8), is right to disapprove of the doing of evil that good may come, but one cannot disapprove that God, through his exceeding power, derive from the permitting of sins greater goods than such as occurred before the sins. It is not that we ought to take pleasure in sin, God forbid! but that we believe the same apostle when he says (Rom. v. 20)

that where sin abounded, grace did much more abound; and we remember that we have gained Jesus Christ himself by reason of sin. Thus we see that the opinion of these prelates tends to maintain that a sequence of things where sin enters in may have been and has been, in effect, better than another sequence without sin.

12. Use has ever been made of comparisons taken from the pleasures of the senses when these are mingled with that which borders on pain, to prove that there is something of like nature in intellectual pleasures. A little acid, sharpness or bitterness is often more pleasing than sugar; shadows enhance colours; and even a dissonance in the right place gives relief to harmony. We wish to be terrified by rope-dancers on the point of falling and we wish that tragedies shall well-nigh cause us to weep. Do men relish health enough, or thank God enough for it, without having ever been sick? And is it not most often necessary that a little evil render the good more discernible, that is to say, greater?

13. But it will be said that evils are great and many in number in comparison with the good: that is erroneous. It is only want of attention that diminishes our good, and this attention must be given to us through some admixture of evils. If we were usually sick and seldom in good health, we should be wonderfully sensible of that great good and we should be less sensible of our evils. But is it not better, notwithstanding, that health should be usual and sickness the exception? Let us then by our reflexion supply what is lacking in our perception, in order to make the good of health more discernible. Had we not the knowledge of the life to come, I believe there would be few persons who, being at the point of death, were not content to take up life again, on condition of passing through the same amount of good and evil, provided always that it were not the same kind: one would be content with variety, without requiring a better condition than that wherein one had been.

14. When one considers also the fragility of the human body, one looks in wonder at the wisdom and the goodness of the Author of Nature, who has made the body so enduring and its condition so tolerable. That has often made me say that I am not astonished men are sometimes sick, but that I am astonished they are sick so little and not always. This also ought to make us the more esteem the divine contrivance of the mechanism of animals, whose Author

has made machines so fragile and so subject to corruption and yet so capable of maintaining themselves: for it is Nature which cures us rather than medicine. Now this very fragility is a consequence of the nature of things, unless we are to will that this kind of creature, reasoning and clothed in flesh and bones, be not in the world. But that, to all appearance, would be a defect which some philosophers of old would have called *vacuum formarum*, a gap in the order of species.

15. Those whose humour it is to be well satisfied with Nature and with fortune and not to complain about them, even though they should not be the best endowed, appear to me preferable to the other sort; for besides that these complaints are ill founded, it is in effect murmuring against the orders of providence. One must not readily be among the malcontents in the State where one is, and one must not be so at all in the city of God, wherein one can only wrongfully be of their number. The books of human misery, such as that of Pope Innocent III, to me seem not of the most serviceable: evils are doubled by being given an attention that ought to be averted from them, to be turned towards the good which by far preponderates. Even less do I approve books such as that of Abbé Esprit, *On the Falsity of Human Virtues*, of which we have lately been given a summary: for such a book serves to turn everything wrong side out, and cause men to be such as it represents them.

16. It must be confessed, however, that there are disorders in this life, which appear especially in the prosperity of sundry evil men and in the misfortune of many good people. There is a German proverb which even grants the advantage to the evil ones, as if they were commonly the most fortunate:

> *Je krümmer Holz, je bessre Krücke:*
> *Je ärger Schalck, je grösser Glücke.*

And it were to be desired that this saying of Horace should be true in our eyes:

> *Raro antecedentem scelestum*
> *Deseruit pede poena claudo.*

Yet it often comes to pass also, though this perchance not the most often,

That in the world's eyes Heaven is justified,

and that one may say with Claudian:

> *Abstulit hunc tandem Rufini poena tumultum,*
> *Absolvitque deos . . .*

17. But even though that should not happen here, the remedy is all prepared in the other life: religion and reason itself teach us that, and we must not murmur against a respite which the supreme wisdom has thought fit to grant to men for repentance. Yet there objections multiply on another side, when one considers salvation and damnation: for it appears strange that, even in the great future of eternity, evil should have the advantage over good, under the supreme authority of him who is the sovereign good, since there will be many that are called and few that are chosen or are saved. It is true that one sees from some lines of Prudentius (Hymn. ante Somnum),

> *Idem tamen benignus*
> *Ultor retundit iram,*
> *Paucosque non piorum*
> *Patitur perire in aevum,*

that divers men believed in his time that the number of those wicked enough to be damned would be very small. To some indeed it seems that men believed at that time in a sphere between Hell and Paradise; that this same Prudentius speaks as if he were satisfied with this sphere; that St. Gregory of Nyssa also inclines in that direction, and that St. Jerome leans towards the opinion according whereunto all Christians would finally be taken into grace. A saying of St. Paul which he himself gives out as mysterious, stating that all Israel will be saved, has provided much food for reflexion. Sundry pious persons, learned also, but daring, have revived the opinion of Origen, who maintains that good will predominate in due time, in all and everywhere, and that all rational creatures, even the bad angels, will become at last holy and blessed. The book of the eternal Gospel, published lately in German and supported by a great and learned work entitled Ἀποκατάστασις πάντων, has caused much stir over this great paradox. M. le Clerc also has ingeniously pleaded the cause of the Origenists, but without declaring himself for them.

18. There is a man of wit who, pushing my principle of harmony even to arbitrary suppositions that I in no wise approve, has created for himself a theology well-nigh astronomical. He believes that the present confusion in this world below began when the Presiding Angel of the globe of the earth, which was still a sun (that is, a star that was fixed and luminous of itself) committed a sin with some lesser angels of his department, perhaps rising inopportunely against an angel of a greater sun; that simultaneously, by the Pre-established Harmony of the Realms of Nature and of Grace, and consequently by natural causes occurring at the appointed time, our globe was covered with stains, rendered opaque and driven from its place; which has made it become a wandering star or planet, that is, a Satellite of another sun, and even perhaps of that one whose superiority its angel refused to recognize; and that therein consists the fall of Lucifer. Now the chief of the bad angels, who in Holy Scripture is named the prince, and even the god of this world, being, with the angels of his train, envious of that rational animal which walks on the surface of this globe, and which God has set up there perhaps to compensate himself for their fall, strives to render it accessary in their crimes and a participator in their misfortunes. Whereupon Jesus Christ came to save men. He is the eternal Son of God, even as he is his only Son; but (according to some ancient Christians, and according to the author of this hypothesis) having taken upon him at first, from the beginning of things, the most excellent nature among created beings, to bring them all to perfection, he set himself amongst them: and this is the second filiation, whereby he is the first-born of all creatures. This is he whom the Cabalists called Adam Kadmon. Haply he had planted his tabernacle in that great sun which illumines us; but he came at last into this globe where we are, he was born of the Virgin, and took human nature upon him to save mankind from the hands of their enemy and his. And when the time of judgement shall draw near, when the present face of our globe shall be about to perish, he will return to it in visible form, thence to withdraw the good, transplanting them, it may be, into the sun, and to punish here the wicked with the demons that have allured them; then the globe of the earth will begin to burn and will be perhaps a comet. This fire will last for aeons upon aeons. The tail of the comet is intended by the smoke which will rise incessantly, according to the Apocalypse, and this fire will be

hell, or the second death whereof Holy Scripture speaks. But at last hell will render up its dead, death itself will be destroyed; reason and peace will begin to hold sway again in the spirits that had been perverted; they will be sensible of their error, they will adore their Creator, and will even begin to love him all the more for seeing the greatness of the abyss whence they emerge. Simultaneously (by virtue of the *harmonic parallelism* of the Realms of Nature and of Grace) this long and great conflagration will have purged the earth's globe of its stains. It will become again a sun; its Presiding Angel will resume his place with the angels of his train; humans that were damned shall be with them numbered amongst the good angels; this chief of our globe shall render homage to the Messiah, chief of created beings. The glory of this angel reconciled shall be greater than it was before his fall.

> *Inque Deos iterum factorum lege receptus*
> *Aureus aeternum noster regnabit Apollo.*

The vision seemed to me pleasing, and worthy of a follower of Origen: but we have no need of such hypothesis or fictions, where Wit plays a greater part than Revelation, and which even Reason cannot turn to account. For it does not appear that there is one principal place in the known universe deserving in preference to the rest to be the seat of the eldest of created beings; and the sun of our system at least is not it.

19. Holding then to the established doctrine that the number of men damned eternally will be incomparably greater than that of the saved, we must say that the evil could not but seem to be almost as nothing in comparison with the good, when one contemplates the true vastness of the city of God. Coelius Secundus Curio wrote a little book, *De Amplitudine Regni Coelestis*, which was reprinted not long since; but he is indeed far from having apprehended the compass of the kingdom of heaven. The ancients had puny ideas on the works of God, and St. Augustine, for want of knowing modern discoveries, was at a loss when there was question of explaining the prevalence of evil. It seemed to the ancients that there was only one earth inhabited, and even of that men held the antipodes in dread: the remainder of the world was, according to them, a few shining globes and a few crystalline spheres. To-day, whatever bounds are given or not given to the universe, it must be acknowledged that there is an infinite number of globes, as great

as and greater than ours, which have as much right as it to hold rational inhabitants, though it follows not at all that they are human. It is only one planet, that is to say one of the six principal satellites of our sun; and as all fixed stars are suns also, we see how small a thing our earth is in relation to visible things, since it is only an appendix of one amongst them. It may be that all suns are peopled only by blessed creatures, and nothing constrains us to think that many are damned, for few instances or few samples suffice to show the advantage which good extracts from evil. Moreover, since there is no reason for the belief that there are stars everywhere, is it not possible that there may be a great space beyond the region of the stars? Whether it be the Empyrean Heaven, or not, this immense space encircling all this region may in any case be filled with happiness and glory. It can be imagined as like the Ocean, whither flow the rivers of all blessed creatures, when they shall have reached their perfection in the system of the stars. What will become of the consideration of our globe and its inhabitants? Will it not be something incomparably less than a physical point, since our earth is as a point in comparison with the distance of some fixed stars? Thus since the proportion of that part of the universe which we know is almost lost in nothingness compared with that which is unknown, and which we yet have cause to assume, and since all the evils that may be raised in objection before us are in this near nothingness, haply it may be that all evils are almost nothingness in comparison with the good things which are in the universe.

20. But it is necessary also to meet the more speculative and metaphysical difficulties which have been mentioned, and which concern the cause of evil. The question is asked first of all, whence does evil come? *Si Deus est, unde malum? Si non est, unde bonum?* The ancients attributed the cause of evil to *matter*, which they believed uncreate and independent of God: but we, who derive all being from God, where shall we find the source of evil? The answer is, that it must be sought in the ideal nature of the creature, in so far as this nature is contained in the eternal verities which are in the understanding of God, independently of his will. For we must consider that there is an *original imperfection in the creature* before sin, because the creature is limited in its essence; whence ensues that it cannot know all, and that it can deceive itself and commit other errors. Plato said in *Timaeus* that the world originated in Under-

standing united to Necessity. Others have united God and Nature. This can be given a reasonable meaning. God will be the Understanding; and the Necessity, that is, the essential nature of things, will be the object of the understanding, in so far as this object consists in the eternal verities. But this object is inward and abides in the divine understanding. And therein is found not only the primitive form of good, but also the origin of evil: the Region of the Eternal Verities must be substituted for matter when we are concerned with seeking out the source of things.

This region is the ideal cause of evil (as it were) as well as of good: but, properly speaking, the formal character of evil has no *efficient* cause, for it consists in privation, as we shall see, namely, in that which the efficient cause does not bring about. That is why the Schoolmen are wont to call the cause of evil *deficient*.

21. Evil may be taken metaphysically, physically and morally. *Metaphysical evil* consists in mere imperfection, *physical evil* in suffering, and *moral evil* in sin. Now although physical evil and moral evil be not necessary, it is enough that by virtue of the eternal verities they be possible. And as this vast Region of Verities contains all possibilities it is necessary that there be an infinitude of possible worlds, that evil enter into divers of them, and that even the best of all contain a measure thereof. Thus has God been induced to permit evil.

22. But someone will say to me: why speak you to us of 'permitting'? Is it not God that doeth the evil and that willeth it? Here it will be necessary to explain what 'permission' is, so that it may be seen how this term is not employed without reason. But before that one must explain the nature of will, which has its own degrees. Taking it in the general sense, one may say that *will* consists in the inclination to do something in proportion to the good it contains. This will is called *antecedent* when it is detached, and considers each good separately in the capacity of a good. In this sense it may be said that God tends to all good, as good, *ad perfectionem simpliciter simplicem*, to speak like the Schoolmen, and that by an antecedent will. He is earnestly disposed to sanctify and to save all men, to exclude sin, and to prevent damnation. It may even be said that this will is efficacious *of itself (per se)*, that is, in such sort that the effect would ensue if there were not some stronger reason to prevent it: for this will does not pass into final exercise *(ad summum conatum)*, else it would never fail to produce its

full effect, God being the master of all things. Success entire and infallible belongs only to the *consequent will,* as it is called. This it is which is complete; and in regard to it this rule obtains, that one never fails to do what one wills, when one has the power. Now this consequent will, final and decisive, results from the conflict of all the antecedent wills, of those which tend towards good, even as of those which repel evil; and from the concurrence of all these particular wills comes the total will. So in mechanics compound movement results from all the tendencies that concur in one and the same moving body, and satisfies each one equally, in so far as it is possible to do all at one time. It is as if the moving body took equal account of these tendencies, as I once showed in one of the Paris Journals (7 Sept. 1693), when giving the general law of the compositions of movement. In this sense also it may be said that the antecedent will is efficacious in a sense and even effective with success.

23. Thence it follows that God wills *antecedently* the good and *consequently* the best. And as for evil, God wills moral evil not at all, and physical evil or suffering he does not will absolutely. Thus it is that there is no absolute predestination to damnation; and one may say of physical evil, that God wills it often as a penalty owing to guilt, and often also as a means to an end, that is, to prevent greater evils or to obtain greater good. The penalty serves also for amendment and example. Evil often serves to make us savour good the more; sometimes too it contributes to a greater perfection in him who suffers it, as the seed that one sows is subject to a kind of corruption before it can germinate: this is a beautiful similitude, which Jesus Christ himself used.

24. Concerning sin or moral evil, although it happens very often that it may serve as a means of obtaining good or of preventing another evil, it is not this that renders it a sufficient object of the divine will or a legitimate object of a created will. It must only be admitted or *permitted* in so far as it is considered to be a certain consequence of an indispensable duty: as for instance if a man who was determined not to permit another's sin were to fail of his own duty, or as if an officer on guard at an important post were to leave it, especially in time of danger, in order to prevent a quarrel in the town between two soldiers of the garrison who wanted to kill each other.

25. The rule which states, *non esse facienda mala, ut eveniant bona,* and which even forbids the permission of a moral evil with the end

of obtaining a physical good, far from being violated, is here proved, and its source and its reason are demonstrated. One will not approve the action of a queen who, under the pretext of saving the State, commits or even permits a crime. The crime is certain and the evil for the State is open to question. Moreover, this manner of giving sanction to crimes, if it were accepted, would be worse than a disruption of some one country, which is liable enough to happen in any case, and would perchance happen all the more by reason of such means chosen to prevent it. But in relation to God nothing is open to question, nothing can be opposed to *the rule of the best*, which suffers neither exception nor dispensation. It is in this sense that God permits sin: for he would fail in what he owes to himself, in what he owes to his wisdom, his goodness, his perfection, if he followed not the grand result of all his tendencies to good, and if he chose not that which is absolutely the best, notwithstanding the evil of guilt, which is involved therein by the supreme necessity of the eternal verities. Hence the conclusion that God wills all good *in himself antecedently*, that he wills the best *consequently* as an *end*, that he wills what is indifferent, and physical evil, sometimes as a *means*, but that he will only permit moral evil as the *sine quo non* or as a hypothetical necessity which connects it with the best. Therefore the *consequent will* of God, which has sin for its object, is only *permissive*.

26. It is again well to consider that moral evil is an evil so great only because it is a source of physical evils, a source existing in one of the most powerful of creatures, who is also most capable of causing those evils. For an evil will is in its department what the evil principle of the Manichaeans would be in the universe; and reason, which is an image of the Divinity, provides for evil souls great means of causing much evil. One single Caligula, one Nero, has caused more evil than an earthquake. An evil man takes pleasure in causing suffering and destruction, and for that there are only too many opportunities. But God being inclined to produce as much good as possible, and having all the knowledge and all the power necessary for that, it is impossible that in him there be fault, or guilt, or sin; and when he permits sin, it is wisdom, it is virtue.

27. It is indeed beyond question that we must refrain from preventing the sin of others when we cannot prevent their sin without sinning ourselves. But someone will perhaps bring up the

objection that it is God himself who acts and who effects all that is real in the sin of the creature. This objection leads us to consider the *physical co-operation* of God with the creature, after we have examined the *moral co-operation*, which was the more perplexing. Some have believed, with the celebrated Durand de Saint-Pourçain and Cardinal Aureolus, the famous Schoolman, that the co-operation of God with the creature (I mean the physical cooperation) is only general and mediate, and that God creates substances and gives them the force they need; and that thereafter he leaves them to themselves, and does naught but conserve them, without aiding them in their actions. This opinion has been refuted by the greater number of Scholastic theologians, and it appears that in the past it met with disapproval in the writings of Pelagius. Nevertheless a Capuchin named Louis Pereir of Dole, about the year 1630, wrote a book expressly to revive it, at least in relation to free actions. Some moderns incline thereto, and M. Bernier supports it in a little book on freedom and freewill. But one cannot say in relation to God what 'to conserve' is, without reverting to the general opinion. Also it must be taken into account that the action of God in conserving should have some reference to that which is conserved, according to what it is and to the state wherein it is; thus his action cannot be general or indeterminate. These generalities are abstractions not to be found in the truth of individual things, and the conservation of a man standing is different from the conservation of a man seated. This would not be so if conservation consisted only in the act of preventing and warding off some foreign cause which could destroy that which one wishes to conserve; as often happens when men conserve something. But apart from the fact that we are obliged ourselves sometimes to maintain that which we conserve, we must bear in mind that conservation by God consists in the perpetual immediate influence which the dependence of creatures demands. This dependence attaches not only to the substance but also to the action, and one can perhaps not explain it better than by saying, with theologians and philosophers in general, that it is a continued creation.

28. The objection will be made that God therefore now creates man a sinner, he that in the beginning created him innocent. But here it must be said, with regard to the moral aspect, that God being supremely wise cannot fail to observe certain laws, and to

act according to the rules, as well physical as moral, that wisdom has made him choose. And the same reason that has made him create man innocent, but liable to fall, makes him re-create man when he falls; for God's knowledge causes the future to be for him as the present, and prevents him from rescinding the resolutions made.

29. As for physical co-operation, here one must consider the truth which has made already so much stir in the Schools since St. Augustine declared it, that evil is a privation of being, whereas the action of God tends to the positive. This answer is accounted a quibble, and even something chimerical in the minds of many people. But here is an instance somewhat similar, which will serve to disabuse them.

30. The celebrated Kepler and M. Descartes (in his letters) after him have spoken of the 'natural inertia of bodies'; and it is something which may be regarded as a perfect image and even as a sample of the original limitation of creatures, to show that privation constitutes the formal character of the imperfections and disadvantages that are in substance as well as in its actions. Let us suppose that the current of one and the same river carried along with it various boats, which differ among themselves only in the cargo, some being laden with wood, others with stone, and some more, the others less. That being so, it will come about that the boats most heavily laden will go more slowly than the others, provided it be assumed that the wind or the oar, or some other similar means, assist them not at all. It is not, properly speaking, weight which is the cause of this retardation, since the boats are going down and not upwards; but it is the same cause which also increases the weight in bodies that have greater density, which are, that is to say, less porous and more charged with matter that is proper to them: for the matter which passes through the pores, not receiving the same movement, must not be taken into account. It is therefore matter itself which originally is inclined to slowness or privation of speed; not indeed of itself to lessen this speed, having once received it, since that would be action, but to moderate by its receptivity the effect of the impression when it is to receive it. Consequently, since more matter is moved by the same force of the current when the boat is more laden, it is necessary that it go more slowly; and experiments on the impact of bodies, as well as reason, show that twice as much force must be

employed to give equal speed to a body of the same matter but of twice the size. But that indeed would not be necessary if the matter were absolutely indifferent to repose and to movement, and if it had not this natural inertia whereof we have just spoken to give it a kind of repugnance to being moved. Let us now compare the force which the current exercises on boats, and communicates to them, with the action of God, who produces and conserves whatever is positive in creatures, and gives them perfection, being and force: let us compare, I say, the inertia of matter with the natural imperfection of creatures, and the slowness of the laden boat with the defects to be found in the qualities and the action of the creature; and we shall find that there is nothing so just as this comparison. The current is the cause of the boat's movement, but not of its retardation; God is the cause of perfection in the nature and the actions of the creature, but the limitation of the receptivity of the creature is the cause of the defects there are in its action. Thus the Platonists, St. Augustine and the Schoolmen were right to say that God is the cause of the material element of evil which lies in the positive, and not of the formal element, which lies in privation. Even so one may say that the current is the cause of the material element of the retardation, but not of the formal: that is, it is the cause of the boat's speed without being the cause of the limits to this speed. And God is no more the cause of sin than the river's current is the cause of the retardation of the boat. Force also in relation to matter is as the spirit in relation to the flesh; the spirit is willing and the flesh is weak, and spirits act . . .

quantum non noxia corpora tardant.

31. There is, then, a wholly similar relation between such and such an action of God, and such and such a passion or reception of the creature, which in the ordinary course of things is perfected only in proportion to its 'receptivity', such is the term used. And when it is said that the creature depends upon God in so far as it exists and in so far as it acts, and even that conservation is a continual creation, this is true in that God gives ever to the creature and produces continually all that in it is positive, good and perfect, every perfect gift coming from the Father of lights. The imperfections, on the other hand, and the defects in operations spring from the original limitation that the creature could not but

receive with the first beginning of its being, through the ideal reasons which restrict it. For God could not give the creature all without making of it a God; therefore there must needs be different degrees in the perfection of things, and limitations also of every kind.

32. This consideration will serve also to satisfy some modern philosophers who go so far as to say that God is the only agent. It is true that God is the only one whose action is pure and without admixture of what is termed 'to suffer': but that does not preclude the creature's participation in actions, since *the action of the creature* is a modification of the substance, flowing naturally from it and containing a variation not only in the perfections that God has communicated to the creature, but also in the limitations that the creature, being what it is, brings with it. Thus we see that there is an actual distinction between the substance and its modification or accidents, contrary to the opinion of some moderns and in particular of the late Duke of Buckingham, who spoke of that in a little *Discourse on Religion* recently reprinted. Evil is therefore like darkness, and not only ignorance but also error and malice consist formally in a certain kind of privation. Here is an example of error which we have already employed. I see a tower which from a distance appears round although it is square. The thought that the tower is what it appears to be flows naturally from that which I see; and when I dwell on this thought it is an affirmation, it is a false judgement; but if I pursue the examination, if some reflexion causes me to perceive that appearances deceive me, lo and behold, I abandon my error. To abide in a certain place, or not to go further, not to espy some landmark, these are privations.

33. It is the same in respect of malice or ill will. The will tends towards good in general, it must strive after the perfection that befits us, and the supreme perfection is in God. All pleasures have within themselves some feeling of perfection. But when one is limited to the pleasures of the senses, or to other pleasures to the detriment of greater good, as of health, of virtue, of union with God, of felicity, it is in this privation of a further aspiration that the defect consists. In general perfection is positive, it is an absolute reality; defect is privative, it comes from limitation and tends towards new privations. This saying is therefore as true as it is ancient: *bonum ex causa integra, malum ex quolibet defectu*; as also that

which states : *malum causam habet non efficientem, sed deficientem*. And I hope that the meaning of these axioms will be better apprehended after what I have just said.

34. The physical co-operation of God and of creatures with the will contributes also to the difficulties existing in regard to freedom. I am of opinion that our will is exempt not only from constraint but also from necessity. Aristotle has already observed that there are two things in freedom, to wit, spontaneity and choice, and therein lies our mastery over our actions. When we act freely we are not being forced, as would happen if we were pushed on to a precipice and thrown from top to bottom ; and we are not prevented from having the mind free when we deliberate, as would happen if we were given a draught to deprive us of discernment. There is *contingency* in a thousand actions of Nature ; but when there is no judgement in him who acts there is no *freedom*. And if we had judgement not accompanied by any inclination to act, our soul would be an understanding without will.

35. It is not to be imagined, however, that our freedom consists in an indetermination or an indifference of equipoise, as if one must needs be inclined equally to the side of yes and of no and in the direction of different courses, when there are several of them to take. This equipoise in all directions is impossible : for if we were equally inclined towards the courses A, B and C, we could not be equally inclined towards A and towards not A. This equipoise is also absolutely contrary to experience, and in scrutinizing oneself one will find that there has always been some cause or reason inclining us towards the course taken, although very often we be not aware of that which prompts us : just in the same way one is hardly aware why, on issuing from a door, one has placed the right foot before the left or the left before the right.

36. But let us pass to the difficulties. Philosophers agree to-day that the truth of contingent futurities is determinate, that is to say that contingent futurities are future, or that they will be, that they will happen : for it is as sure that the future will be, as it is sure that the past has been. It was true already a hundred years ago that I should write to-day, as it will be true after a hundred years that I have written. Thus the contingent is not, because it is future, any the less contingent ; and *determination*, which would be called certainty if it were known, is not incompatible with contingency. Often the certain and the determinate are taken as one thing,

because a determinate truth is capable of being known: thus it may be said that determination is an objective certainty.

37. This determination comes from the very nature of truth, and cannot injure freedom: but there are other determinations taken from elsewhere, and in the first place from the foreknowledge of God, which many have held to be contrary to freedom. They say that what is foreseen cannot fail to exist, and they say so truly; but it follows not that what is foreseen is necessary, for *necessary truth* is that whereof the contrary is impossible or implies contradiction. Now this truth which states that I shall write to-morrow is not of that nature, it is not necessary. Yet supposing that God foresees it, it is necessary that it come to pass; that is, the consequence is necessary, namely, that it exist, since it has been foreseen; for God is infallible. This is what is termed a *hypothetical necessity*. But our concern is not this necessity: it is an *absolute necessity* that is required, to be able to say that an action is necessary, that it is not contingent, that it is not the effect of a free choice. Besides it is very easily seen that foreknowledge in itself adds nothing to the determination of the truth of contingent futurities, save that this determination is known: and this does not augment the determination or the 'futurition' (as it is termed) of these events, that whereon we agreed at the outset.

38. This answer is doubtless very correct. It is agreed that fore-knowledge in itself does not make truth more determinate; truth is foreseen because it is determinate, because it is true; but it is not true because it is foreseen: and therein the knowledge of the future has nothing that is not also in the knowledge of the past or of the present. But here is what an opponent will be able to say: I grant you that foreknowledge in itself does not make truth more determinate, but it is the cause of the foreknowledge that makes it so. For it needs must be that the foreknowledge of God have its foundation in the nature of things, and this foundation, making the truth *predeterminate*, will prevent it from being contingent and free.

39. It is this difficulty that has caused two parties to spring up, one of the *predeterminators*, the other of the supporters of *mediate knowledge*. The Dominicans and the Augustinians are for pre-determination, the Franciscans and the modern Jesuits on the other hand are for mediate knowledge. These two parties appeared towards the middle of the sixteenth century and a little later.

Molina himself, who is perhaps one of the first, with Fonseca, to have systematized this point, and from whom the others derived their name of Molinists, says in the book that he wrote on the reconciliation of freewill with grace, about the year 1570, that the Spanish doctors (he means principally the Thomists), who had been writing then for twenty years, finding no other way to explain how God could have a certain knowledge of contingent futurities, had introduced predetermination as being necessary to free actions.

40. As for himself, he thought to have found another way. He considers that there are three objects of divine knowledge, the possibles, the actual events and the conditional events that would happen in consequence of a certain condition if it were translated into action. The knowledge of possibilities is what is called the 'knowledge of mere intelligence'; that of events occurring actually in the progress of the universe is called the 'knowledge of intuition'. And as there is a kind of mean between the merely possible and the pure and absolute event, to wit, the conditional event, it can be said also, according to Molina, that there is a mediate knowledge between that of intuition and that of intelligence. Instance is given of the famous example of David asking the divine oracle whether the inhabitants of the town of Keilah, where he designed to shut himself in, would deliver him to Saul, supposing that Saul should besiege the town. God answered yes; whereupon David took a different course. Now some advocates of this mediate knowledge are of opinion that God, foreseeing what men would do of their own accord, supposing they were placed in such and such circumstances, and knowing that they would make ill use of their free will, decrees to refuse them grace and favourable circumstances. And he may justly so decree, since in any case these circumstances and these aids would not have served them aught. But Molina contents himself with finding therein generally a reason for the decrees of God, founded on what the free creature would do in such and such circumstances.

41. I will not enter into all the detail of this controversy; it will suffice for me to give one instance. Certain older writers, not acceptable to St. Augustine and his first disciples, appear to have had ideas somewhat approaching those of Molina. The Thomists and those who call themselves disciples of St. Augustine (but whom their opponents call Jansenists) combat this doctrine on

philosophical and theological grounds. Some maintain that mediate knowledge must be included in the knowledge of mere intelligence. But the principal objection is aimed at the foundation of this knowledge. For what foundation can God have for seeing what the people of Keilah would do? A simple contingent and free act has nothing in itself to yield a principle of certainty, unless one look upon it as predetermined by the decrees of God, and by the causes that are dependent upon them. Consequently the difficulty existing in actual free actions will exist also in conditional free actions, that is to say, God will know them only under the condition of their causes and of his decrees, which are the first causes of things: and it will not be possible to separate such actions from those causes so as to know a contingent event in a way that is independent of the knowledge of its causes. Therefore all must of necessity be traced back to the predetermination of God's decrees, and this mediate knowledge (so it will be said) will offer no remedy. The theologians who profess to be adherents of St. Augustine claim also that the system of the Molinists would discover the source of God's grace in the good qualities of man, and this they deem an infringement of God's honour and contrary to St. Paul's teaching.

42. It would be long and wearisome to enter here into the replies and rejoinders coming from one side and the other, and it will suffice for me to explain how I conceive that there is truth on both sides. For this result I resort to my principle of an infinitude of possible worlds, represented in the region of eternal verities, that is, in the object of the divine intelligence, where all conditional futurities must be comprised. For the case of the siege of Keilah forms part of a possible world, *which differs from ours only in all that is connected with this hypothesis*, and the idea of this possible world represents that which would happen in this case. Thus we have a principle for the certain knowledge of contingent futurities, whether they happen actually or must happen in a certain case. For in the region of the possibles they are represented as they are, namely, as free contingencies. Therefore neither the foreknowledge of contingent futurities nor the foundation for the certainty of this foreknowledge should cause us perplexity or seem to prejudice freedom. And though it were true and possible that contingent futurities consisting in free actions of reasonable creatures were entirely independent of the decrees of God and of external causes,

there would still be means of foreseeing them; for God would see them as they are in the region of the possibles, before he decrees to admit them into existence.

43. But if the foreknowledge of God has nothing to do with the dependence or independence of our free actions, it is not so with the foreordinance of God, his decrees, and the sequence of causes which, as I believe, always contribute to the determination of the will. And if I am for the Molinists in the first point, I am for the predeterminators in the second, provided always that pre-determination be taken as not necessitating. In a word, I am of opinion that the will is always more inclined towards the course it adopts, but that it is never bound by the necessity to adopt it. That it will adopt this course is certain, but it is not necessary. The case corresponds to that of the famous saying, *Astra inclinant, non necessitant*, although here the similarity is not complete. For the event towards which the stars tend (to speak with the common herd, as if there were some foundation for astrology) does not always come to pass, whereas the course towards which the will is more inclined never fails to be adopted. Moreover the stars would form only a part of the inclinations that co-operate in the event, but when one speaks of the greater inclination of the will, one speaks of the result of all the inclinations. It is almost as we have spoken above of the consequent will in God, which results from all the antecedent wills.

44. Nevertheless, objective certainty or determination does not bring about the necessity of the determinate truth. All philo-sophers acknowledge this, asserting that the truth of contingent futurities is determinate, and that nevertheless they remain con-tingent. The thing indeed would imply no contradiction in itself if the effect did not follow; and therein lies contingency. The better to understand this point, we must take into account that there are two great principles of our arguments. The one is the principle of *contradiction*, stating that of two contradictory pro-positions the one is true, the other false; the other principle is that of the *determinant reason*: it states that nothing ever comes to pass without there being a cause or at least a reason determining it, that is, something to give an *a priori* reason why it is existent rather than non-existent, and in this wise rather than in any other. This great principle holds for all events, and a contrary instance will never be supplied: and although more often than not we are

insufficiently acquainted with these determinant reasons, we perceive nevertheless that there are such. Were it not for this great principle we could never prove the existence of God, and we should lose an infinitude of very just and very profitable arguments whereof it is the foundation; moreover, it suffers no exception, for otherwise its force would be weakened. Besides, nothing is so weak as those systems where all is unsteady and full of exceptions. That fault cannot be laid to the charge of the system I approve, where everything happens in accordance with general rules that at most are mutually restrictive.

45. We must therefore not imagine with some Schoolmen, whose ideas tend towards the chimerical, that free contingent futurities have the privilege of exemption from this general rule of the nature of things. There is always a prevailing reason which prompts the will to its choice, and for the maintenance of freedom for the will it suffices that this reason should incline without necessitating. That is also the opinion of all the ancients, of Plato, of Aristotle, of St. Augustine. The will is never prompted to action save by the representation of the good, which prevails over the opposite representations. This is admitted even in relation to God, the good angels and the souls in bliss: and it is acknowledged that they are none the less free in consequence of that. God fails not to choose the best, but he is not constrained so to do: nay, more, there is no necessity in the object of God's choice, for another sequence of things is equally possible. For that very reason the choice is free and independent of necessity, because it is made between several possibles, and the will is determined only by the preponderating goodness of the object. This is therefore not a defect where God and the saints are concerned: on the contrary, it would be a great defect, or rather a manifest absurdity, were it otherwise, even in men here on earth, and if they were capable of acting without any inclining reason. Of such absurdity no example will ever be found; and even supposing one takes a certain course out of caprice, to demonstrate one's freedom, the pleasure or advantage one thinks to find in this conceit is one of the reasons tending towards it.

46. There is therefore a freedom of contingency or, in a way, of indifference, provided that by 'indifference' is understood that nothing necessitates us to one course or the other; but there is never any *indifference of equipoise*, that is, where all is completely

even on both sides, without any inclination towards either. In-numerable great and small movements, internal and external, co-operate with us, for the most part unperceived by us. And I have already said that when one leaves a room there are such and such reasons determining us to put the one foot first, without pausing to reflect. For there is not everywhere a slave, as in Tri-malchio's house in Petronius, to cry to us: the right foot first. All that we have just said agrees entirely also with the maxims of the philosophers, who teach that a cause cannot act without having a disposition towards action. It is this disposition which contains a predetermination, whether the doer have received it from without, or have had it in consequence of his own antecedent character.

47. Thus we have no need to resort, in company with some new Thomists, to a new immediate predetermination by God, such as may cause the free creature to abandon his indifference, and to a decree of God for predetermining the creature, making it possible for God to know what the creature will do: for it suffices that the creature be predetermined by its preceding state, which inclines it to one course more than to the other. Moreover, all these con-nexions of the actions of the creature and of all creatures were represented in the divine understanding, and known to God through the knowledge of mere intelligence, before he had decreed to give them existence. Thus we see that, in order to account for the foreknowledge of God, one may dispense with both the mediate knowledge of the Molinists and the predetermination which a Bañez or an Alvarez (writers otherwise of great profundity) have taught.

48. By this false idea of an indifference of equipoise the Molin-ists were much embarrassed. They were asked not only how it was possible to know in what direction a cause absolutely indeter-minate would be determined, but also how it was possible that there should finally result therefrom a determination for which there is no source: to say with Molina that it is the privilege of the free cause is to say nothing, but simply to grant that cause the privilege of being chimerical. It is pleasing to see their harassed efforts to emerge from a labyrinth whence there is absolutely no means of egress. Some teach that the will, before it is determined formally, must be determined virtually, in order to emerge from its state of equipoise; and Father Louis of Dole, in his book on the *Co-operation of God*, quotes Molinists who attempt to take refuge

in this expedient: for they are compelled to acknowledge that the cause must needs be disposed to act. But they gain nothing, they only defer the difficulty: for they will still be asked how the free cause comes to be determined virtually. They will therefore never extricate themselves without acknowledging that there is a predetermination in the preceding state of the free creature, which inclines it to be determined.

49. In consequence of this, the case also of Buridan's ass between two meadows, impelled equally towards both of them, is a fiction that cannot occur in the universe, in the order of Nature, although M. Bayle be of another opinion. It is true that, if the case were possible, one must say that the ass would starve himself to death: but fundamentally the question deals in the impossible, unless it be that God bring the thing about expressly. For the universe cannot be halved by a plane drawn through the middle of the ass, which is cut vertically through its length, so that all is equal and alike on both sides, in the manner wherein an ellipse, and every plane figure of the number of those I term 'ambidexter', can be thus halved, by any straight line passing through its centre. Neither the parts of the universe nor the viscera of the animal are alike nor are they evenly placed on both sides of this vertical plane. There will therefore always be many things in the ass and outside the ass, although they be not apparent to us, which will determine him to go on one side rather than the other. And although man is free, and the ass is not, nevertheless for the same reason it must be true that in man likewise the case of a perfect equipoise between two courses is impossible. Furthermore it is true that an angel, or God certainly, could always account for the course man has adopted, by assigning a cause or a predisposing reason which has actually induced him to adopt it: yet this reason would often be complex and incomprehensible to ourselves, because the concatenation of causes linked together is very long.

50. Hence it is that the reason M. Descartes has advanced to prove the independence of our free actions, by what he terms an intense inward sensation, has no force. We cannot properly speaking be sensible of our independence, and we are not aware always of the causes, often imperceptible, whereon our resolution depends. It is as though the magnetic needle took pleasure in turning towards the north: for it would think that it was turning independently of any other cause, not being aware of the imperceptible

movements of the magnetic matter. Nevertheless we shall see later in what sense it is quite true that the human soul is altogether its own natural principle in relation to its actions, dependent upon itself and independent of all other creatures.

51. As for *volition* itself, to say that it is an object of free will is incorrect. We will to act, strictly speaking, and we do not will to will; else we could still say that we will to have the will to will, and that would go on to infinity. Besides, we do not always follow the latest judgement of practical understanding when we resolve to will; but we always follow, in our willing, the result of all the inclinations that come from the direction both of reasons and passions, and this often happens without an express judgement of the understanding.

52. All is therefore certain and determined beforehand in man, as everywhere else, and the human soul is a kind of *spiritual automaton*, although contingent actions in general and free action in particular are not on that account necessary with an absolute necessity, which would be truly incompatible with contingency. Thus neither futurition in itself, certain as it is, nor the infallible prevision of God, nor the predetermination either of causes or of God's decrees destroys this contingency and this freedom. That is acknowledged in respect of futurition and prevision, as has already been set forth. Since, moreover, God's decree consists solely in the resolution he forms, after having compared all possible worlds, to choose that one which is the best, and bring it into existence together with all that this world contains, by means of the all-powerful word *Fiat*, it is plain to see that this decree changes nothing in the constitution of things: God leaves them just as they were in the state of mere possibility, that is, changing nothing either in their essence or nature, or even in their accidents, which are represented perfectly already in the idea of this possible world. Thus that which is contingent and free remains no less so under the decrees of God than under his prevision.

53. But could God himself (it will be said) then change nothing in the world? Assuredly he could not now change it, without derogation to his wisdom, since he has foreseen the existence of this world and of what it contains, and since, likewise, he has formed this resolution to bring it into existence: for he cannot be mistaken nor repent, and it did not behove him to from an imperfect resolution applying to one part and not the

whole. Thus, all being ordered from the beginning, it is only because of this hypothetical necessity, recognized by everyone, that after God's prevision or after his resolution nothing can be changed: and yet the events in themselves remain contingent. For (setting aside this supposition of the futurition of the thing and of the prevision or of the resolution of God, a supposition which already lays it down as a fact that the thing will happen, and in accordance with which one must say, 'Unumquodque, quando est, oportet esse, aut unumquodque, siquidem erit, oportet futurum esse'), the event has nothing in it to render it necessary and to suggest that no other thing might have happened in its stead. And as for the connexion between causes and effects, it only inclined, without necessitating, the free agency, as I have just explained; thus it does not produce even a hypothetical necessity, save in conjunction with something from outside, to wit, this very maxim, that the prevailing inclination always triumphs.

54. It will be said also that, if all is ordered, God cannot then perform miracles. But one must bear in mind that the miracles which happen in the world were also enfolded and represented as possible in this same world considered in the state of mere possibility; and God, who has since performed them, when he chose this world had even then decreed to perform them. Again the objection will be made that vows and prayers, merits and demerits, good and bad actions avail nothing, since nothing can be changed. This objection causes most perplexity to people in general, and yet it is purely a sophism. These prayers, these vows, these good or bad actions that occur to-day were already before God when he formed the resolution to order things. Those things which happen in this existing world were represented, with their effects and their consequences, in the idea of this same world, while it was still possible only; they were represented therein, attracting God's grace whether natural or supernatural, requiring punishments or rewards, just as it has happened actually in this world since God chose it. The prayer or the good action were even then an *ideal cause* or *condition*, that is, an inclining reason able to contribute to the grace of God, or to the reward, as it now does in reality. Since, moreover, all is wisely connected together in the world, it is clear that God, foreseeing that which would happen freely, ordered all other things on that basis beforehand, or (what is

the same) he chose that possible world in which everything was ordered in this fashion.

55. This consideration demolishes at the same time what the ancients called the 'Lazy Sophism' (λόγος ἄργος) which ended in a decision to do nothing: for (people would say) if what I ask is to happen it will happen even though I should do nothing; and if it is not to happen it will never happen, no matter what trouble I take to achieve it. This necessity, supposedly existent in events, and detached from their causes, might be termed *Fatum Mahometanum*, as I have already observed above, because a similar line of reasoning, so it is said, causes the Turks not to shun places ravaged by plague. But the answer is quite ready: the effect being certain, the cause that shall produce it is certain also; and if the effect comes about it will be by virtue of a proportionate cause. Thus your laziness perchance will bring it about that you will obtain naught of what you desire, and that you will fall into those misfortunes which you would by acting with care have avoided. We see, therefore, that the *connexion of causes with effects*, far from causing an unendurable fatality, provides rather a means of obviating it. There is a German proverb which says that death will ever have a cause; and nothing is so true. You will die on that day (let us presume it is so, and that God foresees it): yes, without doubt; but it will be because you will do what shall lead you thither. It is likewise with the chastisements of God, which also depend upon their causes. And it will be apposite in this connexion to quote this famous passage from St. Ambrose (in cap. I *Lucae*), 'Novit Dominus mutare sententiam, si tu noveris mutare delictum', which is not to be understood as of reprobation, but of denunciation, such as that which Jonah dealt out for God to the Ninevites. This common saying: 'Si non es praedestinatus, fac ut praedestineris', must not be taken literally, its true sense being that he who has doubts of his predestination need only do what is required for him to obtain it by the grace of God. The sophism which ends in a decision to trouble oneself over nothing will haply be useful sometimes to induce certain people to face danger fearlessly. It has been applied in particular to Turkish soldiers: but it seems that hashish is a more important factor than this sophism, not to mention the fact that this resolute spirit in the Turks has greatly belied itself in our days.

56. A learned physician of Holland named Johan van Beverwyck took the trouble to write *De Termino Vitae* and to collect

sundry answers, letters and discourses of some learned men of his time on this subject. This collection has been printed, and it is astonishing to see there how often people are misled, and how they have confused a problem which, properly speaking, is the easiest in the world. After that it is no wonder that there are very many doubts which the human race cannot abandon. The truth is that people love to lose themselves, and this is a kind of ramble of the mind, which is unwilling to subject itself to attention, to order, to rules. It seems as though we are so accustomed to games and jesting that we play the fool even in the most serious occupations, and when we least think to do so.

57. I fear that in the recent dispute between the theologians of the Augsburg Confession, *De Termino Paenitentiae Peremptorio*, which has called forth so many treatises in Germany, some misunderstanding, though of a different nature, has slipped in. The terms prescribed by the laws are amongst lawyers known as *fatalia*. It may be said, in a sense, that the *peremptory term*, prescribed to man for his repentance and amendment, is certain in the sight of God, with whom all is certain. God knows when a sinner will be so hardened that thereafter nothing can be done for him: not indeed that it would be impossible for him to do penance or that sufficient grace needs must be refused to him after a certain term, a grace that never fails; but because there will be a time whereafter he will no more approach the ways of salvation. But we never have certain marks for recognizing this term, and we are never justified in considering a man utterly abandoned: that would be to pass a rash judgement. It were better always to have room for hope; and this is an occasion, with a thousand others, where our ignorance is beneficial.

> *Prudens futuri temporis exitum*
> *Caliginosa nocte premit Deus.*

58. The whole future is doubtless determined: but since we know not what it is, nor what is foreseen or resolved, we must do our duty, according to the reason that God has given us and according to the rules that he has prescribed for us; and thereafter we must have a quiet mind, and leave to God himself the care for the outcome. For he will never fail to do that which shall be the best, not only in general but also in particular, for those who have true confidence in him, that is, a confidence composed of

true piety, a lively faith and fervent charity, by virtue of which we will, as far as in us lies, neglect nothing appertaining to our duty and his service. It is true that we cannot 'render service' to him, for he has need of nothing: but it is 'serving him', in our parlance, when we strive to carry out his presumptive will, co-operating in the good as it is known to us, wherever we can contribute thereto. For we must always presume that God is prompted towards the good we know, until the event shows us that he had stronger reasons, although perhaps unknown to us, which have made him subordinate this good that we sought to some other greater good of his own designing, which he has not failed or will not fail to effect.

59. I have just shown how the action of the will depends upon its causes; that there is nothing so appropriate to human nature as this dependence of our actions; and that otherwise one would slip into a preposterous and unendurable fatality, namely into the *Fatum Mahometanum*, which is the worst of all because it over-throws foresight and good counsel. It is well to show, notwith-standing, how this dependence of voluntary actions does not fundamentally preclude the existence within us of a wonderful *spontaneity*, which in a certain sense makes the soul in its resolves independent of the physical influence of all other creatures. This spontaneity, hitherto little recognized, which exalts our command over our actions to the highest pitch, is a consequence of the System of Pre-established Harmony, of which I must give some explana-tion here. The Scholastic philosophers believed that there was a reciprocal physical influence between body and soul: but since it has been recognized that thought and dimensional mass have no mutual connexion, and that they are creatures differing *toto genere*, many moderns have acknowledged that there is no *physical communication* between soul and body, despite the *metaphysical communication* always subsisting, which causes soul and body to compose one and the same *suppositum*, or what is called a person. This physical communication, if there were such, would cause the soul to change the degree of speed and the directional line of some motions that are in the body, and *vice versa* the body to change the sequence of the thoughts that are in the soul. But this effect cannot be inferred from any notion conceived in the body and in the soul; though nothing be better known to us than the soul, since it is inmost to us, that is to say inmost to itself.

60. M. Descartes wished to compromise and to make a part of the body's action dependent upon the soul. He believed in the existence of a rule of Nature to the effect, according to him, that the same quantity of movement is conserved in bodies. He deemed it not possible that the influence of the soul should violate this law of bodies, but he believed that the soul notwithstanding might have power to change the direction of the movements that are made in the body; much as a rider, though giving no force to the horse he mounts, nevertheless controls it by guiding that force in any direction he pleases. But as that is done by means of the bridle, the bit, the spurs and other material aids, it is conceivable how that can be; there are, however, no instruments such as the soul may employ for this result, nothing indeed either in the soul or in the body, that is, either in thought or in the mass, which may serve to explain this change of the one by the other. In a word, that the soul should change the quantity of force and that it should change the line of direction, both these things are equally inexplicable.

61. Moreover, two important truths on this subject have been discovered since M. Descartes' day. The first is that the quantity of absolute force which is in fact conserved is different from the quantity of movement, as I have demonstrated elsewhere. The second discovery is that the same direction is still conserved in all bodies together that are assumed as interacting, in whatever way they come into collision. If this rule had been known to M. Descartes, he would have taken the direction of bodies to be as independent of the soul as their force; and I believe that that would have led direct to the Hypothesis of Pre-established Harmony, whither these same rules have led me. For apart from the fact that the physical influence of one of these substances on the other is inexplicable, I recognized that without a complete derangement of the laws of Nature the soul could not act physically upon the body. And I did not believe that one could here listen to philosophers, competent in other respects, who produce a God, as it were, *ex machina*, to bring about the final solution of the piece, maintaining that God exerts himself deliberately to move bodies as the soul pleases, and to give perceptions to the soul as the body requires. For this system, which is called that of *occasional causes* (because it teaches that God acts on the body at the instance of the soul, and *vice versa*), besides introducing perpetual miracles to

establish communication between these two substances, does not obviate the derangement of the natural laws obtaining in each of these same substances, which, in the general opinion, their mutual influence would cause.

62. Being on other considerations already convinced of the principle of Harmony in general, I was in consequence convinced likewise of the *preformation* and the Pre-established Harmony of all things amongst themselves, of that between nature and grace, between the decrees of God and our actions foreseen, between all parts of matter, and even between the future and the past, the whole in conformity with the sovereign wisdom of God, whose works are the most harmonious it is possible to conceive. Thus I could not fail to arrive at the system which declares that God created the soul in the beginning in such a fashion that it must produce and represent to itself successively that which takes place within the body, and the body also in such a fashion that it must do of itself that which the soul ordains. Consequently the laws that connect the thoughts of the soul in the order of final causes and in accordance with the evolution of perceptions must produce pictures that meet and harmonize with the impressions of bodies on our organs; and likewise the laws of movements in the body, which follow one another in the order of efficient causes, meet and so harmonize with the thoughts of the soul that the body is induced to act at the time when the soul wills it.

63. Far from its being prejudicial, nothing can be more favourable to freedom than that system. And M. Jacquelot has demonstrated well in his book on the *Conformity of Faith with Reason*, that it is just as if he who knows all that I shall order a servant to do the whole day long on the morrow made an automaton entirely resembling this servant, to carry out to-morrow at the right moment all that I should order; and yet that would not prevent me from ordering freely all that I should please, although the action of the automaton that would serve me would not be in the least free.

64. Moreover, since all that passes in the soul depends, according to this system, only upon the soul, and its subsequent state is derived only from it and from its present state, how can one give it a greater *independence*? It is true that there still remains some imperfection in the constitution of the soul. All that happens to the soul depends upon it, but depends not always upon its will; that

were too much. Nor are such happenings even recognized always by its understanding or perceived with distinctness. For there is in the soul not only an order of distinct perceptions, forming its dominion, but also a series of confused perceptions or passions, forming its bondage: and there is no need for astonishment at that; the soul would be a Divinity if it had none but distinct perceptions. It has nevertheless some power over these confused perceptions also, even if in an indirect manner. For although it cannot change its passions forthwith, it can work from afar towards that end with enough success, and endue itself with new passions and even habits. It even has a like power over the more distinct perceptions, being able to endue itself indirectly with opinions and intentions, and to hinder itself from having this one or that, and stay or hasten its judgement. For we can seek means beforehand to arrest ourselves, when occasion arises, on the sliding step of a rash judgement; we can find some incident to justify postponement of our resolution even at the moment when the matter appears ready to be judged. Although our opinion and our act of willing be not directly objects of our will (as I have already observed), one sometimes, takes measures nevertheless, to will and even to believe in due time, that which one does not will, or believe, now. So great is the profundity of the spirit of man.

65. And now, to bring to a conclusion this question of *spontaneity*, it must be said that, on a rigorous definition, the soul has within it the principle of all its actions, and even of all its passions, and that the same is true in all the simple substances scattered throughout Nature, although there be freedom only in those that are intelligent. In the popular sense notwithstanding, speaking in accordance with appearances, we must say that the soul depends in some way upon the body and upon the impressions of the senses: much as we speak with Ptolemy and Tycho in everyday converse, and think with Copernicus, when it is a question of the rising and the setting of the sun.

66. One may however give a true and philosophic sense to this *mutual dependence* which we suppose between the soul and the body. It is that the one of these two substances depends upon the other ideally, in so far as the reason of that which is done in the one can be furnished by that which is in the other. This had already happened when God ordered beforehand the harmony that there

would be between them. Even so would that automaton, that should fulfil the servant's function, depend upon me *ideally*, in virtue of the knowledge of him who, foreseeing my future orders, would have rendered it capable of serving me at the right moment all through the morrow. The knowledge of my future intentions would have actuated this great craftsman, who would accordingly have fashioned the automaton: my influence would be objective, and his physical. For in so far as the soul has perfection and distinct thoughts, God has accommodated the body to the soul, and has arranged beforehand that the body is impelled to execute its orders. And in so far as the soul is imperfect and as its perceptions are confused, God has accommodated the soul to the body, in such sort that the soul is swayed by the passions arising out of corporeal representations. This produces the same effect and the same appearance as if the one depended immediately upon the other, and by the agency of a physical influence. Properly speaking, it is by its confused thoughts that the soul represents the bodies which encompass it. The same thing must apply to all that we understand by the actions of simple substances one upon another. For each one is assumed to act upon the other in proportion to its perfection, although this be only ideally, and in the reasons of things, as God in the beginning ordered one substance to accord with another in proportion to the perfection or imperfection that there is in each. (Withal action and passion are always reciprocal in creatures, because one part of the reasons which serve to explain clearly what is done, and which have served to bring it into existence, is in the one of these substances, and another part of these reasons is in the other, perfections and imperfections being always mingled and shared.) Thus it is we attribute *action* to the one, and *passion* to the other.

67. But after all, whatsoever dependence be conceived in voluntary actions, and even though there were an absolute and mathematical necessity (which there is not) it would not follow that there would not be a sufficient degree of freedom to render rewards and punishments just and reasonable. It is true that generally we speak as though the necessity of the action put an end to all merit and all demerit, all justification for praise and blame, for reward and punishment: but it must be admitted that this conclusion is not entirely correct. I am very far from sharing the opinions of Bradwardine, Wyclif, Hobbes and Spinoza, who

advocate, so it seems, this entirely mathematical necessity, which I think I have adequately refuted, and perhaps more clearly than is customary. Yet one must always bear testimony to the truth and not impute to a dogma anything that does not result from it. Moreover, these arguments prove too much, since they would prove just as much against hypothetical necessity, and would justify the lazy sophism. For the absolute necessity of the sequence of causes would in this matter add nothing to the infallible certainty of a hypothetical necessity.

68. In the first place, therefore, it must be agreed that it is permitted to kill a madman when one cannot by other means defend oneself. It will be granted also that it is permitted, and often even necessary, to destroy venomous or very noxious animals, although they be not so by their own fault.

69. Secondly, one inflicts punishments upon a beast, despite its lack of reason and freedom, when one deems that this may serve to correct it: thus one punishes dogs and horses, and indeed with much success. Rewards serve us no less in the managing of animals: when an animal is hungry, the food that is given to him causes him to do what otherwise would never be obtained from him.

70. Thirdly, one would inflict even on beasts capital punishments (where it is no longer a question of correcting the beast that is punished) if this punishment could serve as an example, or inspire terror in others, to make them cease from evil doing. Rorarius, in his book on reason in beasts, says that in Africa they crucified lions, in order to drive away other lions from the towns and frequented places, and that he had observed in passing through the province of Jülich that they hanged wolves there in order to ensure greater safety for the sheepfolds. There are people in the villages also who nail birds of prey to the doors of houses, with the idea that other birds of the same kind will then not so readily appear. These measures would always be justified if they were of any avail.

71. Then, in the fourth place, since experience proves that the fear of chastisements and the hope of rewards serves to make men abstain from evil and strive to do good, one would have good reason to avail oneself of such, even though men were acting under necessity, whatever the necessity might be. The objection will be raised that if good or evil is necessary it is useless to avail oneself of means to obtain it or to hinder it: but the answer has already been

given above in the passage combating the lazy sophism. If good or evil were a necessity without these means, then such means would be unavailing; but it is not so. These goods and evils come only with the aid of these means, and if these results were necessary the means would be a part of the causes rendering them necessary, since experience teaches us that often fear or hope hinders evil or advances good. This objection, then, differs hardly at all from the lazy sophism, which we raise against the certainty as well as the necessity of future events. Thus one may say that these objections are directed equally against hypothetical necessity and absolute necessity, and that they prove as much against the one as against the other, that is to say, nothing at all.

72. There was a great dispute between Bishop Bramhall and Mr. Hobbes, which began when they were both in Paris, and which was continued after their return to England; all the parts of it are to be found collected in a quarto volume published in London in the year 1656. They are all in English, and have not been translated as far as I know, nor inserted in the Collection of Works in Latin by Mr. Hobbes. I had already read these writings, and have obtained them again since. And I had observed at the outset that he had not at all proved the absolute necessity of all things, but had shown sufficiently that necessity would not overthrow all the rules of divine or human justice, and would not prevent altogether the exercise of this virtue.

73. There is, however, a kind of justice and a certain sort of rewards and of punishments which appear not so applicable to those who should act by an absolute necessity, supposing such necessity existed. It is that kind of justice which has for its goal neither improvement nor example, nor even redress of the evil. This justice has its foundation only in the fitness of things, which demands a certain satisfaction for the expiation of an evil action. The Socinians, Hobbes and some others do not admit this punitive justice, which properly speaking is avenging justice. God reserves it for himself in many cases; but he does not fail to grant it to those who are entitled to govern others, and he exercises it through their agency, provided that they act under the influence of reason and not of passion. The Socinians believe it to be without foundation, but it always has some foundation in that fitness of things which gives satisfaction not only to the injured but also to the wise who see it; even as a beautiful piece of music, or again a good

piece of architecture, satisfies cultivated minds. And the wise law-giver having threatened, and having, so to speak, promised a chastisement, it befits his consistency not to leave the action completely unpunished, even though the punishment would no longer avail to correct anyone. But even though he should have promised nothing, it is enough that there is a fitness of things which could have prompted him to make this promise, since the wise man likewise promises only that which is fitting. And one may even say that there is here a certain compensation of the mind, which would be scandalized by disorder if the chastisement did not contribute towards restoring order. One can also consult what Grotius wrote against the Socinians, of the satisfaction of Jesus Christ, and the answer of Crellius thereto.

74. Thus it is that the pains of the damned continue, even when they no longer serve to turn them away from evil, and that likewise the rewards of the blessed continue, even when they no longer serve for strengthening them in good. One may say nevertheless that the damned ever bring upon themselves new pains through new sins, and that the blessed ever bring upon themselves new joys by new progress in goodness: for both are founded on the *principle of the fitness of things*, which has seen to it that affairs were so ordered that the evil action must bring upon itself a chastisement. There is good reason to believe, following the parallelism of the two realms, that of final causes and that of efficient causes, that God has established in the universe a connexion between punishment or reward and bad or good action, in accordance wherewith the first should always be attracted by the second, and virtue and vice obtain their reward and their punishment in consequence of the natural sequence of things, which contains still another kind of pre-established harmony than that which appears in the communication between the soul and the body. For, in a word, all that God does, as I have said already, is harmonious to perfection. Perhaps then this principle of the fitness of things would no longer apply to beings acting without true freedom or exemption from absolute necessity; and in that case corrective justice alone would be administered, and not punitive justice. That is the opinion of the famous Conringius, in a dissertation he published on what is just. And indeed, the reasons Pomponazzi employed in his book on fate, to prove the usefulness of chastisements and rewards, even though all should come about in our

actions by a fatal necessity, concern only amendment and not satisfaction, κόλασιν οὐ τιμωρίαν. Moreover, it is only for the sake of outward appearances that one destroys animals accessary to certain crimes, as one razes the houses of rebels, that is, to inspire terror. Thus it is an act of corrective justice, wherein punitive iustice has no part at all.

75. But we will not amuse ourselves now by discussing a question more curious than necessary, since we have shown sufficiently that there is no such necessity in voluntary actions. Nevertheless it was well to show that *imperfect freedom* alone, that is, freedom which is exempt only from constraint, would suffice as foundation for chastisements and rewards of the kind conducive to the avoidance of evil, and to amendment. One sees also from this that some persons of intelligence, who persuade themselves that everything is necessary, are wrong in saying that none must be praised or blamed, rewarded or punished. Apparently they say so only to exercise their wit: the pretext is that all being necessary nothing would be in our power. But this pretext is ill founded: necessary actions would be still in our power, at least in so far as we could perform them or omit them, when the hope or the fear of praise or blame, of pleasure or pain prompted our will thereto, whether they prompted it of necessity, or in prompting it they left spontaneity, contingency and freedom all alike unimpaired. Thus praise and blame, rewards and punishments would preserve always a large part of their use, even though there were a true necessity in our actions. We can praise and blame also natural good and bad qualities, where the will has no part—in a horse, in a diamond, in a man; and he who said of Cato of Utica that he acted virtuously through the goodness of his nature, and that it was impossible for him to behave otherwise, thought to praise him the more.

76. The difficulties which I have endeavoured up to now to remove have been almost all common to natural and revealed theology. Now it will be necessary to come to a question of revealed theology, concerning the election or the reprobation of men, with the dispensation or use of divine grace in connexion with these acts of the mercy or the justice of God. But when I answered the preceding objections, I opened up a way to meet those that remain. This confirms the observation I made thereon (*Preliminary Dissertation*, 43) that there is rather a conflict between the

true reasons of natural theology and the false reasons of human appearances, than between revealed faith and reason. For on this subject scarcely any difficulty arises that is new, and not deriving its origin from those which can be placed in the way of the truths discerned by reason.

77. Now as theologians of all parties are divided among themselves on this subject of predestination and grace, and often give different answers to the same objections, according to their various principles, one cannot avoid touching on the differences which prevail among them. One may say in general that some look upon God more metaphysically and others more morally: and it has already been stated on other occasions that the Counter-Remonstrants took the first course and the Remonstrants the second. But to act rightly we must affirm alike on one side the independence of God and the dependence of creatures, and on the other side the justice and goodness of God, which makes him dependent upon himself, his will upon his understanding or his wisdom.

78. Some gifted and well-intentioned authors, desiring to show the force of the reasons advocated by the two principal parties, in order to persuade them to a mutual tolerance, deem that the whole controversy is reduced to this essential point, namely: What was God's principal aim in making his decrees with regard to man? Did he make them solely in order to show forth his glory by manifesting his attributes, and forming, to that end, the great plan of creation and providence? Or has he had regard rather to the voluntary movements of intelligent substances which he designed to create, considering what they would will and do in the different circumstances and situations wherein he might place them, so as to form a fitting resolve thereupon? It appears to me that the two answers to this great question thus given as opposites to one another are easy to reconcile, and that in consequence the two parties would be agreed in principle, without any need of tolerance, if all were reduced to this point. In truth God, in designing to create the world, purposed solely to manifest and communicate his perfections in the way that was most efficacious, and most worthy of his greatness, his wisdom and his goodness. But that very purpose pledged him to consider all the actions of creatures while still in the state of pure possibility, that he might form the most fitting plan. He is like a great architect whose aim

in view is the satisfaction or the glory of having built a beautiful palace, and who considers all that is to enter into this construction: the form and the materials, the place, the situation, the means, the workmen, the expense, before he forms a complete resolve. For a wise person in laying his plans cannot separate the end from the means; he does not contemplate any end without knowing if there are means of attaining thereto.

79. I know not whether there are also perchance persons who imagine that, God being the absolute master of all things, one can thence infer that everything outside him is indifferent to him, that he considers himself alone, without concern for others, and that thus he has made some happy and others unhappy without any cause, without choice, without reason. But to teach so about God were to deprive him of wisdom and of goodness. We need only observe that he considers himself and neglects nothing of what he owes to himself, to conclude that he considers his creatures also, and that he uses them in the manner most consistent with order. For the more a great and good prince is mindful of his glory, the more he will think of making his subjects happy, even though he were the most absolute of all monarchs, and though his subjects were slaves from birth, bondsmen (in lawyers' parlance), people entirely in subjection to arbitrary power. Calvin himself and some others of the greatest defenders of the absolute decree rightly maintained that God had *great and just reasons* for his election and the dispensation of his grace, although these reasons be unknown to us in detail: and we must judge charitably that the most rigid predestinators have too much reason and too much piety to depart from this opinion.

80. There will therefore be no argument for debate on that point (as I hope) with people who are at all reasonable. But there will always be argument among those who are called Universalists and Particularists, according to what they teach of the grace and the will of God. Yet I am somewhat inclined to believe that the heated dispute between them on the will of God to save all men, and on that which depends upon it (when one keeps separate the doctrine *de Auxiliis*, or of the assistance of grace), rests rather in expressions than in things. For it is sufficient to consider that God, as well as every wise and beneficent mind, is inclined towards all possible good, and that this inclination is proportionate to the excellence of the good. Moreover, this results (if we take the matter

precisely and in itself) from an 'antecedent will', as it is termed, which, however, is not always followed by its complete effect, because this wise mind must have many other inclinations besides. Thus it is the result of all the inclinations together that makes his will complete and decretory, as I have already explained. One may therefore very well say with ancient writers that God wills to save all men according to his antecedent will, but not according to his consequent will, which never fails to be followed by its effect. And if those who deny this universal will do not allow that the antecedent inclination be called a will, they are only troubling themselves about a question of name.

81. But there is a question more serious in regard to pre-destination to eternal life and to all other destination by God, to wit, whether this destination is absolute or respective. There is destination to good and destination to evil; and as evil is moral or physical, theologians of all parties agree that there is no destina-tion to moral evil, that is to say, that none is destined to sin. As for the greatest physical evil, which is damnation, one can distin-guish between destination and predestination: for predestination appears to contain within itself an absolute destination, which is anterior to the consideration of the good or evil actions of those whom it concerns. Thus one may say that the reprobate are *destined* to be condemned, because they are known to be impenitent. But it cannot so well be said that the reprobate are *predestined* to damnation: for there is no *absolute* reprobation, its foundation being final foreseen impenitence.

82. It is true that there are writers who maintain that God, wishing to manifest his mercy and his justice in accordance with reasons worthy of him, but unknown to us, chose the elect, and in consequence rejected the damned, prior to all thought of sin, even of Adam, that after this resolve he thought fit to permit sin in order to be able to exercise these two virtues, and that he has bestowed grace in Jesus Christ to some in order to save them, while he has refused it to others in order to be able to punish them. Hence these writers are named 'Supralapsarians', because the decree to punish precedes, according to them, the knowledge of the future existence of sin. But the opinion most common to-day amongst those who are called Reformed, and one that is favoured by the Synod of Dordrecht, is that of the 'Infralapsarians', corresponding somewhat to the conception of St. Augustine. For

he asserts that God having resolved to permit the sin of Adam and the corruption of the human race, for reasons just but hidden, his mercy made him choose some of the corrupt mass to be freely saved by the merit of Jesus Christ, and his justice made him resolve to punish the others by the damnation that they deserved. That is why, with the Schoolmen, only the saved were called *Praedestinati* and the damned were called *Praesciti*. It must be admitted that some Infralapsarians and others speak sometimes of predestination to damnation, following the example of Fulgentius and of St. Augustine himself: but that signifies the same as destination to them, and it avails nothing to wrangle about words. That pretext, notwithstanding, was in time past used for maltreating that Godescalc who caused a stir about the middle of the ninth century, and who took the name of Fulgentius to indicate that he followed that author.

83. As for the destination of the elect to eternal life, the Protestants, as well as those of the Roman Church, dispute much among themselves as to whether election is absolute or is founded on the prevision of final living faith. Those who are called Evangelicals, that is, those of the Augsburg Confession, hold the latter opinion: they believe that one need not go into the hidden causes of election while one may find a manifest cause of it shown in Holy Scripture, which is faith in Jesus Christ; and it appears to them that the prevision of the cause is also the cause of the prevision of the effect. Those who are called Reformed are of a different opinion: they admit that salvation comes from faith in Jesus Christ, but they observe that often the cause anterior to the effect in execution is posterior in intention, as when the cause is the means and the effect is the end. Thus the question is, whether faith or salvation is anterior in the intention of God, that is, whether God's design is rather to save man than to make him a believer.

84. Hence we see that the question between the Supralapsarians and the Infralapsarians in part, and again between them and the Evangelicals, comes back to a right conception of the order that is in God's decrees. Perhaps one might put an end to this dispute at once by saying that, properly speaking, all the decrees of God that are here concerned are simultaneous, not only in respect of time, as everyone agrees, but also *in signo rationis*, or in the order of nature. And indeed, the Formula of Concord, building upon some passages

of St. Augustine, comprised in the same Decree of Election salvation and the means that conduce to it. To demonstrate this synchronism of destinations or of decrees with which we are concerned, we must revert to the expedient that I have employed more than once, which states that God, before decreeing anything, considered among other possible sequences of things that one which he afterwards approved. In the idea of this is represented how the first parents sin and corrupt their posterity; how Jesus Christ redeems the human race; how some, aided by such and such graces, attain to final faith and to salvation; and how others, with or without such or other graces, do not attain thereto, continue in sin, and are damned. God grants his sanction to this sequence only after having entered into all its detail, and thus pronounces nothing final as to those who shall be saved or damned without having pondered upon everything and compared it with other possible sequences. Thus God's pronouncement concerns the whole sequence at the same time; he simply decrees its existence. In order to save other men, or in a different way, he must needs choose an altogether different sequence, seeing that all is connected in each sequence. In this conception of the matter, which is that most worthy of the All-wise, all whose actions are connected together to the highest possible degree, there would be only one total decree, which is to create such a world. This total decree comprises equally all the particular decrees, without setting one of them before or after another. Yet one may say also that each particular act of antecedent will entering into the total result has its value and order, in proportion to the good whereto this act inclines. But these acts of antecedent will are not called decrees, since they are not yet inevitable, the outcome depending upon the total result. According to this conception of things, all the difficulties that can here be made amount to the same as those I have already stated and removed in my inquiry concerning the origin of evil.

85. There remains only one important matter of discussion, which has its peculiar difficulties. It is that of the dispensation of the means and circumstances contributing to salvation and to damnation. This comprises amongst others the subject of the Aids of Grace (*de auxiliis gratiae*), on which Rome (since the Congregation *de Auxiliis* under Clement VIII, when a debate took place between the Dominicans and the Jesuits) does not readily permit

books to be published. Everyone must agree that God is altogether good and just, that his goodness makes him contribute the least possible to that which can render men guilty, and the most possible to that which serves to save them (possible, I say, subject to the general order of things); that his justice prevents him from condemning innocent men, and from leaving good actions without reward; and that he even keeps an exact proportion in punishments and rewards. Nevertheless, this idea that one should have of the goodness and the justice of God does not appear enough in what we know of his actions with regard to the salvation and the damnation of men: and it is that which makes difficulties concerning sin and its remedies.

86. The first difficulty is how the soul could be infected with original sin, which is the root of actual sins, without injustice on God's part in exposing the soul thereto. This difficulty has given rise to three opinions on the origin of the soul itself. The first is that of the *pre-existence of human souls* in another world or in another life, where they had sinned and on that account had been condemned to this prison of the human body, an opinion of the Platonists which is attributed to Origen and which even to-day finds adherents. Henry More, an English scholar, advocated something like this dogma in a book written with that express purpose. Some of those who affirm this pre-existence have gone as far as metempsychosis. The younger van Helmont held this opinion, and the ingenious author of some metaphysical *Meditations*, published in 1678 under the name of William Wander, appears to have some leaning towards it. The second opinion is that of *Traduction*, as if the soul of children were engendered (*per traducem*) from the soul or souls of those from whom the body is engendered. St. Augustine inclined to this judgement the better to explain original sin. This doctrine is taught also by most of the theologians of the Augsburg Confession. Nevertheless it is not completely established among them, since the Universities of Jena and Helmstedt, and others besides, have long been opposed to it. The third opinion, and that most widely accepted to-day, is that of *Creation*: it is taught in the majority of the Christian Schools, but it is fraught with the greatest difficulty in respect of original sin.

87. Into this controversy of theologians on the origin of the human soul has entered the philosophic dispute on *the origin of forms*. Aristotle and scholastic philosophy after him called *Form*

that which is a principle of action and is found in that which acts. This inward principle is either substantial, being then termed 'Soul', when it is in an organic body, or accidental, and customarily termed 'Quality'. The same philosopher gave to the soul the generic name of 'Entelechy' or *Act*. This word 'Entelechy' apparently takes its origin from the Greek word signifying 'perfect', and hence the celebrated Ermolao Barbaro expressed it literally in Latin by *perfectihabia*: for Act is a realization of potency. And he had no need to consult the Devil, as men say he did, in order to learn that. Now the Philosopher of Stagira supposes that there are two kinds of Act, the permanent act and the successive act. The permanent or lasting act is nothing but the Substantial or Accidental Form: the substantial form (as for example the soul) is altogether permanent, at least according to my judgement, and the accidental is only so for a time. But the altogether momentary act, whose nature is transitory, consists in action itself. I have shown elsewhere that the notion of Entelechy is not altogether to be scorned, and that, being permanent, it carries with it not only a mere faculty for action, but also that which is called 'force', 'effort', 'conatus', from which action itself must follow if nothing prevents it. Faculty is only an *attribute*, or rather sometimes a mode; but force, when it is not an ingredient of substance itself (that is, force which is not primitive but derivative), is a *quality*, which is distinct and separable from substance. I have shown also how one may suppose that the soul is a primitive force which is modified and varied by derivative forces or qualities, and exercised in actions.

88. Now philosophers have troubled themselves exceedingly on the question of the origin of substantial forms. For to say that the compound of form and matter is produced and that the form is only *comproduced* means nothing. The common opinion was that forms were derived from the potency of matter, this being called *Eduction*. That also meant in fact nothing, but it was explained in a sense by a comparison with shapes: for that of a statue is produced only by removal of the superfluous marble. This comparison might be valid if form consisted in a mere limitation, as in the case of shape. Some have thought that forms were sent from heaven, and even created expressly, when bodies were produced. Julius Scaliger hinted that it was possible that forms were rather derived from the active potency of the efficient cause (that is to

say, either from that of God in the case of Creation or from that of other forms in the case of generation), than from the passive potency of matter. And that, in the case of generation, meant a return to traduction. Daniel Sennert, a famous doctor and physicist at Wittenberg, cherished this opinion, particularly in relation to animate bodies which are multiplied through seed. A certain Julius Caesar della Galla, an Italian living in the Low Countries, and a doctor of Groningen named Johan Freitag wrote with much vehemence in opposition to Sennert. Johann Sperling, a professor at Wittenberg, made a defence of his master, and finally came into conflict with Johann Zeisold, a professor at Jena, who upheld the belief that the human soul is created.

89. But traduction and eduction are equally inexplicable when it is a question of finding the origin of the soul. It is not the same with accidental forms, since they are only modifications of the substance, and their origin may be explained by eduction, that is, by variation of limitations, in the same way as the origin of shapes. But it is quite another matter when we are concerned with the origin of a substance, whose beginning and destruction are equally difficult to explain. Sennert and Sperling did not venture to admit the subsistence and the indestructibility of the souls of beasts or of other primitive forms, although they allowed that they were indivisible and immaterial. But the fact is that they confused indestructibility with immortality, whereby is understood in the case of man that not only the soul but also the personality subsists. In saying that the soul of man is immortal one implies the subsistence of what makes the identity of the person, something which retains its moral qualities, conserving the *consciousness*, or the reflective inward feeling, of what it is: thus it is rendered susceptible to chastisement or reward. But this conservation of personality does not occur in the souls of beasts: that is why I prefer to say that they are imperishable rather than to call them immortal. Yet this misapprehension appears to have been the cause of a great inconsistency in the doctrine of the Thomists and of other good philosophers: they recognized the immateriality or indivisibility of all souls, without being willing to admit their indestructibility, greatly to the prejudice of the immortality of the human soul. John Scot, that is, the Scotsman (which formerly signified Hibernian or Erigena), a famous writer of the time of Louis the Debonair and of his sons, was for the conservation of all

souls: and I see not why there should be less objection to making the atoms of Epicurus or of Gassendi endure, than to affirming the subsistence of all truly simple and indivisible substances, which are the sole and true atoms of Nature. And Pythagoras was right in saying generally, as Ovid makes him say:

Morte carent animae.

90. Now as I like maxims which hold good and admit of the fewest exceptions possible, here is what has appeared to me most reasonable in every sense on this important question. I consider that souls and simple substances altogether cannot begin except by creation, or end except by annihilation. Moreover, as the formation of organic animate bodies appears explicable in the order of nature only when one assumes a *preformation* already organic, I have thence inferred that what we call generation of an animal is only a transformation and augmentation. Thus, since the same body was already furnished with organs, it is to be supposed that it was already animate, and that it had the same soul: so I assume *vice versa*, from the conservation of the soul when once it is created, that the animal is also conserved, and that apparent death is only an envelopment, there being no likelihood that in the order of nature souls exist entirely separated from all body, or that what does not begin naturally can cease through natural forces.

91. Considering that so admirable an order and rules so general are established in regard to animals, it does not appear reasonable that man should be completely excluded from that order, and that everything in relation to his soul should come about in him by miracle. Besides I have pointed out repeatedly that it is of the essence of God's wisdom that all should be harmonious in his works, and that nature should be parallel with grace. It is thus my belief that those souls which one day shall be human souls, like those of other species, have been in the seed, and in the progenitors as far back as Adam, and have consequently existed since the beginning of things, always in a kind of organic body. On this point it seems that M. Swammerdam, Father Malebranche, M. Bayle, Mr. Pitcairne, M. Hartsoeker and numerous other very able persons share my opinion. This doctrine is also sufficiently confirmed by the microscope observations of M. Leeuwenhoek and other good observers. But it also for divers reasons appears likely

to me that they existed then as sentient or animal souls only, endowed with perception and feeling, and devoid of reason. Further I believe that they remained in this state up to the time of the generation of the man to whom they were to belong, but that then they received reason, whether there be a natural means of raising a sentient soul to the degree of a reasoning soul (a thing I find it difficult to imagine) or whether God may have given reason to this soul through some special operation, or (if you will) by a kind of *transcreation*. This latter is easier to admit, inasmuch as revelation teaches much about other forms of immediate operation by God upon our souls. This explanation appears to remove the obstacles that beset this matter in philosophy or theology. For the difficulty of the origin of forms thus disappears completely; and besides it is much more appropriate to divine justice to give the soul, already corrupted *physically* or on the animal side by the sin of Adam, a new perfection which is reason, than to put a reasoning soul, by creation or otherwise, in a body wherein it is to be corrupted *morally*.

92. Now the soul being once under the domination of sin, and ready to commit sin in actual fact as soon as the man is fit to exercise reason, a new question arises, to wit: whether this tendency in a man who has not been regenerated by baptism suffices to damn him, even though he should never come to commit sin, as may happen, and happens often, whether he die before reaching years of discretion or he become dull of sense before he has made use of his reason. St. Gregory of Nazianzos is supposed to have denied this (*Orat. de Baptismo*); but St. Augustine is for the affirmative, and maintains that original sin of itself is sufficient to earn the flames of hell, although this opinion is, to say the least, very harsh. When I speak here of damnation or of hell, I mean pains, and not mere deprivation of supreme felicity; I mean *poenam sensus, non damni*. Gregory of Rimini, General of the Augustinians, with a few others followed St. Augustine in opposition to the accepted opinion of the Schools of his time, and for that reason he was called the torturer of children, *tortor infantum*. The Schoolmen, instead of sending them into the flames of hell, have assigned to them a special Limbo, where they do not suffer, and are only punished by privation of the beatific vision. The Revelations of St. Birgitta (as they are called), much esteemed in Rome, also uphold this dogma. Salmeron and Molina, and before them

Ambrose Catharin and others, grant them a certain natural bliss; and Cardinal Sfondrati, a man of learning and piety, who approves this, latterly went so far as to prefer in a sense their state, which is the state of happy innocence, to that of a sinner saved, as we may see in his *Nodus Praedestinationis Solutus*. That, however, seems to go too far. Certainly a soul truly enlightened would not wish to sin, even though it could by this means obtain all imaginable pleasures. But the case of choosing between sin and true bliss is simply chimerical, and it is better to obtain bliss (even after repentance) than to be deprived of it for ever.

93. Many prelates and theologians of France who are well pleased to differ from Molina, and to join with St. Augustine, seem to incline towards the opinion of this great doctor, who condemns to eternal flames children that die in the age of innocence before having received baptism. This is what appears from the letter mentioned above, written by five distinguished prelates of France to Pope Innocent XII, against that posthumous book by Cardinal Sfondrati. But therein they did not venture to condemn the doctrine of the purely privative punishment of children dying without baptism, seeing it approved by the venerable Thomas Aquinas, and by other great men. I do not speak of those who are called on one side Jansenists and on the other disciples of St. Augustine, for they declare themselves entirely and firmly for the opinion of this Father. But it must be confessed that this opinion has not sufficient foundation either in reason or in Scripture, and that it is outrageously harsh. M. Nicole makes rather a poor apology for it in his book on the *Unity of the Church*, written to oppose M. Jurieu, although M. Bayle takes his side in chapter 178 of the *Reply to the Questions of a Provincial*, vol. III. M. Nicole makes use of this pretext, that there are also other dogmas in the Christian religion which appear harsh. On the one hand, however, that does not lead to the conclusion that these instances of harshness may be multiplied without proof; and on the other we must take into account that the other dogmas mentioned by M. Nicole, namely original sin and eternity of punishment, are only harsh and unjust to outward appearance, while the damnation of children dying without actual sin and without regeneration would in truth be harsh, since it would be in effect the damning of innocents. For that reason I believe that the party which advocates this opinion will never altogether have the upper hand in the

Roman Church itself. Evangelical theologians are accustomed to speak with fair moderation on this question, and to surrender these souls to the judgement and the clemency of their Creator. Nor do we know all the wonderful ways that God may choose to employ for the illumination of souls.

94. One may say that those who condemn for original sin alone, and who consequently condemn children dying unbaptized or outside the Covenant, fall, in a sense, without being aware of it, into a certain attitude to man's inclination and God's foreknowledge which they disapprove in others. They will not have it that God should refuse his grace to those whose resistance to it he foresees, nor that this expectation and this tendency should cause the damnation of these persons: and yet they claim that the tendency which constitutes original sin, and in which God foresees that the child will sin as soon as he shall reach years of discretion, suffices to damn this child beforehand. Those who maintain the one and reject the other do not preserve enough uniformity and connexion in their dogmas.

95. There is scarcely less difficulty in the matter of those who reach years of discretion and plunge into sin, following the inclination of corrupt nature, if they receive not the succour of the grace necessary for them to stop on the edge of the precipice, or to drag themselves from the abyss wherein they have fallen. For it seems hard to damn them eternally for having done that which they had no power to prevent themselves from doing. Those that damn even children, who are without discretion, trouble themselves even less about adults, and one would say that they have become callous through the very expectation of seeing people suffer. But it is not the same with other theologians, and I would be rather on the side of those who grant to all men a grace sufficient to draw them away from evil, provided they have a sufficient tendency to profit by this succour, and not to reject it voluntarily. The objection is made that there has been and still is a countless multitude of men, among civilized peoples and among barbarians, who have never had this knowledge of God and of Jesus Christ which is necessary for those who would tread the wonted paths to salvation. But without excusing them on the plea of a sin purely philosophical, and without stopping at a mere penalty of privation, things for which there is no opportunity of discussion here, one may doubt the fact: for how do we know whether they

do not receive ordinary or extraordinary succour of kinds unknown to us? This maxim, *Quod facienti, quod in se est, non denegatur gratia necessaria*, appears to me to have eternal truth. Thomas Aquinas, Archbishop Bradwardine and others have hinted that, in regard to this, something comes to pass of which we are not aware. (Thom. quest. XIV, *De Veritate*, artic. XI, ad I et alibi. Bradwardine, *De Causa Dei*, non procul ab initio.) And sundry theologians of great authority in the Roman Church itself have taught that a sincere act of the love of God above all things, when the grace of Jesus Christ arouses it, suffices for salvation. Father Francis Xavier answered the Japanese that if their ancestors had used well their natural light God would have given them the grace necessary for salvation; and the Bishop of Geneva, Francis of Sales, gives full approval to this answer (Book 4, *On the Love of God*, ch. 5).

96. This I pointed out some time ago to the excellent M Pélisson, to show him that the Roman Church, going further than the Protestants, does not damn utterly those who are outside its communion, and even outside Christianity, by using as its only criterion explicit faith. Nor did he refute it, properly speaking, in the very kind answer he gave me, and which he published in the fourth part of his *Reflexions*, also doing me the honour of adding to it my letter. I offered him then for consideration what a famous Portuguese theologian, by name Jacques Payva Andradius, envoy to the Council of Trent, wrote concerning this, in opposition to Chemnitz, during this same Council. And now, without citing many other authors of eminence, I will content myself with naming Father Friedrich Spee, the Jesuit, one of the most excellent in his Society, who also held this common opinion upon the efficacy of the love of God, as is apparent in the preface to the admirable book which he wrote in Germany on the Christian virtues. He speaks of this observation as of a highly important secret of piety, and expatiates with great clearness upon the power of divine love to blot out sin, even without the intervention of the Sacraments of the Catholic Church, provided one scorn them not, for that would not at all be compatible with this love. And a very great personage, whose character was one of the most lofty to be found in the Roman Church, was the first to make me acquainted with it. Father Spee was of a noble family of Westphalia (it may be said in passing) and he died in the odour of sanctity, according

to the testimony of him who published this book in Cologne with the approval of the Superiors.

97. The memory of this excellent man ought to be still precious to persons of knowledge and good sense, because he is the author of the book entitled: *Cautio Criminalis circa Processus contra Sagas*, which has caused much stir, and has been translated into several languages. I learnt from the Grand Elector of Mainz, Johann Philipp von Schönborn, uncle of His Highness the present Elector, who walks gloriously in the footsteps of that worthy predecessor, the story that follows. That Father was in Franconia when there was a frenzy there for burning alleged sorcerers. He accompanied even to the pyre many of them, all of whom he recognized as being innocent, from their confessions and the researches that he had made thereon. Therefore in spite of the danger incurred at that time by one telling the truth in this matter, he resolved to compile this work, without however naming himself. It bore great fruit and on this matter converted that Elector, at that time still a simple canon and afterwards Bishop of Würzburg, finally also Archbishop of Mainz, who, as soon as he came to power, put an end to these burnings. Therein he was followed by the Dukes of Brunswick, and finally by the majority of the other princes and states of Germany.

98. This digression appeared to me to be seasonable, because that writer deserves to be more widely known. Returning now to the subject I make a further observation. Supposing that to-day a knowledge of Jesus Christ according to the flesh is absolutely necessary to salvation, as indeed it is safest to teach, it will be possible to say that God will give that knowledge to all those who do, humanly speaking, that which in them lies, even though God must needs give it by a miracle. Moreover, we cannot know what passes in souls at the point of death; and if sundry learned and serious theologians claim that children receive in baptism a kind of faith, although they do not remember it afterwards when they are questioned about it, why should one maintain that nothing of a like nature, or even more definite, could come about in the dying, whom we cannot interrogate after their death? Thus there are countless paths open to God, giving him means of satisfying his justice and his goodness: and the only thing one may allege against this is that we know not what way he employs; which is far from being a valid objection.

177

99. Let us pass on to those who lack not power to amend, but good will. They are doubtless not to be excused; but there always remains a great difficulty concerning God, since it rested with him to give them this same good will. He is the master of wills, the hearts of kings and those of all other men are in his hand. Holy Scripture goes so far as to say that God at times hardened the wicked in order to display his power by punishing them. This hardening is not to be taken as meaning that God inspires men with a kind of anti-grace, that is, a kind of repugnance to good, or even an inclination towards evil, just as the grace that he gives is an inclination towards good. It is rather that God, having considered the sequence of things that he established, found it fitting, for superior reasons, to permit that Pharaoh, for example, should be in such *circumstances* as should increase his wickedness, and divine wisdom willed to derive a good from this evil.

100. Thus it all often comes down to *circumstances*, which form a part of the combination of things. There are countless examples of small circumstances serving to convert or to pervert. Nothing is more widely known than the *Tolle, lege* (Take and read) cry which St. Augustine heard in a neighbouring house, when he was pondering on what side he should take among the Christians divided into sects, and saying to himself,

Quod vitae sectabor iter?

This brought him to open at random the book of the Holy Scriptures which he had before him, and to read what came before his eyes: and these were words which finally induced him to give up Manichaeism. The good Steno, a Dane, who was titular Bishop of Titianopolis, Vicar Apostolic (as they say) of Hanover and the region around, when there was a Duke Regent of his religion, told us that something of that kind had happened to him. He was a great anatomist and deeply versed in natural science; but he unfortunately gave up research therein, and from being a great physicist he became a mediocre theologian. He would almost listen to nothing more about the marvels of Nature, and an express order from the Pope *in virtute sanctae obedientiae* was needed to extract from him the observations M. Thévenot asked of him. He told us then that what had greatly helped towards inducing him to place himself on the side of the Roman Church had been the voice of a lady in Florence, who had cried out to him from a window:

'Go not on the side where you are about to go, sir, go on the other side.' 'That voice struck me,' he told us, 'because I was just meditating upon religion.' This lady knew that he was seeking a man in the house where she was, and, when she saw him making his way to the other house, wished to point out where his friend's room was.

101. Father John Davidius, the Jesuit, wrote a book entitled *Veridicus Christianus*, which is like a kind of *Bibliomancy*, where one takes passages at random, after the pattern of the *Tolle, lege* of St. Augustine, and it is like a devotional game. But the chances to which, in spite of ourselves, we are subject, play only too large a part in what brings salvation to men, or removes it from them. Let us imagine twin Polish children, the one taken by the Tartars, sold to the Turks, brought to apostasy, plunged in impiety, dying in despair; the other saved by some chance, falling then into good hands to be educated properly, permeated by the soundest truths of religion, exercised in the virtues that it commends to us, dying with all the feelings of a good Christian. One will lament the misfortune of the former, prevented perhaps by a slight circumstance from being saved like his brother, and one will marvel that this slight chance should have decided his fate for eternity.

102. Someone will perchance say that God foresaw by mediate knowledge that the former would have been wicked and damned even if he had remained in Poland. There are perhaps conjunctures wherein something of the kind takes place. But will it therefore be said that this is a general rule, and that not one of those who were damned amongst the pagans would have been saved if he had been amongst Christians? Would that not be to contradict our Lord, who said that Tyre and Sidon would have profited better by his preaching, if they had had the good fortune to hear it, than Capernaum?

103. But were one to admit even here this use of mediate knowledge against all appearances, this knowledge still implies that God considers what a man would do in such and such circumstances; and it always remains true that God could have placed him in other circumstances more favourable, and given him inward or outward succour capable of vanquishing the most abysmal wickedness existing in any soul. I shall be told that God is not bound to do so, but that is not enough; it must be added that greater reasons prevent him from making all his goodness felt by

all. Thus there must needs be choice; but I do not think one must seek the reason altogether in the good or bad nature of men. For if with some people one assume that God, choosing the plan which produces the most good, but which involves sin and damnation, has been prompted by his wisdom to choose the best natures in order to make them objects of his grace, this grace would not sufficiently appear to be a free gift. Accordingly man will be distinguishable by a kind of inborn merit, and this assumption seems remote from the principles of St. Paul, and even from those of Supreme Reason.

104. It is true that there are reasons for God's choice, and the consideration of the object, that is, the nature of man, must needs enter therein; but it does not seem that this choice can be subjected to a rule such as we are capable of conceiving, and such as may flatter the pride of men. Some famous theologians believe that God offers more grace, and in a more favourable way, to those whose resistance he foresees will be less, and that he abandons the rest to their self-will. We may readily suppose that this is often the case, and this expedient, among those which make man distinguishable by anything favourable in his nature, is the farthest removed from Pelagianism. But I would not venture, notwithstanding, to make of it a universal rule. Moreover, that we may not have cause to vaunt ourselves, it is necessary that we be ignorant of the reasons for God's choice. Those reasons are too diverse to become known to us; and it may be that God at times shows the power of his grace by overcoming the most obstinate resistance, to the end that none may have cause either to despair or to be puffed up. St. Paul, as it would seem, had this in mind when he offered himself as an example. God, he said, has had mercy upon me, to give a great example of his patience.

105. It may be that fundamentally all men are equally bad, and consequently incapable of being distinguished the one from the other through their good or less bad natural qualities; but they are not bad all in the same way: for there is an inherent individual difference between souls, as the Pre-established Harmony proves. Some are more or less inclined towards a particular good or a particular evil, or towards their opposites, all in accordance with their natural dispositions. But since the general plan of the universe, chosen by God for superior reasons, causes men to be in different circumstances, those who meet with such as are more

favourable to their nature will become more readily the least wicked, the most virtuous, the most happy; yet it will be always by aid of the influence of that inward grace which God unites with the circumstances. Sometimes it even comes to pass, in the progress of human life, that a more excellent nature succeeds less, for lack of cultivation or opportunities. One may say that men are chosen and ranged not so much according to their excellence as according to their conformity with God's plan. Even so it may occur that a stone of lesser quality is made use of in a building or in a group because it proves to be the particular one for filling a certain gap.

106. But, in fine, all these attempts to find reasons, where there is no need to adhere altogether to certain hypotheses, serve only to make clear to us that there are a thousand ways of justifying the conduct of God. All the disadvantages we see, all the obstacles we meet with, all the difficulties one may raise for oneself, are no hindrance to a belief founded on reason, even when it cannot stand on conclusive proof, as has been shown and will later become more apparent, that there is nothing so exalted as the wisdom of God, nothing so just as his judgements, nothing so pure as his holiness, and nothing more vast than his goodness.

ESSAYS

ON THE JUSTICE OF GOD

AND THE FREEDOM OF MAN

IN THE ORIGIN OF EVIL

PART TWO

107. **H**ITHERTO I have devoted myself to giving a full and clear exposition of this whole subject: and although I have not yet spoken of M. Bayle's objections in particular, I have endeavoured to anticipate them, and to suggest ways of answering them. But as I have taken upon myself the task of meeting them in detail, not only because there will perhaps still be passages calling for elucidation, but also because his arguments are usually full of wit and erudition, and serve to throw greater light on this controversy, it will be well to give an account of the chief objections that are dispersed through his works, and to add my answers. At the beginning I observed 'that God co-operates in moral evil, and in physical evil, and in each of them both morally and physically; and that man co-operates therein also morally and physically in a free and active way, becoming in consequence subject to blame and punishment'. I have shown also that each point has its own difficulty; but the greatest of these lies in maintaining that God co-operates morally in moral evil, that is, in sin, without being the originator of the sin, and even without being accessary thereto.

108. He does this by *permitting* it justly, and by *directing* it wisely towards the good, as I have shown in a manner that appears tolerably intelligible. But as it is here principally that M. Bayle

undertakes to discomfit those who maintain that there is nothing in faith which cannot be harmonized with reason, it is also here especially I must show that my dogmas are fortified (to make use of his own allegory) with a rampart, even of reasons, which is able to resist the fire of his strongest batteries. He has ranged them against me in chapter 144 of his *Reply to the Questions of a Provincial* (vol. III, p. 812), where he includes the theological doctrine in seven propositions and opposes thereto nineteen philosophic maxims, like so many large cannon capable of breaching my rampart. Let us begin with the theological propositions.

109. I. 'God,' he says, 'the Being eternal and necessary, infinitely good, holy, wise and powerful, possesses from all eternity a glory and a bliss that can never either increase or diminish.' This proposition of M. Bayle's is no less philosophical than theological. To say that God possesses a 'glory' when he is alone, that depends upon the meaning of the term. One may say, with some, that glory is the satisfaction one finds in being aware of one's own perfections; and in this sense God possesses it always. But when glory signifies that others become aware of these perfections, one may say that God acquires it only when he reveals himself to intelligent creatures; even though it be true that God thereby gains no new good, and it is rather the rational creatures who thence derive advantage, when they apprehend aright the glory of God.

110. II. 'He resolved freely upon the production of creatures, and he chose from among an infinite number of possible beings those whom it pleased him to choose, to give them existence, and to compose the universe of them, while he left all the rest in nothingness.' This proposition is also, just like the preceding one, in close conformity with that part of philosophy which is called natural theology. One must dwell a little on what is said here, that he chose the possible beings 'whom it pleased him to choose'. For it must be borne in mind that when I say, 'that pleases me', it is as though I were saying, 'I find it good'. Thus it is the ideal goodness of the object which pleases, and which makes me choose it among many others which do not please or which please less, that is to say, which contain less of that goodness which moves me. Now it is only the genuinely good that is capable of pleasing God: and consequently that which pleases God most, and which meets his choice, is the best.

111. III. 'Human nature having been among the Beings that he willed to produce, he created a man and a woman, and granted them amongst other favours free will, so that they had the power to obey him; but he threatened them with death if they should disobey the order that he gave them to abstain from a certain fruit.' This proposition is in part revealed, and should be admitted without difficulty, provided that *free will* be understood properly, according to the explanation I have given.

112. IV. 'They ate thereof nevertheless, and thenceforth they were condemned, they and all their posterity, to the miseries of this life, to temporal death and eternal damnation, and made subject to such a tendency to sin that they abandoned themselves thereto endlessly and without ceasing.' There is reason to suppose that the forbidden action by itself entailed these evil results in accordance with a natural effect, and that it was for that very reason, and not by a purely arbitrary decree, that God had forbidden it: much as one forbids knives to children. The famous Fludde or de Fluctibus, an Englishman, once wrote a book *De Vita, Morte et Resurrectione* under the name of R. Otreb, wherein he maintained that the fruit of the forbidden tree was a poison: but we cannot enter into this detail. It suffices that God forbade a harmful thing; one must not therefore suppose that God acted here simply in the character of a legislator who enacts a purely positive law, or of a judge who imposes and inflicts a punishment by an order of his will, without any connexion between the evil of guilt and the evil of punishment. And it is not necessary to suppose that God in justifiable annoyance deliberately put a corruption in the soul and the body of man, by an extraordinary action, in order to punish him: much as the Athenians gave hemlock-juice to their criminals. M. Bayle takes the matter thus: he speaks as if the original corruption had been put in the soul of the first man by an order and operation of God. It is that which calls forth his objection (*Reply to the Questions of a Provincial*, vol. III, ch. 178, p. 1218) 'that reason would not commend the monarch who, in order to chastise a rebel, condemned him and his descendants to have a tendency towards rebellion'. But this chastisement happens naturally to the wicked, without any ordinance of a legislator, and they become addicted to evil. If drunkards begot children inclined to the same vice, by a natural consequence of what takes place in bodies, that would be a punishment of their progenitors,

but it would not be a penalty of law. There is something comparable to this in the consequences of the first man's sin. For the contemplation of divine wisdom leads us to believe that the realm of nature serves that of grace; and that God as an Architect has done all in a manner befitting God considered as a Monarch. We do not sufficiently know the nature of the forbidden fruit, or that of the action, or its effects, to judge of the details of this matter: nevertheless we must do God justice so far as to believe that it comprised something other than what painters depict for us.

113. V. 'It has pleased him by his infinite mercy to deliver a very few men from this condemnation; and, leaving them exposed during this life to the corruption of sin and misery, he has given them aids which enable them to obtain the never-ending bliss of paradise.' Many in the past have doubted, as I have already observed, whether the number of the damned is so great as is generally supposed; and it appears that they believed in the existence of some intermediate state between eternal damnation and perfect bliss. But we have no need of these opinions, and it is enough to keep to the ideas accepted in the Church. In this connexion it is well to observe that this proposition of M. Bayle's is conceived in accordance with the principles of sufficient grace, given to all men, and sufficing them provided that they have good will. Although M. Bayle holds the opposite opinion, he wished (as he states in the margin) to avoid the terms that would not agree with a system of decrees subsequent to the prevision of contingent events.

114. VI. 'He foresaw from eternity all that which should happen, he ordered all things and placed them each one in its own place, and he guides and controls them continually, according to his pleasure. Thus nothing is done without his permission or against his will, and he can prevent, as seems good to him, as much and as often as seems good to him, all that does not please him, and in consequence sin, which is the thing in the world that most offends him and that he most detests; and he can produce in each human soul all the thoughts that he approves.' This thesis is also purely philosophic, that is, recognizable by the light of natural reason. It is opportune also, as one has dwelt in thesis II on *that which pleases*, to dwell here upon *that which seems good*, that is, upon that which God finds good to do. He can avoid or put away as 'seems good to him' all 'that does not please him'. Nevertheless it must be borne in mind that some objects of his aversion, such as

certain evils, and especially sin, which his antecedent will repelled, could only have been rejected by his consequent or decretory will, in so far as it was prompted by the rule of the best, which the All-wise must choose after having taken all into account. When one says 'that sin offends God most, and that he detests it most', these are human ways of speaking. God cannot, properly speaking, be *offended*, that is, injured, disturbed, disquieted or angered; and he *detests* nothing of that which exists, in the sense that to detest something is to look upon it with abomination and in a way that causes us disgust, that greatly pains and distresses us; for God cannot suffer either vexation, or grief or discomfort; he is always altogether content and at ease. Yet these expressions in their true sense are justified. The supreme goodness of God causes his antecedent will to repel all evil, but moral evil more than any other: it only admits evil at all for irresistible superior reasons, and with great correctives which repair its ill effects to good advantage. It is true also that God could produce in each human soul all the thoughts that he approves: but this would be to act by miracles, more than his most perfectly conceived plan admits.

115. VII. 'He offers grace to people that he knows are destined not to accept it, and so destined by this refusal to make themselves more criminal than they would be if he had not offered them that grace; he assures them that it is his ardent wish that they accept it, and he does not give them the grace which he knows they would accept.' It is true that these people become more criminal through their refusal than if one had offered them nothing, and that God knows this. Yet it is better to permit their crime than to act in a way which would render God himself blameworthy, and provide the criminals with some justification for the complaint that it was not possible for them to do better, even though they had or might have wished it. God desires that they receive such grace from him as they are fit to receive, and that they accept it; and he desires to give them in particular that grace whose acceptance by them he foresees: but it is always by a will antecedent, detached or particular, which cannot always be carried out in the general plan of things. This thesis also is among the number of those which philosophy establishes no less than revelation, like three others of the seven that we have just stated here, the third, fourth and fifth being the only ones where revelation is necessary.

116. Here now are the nineteen philosophic maxims which M. Bayle opposes to the seven theological propositions.

I. 'As the infinitely perfect Being finds in himself a glory and a bliss that can never either diminish or increase, his goodness alone has determined him to create this universe: neither the ambition to be praised, nor any interested motive of preserving or augmenting his bliss and his glory, has had any part therein.' This maxim is very good: praises of God do him no service, but they are of service to the men who praise him, and he desired their good. Nevertheless, when one says that *goodness* alone determined God to create this universe, it is well to add that his GOODNESS prompted him *antecedently* to create and to produce all possible good; but that his WISDOM made the choice and caused him to select the best *consequently*; and finally that his POWER gave him the means to carry out *actually* the great design which he had formed.

117. II. 'The goodness of the infinitely perfect Being is infinite, and would not be infinite if one could conceive of a goodness greater than this. This characteristic of infinity is proper also to all his other perfections, to love of virtue, hatred of vice, etc., they must be the greatest one can imagine. (See M. Jurieu in the first three sections of the *Judgement on Methods*, where he argues constantly upon this principle, as upon a primary notion. See also in Wittich, *De Providentia Dei*, n. 12, these words of St. Augustine, lib. I, *De Doctrina Christiana*, c. 7: "Cum cogitatur Deus, ita cogitatur, ut aliquid, quo nihil melius sit atque sublimius. Et paulo post: Nec quisquam inveniri potest, qui hoc Deum credat esse, quo melius aliquid est.")'

This maxim is altogether to my liking, and I draw from it this conclusion, that God does the very best possible: otherwise the exercise of his goodness would be restricted, and that would be restricting his *goodness* itself, if it did not prompt him to the best, if he were lacking in good will. Or again it would be restricting his *wisdom* and his *power*, if he lacked the knowledge necessary for discerning the best and for finding the means to obtain it, or if he lacked the strength necessary for employing these means. There is, however, ambiguity in the assertion that love of virtue and hatred of vice are infinite in God: if that were absolutely and unreservedly true, in practice there would be no vice in the world. But although each one of God's perfections is infinite in itself, it is exercised only in proportion to the object and as the nature of things prompts it.

Thus love of the best in the whole carries the day over all other individual inclinations or hatreds; it is the only impulse whose very exercise is absolutely infinite, nothing having power to prevent God from declaring himself for the best; and some vice being combined with the best possible plan, God permits it.

118. III. 'An infinite goodness having guided the Creator in the production of the world, all the characteristics of knowledge, skill, power and greatness that are displayed in his work are destined for the happiness of intelligent creatures. He wished to show forth his perfections only to the end that creatures of this kind should find their felicity in the knowledge, the admiration and the love of the Supreme Being.'

This maxim appears to me not sufficiently exact. I grant that the happiness of intelligent creatures is the principal part of God's design, for they are most like him; but nevertheless I do not see how one can prove that to be his sole aim. It is true that the realm of nature must serve the realm of grace: but, since all is connected in God's great design, we must believe that the realm of grace is also in some way adapted to that of nature, so that nature preserves the utmost order and beauty, to render the combination of the two the most perfect that can be. And there is no reason to suppose that God, for the sake of some lessening of moral evil, would reverse the whole order of nature. Each perfection or imperfection in the creature has its value, but there is none that has an infinite value. Thus the moral or physical good and evil of rational creatures does not infinitely exceed the good and evil which is simply metaphysical, namely that which lies in the perfection of the other creatures; and yet one would be bound to say this if the present maxim were strictly true. When God justified to the Prophet Jonah the pardon that he had granted to the inhabitants of Nineveh, he even touched upon the interest of the beasts who would have been involved in the ruin of this great city. No substance is absolutely contemptible or absolutely precious before God. And the abuse or the exaggerated extension of the present maxim appears to be in part the source of the difficulties that M. Bayle puts forward. It is certain that God sets greater store by a man than a lion; nevertheless it can hardly be said with certainty that God prefers a single man in all respects to the whole of lion-kind. Even should that be so, it would by no means follow that the interest of a certain number of men would prevail over the consideration of a general disorder diffused through an infinite number of creatures. This opinion would be a remnant of the old and somewhat discredited maxim, that all is made solely for man.

119. IV. 'The benefits he imparts to the creatures that are capable of felicity tend only to their happiness. He therefore does not permit that these should serve to make them unhappy, and, if the wrong use that they made of them were capable of destroying them, he would give them sure means of always using them well. Otherwise they would not be true benefits, and his goodness would be smaller than that we can conceive of in another benefactor. (I mean, in a Cause that united with its gifts the sure skill to make good use of them.)'

There already is the abuse or the ill effect of the preceding maxim. It is not strictly true (though it appear plausible) that the benefits God imparts to the creatures who are capable of felicity tend solely to their happiness. All is connected in Nature; and if a skilled artisan, an engineer, an architect, a wise politician often makes one and the same thing serve several ends, if he makes a double hit with a single throw, when that can be done conveniently, one may say that God, whose wisdom and power are perfect, does so always. That is husbanding the ground, the time, the place, the material, which make up as it were his outlay. Thus God has more than one purpose in his projects. The felicity of all rational creatures is one of the aims he has in view; but it is not his whole aim, nor even his final aim. Therefore it happens that the unhappiness of some of these creatures may come about *by concomitance*, and as a result of other greater goods: this I have already explained, and M. Bayle has to some extent acknowledged it. The goods as such, considered in themselves, are the object of the antecedent will of God. God will produce as much reason and knowledge in the universe as his plan can admit. One can conceive of a mean between an antecedent will altogether pure and primitive, and a consequent and final will. The *primitive antecedent will* has as its object each good and each evil in itself, detached from all combination, and tends to advance the good and prevent the evil. The *mediate will* relates to combinations, as when one attaches a good to an evil: then the will will have some tendency towards this combination when the good exceeds the evil therein. But the *final and decisive will* results from consideration of all the goods and all the evils that enter into our deliberation, it results from a total combination. This shows that a mediate will, although it may in a sense pass as consequent in relation to a pure and primitive antecedent will, must be considered antecedent in relation to the final and decretory will. God gives reason to the human race; misfortunes arise thence by concomitance. His pure antecedent will tends towards giving reason, as a great good, and preventing the evils in question. But when it is a question of the evils that accompany this gift which God has made to us of reason, the compound, made up of the combination of reason and of these evils, will be the object of a mediate will of God, which will tend towards producing or preventing this compound, according as the good or the evil prevails therein. But even though it should prove that reason did more harm than good to men (which, however, I do not admit), whereupon the mediate will of God would discard it with all its concomitants, it might still be the case that it was more in accordance with the perfection of the universe to give reason to men, notwithstanding all the evil consequences which it might have with reference to them. Consequently, the final will or the decree of God, resulting from all the considerations he can have, would be to give it to them. And, far from being subject to blame for this, he would be blameworthy if he did not so. Thus the evil, or the mixture of goods and evils wherein the evil prevails, happens only *by concomitance*, because it is connected with greater goods that are outside this mixture. This mixture, therefore, or this compound, is not to be conceived as a grace or as a gift from God to us; but the good that is found mingled therein will nevertheless be good. Such is God's gift of reason to those who make ill use thereof. It is always a good in itself; but the combination of this good with the evils that proceed from its abuse is not a good with regard to those who in consequence thereof become unhappy. Yet it comes to be by concomitance, because it serves a greater good in relation to the universe. And it is doubtless that which prompted God to give reason to those who have made it an instrument of their unhappiness. Or, to put it more precisely, in accordance with my system God, having found among the possible beings some rational creatures who misuse their reason, gave existence to those who are included in the best possible plan of the universe. Thus nothing prevents us from admitting that God grants goods which turn into evil by the fault of men, this often happening to men in just punishment of the misuse they had made of God's grace. Aloysius Novarinus wrote a book *De Occultis Dei Beneficiis*: one could write one *De Occultis Dei Poenis*. This saying of Claudian would be in place here with regard to some persons:

> *Tolluntur in altum,*
> *Ut lapsu graviore ruant.*

But to say that God should not give a good which he knows an evil will will abuse, when the general plan of things demands that he give it; or again to say that he should give certain means for preventing it, contrary to this same general order: that is to wish (as I have observed already) that God himself become blameworthy in order to prevent man from being so. To object, as people do here, that the goodness of God would be smaller than that of another benefactor who would give a more useful gift, is to overlook the fact that the goodness of a benefactor is not measured by a single benefit. It may well be that a gift from a private person is greater than one from a prince, but the gifts of this private person all taken together will be much inferior to the prince's gifts all together. Thus one can esteem fittingly the good things done by God only when one considers their whole extent by relating them to the entire universe. Moreover, one may say that the gifts given in the expectation that they will harm are the gifts of an enemy, ἐχθρῶν δῶρα ἄδωρα,

> *Hostibus eveniant talia dona meis.*

But that applies to when there is malice or guilt in him who gives them, as there was in that Eutrapelus of whom Horace speaks, who did good to people in order to give them the means of destroying themselves. His design was evil, but God's design cannot be better than it is. Must God spoil his system, must there be less beauty, perfection and reason in the universe, because there are people who misuse reason? The common sayings are in place here: *Abusus non tollit usum*; there is *scandalum datum et scandalum acceptum*.

120. V. 'A maleficent being is very capable of heaping magnificent gifts upon his enemies, when he knows that they will make thereof a use that will destroy them. It therefore does not beseem the infinitely good Being to give to creatures a free will, whereof, as he knows for certain, they would make a use that would render them unhappy. Therefore if he gives them free will he combines with it the art of using it always opportunely, and permits not that

they neglect the practice of this art in any conjuncture; and if there were no sure means of determining the good use of this free will, he would rather take from them this faculty, than allow it to be the cause of their unhappiness. That is the more manifest, as free will is a grace which he has given them of his own choice and without their asking for it; so that he would be more answerable for the unhappiness it would bring upon them than if he had only granted it in response to their importunate prayers.'

What was said at the end of the remark on the preceding maxim ought to be repeated here, and is sufficient to counter the present maxim. Moreover, the author is still presupposing that false maxim advanced as the third, stating that the happiness of rational creatures is the sole aim of God. If that were so, perhaps neither sin nor unhappiness would ever occur, even by concomitance. God would have chosen a sequence of possibles where all these evils would be excluded. But God would fail in what is due to the universe, that is, in what he owes to himself. If there were only spirits they would be without the required connexion, without the order of time and place. This order demands matter, movement and its laws; to adjust these to spirits in the best possible way means to return to our world. When one looks at things only in the mass, one imagines to be practicable a thousand things that cannot properly take place. To wish that God should not give free will to rational creatures is to wish that there be none of these creatures; and to wish that God should prevent them from misusing it is to wish that there be none but these creatures alone, together with what was made for them only. If God had none but these creatures in view, he would doubtless prevent them from destroying themselves. One may say in a sense, however, that God has given to these creatures the art of always making good use of their free will, for the natural light of reason is this art. But it would be necessary always to have the will to do good, and often creatures lack the means of giving themselves the will they ought to have; often they even lack the will to use those means which indirectly give a good will. Of this I have already spoken more than once. This fault must be admitted, and one must even acknowledge that God would perhaps have been able to exempt creatures from that fault, since there is nothing to prevent, so it seems, the existence of some whose nature it would be always to have good will. But I reply that it is not necessary, and that it was not feasible for all rational creatures to have so great a perfection, and such as would bring them so close to the Divinity. It may even be that that can only be made possible by a special divine grace. But in this case, would it be proper for God to grant it to all, that is, always to act miraculously in respect of all rational creatures? Nothing would be less rational than these perpetual miracles. There are degrees among creatures: the general order requires it. And it appears quite consistent with the order of divine government that the great privilege of strengthening in the good should be granted more easily to those who had a good will when they were in a more imperfect state, in the state of struggle and of pilgrimage, *in Ecclesia militante, in statu viatorum*. The good angels themselves were not created incapable of sin. Nevertheless I would not dare to assert that there are no blessed creatures born, or such as are sinless and holy by their nature. There are perhaps people who give this privilege to the Blessed Virgin, since, moreover, the Roman Church to-day places her above the angels. But it suffices us that the universe is very great and very varied: to wish to limit it is to have little knowledge thereof. 'But', M. Bayle goes on, 'God has given free will to creatures capable of sinning, without their having asked him for this grace. And he who gave such a gift would be more answerable for the unhappiness that it brought upon those who made use of it, than if he had granted it only in response to their importunate prayers.' But importunity in prayers makes no difference to God; he knows better than we what we need, and he only grants what serves the interest of the whole. It seems that M. Bayle here makes free will consist in the faculty for sinning; yet he acknowledges elsewhere that God and the Saints are free, without having this faculty. However that may be, I have already shown fully that God, doing what his wisdom and his goodness combined ordain, is not answerable for the evil that he permits. Even men, when they do their duty, are not answerable for consequences, whether they foresee them or not.

121. VI. 'It is as sure a means of taking a man's life to give him a silk cord that one knows certainly he will make use of freely to strangle himself, as to plant a few dagger thrusts in his body. One desires his death not less when one makes use of the first way, than when one employs the second: it even seems as though one desires it with a more malicious intention, since one tends to leave to him the whole trouble and the whole blame of his destruction.'

Those who write treatises on Duties (De Officiis) as, for instance, Cicero, St. Ambrose, Grotius, Opalenius, Sharrok, Rachelius, Pufendorf, as well as the Casuists, teach that there are cases where one is not obliged to return to its owner a thing deposited: for example, one will not give back a dagger when one knows that he who has deposited it is about to stab someone. Let us pretend that I have in my hands the fatal draught that Meleager's mother will make use of to kill him; the magic javelin that Cephalus will unwittingly employ to kill his Procris; the horses of Theseus that will tear to pieces Hippolytus, his son: these things are demanded back from me, and I am right in refusing them, knowing the use that will be made of them. But how will it be if a competent judge orders me to restore them, when I cannot prove to him what I know of the evil consequences that restitution will have, Apollo perchance having given to me, as to Cassandra, the gift of prophecy under the condition that I shall not be believed? I should then be compelled to make restitution, having no alternative other than my own destruction: thus I cannot escape from contributing towards the evil. Another comparison: Jupiter promises Semele, the Sun Phaeton, Cupid Psyche to grant whatever favour the other shall ask. They swear by the Styx,

Di cujus jurare timent et fallere Numen.

One would gladly stop, but too late, the request half heard,

Voluit Deus ora loquentis
Opprimere; exierat jam vox properata sub auras.

One would gladly draw back after the request was made, making vain remonstrances; but they press you, they say to you: 'Do you make oaths that you will not keep?' The law of the Styx is inviolable, one must needs submit to it; if one has erred in making the oath, one would err more in not keeping it; the promise must be fulfilled, however harmful it may be to him who exacts it. It would be ruinous to you if you did not fulfil it. It seems as though the moral of these fables implies that a supreme necessity may constrain one to comply with evil. God, in truth, knows no other judge that can compel him to give what may turn to evil, he is not like Jupiter who fears the Styx. But his own wisdom is the greatest judge that he can find, there is no appeal from its judgements: they are the decrees of destiny. The eternal verities, objects of his wisdom, are more inviolable than the Styx. These laws and this judge do not constrain: they are stronger, for they persuade. Wisdom only shows God the best possible exercise of his goodness: after that, the evil that occurs is an inevitable result of the best. I will add something stronger: To permit the evil, as God permits it, is the greatest goodness.

Si mala sustulerat, non erat ille bonus.

One would need to have a bent towards perversity to say after this that it is more malicious to leave to someone the whole trouble and the whole blame of his destruction. When God does leave it to a man, it has belonged to him since before his existence; it was already in the idea of him as still merely possible, before the decree of God which makes him to exist. Can one, then, leave it or give it to another? There is the whole matter.

122. VII. 'A true benefactor gives promptly, and does not wait to give until those he loves have suffered long miseries from the privation of what he could have imparted to them at first very easily, and without causing any inconvenience to himself. If the limitation of his forces does not permit him to do good without inflicting pain or some other inconvenience, he acquiesces in this, but only regretfully, and he never employs this way of rendering service when he can render it without mingling any kind of evil in his favours. If the profit one could derive from the evils he inflicted could spring as easily from an unalloyed good as from those evils, he would take the straight road of unalloyed good, and not the indirect road that would lead from the evil to the good. If he showers riches and honours, it is not to the end that those who have enjoyed them, when they come to lose them, should be all the more deeply afflicted in proportion to their previous experience of pleasure, and that thus they should become more unhappy than the persons who have always been deprived of these advantages. A malicious being would shower good things at such a price upon the people for whom he had the most hatred.'

(Compare this passage of Aristotle, *Rhetor.*, 1. 2, c. 23, p. m. 446:
οἷον εἰ δοίη ἄν τις τινι ἵνα ἀφελόμενος λειπήσῃ · ὅθεν καὶ τοῦτ' εἴρηται,

πολλοῖς ὁ δαίμων οὐ κατ' εὐνοίαν φέρων
Μέγαλα δίδωσιν εὐτυχήματ', ἀλλ' ἵνα
τὰς συμφορὰς λάβωσιν ἐπιφανεστέρας.

Id est: Veluti si quis alicui aliquid det, ut (postea) hoc (ipsi) erepto (ipsum) afficiat dolore. Unde etiam illud est dictum:

> *Bona magna multis non amicus dat Deus,*
> *Insigniore ut rursus his privet malo.*)

All these objections depend almost on the same sophism; they change and mutilate the fact, they only half record things: God has care for men, he loves the human race, he wishes it well, nothing so true. Yet he allows men to fall, he often allows them to perish, he gives them goods that tend towards their destruction; and when he makes someone happy, it is after many sufferings: where is his affection, where is his goodness or again where is his power? Vain objections, which suppress the main point, which ignore the fact that it is of God one speaks. It is as though one were speaking of a mother, a guardian, a tutor, whose well-nigh only care is concerned with the upbringing, the preservation, the happiness of the person in question, and who neglect their duty. God takes care of the universe, he neglects nothing, he chooses what is best on the whole. If in spite of all that someone is wicked and unhappy, it behoved him to be so. God (so they say) could have given happiness to all, he could have given it promptly and easily, and without causing himself any inconvenience, for he can do all. But should he? Since he does not so, it is a sign that he had to act altogether differently. If we infer from this either that God only regretfully, and owing to lack of power, fails to make men happy and to give the good first of all and without admixture of evil, or else that he lacks the good will to give it unreservedly and for good and all, then we are comparing our true God with the God of Herodotus, full of envy, or with the demon of the poet whose iambics Aristotle quotes, and I have just translated into Latin, who gives good things in order that he may cause more affliction by taking them away. That would be trifling with God in perpetual anthropomorphisms, representing him as a man who must give himself up completely to one particular business, whose goodness must be chiefly exercised upon those objects alone which are known to us, and who lacks either aptitude or good will. God is not lacking therein, he could do the good that we would desire; he even wishes it, taking it separately, but he must not do it in preference to other greater goods which are opposed to it. Moreover, one has no cause to complain of the fact that usually one attains salvation only through many sufferings, and by bearing the cross of Jesus Christ. These evils serve to make the elect imitators of their master, and to increase their happiness.

123. VIII. 'The greatest and the most substantial glory that he who is the master of others can gain is to maintain amongst them virtue, order, peace, contentment of mind. The glory that he would derive from their unhappiness can be nothing but a false glory.'

If we knew the city of God just as it is, we should see that it is the most perfect state which can be devised; that virtue and happiness reign there, as far as is possible, in accordance with the laws of the best; that sin and unhappiness (whose entire exclusion from the nature of things reasons of the supreme order did not permit), are well-nigh nothing there in comparison with the good, and even are of service for greater good. Now since these evils were to exist, there must needs be some appointed to be subject to them, and we are those people. If it were others, would there not be the same appearance of evil? Or rather, would not these others be those known as We? When God derives some glory from the evil through having made it serve a greater good, it was proper that he should derive that glory. It is not therefore a false glory, as would be that of a prince who overthrew his state in order to have the honour of setting it up again.

124. IX. 'The way whereby that master can give proof of greatest love for virtue is to cause it, if he can, to be always practised without any mixture of vice. If it is easy for him to procure for his subjects this advantage, and nevertheless he permits vice to raise its head, save that he punishes it finally after having long tolerated it, his affection for virtue is not the greatest one can conceive; it is therefore not infinite.'

I am not yet half way through the nineteen maxims, and already I am weary of refuting, and making the same answer always. M. Bayle multiplies unnecessarily his so-called maxims in opposition to my dogmas. If things connected together may be separated, the parts from their whole, the human kind from the universe, God's attributes the one from the other, power from wisdom, it may be said that God *can cause* virtue to be in the world without any mixture of vice, and even that he can do so *easily*. But, since he has permitted vice, it must be that that order of the universe which was found preferable to every other plan required it. One must believe that it is not permitted to do otherwise, since it is not possible to do better. It is a hypothetical necessity, a moral necessity, which, far from being contrary to freedom, is the effect of its choice. *Quae rationi contraria sunt, ea nec fieri a Sapiente posse credendum est.* The objection is made here, that God's affection for virtue is therefore not the greatest which can be conceived, that it is not *infinite*. To that an answer has already been given on the second maxim, in the assertion that God's affection for any created thing whatsoever is proportionate to the value of the thing. Virtue is the noblest quality of created things, but it is not the only good quality of creatures. There are innumerable others which attract the inclination of God: from all these inclinations there results the most possible good, and it turns out that if there were only virtue, if there were only rational creatures, there would be less good. Midas proved to be less rich when he had only gold. And besides, wisdom must vary. To multiply one and the same thing only would be superfluity, and poverty too. To have a thousand well-bound Vergils in one's library, always to sing the airs from the opera of Cadmus and Hermione, to break all the china in order only to have cups of gold, to have only diamond buttons, to eat nothing but partridges, to drink only Hungarian or Shiraz wine—would one call that reason? Nature had need of animals, plants, inanimate bodies; there are in these creatures, devoid of reason, marvels which serve for exercise of the reason. What would an intelligent creature do if there were no unintelligent things? What would it think of, if there were neither movement, nor matter, nor sense? If it had only distinct thoughts it would be a God, its wisdom would be without bounds: that is one of the results of my meditations. As soon as there is a mixture of confused thoughts, there is sense, there is matter. For these confused thoughts come from the relation of all things one to the other by way of duration and extent. Thus it is that in my philosophy there is no rational creature without some organic body, and there is no created spirit entirely detached from matter. But these organic bodies vary no less in perfection than the spirits to which they belong. Therefore, since God's wisdom must nave a world of bodies, a world of substances capable of perception and incapable of reason; since, in short, it was necessary to choose from all the things possible what produced the best effect together, and since vice entered in by this door, God would not have been altogether good, altogether wise if he had excluded it.

125. X. 'The way to evince the greatest hatred for vice is not indeed to allow it to prevail for a long time and then chastise it, but to crush it before its birth, that is, prevent it from showing itself anywhere. A king, for example, who put his finances in such good order that no malversation was ever committed, would thus display more hatred for the wrong done by factionaries than if, after having suffered them to batten on the blood of the people, he had them hanged.'

It is always the same song, it is anthropomorphism pure and simple. A king should generally have nothing so much at heart as to keep his subjects free from oppression. One of his greatest interests is to bring good order into his finances. Nevertheless there are times when he is obliged to tolerate vice and disorders. He has a great war on his hands, he is in a state of exhaustion, he has no choice of generals, it is necessary to humour those he has, those possessed of great authority with the soldiers: a Braccio, a Sforza, a Wallenstein. He lacks money for the most pressing needs, it is necessary to turn to great financiers, who have an established credit, and he must at the same time connive at their malversations. It is true that this unfortunate necessity arises most often from previous errors. It is not the same with God: he has need of no man, he commits no error, he always does the best. One cannot even wish that things may go better, when one understands them: and it would be a vice in the Author of things if he wished to change anything whatsoever in them, if he wished to exclude the vice that was found there. Is this State with perfect government, where good is willed and performed as far as it is possible, where evil even serves the greatest good, comparable with the State of a prince whose affairs are in ruin and who escapes as best he can? Or with that of a prince who encourages oppression in order to punish it, and who delights to see the little men with begging bowls and the great on scaffolds?

126. XI. 'A ruler devoted to the interests of virtue, and to the good of his subjects, takes the utmost care to ensure that they never disobey his laws; and if he must needs chastise them for their disobedience, he sees to it that the penalty cures them of the inclination to evil, and restores in their soul a strong and constant tendency towards good: so far is he from any desire that the penalty for the error should incline them more and more towards evil.'

To make men better, God does all that is due, and even all that can be done on his side without detriment to what is due. The most usual aim of punishment is amendment; but it is not the sole aim, nor that which God always intends. I have said a word on that above. Original sin, which disposes men towards evil, is not merely a penalty for the first sin; it is a natural consequence thereof. On that too a word has been said, in the course of an observation on the fourth theological proposition. It is like drunkenness, which is a penalty for excess in drinking and is at the same time a natural consequence that easily leads to new sins.

127. XII. 'To permit the evil that one could prevent is not to care whether it be committed or not, or is even to wish that it be committed.'

By no means. How many times do men permit evils which they could prevent if they turned all their efforts in that direction? But other more important cares prevent them from doing so. One will rarely resolve upon adjusting irregularities in the coinage while one is involved in a great war. And the action of an English Parliament in this direction a little before the Peace of Ryswyck will be rather praised than imitated. Can one conclude from this that the State has no anxiety about this irregularity, or even that it desires it? God has a far stronger reason, and one far more worthy of him, for tolerating evils. Not only does he derive from them greater goods, but he finds them connected with the greatest goods of all those that are possible: so that it would be a fault not to permit them.

128. XIII. 'It is a very great fault in those who govern, if they do not care whether there be disorder in their States or not. The fault is still greater if they wish and even desire disorder there. If by hidden and indirect, but infallible, ways they stirred up a sedition in their States to bring them to the brink of ruin, in order to gain for themselves the glory of showing that they have the courage and the prudence necessary for saving a great kingdom on the point of perishing, they would be most deserving of condemnation. But if they stirred up this sedition because there were no other means than that, of averting the total ruin of their subjects and of strengthening on new foundations, and for several centuries, the happiness of nations, one must needs lament the unfortunate necessity (see above, pp. 146, 147, what has been said of the

force of necessity) to which they were reduced, and praise them for the use that they made thereof.'

This maxim, with divers others set forth here, is not applicable to the government of God. Not to mention the fact that it is only the disorders of a very small part of his kingdom which are brought up in objection, it is untrue that he has no anxiety about evils, that he desires them, that he brings them into being, to have the glory of allaying them. God wills order and good; but it happens sometimes that what is disorder in the part is order in the whole. I have already stated this legal axiom: *Incivile est nisi tota lege inspecta judicare*. The permission of evils comes from a kind of moral necessity: God is constrained to this by his wisdom and by his goodness; *this necessity is happy*, whereas that of the prince spoken of in the maxim is *unhappy*. His State is one of the most corrupt; and the government of God is the best State possible.

129. XIV. 'The permission of a certain evil is only excusable when one cannot remedy it without introducing a greater evil; but it cannot be excusable in those who have in hand a remedy more efficacious against this evil, and against all the other evils that could spring from the suppression of this one.'

The maxim is true, but it cannot be brought forward against the government of God. Supreme reason constrains him to permit the evil. If God chose what would not be the best absolutely and in all, that would be a greater evil than all the individual evils which he could prevent by this means. This wrong choice would destroy his wisdom and his goodness.

130. XV. 'The Being infinitely powerful, Creator of matter and of spirits, makes whatever he wills of this matter and these spirits. There is no situation or shape that he cannot communicate to spirits. If he then permitted a physical or a moral evil, this would not be for the reason that otherwise some other still greater physical or moral evil would be altogether inevitable. None of those reasons for the mixture of good and evil which are founded on the limitation of the forces of benefactors can apply to him.'

It is true that God makes of matter and of spirits whatever he wills; but he is like a good sculptor, who will make from his block of marble only that which he judges to be the best, and who judges well. God makes of matter the most excellent of all possible machines; he makes of spirits the most excellent of all governments conceivable; and over and above all that, he establishes for their union the most perfect of all harmonies, according to the system I have proposed. Now since physical evil and moral evil occur in this perfect work, one must conclude (contrary to M. Bayle's assurance here) that *otherwise a still greater evil would have been altogether inevitable*. This great evil would be that God would have chosen ill if he had chosen otherwise than he has chosen. It is true that God is infinitely powerful; but his power is indeterminate, goodness and wisdom combined determine him to produce the best. M. Bayle makes elsewhere an objection which is peculiar to him, which he derives from the opinions of the modern Cartesians. They say that God could have given to souls what thoughts he would, without making them depend upon any relation to the body: by this means souls would be spared a great number of evils which only spring from derangement of the body. More will be said of this later; now it is sufficient to bear in mind that God cannot establish a system ill-connected and full of dissonances. It is to some extent the nature of souls to represent bodies.

131. XVI. 'One is just as much the cause of an event when one brings it about in moral ways, as when one brings it about in physical ways. A Minister of State, who, without going out of his study, and simply by utilizing the passions of the leaders of a faction, overthrew all their plots, would thus be bringing about the ruin of this faction, no less than if he destroyed it by a surprise attack.'

I have nothing to say against this maxim. Evil is always attributed to moral causes, and not always to physical causes. Here I observe simply that if I could not prevent the sin of others except by committing a sin myself, I should be justified in permitting it, and I should not be accessary thereto, or its moral cause. In God, every fault would represent a sin; it would be even more than sin, for it would destroy Divinity. And it would be a great fault in him not to choose the best. I have said so many times. He would then prevent sin by something worse than all sins.

132. XVII. 'It is all the same whether one employ a necessary cause, or employ a free cause while choosing the moments when one knows it to be determined. If I imagine that gunpowder has the power to ignite or not to ignite when fire touches it, and if I know for certain that it will be disposed to ignite at eight o'clock in the morning, I shall be just as much the cause of its effects if I apply the fire to it at that hour, as I should be in assuming, as is

the case, that it is a necessary cause. For where I am concerned it would no longer be a free cause. I should be catching it at the moment when I knew it to be necessitated by its own choice. It is impossible for a being to be free or indifferent with regard to that to which it is already determined, and at the time when it is determined thereto. All that which exists exists of necessity while it exists. (Τὸ εἶναι τὸ ὂν ὅταν ᾖ, καὶ τὸ μὴ ὂν μὴ εἶναι ὅταν μὴ ᾖ, ἀνάγκη. "Necesse est id quod est, quando est, esse; et id quod non est, quando non est, non esse": Arist., *De Interpret.*, cap. 9. The Nominalists have adopted this maxim of Aristotle. Scotus and sundry other Schoolmen appear to reject it, but fundamentally their distinctions come to the same thing. See the Jesuits of Coimbra on this passage from Aristotle, p. 380 *et seq.*)'

This maxim may pass also; I would wish only to change something in the phraseology. I would not take 'free' and 'indifferent' for one and the same thing, and would not place 'free' and 'determined' in antithesis. One is never altogether indifferent with an indifference of equipoise; one is always more inclined and consequently more determined on one side than on another: but one is never necessitated to the choice that one makes. I mean here a *necessity* absolute and metaphysical; for it must be admitted that God, that wisdom, is prompted to the best by a *moral* necessity. It must be admitted also that one is necessitated to the choice by a hypothetical necessity, when one actually makes the choice; and even before one is necessitated thereto by the very truth of the futurition, since one will do it. These hypothetical necessities do no harm. I have spoken sufficiently on this point already.

133. XVIII. 'When a whole great people has become guilty of rebellion, it is not showing clemency to pardon the hundred thousandth part, and to kill all the rest, not excepting even babes and sucklings.'

It seems to be assumed here that there are a hundred thousand times more damned than saved, and that children dying unbaptized are included among the former. Both these points are disputed, and especially the damnation of these children. I have spoken of this above. M. Bayle urges the same objection elsewhere (*Reply to the Questions of a Provincial*, vol. III, ch. 178, p. 1223): 'We see clearly', he says, 'that the Sovereign who wishes to exercise both justice and clemency when a city has revolted must be content with the punishment of a small number of mutineers, and pardon all the rest. For if the number of those who are chastised is as a thousand to one, in comparison with those whom he freely pardons, he cannot be accounted mild, but, on the contrary, cruel. He would assuredly be accounted an abominable tyrant if he chose punishments of long duration, and if he eschewed bloodshed only because he was convinced that men would prefer death to a miserable life; and if, finally, the desire to take revenge were more responsible for his severities than the desire to turn to the service of the common weal the penalty that he would inflict on almost all the rebels. Criminals who are executed are considered to expiate their crimes so completely by the loss of their life, that the public requires nothing more, and is indignant when executioners are clumsy. These would be stoned if they were known deliberately to give repeated strokes of the axe; and the judges who are present at the execution would not be immune from danger if they were thought to take pleasure in this evil sport of the executioners, and to have surreptitiously urged them to practise it.' (Note that this is not to be understood as strictly universal. There are cases where the people approve of the slow killing of certain criminals, as when Francis I thus put to death some persons accused of heresy after the notorious Placards of 1534. No pity was shown to Ravaillac, who was tortured in divers horrible ways. See the *French Mercury*, vol. I, fol. m., 455 *et seq.* See also Pierre Matthieu in his *History of the Death of Henry IV*; and do not forget what he says on page m. 99 concerning the discussion by the judges with regard to the torture of this parricide.) 'Finally it is an exceptionally notorious fact that Rulers who should be guided by St. Paul, I mean who should condemn to the extreme penalty all those whom he condemns to eternal death, would be accounted enemies of the human kind and destroyers of their communities. It is incontestable that their laws, far from being fitted, in accordance with the aim of legislators, to uphold society, would be its complete ruin. (Apply here these words of Pliny the Younger, *Epist.*, 22, lib. 8: Mandemus memoriae quod vir mitissimus, et ob hoc quoque maximus, Thrasea crebro dicere solebat, Qui vitia odit, homines odit.)' He adds that it was said of the laws of Draco, an Athenian lawgiver, that they had not been written with ink, but with blood, because they punished all sins with the extreme penalty, and because damnation is a penalty even worse than death. But it must be borne in mind that damnation is a consequence of sin. Thus I once answered a friend, who raised as an objection the disproportion existing between an eternal punishment and a limited crime, that there is no injustice when the continuation of the punishment is only a result of the continuation of the sin. I will speak further on this point later. As for the number of the damned, even though it should be incomparably greater among men than the number of the saved, that would not preclude the possibility that in the universe the happy creatures infinitely outnumber those who are unhappy. Such examples as that of a prince who punishes only the leaders of rebels or of a general who has a regiment decimated, are of no importance here. Self-interest compels the prince and the general to pardon the guilty, even though they should remain wicked. God only pardons those who become better: he can distinguish them; and this severity is more consistent with perfect justice. But if anyone asks why God gives not to all the grace of conversion, the question is of a different nature, having no relation to the present maxim. I have already answered it in a sense, not in order to find God's reasons, but to show that he cannot lack such, and that there are no opposing reasons of any validity. Moreover, we know that sometimes whole cities are destroyed and the inhabitants put to the sword, to inspire terror in the rest. That may serve to shorten a great war or a rebellion, and would mean a saving of blood through the shedding of it: there is no decimation there. We cannot assert, indeed, that the wicked of our globe are punished so severely in order to intimidate the inhabitants of the other globes and to make them better. Yet an abundance of reasons in the universal harmony which are unknown to us, because we know not sufficiently the extent of the city of God, nor the form of the general republic of spirits, nor even the whole architecture of bodies, may produce the same effect.

134. XIX. 'Those physicians who chose, among many remedies capable of curing a sick man, whereof divers were such as they well knew he would take with enjoyment, precisely that one which they knew he would refuse to take, would vainly urge and pray him not to refuse it; we should still have just cause for thinking that they had no desire to cure him: for if they wished to do so, they would choose for him among those good medicines one which they knew he would willingly swallow. If, moreover, they knew that rejection of the remedy they offered him would augment his

sickness to the point of making it fatal, one could not help saying that, despite all their exhortations, they must certainly be desirous of the sick man's death.'

God wishes to save all men: that means that he would save them if men themselves did not prevent it, and did not refuse to receive his grace; and he is not bound or prompted by reason always to overcome their evil will. He does so sometimes nevertheless, when superior reasons allow of it, and when his consequent and decretory will, which results from all his reasons, makes him resolve upon the election of a certain number of men. He gives aids to all for their conversion and for perseverance, and these aids suffice in those who have good will, but they do not always suffice to give good will. Men obtain this good will either through particular aids or through circumstances which cause the success of the general aids. God cannot refrain from offering other remedies which he knows men will reject, bringing upon themselves all the greater guilt: but shall one wish that God be unjust in order that man may be less criminal? Moreover, the grace that does not serve the one may serve the other, and indeed always serves the totality of God's plan, which is the best possible in conception. Shall God not give the rain, because there are low-lying places which will be thereby incommoded? Shall the sun not shine as much as it should for the world in general, because there are places which will be too much dried up in consequence? In short, all these comparisons, spoken of in these maxims that M. Bayle has just given, of a physician, a benefactor, a minister of State, a prince, are exceedingly lame, because it is well known what their duties are and what can and ought to be the object of their cares: they have scarce more than the one affair, and they often fail therein through negligence or malice. God's object has in it something infinite, his cares embrace the universe: what we know thereof is almost nothing, and we desire to gauge his wisdom and his goodness by our knowledge. What temerity, or rather what absurdity! The objections are on false assumptions; it is senseless to pass judgement on the point of law when one does not know the matter of fact. To say with St. Paul, *O altitudo divitiarum et sapientiae,* is not renouncing reason, it is rather employing the reasons that we know, for they teach us that immensity of God whereof the Apostle speaks. But therein we confess our ignorance of the facts, and we acknowledge, moreover, before we see it, that

God does all the best possible, in accordance with the infinite wisdom which guides his actions. It is true that we have already before our eyes proofs and tests of this, when we see something entire, some whole complete in itself, and isolated, so to speak, among the works of God. Such a whole, shaped as it were by the hand of God, is a plant, an animal, a man. We cannot wonder enough at the beauty and the contrivance of its structure. But when we see some broken bone, some piece of animal's flesh, some sprig of a plant, there appears to be nothing but confusion, unless an excellent anatomist observe it: and even he would recognize nothing therein if he had not before seen like pieces attached to their whole. It is the same with the government of God: that which we have been able to see hitherto is not a large enough piece for recognition of the beauty and the order of the whole. Thus the very nature of things implies that this order in the Divine City, which we see not yet here on earth, should be an object of our faith, of our hope, of our confidence in God. If there are any who think otherwise, so much the worse for them, they are malcontents in the State of the greatest and the best of all monarchs; and they are wrong not to take advantage of the examples he has given them of his wisdom and his infinite goodness, whereby he reveals himself as being not only wonderful, but also worthy of love beyond all things.

135. I hope it will be found that nothing of what is comprised in the nineteen maxims of M. Bayle, which we have just considered, has been left without a necessary answer. It is likely that, having often before meditated on this subject, he will have put there all his strongest convictions touching the moral cause of moral evil. There are, however, still sundry passages here and there in his works which it will be well not to pass over in silence. Very often he exaggerates the difficulty which he assumes with regard to freeing God from the imputation of sin. He observes (*Reply to the Questions of a Provincial*, ch. 161, p. 1024) that Molina, if he reconciled free will with foreknowledge, did not reconcile the goodness and the holiness of God with sin. He praises the sincerity of those who bluntly declare (as he claims Piscator did) that everything is to be traced back to the will of God, and who maintain that God could not but be just, even though he were the author of sin, even though he condemned innocence. And on the other side, or in other passages, he seems to show more approval

of the opinions of those who preserve God's goodness at the expense of his greatness, as Plutarch does in his book against the Stoics. 'It was more reasonable', he says, 'to say' (with the Epicureans) 'that innumerable parts' (or atoms flying about at haphazard through an infinite space) 'by their force prevailed over the weakness of Jupiter and, in spite of him and against his nature and will, did many bad and irrational things, than to agree that there is neither confusion nor wickedness but he is the author thereof.' What may be said for both these parties, Stoics and Epicureans, appears to have led M. Bayle to the ἐπέχειν of the Pyrrhonians, the suspension of his judgement in respect of reason, so long as faith is set apart; and to that he professes sincere submission.

136. Pursuing his arguments, however, he has gone as far as attempting almost to revive and reinforce those of the disciples of Manes, a Persian heretic of the third century after Christ, or of a certain Paul, chief of the Manichaeans in Armenia in the seventh century, from whom they were named Paulicians. All these heretics renewed what an ancient philosopher of Upper Asia, known under the name of Zoroaster, had taught, so it is said, of two intelligent principles of all things, the one good, the other bad, a dogma that had perhaps come from the Indians. Among them numbers of people still cling to their error, one that is exceedingly prone to overtake human ignorance and superstition, since very many barbarous peoples, even in America, have been deluded by it, without having had need of philosophy. The Slavs (according to Helmold) had their Zernebog or black God. The Greeks and Romans, wise as they seem to be, had a Vejovis or Anti-Jupiter, otherwise called Pluto, and numerous other maleficent divinities. The Goddess Nemesis took pleasure in abasing those who were too fortunate; and Herodotus in some passages hints at his belief that all Divinity is envious; which, however, is not in harmony with the doctrine of the two principles.

137. Plutarch, in his treatise *On Isis and Osiris*, knows of no writer more ancient than Zoroaster the magician, as he calls him, that is likely to have taught the two principles. Trogus or Justin makes him a King of the Bactrians, who was conquered by Ninus or Semiramis; he attributes to him the knowledge of astronomy and the invention of magic. But this magic was apparently the religion of the fire-worshippers: and it appears that he looked upon

light and heat as the good principle, while he added the evil, that is to say, opacity, darkness, cold. Pliny cites the testimony of a certain Hermippus, an interpreter of Zoroaster's books, according to whom Zoroaster was a disciple in the art of magic to one named Azonacus; unless indeed this be a corruption of Oromases, of whom I shall speak presently, and whom Plato in the *Alcibiades* names as the father of Zoroaster. Modern Orientals give the name Zerdust to him whom the Greeks named Zoroaster; he is regarded as corresponding to Mercury, because with some nations Wednesday (*mercredi*) takes its name from him. It is difficult to disentangle the story of Zoroaster and know exactly when he lived. Suidas puts him five hundred years before the taking of Troy. Some Ancients cited by Pliny and Plutarch took it to be ten times as far back. But Xanthus the Lydian (in the preface to Diogenes Laertius) put him only six hundred years before the expedition of Xerxes. Plato declares in the same passage, as M. Bayle observes, that the magic of Zoroaster was nothing but the study of religion. Mr. Hyde in his book on the religion of the ancient Persians tries to justify this magic, and to clear it not only of the crime of impiety but also of idolatry. Fire-worship prevailed among the Persians and the Chaldaeans also; it is thought that Abraham left it when he departed from Ur of the Chaldees. Mithras was the sun and he was also the God of the Persians; and according to Ovid's account horses were offered in sacrifice to him,

> *Placat equo Persis radiis Hyperiona cinctum,*
> *Ne detur celeri victima tarda Deo.*

But Mr. Hyde believes that they only made use of the sun and fire in their worship as symbols of the Divinity. It may be necessary to distinguish, as elsewhere, between the Wise and the Multitude. There are in the splendid ruins of Persepolis or of Tschelminaar (which means forty columns) sculptured representations of their ceremonies. An ambassador of Holland had had them sketched at very great cost by a painter, who had devoted a considerable time to the task: but by some chance or other these sketches fell into the hands of a well-known traveller, M. Chardin, according to what he tells us himself. It would be a pity if they were lost. These ruins are one of the most ancient and most beautiful monuments of the earth; and in this respect I wonder at such lack of curiosity in a century so curious as ours.

138. The ancient Greeks and the modern Orientals agree in saying that Zoroaster called the good God Oromazes, or rather Oromasdes, and the evil God Arimanius. When I pondered on the fact that great princes of Upper Asia had the name of Hormisdas and that Irminius or Herminius was the name of a god or ancient hero of the Scythian Celts, that is, of the Germani, it occurred to me that this Arimanius or Irminius might have been a great conqueror of very ancient time coming from the west, just as Genghis Khan and Tamburlaine were later, coming from the east. Arimanius would therefore have come from the north-west, that is, from Germania and Sarmatia, through the territory of the Alani and Massagetae, to raid the dominions of one Ormisdas, a great king in Upper Asia, just as other Scythians did in the days of Cyaxares, King of the Medes, according to the account given by Herodotus. The monarch governing civilized peoples, and working to defend them against the barbarians, would have gone down to posterity, amongst the same peoples, as the good god; but the chief of these devastators will have become the symbol of the evil principle: that is altogether reasonable. It appears from this same mythology that these two princes contended for long, but that neither of them was victorious. Thus they both held their own, just as the two principles shared the empire of the world according to the hypothesis attributed to Zoroaster.

139. It remains to be proved that an ancient god or hero of the Germani was called Herman, Arimanius or Irminius. Tacitus relates that the three tribes which composed Germania, the Ingaevones, the Istaevones and the Herminones or Hermiones, were thus named from the three sons of Mannus. Whether that be true or not, he wished in any case to indicate that there was a hero named Herminius, from whom he was told the Herminones were named. Herminones, Hermenner, Hermunduri all mean the same, that is, Soldiers. Even in the Dark Ages Arimanni were *viri militares*, and there is *feudum Arimandiae* in Lombard law.

140. I have shown elsewhere that apparently the name of one part of Germania was given to the whole, and that from these Herminones or Hermunduri all the Teutonic peoples were named *Hermanni* or *Germani*. The difference between these two words is only in the force of the aspiration: there is the same difference of initial letter between the *Germani* of the Latins and *Hermanos* of the Spaniards, or in the *Gammarus* of the Latins and the *Hummer* (that is,

marine crayfish) of the Low Germans. Besides it is very usual for
one part of a nation to give the name to the whole: so all the
Germani were called Alemanni by the French, and yet this,
according to the old nomenclature, only applied to the Suabians
and the Swiss. Although Tacitus did not actually know the origin
of the name of the Germani, he said something which supports my
opinion, when he observed that it was a name which inspired
terror, taken or given *ob metum*. In fact it signifies a warrior:
Heer, Hari is army, whence comes *Hariban*, or 'call to Haro', that is,
a general order to be with the army, since corrupted into *Arrière-
ban*. Thus Hariman or Ariman, German *Guerre-man*, is a soldier.
For as *Hari, Heer* means army, so *Wehr* signifies arms, *Wehren* to
fight, to make war, the word *Guerre, Guerra* coming doubtless from
the same source. I have already spoken of the *feudum Arimandiae*:
not only did Herminones or Germani signify the same, but also
that ancient Herman, so-called son of Mannus, appears to have
been given this name as being pre-eminently a warrior.

141. Now it is not the passage in Tacitus only which indicates
for us this god or hero: we cannot doubt the existence of one of this
name among these peoples, since Charlemagne found and
destroyed near the Weser the column called *Irminsäule*, erected in
honour of this god. And that combined with the passage in
Tacitus leaves us with the conclusion that it was not that
famous Arminius who was an enemy of the Romans, but a
much greater and more ancient hero, that this cult concerned.
Arminius bore the same name as those who are called Hermann
to-day. Arminius was not great enough, nor fortunate enough, nor
well enough known throughout Germania to attain to the honour
of a public cult, even at the hands of remote tribes, like the Saxons,
who came long after him into the country of the Cherusci. And
our Arminius, taken by the Asiatics for the evil God, provides
ample confirmation of my opinion. For in these matters conjec-
tures confirm one another without any logical circle, when their
foundations tend towards one and the same end.

142. It is not beyond belief that the Hermes (that is, Mercury)
of the Greeks is the same Herminius or Arimanius. He may have
been an inventor or promoter of the arts and of a slightly more
civilized life among his own people and in the countries where he
held supremacy, while amongst his enemies he was looked upon
as the author of confusion. Who knows but that he may have

ESSAYS ON THE JUSTICE OF GOD AND THE

penetrated even into Egypt, like the Scythians who in pursuit of
Sesostris came nearly so far. Theut, Menes and Hermes were
known and revered in Egypt. They might have been Tuiscon, his
son Mannus and Herman, son of Mannus, according to the
genealogy of Tacitus. Menes is held to be the most ancient king of
the Egyptians; 'Theut' was with them a name for Mercury. At
least Theut or Tuiscon, from whom Tacitus derives the descent of
the Germani, and from whom the Teutons, *Tuitsche* (that is,
Germani) even to-day have their name, is the same as that
Teutates who according to Lucan was worshipped by the Gauls,
and whom Caesar took *pro Dite Patre*, for Pluto, because of the
resemblance between his Latin name and that of *Teut* or *Thiet,
Titan, Theodon*; this in ancient times signified men, people, and
also an excellent man (like the word ' baron '), in short, a prince.
There are authorities for all these significations: but one must not
delay over this point. Herr Otto Sperling, who is well known for
various learned writings, but has many more in readiness to
appear, in a special dissertation has treated the question of this
Teutates, God of the Celts. Some observations which I imparted
to him on that subject have been published, with his reply, in the
Literary News of the Baltic Sea. He interprets this passage from Lucan
somewhat otherwise than I do:

> *Teutates, pollensque feris altaribus Hesus,*
> *Et Tamaris Scythicae non mitior ara Dianae.*

Hesus was, it appears, the God of War, who was called Ares by the
Greeks and Erich by the ancient Germani, whence still remains
Erichtag, Tuesday. The letters R and S, which are produced by
the same organ, are easily interchanged, for instance: *Moor* and
Moos, Geren and *Gesen, Er war* and *Er was, Fer, Hierro, Eiron, Eisen.*
Likewise *Papisius, Valesius, Fusius,* instead of *Papirius, Valerius,
Furius,* with the ancient Romans. As for Taramis or perhaps
Taranis, one knows that *Taran* was the thunder, or the God of
Thunder, with the ancient Celts, called *Thor* by the Germani of
the north; whence the English have preserved the name 'Thurs-
day', *jeudi, diem Jovis*. And the passage from Lucan means that the
altar of Taran, God of the Celts, was not less cruel than that of
Diana in Tauris: *Taranis aram non mitiorem ara Dianae Scythicae
fuisse.*

143. It is also not impossible that there was a time when the

western or Celtic princes made themselves masters of Greece, of
Egypt and a good part of Asia, and that their cult remained in
those countries. When one considers with what rapidity the Huns,
the Saracens and the Tartars gained possession of a great part of
our continent one will be the less surprised at this; and it is confirmed
by the great number of words in the Greek and German tongues
which correspond so closely. Callimachus, in a hymn in honour of
Apollo, seems to imply that the Celts who attacked the Temple at
Delphi, under their Brennus, or chief, were descendants of the
ancient Titans and Giants who made war on Jupiter and the other
gods, that is to say, on the Princes of Asia and of Greece. It may
be that Jupiter is himself descended from the Titans or Theodons,
that is, from the earlier Celto-Scythian princes; and the material
collected by the late Abbé de la Charmoye in his *Celtic Origins*
conforms to that possibility. Yet there are opinions on other
matters in this work by this learned writer which to me do not
appear probable, especially when he excludes the Germani from
the number of the Celts, not having recalled sufficiently the facts
given by ancient writers and not being sufficiently aware of the
relation between the ancient Gallic and Germanic tongues. Now
the so-called Giants, who wished to scale the heavens, were new
Celts who followed the path of their ancestors; and Jupiter,
although of their kindred, as it were, was constrained to resist
them. Just so did the Visigoths established in Gallic territory
resist, together with the Romans, other peoples of Germania and
Scythia, who succeeded them under Attila their leader, he being
at that time in control of the Scythian, Sarmatic and Germanic
tribes from the frontiers of Persia up to the Rhine. But the pleasure
one feels when one thinks to find in the mythologies of the gods
some trace of the old history of fabulous times has perhaps carried
me too far, and I know not whether I shall have been any more
successful than Goropius Becanus, Schrieckius, Herr Rudbeck
and the Abbé de la Charmoye.

144. Let us return to Zoroaster, who led us to Oromasdes and
Arimanius, the sources of good and evil, and let us assume that
he looked upon them as two eternal principles opposed to each
other, although there is reason to doubt this assumption. It is
thought that Marcion, disciple of Cerdon, was of this opinion
before Manes. M. Bayle acknowledges that these men used lament-
able arguments; but he thinks that they did not sufficiently

recognize their advantages or know how to apply their principal instrument, which was the difficulty over the origin of evil. He believes that an able man on their side would have thoroughly embarrassed the orthodox, and it seems as though he himself, failing any other, wished to undertake a task so unnecessary in the opinion of many people. 'All the hypotheses' (he says, *Dictionary*, v., 'Marcion', p. 2039) 'that Christians have established parry but poorly the blows aimed at them: they all triumph when they act on the offensive; but they lose their whole advantage when they have to sustain the attack.' He confesses that the 'Dualists' (as with Mr. Hyde he calls them), that is, the champions of two principles, would soon have been routed by *a priori* reasons, taken from the nature of God; but he thinks that they triumph in their turn when one comes to the *a posteriori* reasons, which are taken from the existence of evil.

145. He treats of the matter with abundant detail in his *Dictionary*, article 'Manichaeans', p. 2025, which we must examine a little, in order to throw greater light upon this subject: 'The surest and clearest ideas of order teach us', he says, 'that a Being who exists through himself, who is necessary, who is eternal, must be single, infinite, all powerful, and endowed with all kinds of perfections.' This argument deserves to have been developed more completely. 'Now it is necessary to see', he goes on, 'if the phenomena of nature can be conveniently explained by the hypothesis of one single principle.' I have explained it sufficiently by showing that there are cases where some disorder in the part is necessary for producing the greatest order in the whole. But it appears that M. Bayle asks a little too much: he wishes for a detailed exposition of how evil is connected with the best possible scheme for the universe. That would be a complete explanation of the phenomena: but I do not undertake to give it; nor am I bound to do so, for there is no obligation to do that which is impossible for us in our existing state. It is sufficient for me to point out that there is nothing to prevent the connexion of a certain individual evil with what is the best on the whole. This incomplete explanation, leaving something to be discovered in the life to come, is sufficient for answering the objections, though not for a comprehension of the matter.

146. 'The heavens and all the rest of the universe', adds M. Bayle, 'preach the glory, the power, the oneness of God.' Thence

the conclusion should have been drawn that this is the case (as I have already observed above) because there is seen in these objects something entire and isolated, so to speak. Every time we see such a work of God, we find it so perfect that we must wonder at the contrivance and the beauty thereof: but when we do not see an entire work, when we only look upon scraps and fragments, it is no wonder if the good order is not evident there. Our planetary system composes such an isolated work, which is complete also when it is taken by itself; each plant, each animal, each man furnishes one such work, to a certain point of perfection: one recognizes therein the wonderful contrivance of the author. But the human kind, so far as it is known to us, is only a fragment, only a small portion of the City of God or of the republic of Spirits, which has an extent too great for us, and whereof we know too little, to be able to observe the wonderful order therein. 'Man alone,' says M. Bayle, 'that masterpiece of his Creator among things visible, man alone, I say, gives rise to great objections with regard to the oneness of God.' Claudian made the same observation, unburdening his heart in these well-known lines:

Saepe mihi dubiam traxit sententia mentem, etc.

But the harmony existing in all the rest allows of a strong presumption that it would exist also in the government of men, and generally in that of Spirits, if the whole were known to us. One must judge the works of God as wisely as Socrates judged those of Heraclitus in these words: What I have understood thereof pleases me; I think that the rest would please me no less if I understood it.

147. Here is another particular reason for the disorder apparent in that which concerns man. It is that God, in giving him intelligence, has presented him with an image of the Divinity. He leaves him to himself, in a sense, in his small department, *ut Spartam quam nactus est ornet*. He enters there only in a secret way, for he supplies being, force, life, reason, without showing himself. It is there that free will plays its game: and God makes game (so to speak) of these little Gods that he has thought good to produce, as we make game of children who follow pursuits which we secretly encourage or hinder according as it pleases us. Thus man is there like a little god in his own world or *Microcosm*, which he governs

after his own fashion: he sometimes performs wonders therein, and his art often imitates nature.

> *Jupiter in parvo cum cerneret aethera vitro,*
> *Risit et ad Superos talia dicta dedit:*
> *Huccine mortalis progressa potentia, Divi?*
> *Jam meus in fragili luditur orbe labor.*
> *Jura poli rerumque fidem legesque Deorum*
> *Cuncta Syracusius transtulit arte Senex.*
> *Quid falso insontem tonitru Salmonea miror?*
> *Aemula Naturae est parva reperta manus.*

But he also commits great errors, because he abandons himself to the passions, and because God abandons him to his own way. God punishes him also for such errors, now like a father or tutor, training or chastising children, now like a just judge, punishing those who forsake him: and evil comes to pass most frequently when these intelligences or their small worlds come into collision. Man finds himself the worse for this, in proportion to his fault; but God, by a wonderful art, turns all the errors of these little worlds to the greater adornment of his great world. It is as in those devices of perspective, where certain beautiful designs look like mere confusion until one restores them to the right angle of vision or one views them by means of a certain glass or mirror. It is by placing and using them properly that one makes them serve as adornment for a room. Thus the apparent deformities of our little worlds combine to become beauties in the great world, and have nothing in them which is opposed to the oneness of an infinitely perfect universal principle: on the contrary, they increase our wonder at the wisdom of him who makes evil serve the greater good.

148. M. Bayle continues: 'that man is wicked and miserable; that there are everywhere prisons and hospitals; that history is simply a collection of the crimes and calamities of the human race.' I think that there is exaggeration in that: there is incomparably more good than evil in the life of men, as there are incomparably more houses than prisons. With regard to virtue and vice, a certain mediocrity prevails. Machiavelli has already observed that there are few very wicked and very good men, and that this causes the failure of many great enterprises. I find it a great fault in historians that they keep their mind on the evil more

than on the good. The chief end of history, as also of poetry, should be to teach prudence and virtue by examples, and then to display vice in such a way as to create aversion to it and to prompt men to avoid it, or serve towards that end.

149. M. Bayle avows: 'that one finds everywhere both moral good and physical good, some examples of virtue, some examples of happiness, and that this is what makes the difficulty. For if there were only wicked and unhappy people', he says, 'there would be no need to resort to the hypothesis of the two principles.' I wonder that this admirable man could have evinced so great an inclination towards this opinion of the two principles; and I am surprised at his not having taken into account that this romance of human life, which makes the universal history of the human race, lay fully devised in the divine understanding, with innumerable others, and that the will of God only decreed its existence because this sequence of events was to be most in keeping with the rest of things, to bring forth the best result. And these apparent faults in the whole world, these spots on a Sun whereof ours is but a ray, rather enhance its beauty than diminish it, contributing towards that end by obtaining a greater good. There are in truth two principles, but they are both in God, to wit, his understanding and his will. The understanding furnishes the principle of evil, without being sullied by it, without being evil; it represents natures as they exist in the eternal verities; it contains within it the reason wherefore evil is permitted: but the will tends only towards good. Let us add a third principle, namely power; it precedes even understanding and will, but it operates as the one displays it and as the other requires it.

150. Some (like Campanella) have called these three perfections of God the three primordialities. Many have even believed that there was therein a secret connexion with the Holy Trinity: that power relates to the Father, that is, to the source of Divinity, wisdom to the Eternal Word, which is called λόγος by the most sublime of the Evangelists, and will or Love to the Holy Spirit. Well-nigh all the expressions or comparisons derived from the nature of the intelligent substance tend that way.

151. It seems to me that if M. Bayle had taken into account what I have just said of the principles of things, he would have answered his own questions, or at the least he would not have continued to ask, as he does in these which follow: 'If man is the work

of a single principle supremely good, supremely holy, supremely powerful, can he be subject to diseases, to cold, heat, hunger, thirst, pain, grief? Can he have so many evil tendencies? Can he commit so many crimes? Can supreme goodness produce an unhappy creature? Shall not supreme power, united to an infinite goodness, shower blessings upon its work, and shall it not banish all that might offend or grieve?' Prudentius in his *Hamartigenia* presented the same difficulty:

> *Si non vult Deus esse malum, cur non vetat? inquit.*
> *Non refert auctor fuerit, factorve malorum.*
> *Anne opera in vitium sceleris pulcherrima verti,*
> *Cum possit prohibere, sinat; quod si velit omnes*
> *Innocuos agere Omnipotens, ne sancta voluntas*
> *Degeneret, facto nec se manus inquinet ullo?*
> *Condidit ergo malum Dominus, quod spectat ab alto,*
> *Et patitur fierique probat, tanquam ipse crearit.*
> *Ipse creavit enim, quod si discludere possit,*
> *Non abolet, longoque sinit grassarier usu.*

But I have already answered that sufficiently. Man is himself the source of his evils: just as he is, he was in the divine idea. God, prompted by essential reasons of wisdom, decreed that he should pass into existence just as he is. M. Bayle would perchance have perceived this origin of evil in the form in which I demonstrate it here, if he had herein combined the wisdom of God with his power, his goodness and his holiness. I will add, in passing, that his *holiness* is nothing other than the highest degree of goodness, just as the crime which is its opposite is the worst of all evil.

152. M. Bayle places the Greek philosopher Melissus, champion of the oneness of the first principle (and perhaps even of the oneness of substance) in conflict with Zoroaster, as with the first originator of duality. Zoroaster admits that the hypothesis of Melissus is more consistent with order and *a priori* reasons, but he denies its conformity with experience and *a posteriori* reasons. 'I surpass you', he said, 'in the explanation of phenomena, which is the principal mark of a good system.' But, in my opinion, it is not a very good explanation of a phenomenon to assign to it an *ad hoc* principle: to evil, a *principium maleficum*, to cold, a *primum frigidum*; there is nothing so easy and nothing so dull. It is well-nigh as if someone were to say that the

Peripatetics surpass the new mathematicians in the explanation of the phenomena of the stars, by giving them *ad hoc* intelligences to guide them. According to that, it is quite easy to conceive why the planets make their way with such precision; whereas there is need of much geometry and reflexion to understand how from the gravity of the planets, which bears them towards the sun, combined with some whirlwind which carries them along, or with their own motive force, can spring the elliptic movement of Kepler, which satisfies appearances so well. A man incapable of relishing deep speculations will at first applaud the Peripatetics and will treat our mathematicians as dreamers. Some old Galenist will do the same with regard to the faculties of the Schoolmen: he will admit a chylific, a chymific and a sanguific, and he will assign one of these *ad hoc* to each operation; he will think he has worked wonders, and will laugh at what he will call the chimeras of the moderns, who claim to explain through mechanical structure what passes in the body of an animal.

153. The explanation of the cause of evil by a particular principle, *per principium maleficum*, is of the same nature. Evil needs no such explanation, any more than do cold and darkness: there is neither *primum frigidum* nor principle of darkness. Evil itself comes only from privation; the positive enters therein only by concomitance, as the active enters by concomitance into cold. We see that water in freezing is capable of breaking a gun-barrel wherein it is confined; and yet cold is a certain privation of force, it only comes from the diminution of a movement which separates the particles of fluids. When this separating motion becomes weakened in the water by the cold, the particles of compressed air concealed in the water collect; and, becoming larger, they become more capable of acting outwards through their buoyancy. The resistance which the surfaces of the proportions of air meet in the water, and which opposes the force exerted by these portions towards dilation, is far less, and consequently the effect of the air greater, in large air-bubbles than in small, even though these small bubbles combined should form as great a mass as the large. For the resistances, that is, the surfaces, increase by the *square*, and the forces, that is, the contents or the volumes of the spheres of compressed air, increase by the *cube*, of their diameters. Thus it is *by accident* that privation involves action and force. I have already shown how privation is enough to cause error and malice, and

how God is prompted to permit them, despite that there be no malignity in him. Evil comes from privation; the positive and action spring from it by accident, as force springs from cold.

154. The statement that M. Bayle attributes to the Paulicians, p. 2323, is not conclusive, to wit, that free will must come from two principles, to the end that it may have power to turn towards good and towards evil: for, being simple in itself, it should rather have come from a neutral principle if this argument held good. But free will tends towards good, and if it meets with evil it is by accident, for the reason that this evil is concealed beneath the good, and masked, as it were. These words which Ovid ascribes to Medea,

Video meliora proboque,
Deteriora sequor,

imply that the morally good is mastered by the agreeably good, which makes more impression on souls when they are disturbed by the passions.

155. Furthermore, M. Bayle himself supplies Melissus with a good answer; but a little later he disputes it. Here are his words, p. 2025: 'If Melissus consults the notions of order, he will answer that man was not wicked when God made him; he will say that man received from God a happy state, but that not having followed the light of conscience, which in accordance with the intention of its author should have guided him along the path of virtue, he has become wicked, and has deserved that God the supremely good should make him feel the effects of his anger. It is therefore not God who is the cause of moral evil: but he is the cause of physical evil, that is, of the punishment of moral evil. And this punishment, far from being incompatible with the supremely good principle, of necessity emanates from that one of its attributes, I mean its justice, which is not less essential to it than its goodness. This answer, the most reasonable that Melissus can give, is fundamentally good and sound, but it may be disputed by something more specious and more dazzling. For indeed Zoroaster objects that the infinitely good principle ought to have created man not only without actual evil, but also without the inclination towards evil; that God, having foreseen sin with all its consequences, ought to have prevented it; that he ought to have impelled man to moral good, and not to have allowed him any force for tending towards crime.' That is quite easy to say, but it is not

practicable if one follows the principles of order: it could not have been accomplished without perpetual miracles. Ignorance, error and malice follow one another naturally in animals made as we are: should this species, then, have been missing in the universe? I have no doubt but that it is too important there, despite all its weaknesses, for God to have consented to its abolition.

156. M. Bayle, in the article entitled 'Paulicians' inserted by him in his *Dictionary*, follows up the pronouncements he made in the article on the Manichaeans. According to him (p. 2330, lit. H) the orthodox seem to admit two first principles, in making the devil the originator of sin. M. Becker, a former minister of Amsterdam, author of the book entitled *The World Bewitched*, has made use of this idea in order to demonstrate that one should not assign such power and authority to the Devil as would allow of his comparison with God. Therein he is right: but he pushes the conclusions too far. And the author of the book entitled 'Ἀποκατάστασις Πάντων believes that if the Devil had never been vanquished and despoiled, if he had always kept his prey, if the title of invincible had belonged to him, that would have done injury to the glory of God. But it is a poor advantage to keep those whom one has led astray in order to share their punishment for ever. And as for the cause of evil, it is true that the Devil is the author of sin. But the origin of sin comes from farther away, its source is in the original imperfection of creatures: that renders them capable of sinning, and there are circumstances in the sequence of things which cause this power to evince itself in action.

157. The devils were angels like the rest before their fall, and it is thought that their leader was one of the chief among angels; but Scripture is not explicit enough on that point. The passage of the Apocalypse that speaks of the struggle with the Dragon, as of a vision, leaves much in doubt, and does not sufficiently develop a subject which by the other sacred writers is hardly mentioned. It is not in place here to enter into this discussion, and one must still admit that the common opinion agrees best with the sacred text. M. Bayle examines some replies of St. Basil, of Lactantius and others on the origin of evil. As, however, they are concerned with physical evil, I postpone discussion thereof, and I will proceed with the examination of the difficulties over the moral cause of moral evil, which arise in several passages of the works of our gifted author.

158. He disputes the *permission* of this evil, he would wish one to admit that God *wills* it. He quotes these words of Calvin (on Genesis, ch. 3): 'The ears of some are offended when one says that God willed it. But I ask you, what else is the permission of him who is entitled to forbid, or rather who has the thing in his own hands, but an act of will?' M. Bayle explains these words of Calvin, and those which precede them, as if he admitted that God willed the fall of Adam, not in so far as it was a crime, but under some other conception that is unknown to us. He quotes casuists who are somewhat lax, who say that a son can desire the death of his father, not in so far as it is an evil for himself but in so far as it is a good for his heirs (*Reply to the Questions of a Provincial*, ch. 147, p. 850). It seems to me that Calvin only says that God willed man's fall for some reason unknown to us. In the main, when it is a question of a decisive will, that is, of a decree, these distinctions are useless: one wills the action with all its qualities, if it is true that one wills it. But when it is a crime, God can only will the permission of it: the crime is neither an end nor a means, it is only a *conditio sine qua non*; thus it is not the object of a direct will, as I have already demonstrated above. God cannot prevent it without acting against what he owes to himself, without doing something that would be worse than the crime of man, without violating the rule of the best; and that would be to destroy divinity, as I have already observed. God is therefore bound by a moral necessity, which is in himself, to permit moral evil in creatures. There is precisely the case wherein the will of a wise mind is only permissive. I have already said this: he is bound to permit the crime of others when he cannot prevent it without himself failing in that which he owes to himself.

159. 'But among all these infinite combinations', says M. Bayle (p. 853), 'it pleased God to choose one wherein Adam was to sin, and by his decree he made it, in preference to all the others, the plan that should come to pass.' Very good; that is speaking my language; so long as one applies it to the combinations which compose the whole universe. 'You will therefore never make us understand', he adds, 'how God did not will that Eve and Adam should sin, since he rejected all the combinations wherein they would not have sinned.' But the thing is in general very easy to understand, from all that I have just said. This combination that makes the whole universe is the best; God therefore could not

refrain from choosing it without incurring a lapse, and rather than incur such, a thing altogether inappropriate to him, he permits the lapse or the sin of man which is involved in this combination.

160. M. Jacquelot, with other able men, does not differ in opinion from me, when for example he says, p. 186 of his treatise on the *Conformity of Faith with Reason*: 'Those who are puzzled by these difficulties seem to be too limited in their outlook, and to wish to reduce all God's designs to their own interests. When God formed the universe, his whole prospect was himself and his own glory, so that if we had knowledge of all creatures, of their diverse combinations and of their different relations, we should understand without difficulty that the universe corresponds perfectly to the infinite wisdom of the Almighty.' He says elsewhere (p. 232): 'Supposing the impossible, that God could not prevent the wrong use of free will without destroying it, it will be agreed that since his wisdom and his glory determined him to form free creatures this powerful reason must have prevailed over the grievous consequences which their freedom might have.' I have endeavoured to develop this still further through *the reason of the best and the moral necessity* which led God to make this choice, despite the sin of some creatures which is involved therein. I think that I have cut down to the root of the difficulty; nevertheless I am well pleased, for the sake of throwing more light on the matter, to apply my principle of solution to the peculiar difficulties of M. Bayle.

161. Here is one, set forth in these terms (ch. 148, p. 856): 'Would it in a prince be a mark of his kindness: 1. To give to a hundred messengers as much money as is needed for a journey of two hundred leagues? 2. To promise a recompense to all those who should finish the journey without having borrowed anything, and to threaten with imprisonment all those whom their money should not have sufficed? 3. To make choice of a hundred persons, of whom he would know for certain that there were but two who should earn the recompense, the ninety-eight others being destined to find on the way either a mistress or a gamester or some other thing which would make them incur expenses, and which he would himself have been at pains to dispose in certain places along their path? 4. To imprison actually ninety-eight of these messengers on the moment of their return? Is it not abundantly evident that he would have no kindness for them, and that on the contrary he would intend for them, not the proposed recompense,

but prison? They would deserve it, certainly; but he who had wished them to deserve it and placed them in the sure way towards deserving it, should he be worthy of being called kind, on the pretext that he had recompensed the two others?' It would doubtless not be on that account that he earned the title of 'kind'. Yet other circumstances may contribute, which would avail to render him worthy of praise for having employed this artifice in order to know those people, and to make trial of them; just as Gideon made use of some extraordinary means of choosing the most valiant and the least squeamish among his soldiers. And even if the prince were to know already the disposition of all these messengers, may he not put them to this test in order to make them known also to the others? Even though these reasons be not applicable to God, they make it clear, nevertheless, that an action like that of this prince may appear preposterous when it is detached from the circumstances indicating its cause. All the more must one deem that God has acted well, and that we should see this if we fully knew of all that he has done.

162. M. Descartes, in a letter to the Princess Elizabeth (vol. 1, letter 10) has made use of another comparison to reconcile human freedom with the omnipotence of God. 'He imagines a monarch who has forbidden duels, and who, knowing for certain that two noblemen, if they meet, will fight, takes sure steps to bring about their meeting. They meet indeed, they fight: their disobedience of the law is an effect of their free will, they are punishable. What a king can do in such a case (he adds) concerning some free actions of his subjects, God, who has infinite foreknowledge and power, certainly does concerning all those of men. Before he sent us into this world he knew exactly what all the tendencies of our will would be: he has endued us therewith, he also has disposed all other things that are outside us, to cause such and such objects to present themselves to our senses at such and such a time. He knew that as a result of this our free will would determine us toward some particular thing, and he has willed it thus; but he has not for that willed to constrain our free will thereto. In this king one may distinguish two different degrees of will, the one whereby he willed that these noblemen should fight, since he brought about their meeting, and the other whereby he did not will it, since he forbade duels. Even so theologians distinguish in God an absolute and independent will, whereby he wills that all things be done

just as they are done, and another which is relative, and which concerns the merit or demerit of men, whereby he wills that his Laws be obeyed' (Descartes, letter 10 of vol. 1, pp. 51, 52. Compare with that the quotation made by M. Arnauld, vol. 2, p. 288 *et seqq.* of his *Reflexions on the System of Malebranche*, from Thomas Aquinas, on the antecedent and consequent will of God).

163. Here is M. Bayle's reply to that (*Reply to the Questions of a Provincial*, ch. 154, p. 943): 'This great philosopher is much mistaken, it seems to me. There would not be in this monarch any degree of will, either small or great, that these two noblemen should obey the law, and not fight. He would will entirely and solely that they should fight. That would not exculpate them, they would only follow their passion, they would be unaware that they conformed to the will of their sovereign: but he would be in truth the moral cause of their encounter, and he would not more entirely wish it supposing he were to inspire them with the desire or to give them the order for it. Imagine to yourself two princes each of whom wishes his eldest son to poison himself. One employs constraint, the other contents himself with secretly causing a grief that he knows will be sufficient to induce his son to poison himself. Will you be doubtful whether the will of the latter is less complete than the will of the former? M. Descartes is therefore assuming an unreal fact and does not at all solve the difficulty.'

164. One must confess that M. Descartes speaks somewhat crudely of the will of God in regard to evil in saying not only that God knew that our free will would determine us toward some particular thing, but also *that he also wished it*, albeit he did not will to constrain the will thereto. He speaks no less harshly in the eighth letter of the same volume, saying that not the slightest thought enters into the mind of a man which God does not *will*, and has not willed from all eternity, to enter there. Calvin never said anything harsher; and all that can only be excused if it is to be understood of a permissive will. M. Descartes' solution amounts to the distinction between the will expressed in the sign and the will expressive of the good pleasure (*inter voluntatem signi et bene-placiti*) which the moderns have taken from the Schoolmen as regards the terms, but to which they have given a meaning not usual among the ancients. It is true that God may command something and yet not will that it be done, as when he commanded Abraham to sacrifice his son: he willed the obedience, and he did not

will the action. But when God commands the virtuous action and forbids the sin, he wills indeed that which he ordains, but it is only by an antecedent will, as I have explained more than once.

165. M. Descartes' comparison is therefore not satisfactory; but it may be made so. One must make some change in the facts, inventing some reason to oblige the prince to cause or permit the two enemies to meet. They must, for instance, be together in the army or in other obligatory functions, a circumstance the prince himself cannot hinder without endangering his State. For example, the absence of either of them might be responsible for the disappearance of innumerable persons of his party from the army or cause grumbling among the soldiers and give rise to some great disturbance. In this case, therefore, one may say that the prince does not will the duel: he knows of it, but he permits it notwithstanding, for he prefers permitting the sin of others to committing one himself. Thus this corrected comparison may serve, provided that one observe the difference between God and the prince. The prince is forced into this permission by his powerlessness; a more powerful monarch would have no need of all these considerations; but God, who has power to do all that is possible, only permits sin because it is absolutely impossible to anyone at all to do better. The prince's action is peradventure not free from sorrow and regret. This regret is due to his imperfection, of which he is sensible; therein lies displeasure. God is incapable of such a feeling and finds, moreover, no cause therefor; he is infinitely conscious of his own perfection, and it may even be said that the imperfection in creatures taken individually changes for him into perfection in relation to the whole, and that it is an added glory for the Creator. What more can one wish, when one possesses a boundless wisdom and when one is as powerful as one is wise; when one can do all and when one has the best?

166. Having once understood these things, we are hardened sufficiently, so it seems to me, against the strongest and most spirited objections. I have not concealed them: but there are some we shall merely touch upon, because they are too odious. The Remonstrants and M. Bayle (*Reply to the Questions of a Provincial*, vol. III, ch. 152, end page 919) quote St. Augustine, saying, '*crudelem esse misericordiam velle aliquem miserum esse ut eius miserearis*': in the same sense is cited Seneca *De Benef.*, L. 6, c. 36, 37. I confess that one would have some reason to urge that against those who

believed that God has no other cause for permitting sin than the design to have something wherewith to exercise punitive justice against the majority of men, and his mercy towards a small number of elect. But it must be considered that God had reasons for his permission of sin, more worthy of him and more profound in relation to us. Someone has dared to compare God's course of action with that of a Caligula, who has his edicts written in so small a hand and has them placarded in so high a place that it is not possible to read them; with that of a mother who neglects her daughter's honour in order to attain her own selfish ends; with that of Queen Catherine de Medicis, who is said to have abetted the love-affairs of her ladies in order to learn of the intrigues of the great; and even with that of Tiberius, who arranged, through the extraordinary services of the executioner, that the law forbidding the subjection of a virgin to capital punishment should no longer apply to the case of Sejanus's daughter. This last comparison was proposed by Peter Bertius, then an Armenian, but finally a member of the Roman communion. And a scandalous comparison has been made between God and Tiberius, which is related at length by Andreas Caroli in his *Memorabilia Ecclesiastica* of the last century, as M. Bayle observes. Bertius used it against the Gomarists. I think that arguments of this kind are only valid against those who maintain that justice is an arbitrary thing in relation to God; or that he has a despotic power which can go so far as being able to condemn innocents; or, in short, that good is not the motive of his actions.

167. At that same time an ingenious satire was composed against the Gomarists, entitled *Fur praedestinatus, de gepredestineerde dief,* wherein there is introduced a thief condemned to be hanged, who attributes to God all the evil he has done; who believes himself predestined to salvation notwithstanding his wicked actions; who imagines that this belief is sufficient for him, and who defeats by arguments *ad hominem* a Counter-remonstrant minister called to prepare him for death: but this thief is finally converted by an old pastor who had been dismissed for his Arminianism, whom the gaoler, in pity for the criminal and for the weakness of the minister, had brought to him secretly. Replies were made to this lampoon, but replies to satires never please as much as the satires themselves. M. Bayle (*Reply to the Questions of a Provincial,* vol. III, ch. 154, p. 938) says that this book was printed in England in the

time of Cromwell, and he appears not to have been informed that it was only a translation of the much older original Flemish. He adds that Dr. George Kendal wrote a confutation of it at Oxford in the year 1657, under the title of *Fur pro Tribunali*, and that the dialogue is there inserted. This dialogue presupposes, contrary to the truth, that the Counter-remonstrants make God the cause of evil, and teach a kind of predestination in the Mahometan manner according to which it does not matter whether one does good or evil, and the assumption that one is predestined assures the fact. They by no means go so far. Nevertheless it is true that there are among them some Supralapsarians and others who find it hard to declare themselves in clear terms upon the justice of God and the principles of piety and morals in man. For they imagine despotism in God, and demand that man be convinced, without reason, of the absolute certainty of his election, a course that is liable to have dangerous consequences. But all those who acknowledge that God produces the best plan, having chosen it from among all possible ideas of the universe; that he there finds man inclined by the original imperfection of creatures to misuse his free will and to plunge into misery; that God prevents the sin and the misery in so far as the perfection of the universe, which is an emanation from his, may permit it: those, I say, show forth more clearly that God's intention is the one most right and holy in the world; that the creature alone is guilty, that his original limitation or imperfection is the source of his wickedness, that his evil will is the sole cause of his misery; that one cannot be destined to salvation without also being destined to the holiness of the children of God, and that all hope of election one can have can only be founded upon the good will infused into one's heart by the grace of God.

168. *Metaphysical considerations* also are brought up against my explanation of the moral cause of moral evil; but they will trouble me less since I have dismissed the objections derived from moral reasons, which were more impressive. These metaphysical considerations concern the nature of the *possible* and of the *necessary*; they go against my fundamental assumption that God has chosen the best of all possible worlds. There are philosophers who have maintained that there is nothing possible except that which actually happens. These are those same people who thought or could have thought that all is necessary unconditionally. Some

were of this opinion because they admitted a brute and blind necessity in the cause of the existence of things: and it is these I have most reason for opposing. But there are others who are mistaken only because they misuse terms. They confuse moral necessity with metaphysical necessity: they imagine that since God cannot help acting for the best he is thus deprived of freedom, and things are endued with that necessity which philosophers and theologians endeavour to avoid. With these writers my dispute is only one of words, provided they admit in very deed that God chooses and does the best. But there are others who go further, they think that God could have done better. This is an opinion which must be rejected: for although it does not altogether deprive God of wisdom and goodness, as do the advocates of blind necessity, it sets bounds thereto, thus derogating from God's supreme perfection.

169. The question of the *possibility of things that do not happen* has already been examined by the ancients. It appears that Epicurus, to preserve freedom and to avoid an absolute necessity, maintained, after Aristotle, that contingent futurities were not susceptible of determinate truth. For if it was true yesterday that I should write to-day, it could therefore not fail to happen, it was already necessary; and, for the same reason, it was from all eternity. Thus all that which happens is necessary, and it is impossible for anything different to come to pass. But since that is not so it would follow, according to him, that contingent futurities have no determinate truth. To uphold this opinion, Epicurus went so far as to deny the first and the greatest principle of the truths of reason, he denied that every assertion was either true or false. Here is the way they confounded him: 'You deny that it was true yesterday that I should write to-day; it was therefore false.' The good man, not being able to admit this conclusion, was obliged to say that it was neither true nor false. After that, he needs no refutation, and Chrysippus might have spared himself the trouble he took to prove the great principle of contradictories, following the account by Cicero in his book *De Fato*: 'Contendit omnes nervos Chrysippus ut persuadeat omne 'Aξίωμα aut verum esse aut falsum. Ut enim Epicurus veretur ne si hoc concesserit, concedendum sit, fato fieri quaecunque fiant; si enim alterum ex aeternitate verum sit, esse id etiam certum; si certum, etiam necessarium; ita et necessitatem et fatum confirmari putat; sic Chrysippus metuit ne non, si non

ESSAYS ON THE JUSTICE OF GOD AND THE

obtinuerit omne quod enuncietur aut verum esse aut falsum, omnia fato fieri possint ex causis aeternis rerum futurarum.' M. Bayle observes (*Dictionary*, article 'Epicurus', let. T, p. 1141) 'that neither of these two great philosophers [Epicurus and Chrysippus] understood that the truth of this maxim, every proposition is true or false, is independent of what is called *fatum*: it could not therefore serve as proof of the existence of the *fatum*, as Chrysippus maintained and as Epicurus feared. Chrysippus could not have conceded, without damaging his own position, that there are propositions which are neither true nor false. But he gained nothing by asserting the contrary: for, whether there be free causes or not, it is equally true that this proposition, The Grand Mogul will go hunting to-morrow, is true or false. Men rightly regarded as ridiculous this speech of Tiresias: All that I shall say will happen or not, for great Apollo confers on me the faculty of prophesying. If, assuming the impossible, there were no God, it would yet be certain that everything the greatest fool in the world should predict would happen or would not happen. That is what neither Chrysippus nor Epicurus has taken into consideration.' Cicero, lib. 1, *De Nat. Deorum*, with regard to the evasions of the Epicureans expressed the sound opinion (as M. Bayle observes towards the end of the same page) that it would be much less shameful to admit that one cannot answer one's opponent, than to have recourse to such answers. Yet we shall see that M. Bayle himself confused the certain with the necessary, when he maintained that the choice of the best rendered things necessary.

170. Let us come now to the possibility of things that do not happen, and I will give the very words of M. Bayle, albeit they are somewhat discursive. This is what he says on the matter in his *Dictionary* (article 'Chrysippus', let. S, p. 929): 'The celebrated dispute on things possible and things impossible owed its origin to the doctrine of the Stoics concerning fate. The question was to know whether, among the things which have never been and never will be, there are some possible; or whether all that is not, all that has never been, all that will never be, was impossible. A famous dialectician of the Megaric Sect, named Diodorus, gave a negative answer to the first of these two questions and an affirmative to the second; but Chrysippus vehemently opposed him. Here are two passages of Cicero (epist. 4, lib. 9, *Ad Familiar.*): "περὶ δυνατῶν me scito κατὰ Διόδωρον κρίνειν. Quapropter si

230

venturus es, scito necesse esse te venire. Sin autem non es, τῶν ἀδυνάτων est te venire. Nunc vide utra te κρίσις magis delectet, Χρυσίππεια ne, an haec; quam noster Diodorus [a Stoic who for a long time had lived in Cicero's house] non concoquebat." This is quoted from a letter that Cicero wrote to Varro. He sets forth more comprehensively the whole state of the question, in the little book *De Fato*. I am going to quote a few pieces (Cic., *De Fato*, p. m. 65): "Vigila, Chrysippe, ne tuam causam, in qua tibi cum Diodoro valente Dialectico magna luctatio est, deseras ... omne ergo quod falsum dicitur in futuro, id fieri non potest. At hoc, Chrysippe, minime vis, maximeque tibi de hoc ipso cum Diodoro certamen est. Ille enim id solum fieri posse dicit, quod aut sit verum, aut futurum sit verum; et quicquid futurum sit, id dicit fieri necesse esse; et quicquid non sit futurum, id negat fieri posse. Tu etiam quae non sint futura, posse fieri dicis, ut frangi hanc gemmam, etiamsi id nunquam futurum sit: neque necesse fuisse Cypselum regnare Corinthi, quamquam id millesimo ante anno Apollinis Oraculo editum esset. ... Placet Diodoro, id solum fieri posse, quod aut verum sit, aut verum futurum sit: qui locus attingit hanc quaestionem, nihil fieri, quod non necesse fuerit; et quicquid fieri possit, id aut esse jam, aut futurum esse: nec magis commutari ex veris in falsa ea posse quae futura sunt, quam ea quae facta sunt: sed in factis immutabilitatem apparere; in futuris quibusdam, quia non apparent, ne inesse quidem videri: ut in eo qui mortifero morbo urgeatur, verum sit, hic morietur hoc morbo: at hoc idem si vere dicatur in eo, in quo tanta vis morbi non appareat, nihilominus futurum sit. Ita fit ut commutatio ex vero in falsum, ne in futuro quidem ulla fieri possit." Cicero makes it clear enough that Chrysippus often found himself in difficulties in this dispute, and that is no matter for astonishment: for the course he had chosen was not bound up with his dogma of fate, and, if he had known how, or had dared, to reason consistently, he would readily have adopted the whole hypothesis of Diodorus. We have seen already that the freedom he assigned to the soul, and his comparison of the cylinder, did not preclude the possibility that in reality all the acts of the human will were unavoidable consequences of fate. Hence it follows that everything which does not happen is impossible, and that there is nothing possible but that which actually comes to pass. Plutarch (*De Stoicor. Repugn.*, pp. 1053, 1054) discomfits him completely, on that point as well as on the dispute with Diodorus, and maintains that his opinion on possibility is altogether contrary to the doctrine of *fatum*. Observe that the most eminent Stoics had written on this matter without following the same path. Arrian (in *Epict.*, lib. 2, c. 29, p. m. 166) named four of them, who are Chrysippus, Cleanthes, Archidemus and Antipater. He evinces great scorn for this dispute; and M. Ménage need not have cited him as a writer who had spoken in commendation of the work of Chrysippus περὶ δυνατῶν ("citatur honorifice apud Arrianum", Menag. in *Laert.*, I, 7, 341) for assuredly these words, "γέγραφε δὲ καὶ Χρύσιππος θαυμαστῶς, etc., de his rebus mira scripsit Chrysippus", etc., are not in that connexion a eulogy. That is shown by the passages immediately before and after it. Dionysius of Halicarnassus (*De Collocat. Verbor.*, c. 17, p. m. 11) mentions two treatises by Chrysippus, wherein, under a title that promised something different, much of the logicians' territory had been explored. The work was entitled "περὶ τῆς συντάξεως τῶν τοῦ λόγου μερῶν, de partium orationis collocatione", and treated only of propositions true and false, possible and impossible, contingent and equivocal, etc., matter that our Schoolmen have pounded down and reduced to its essence. Take note that Chrysippus recognized that past things were necessarily true, which Cleanthes had not been willing to admit. (Arrian, *ubi supra*, p. m. 165.) "Οὐ πᾶν δὲ παρεληλυθὸς ἀληθὲς ἀναγκαῖόν ἐστι, καθάπερ οἱ περὶ Κλεάνθην φέρεσθαι δοκοῦσι. Non omne praeteritum ex necessitate verum est, ut illi qui Cleanthem sequuntur sentiunt." We have already seen (p. 562, col. 2) that Abélard is alleged to have taught a doctrine which resembles that of Diodorus. I think that the Stoics pledged themselves to give a wider range to possible things than to future things, for the purpose of mitigating the odious and frightful conclusions which were drawn from their dogma of fatality.'

It is sufficiently evident that Cicero when writing to Varro the words that have just been quoted (lib. 9, Ep. 4, *Ad Familiar.*) had not enough comprehension of the effect of Diodorus's opinion, since he found it preferable. He presents tolerably well in his book *De Fato* the opinions of those writers, but it is a pity that he has not always added the reasons which they employed. Plutarch in his treatise on the contradictions of the Stoics and M. Bayle are both surprised that Chrysippus was not of the same opinion as Diodorus, since he favours fatality. But Chrysippus and even his master

Cleanthes were on that point more reasonable than is supposed. That will be seen as we proceed. It is open to question whether the past is more necessary than the future. Cleanthes held the opinion that it is. The objection is raised that it is necessary *ex hypothesi* for the future to happen, as it is necessary *ex hypothesi* for the past to have happened. But there is this difference, that it is not possible to act on the past state, that would be a contradiction; but it is possible to produce some effect on the future. Yet the hypothetical necessity of both is the same: the one cannot be changed, the other will not be; and once that is past, it will not be possible for it to be changed either.

171. The famous Pierre Abélard expressed an opinion resembling that of Diodorus in the statement that God can do only that which he does. It was the third of the fourteen propositions taken from his works which were censured at the Council of Sens. It had been taken from the third book of his *Introduction to Theology*, where he treats especially of the power of God. The reason he gave for his statement was that God can do only that which he wills. Now God cannot will to do anything other than that which he does, because, of necessity, he must will whatever is fitting. Hence it follows that all that which he does not, is not fitting, that he cannot will to do it, and consequently that he cannot do it. Abélard admits himself that this opinion is peculiar to him, that hardly anyone shares in it, that it seems contrary to the doctrine of the saints and to reason and derogatory to the greatness of God. It appears that this author was a little too much inclined to speak and to think differently from others: for in reality this was only a dispute about words: he was changing the use of terms. Power and will are different faculties, whose objects also are different; it is confusing them to say that God can do only that which he wills. On the contrary, among various possibles, he wills only that which he finds the best. For all possibles are regarded as objects of power, but actual and existing things are regarded as the objects of his decretory will. Abélard himself acknowledged it. He raises this objection for himself: a reprobate can be saved; but he can only be saved if God saves him. God can therefore save him, and consequently do something that he does not. Abélard answers that it may indeed be said that this man can be saved in respect of the possibility of human nature, which is capable of salvation: but that it may not be said that God can save him in respect of God

himself, because it is impossible that God should do that which he must not do. But Abélard admits that it may very well be said in a sense, speaking absolutely and setting aside the assumption of reprobation, that such an one who is reprobate can be saved, and that thus often that which God does not can be done. He could therefore have spoken like the rest, who mean nothing different when they say that God can save this man, and that he can do that which he does not.

172. The so-called necessity of Wyclif, which was condemned by the Council of Constance, seems to arise simply from this same misunderstanding. I think that men of talent do wrong to truth and to themselves when, without reason, they bring into use new and displeasing expressions. In our own time the celebrated Mr. Hobbes supported this same opinion, that what does not happen is impossible. He proves it by the statement that all the conditions requisite for a thing that shall not exist (*omnia rei non futurae requisita*) are never found together, and that the thing cannot exist otherwise. But who does not see that that only proves a hypothetical impossibility? It is true that a thing cannot exist when a requisite condition for it is lacking. But as we claim to be able to say that the thing can exist although it does not exist, we claim in the same way to be able to say that the requisite conditions can exist although they do not exist. Thus Mr. Hobbes's argument leaves the matter where it is. The opinion which was held concerning Mr. Hobbes, that he taught an absolute necessity of all things, brought upon him much discredit, and would have done him harm even had it been his only error.

173. Spinoza went further: he appears to have explicitly taught a blind necessity, having denied to the Author of Things understanding and will, and assuming that good and perfection relate to us only, and not to him. It is true that Spinoza's opinion on this subject is somewhat obscure: for he grants God thought, after having divested him of understanding, *cogitationem, non intellectum concedit Deo*. There are even passages where he relents on the question of necessity. Nevertheless, as far as one can understand him, he acknowledges no goodness in God, properly speaking, and he teaches that all things exist through the necessity of the divine nature, without any act of choice by God. We will not waste time here in refuting an opinion so bad, and indeed so inexplicable. My own opinion is founded on the nature of the possibles, that is,

of things that imply no contradiction. I do not think that a Spinozist will say that all the romances one can imagine exist actually now, or have existed, or will still exist in some place in the universe. Yet one cannot deny that romances such as those of Mademoiselle de Scudéry, or as *Octavia*, are possible. Let us therefore bring up against him these words of M. Bayle, which please me well, on page 390, 'It is to-day', he says, 'a great embarrassment for the Spinozists to see that, according to their hypothesis, it was as impossible from all eternity that Spinoza, for instance, should not die at The Hague, as it is impossible for two and two to make six. They are well aware that it is a necessary conclusion from their doctrine, and a conclusion which disheartens, affrights, and stirs the mind to revolt, because of the absurdity it involves, diametrically opposed to common sense. They are not well pleased that one should know they are subverting a maxim so universal and so evident as this one: All that which implies contradiction is impossible, and all that which implies no contradiction is possible.'

174. One may say of M. Bayle, 'ubi bene, nemo melius', although one cannot say of him what was said of Origen, 'ubi male, nemo pejus'. I will only add that what has just been indicated as a maxim is in fact the definition of the *possible* and the *impossible*. M. Bayle, however, adds here towards the end a remark which somewhat spoils his eminently reasonable statement. 'Now what contradiction would there be if Spinoza had died in Leyden? Would Nature then have been less perfect, less wise, less powerful?' He confuses here what is impossible because it implies contradiction with what cannot happen because it is not meet to be chosen. It is true that there would have been no contradiction in the supposition that Spinoza died in Leyden and not at The Hague; there would have been nothing so possible: the matter was therefore indifferent in respect of the power of God. But one must not suppose that any event, however small it be, can be regarded as indifferent in respect of his wisdom and his goodness. Jesus Christ has said divinely well that everything is numbered, even to the hairs of our head. Thus the wisdom of God did not permit that this event whereof M. Bayle speaks should happen otherwise than it happened, not as if by itself it would have been more deserving of choice, but on account of its connexion with that entire sequence of the universe which deserved to be given preference. To say that what has already happened was of no interest to the wisdom of

God, and thence to infer that it is therefore not necessary, is to make a false assumption and argue incorrectly to a true conclusion. It is confusing what is necessary by moral necessity, that is, according to the principle of Wisdom and Goodness, with what is so by metaphysical and brute necessity, which occurs when the contrary implies contradiction. Spinoza, moreover, sought a metaphysical necessity in events. He did not think that God was determined by his goodness and by his perfection (which this author treated as chimeras in relation to the universe), but by the necessity of his nature; just as the semicircle is bound to enclose only right angles, without either knowing or willing this. For Euclid demonstrated that all angles enclosed between two straight lines drawn from the extremities of the diameter towards a point on the circumference of the circle are of necessity right angles, and that the contrary implies contradiction.

175. There are people who have gone to the other extreme: under the pretext of freeing the divine nature from the yoke of necessity they wished to regard it as altogether indifferent, with an indifference of equipoise. They did not take into account that just as metaphysical necessity is preposterous in relation to God's actions *ad extra*, so moral necessity is worthy of him. It is a happy necessity which obliges wisdom to do good, whereas indifference with regard to good and evil would indicate a lack of goodness or of wisdom. And besides, the indifference which would keep the will in a perfect equipoise would itself be a chimera, as has been already shown: it would offend against the great principle of the determinant reason.

176. Those who believe that God established good and evil by an arbitrary decree are adopting that strange idea of mere indifference, and other absurdities still stranger. They deprive God of the designation *good*: for what cause could one have to praise him for what he does, if in doing something quite different he would have done equally well? And I have very often been surprised that divers Supralapsarian theologians, as for instance Samuel Rutherford, a Professor of Theology in Scotland, who wrote when the controversies with the Remonstrants were at their height, could have been deluded by so strange an idea. Rutherford (in his *Exercitationes Apologeticae pro Gratia*) says positively that nothing is unjust or morally bad in God's eyes before he has forbidden it: thus without this prohibition it would be a matter of

indifference whether one murdered or saved a man, loved God or hated him, praised or blasphemed him. Nothing is so unreasonable as that. One may teach that God established good and evil by a positive law, or one may assert that there was something good and just before his decree, but that he is not required to conform to it, and that nothing prevents him from acting unjustly and from perhaps condemning innocence: but it all comes to the same thing, offering almost equal dishonour to God. For if justice was established arbitrarily and without any cause, if God came upon it by a kind of hazard, as when one draws lots, his goodness and his wisdom are not manifested in it, and there is nothing at all to attach him to it. If it is by a purely arbitrary decree, without any reason, that he has established or created what we call justice and goodness, then he can annul them or change their nature. Thus one would have no reason to assume that he will observe them always, as it would be possible to say he will observe them on the assumption that they are founded on reasons. The same would hold good more or less if his justice were different from ours, if (for example) it were written in his code that it is just to make the innocent eternally unhappy. According to these principles also, nothing would compel God to keep his word or would assure us of its fulfilment. For why should the law of justice, which states that reasonable promises must be kept, be more inviolable for him than any other laws?

177. All these three dogmas, albeit a little different from one another, namely, (1) that the nature of justice is arbitrary, (2) that it is fixed, but it is not certain that God will observe it, and finally (3) that the justice we know is not that which he observes, destroy the confidence in God that gives us tranquillity, and the love of God that makes our happiness. There is nothing to prevent such a God from behaving as a tyrant and an enemy of honest folk, and from taking pleasure in that which we call evil. Why should he not, then, just as well be the evil principle of the Manichaeans as the single good principle of the orthodox? At least he would be neutral and, as it were, suspended between the two, or even sometimes the one and sometimes the other. That would be as if someone were to say that Oromasdes and Arimanius reign in turns, according to which of the two is the stronger or the more adroit. It is like the saying of a certain Moghul woman. She, so it seems, having heard it said that formerly under Genghis Khan and his

successors her nation had had dominion over most of the North and East, told the Muscovites recently, when M. Isbrand went to China on behalf of the Czar, through the country of those Tartars, that the god of the Moghuls had been driven from Heaven, but that one day he would take his own place again. The true God is always the same: natural religion itself demands that he be essentially as good and wise as he is powerful. It is scarcely more contrary to reason and piety to say that God acts without cognition, than to maintain that he has cognition which does not find the eternal rules of goodness and of justice among its objects, or again to say that he has a will such as heeds not these rules.

178. Some theologians who have written of God's right over creatures appear to have conceded to him an unrestricted right, an arbitrary and despotic power. They thought that would be placing divinity on the most exalted level that may be imagined for it, and that it would abase the creature before the Creator to such an extent that the Creator is bound by no laws of any kind with respect to the creature. There are passages from Twiss, Rutherford and some other Supralapsarians which imply that God cannot sin whatever he may do, because he is subject to no law. M. Bayle himself considers that this doctrine is monstrous and contrary to the holiness of God (*Dictionary*, v. 'Paulicians', p. 2332 *in initio*); but I suppose that the intention of some of these writers was less bad than it seems to be. Apparently they meant by the term right, ἀνυπευθυνίαν, a state wherein one is responsible to none for one's actions. But they will not have denied that God owes to himself what goodness and justice demand of him. On that matter one may see M. Amyraut's *Apology for Calvin*: it is true that Calvin appears orthodox on this subject, and that he is by no means one of the extreme Supralapsarians.

179. Thus, when M. Bayle says somewhere that St. Paul extricates himself from predestination only through the consideration of God's absolute right, and the incomprehensibility of his ways, it is implied that, if one understood them, one would find them consistent with justice, God not being able to use his power otherwise. St. Paul himself says that it is a *depth*, but a depth of wisdom (*altitudo sapientiae*), and *justice* is included in *the goodness of the All-wise*. I find that M. Bayle speaks very well elsewhere on the application of our notions of goodness to the actions of God (*Reply to the Questions of a Provincial*, ch. 81, p. 139): 'One must not assert

here', he says, 'that the goodness of the infinite Being is not subject to the same rules as the goodness of the creature. For if there is in God an attribute that can be called goodness, the marks of goodness in general must apply to him. Now when we reduce goodness to the most general abstraction, we find therein the will to do good. Divide and subdivide into as many kinds as you shall please this general goodness, into infinite goodness, finite goodness, kingly goodness, goodness of a father, goodness of a husband, goodness of a master, you will find in each, as an inseparable attribute, the will to do good.'

180. I find also that M. Bayle combats admirably the opinion of those who assert that goodness and justice depend solely upon the arbitrary choice of God; who suppose, moreover, that if God had been determined by the goodness of things themselves to act, he would be entirely subjected to necessity in his actions, a state incompatible with freedom. That is confusing metaphysical necessity with moral necessity. Here is what M. Bayle says in objection to this error (*Reply*, ch. 89, p. 203): 'The consequence of this doctrine will be, that before God resolved upon creating the world he saw nothing better in virtue than in vice, and that his ideas did not show him that virtue was more worthy of his love than vice. That leaves no distinction between natural right and positive right; there will no longer be anything unalterable or inevitable in morals; it will have been just as possible for God to command people to be vicious as to command them to be virtuous; and one will have no certainty that the moral laws will not one day be abrogated, as the ceremonial laws of the Jews were. This, in a word, leads us straight to the belief that God was the free author, not only of goodness and of virtue, but also of truth and of the essence of things. That is what certain of the Cartesians assert, and I confess that their opinion (see the Continuation of *Divers Thoughts on the Comet*, p. 554) might be of some avail in certain circumstances. Yet it is open to dispute for so many reasons, and subject to consequences so troublesome (see chapter 152 of the same Continuation) that there are scarcely any extremes it were not better to suffer rather than plunge into that one. It opens the door to the most exaggerated Pyrrhonism: for it leads to the assertion that this proposition, three and three make six, is only true where and during the time when it pleases God; that it is perhaps false in some parts of the universe; and that perhaps it will be so among

men in the coming year. All that depends on the free will of God could have been limited to certain places and certain times, like the Judaic ceremonies. This conclusion will be extended to all the laws of the Decalogue, if the actions they command are in their nature divested of all goodness to the same degree as the actions they forbid.'

181. To say that God, having resolved to create man just as he is, could not but have required of him piety, sobriety, justice and chastity, because it is impossible that the disorders capable of overthrowing or disturbing his work can please him, that is to revert in effect to the common opinion. Virtues are virtues only because they serve perfection or prevent the imperfection of those who are virtuous, or even of those who have to do with them. And they have that power by their nature and by the nature of rational creatures, before God decrees to create them. To hold a different opinion would be as if someone were to say that the rules of proportion and harmony are arbitrary with regard to musicians because they occur in music only when one has resolved to sing or to play some instrument. But that is exactly what is meant by being essential to good music: for those rules belong to it already in the ideal state, even when none yet thinks of singing, since it is known that they must of necessity belong to it as soon as one shall sing. In the same way virtues belong to the ideal state of the rational creature before God decrees to create it; and it is for that very reason we maintain that virtues are good by their nature.

182. M. Bayle has inserted a special chapter in his Continuation of *Divers Thoughts on the Comet* (it is chapter 152) where he shows 'that the Christian Doctors teach that there are things which are just antecedently to God's decrees'. Some theologians of the Augsburg Confession censured some of the Reformed who appeared to be of a different opinion; and this error was regarded as if it were a consequence of the absolute decree, which doctrine seems to exempt the will of God from any kind of reason, *ubi stat pro ratione voluntas*. But, as I have observed already on various occasions, Calvin himself acknowledged that the decrees of God are in conformity with justice and wisdom, although the reasons that might prove this conformity in detail are unknown to us. Thus, according to him, the rules of goodness and of justice are anterior to the decrees of God. M. Bayle, in the same place, quotes a passage from the celebrated M. Turretin which draws a

distinction between natural divine laws and positive divine laws. Moral laws are of the first kind and ceremonial of the second. Samuel Desmarests, a celebrated theologian formerly at Groningen, and Herr Strinesius, who is still at Frankfort on the Oder, advocated this same distinction; and I think that it is the opinion most widely accepted even among the Reformed. Thomas Aquinas and all the Thomists were of the same opinion, with the bulk of the Schoolmen and the theologians of the Roman Church. The Casuists also held to that idea: I count Grotius among the most eminent of them, and he was followed in this point by his commentators. Herr Pufendorf appeared to be of a different opinion, which he insisted on maintaining in the face of censure from some theologians; but he need not be taken into account, not having advanced far enough in subjects of this kind. He makes a vigorous protest against the absolute decree, in his *Fecialis divinus*, and yet he approves what is worst in the opinions of the champions of this decree, and without which this decree (as others of the Reformed explain) becomes endurable. Aristotle was very orthodox on this matter of justice, and the Schoolmen followed him: they distinguish, just as Cicero and the Jurists do, between perpetual right, which is binding on all and everywhere, and positive right, which is only for certain times and certain peoples. I once read with enjoyment the *Euthyphro* of Plato, who makes Socrates uphold the truth on that point, and M. Bayle has called attention to the same passage.

183. M. Bayle himself upholds this truth with considerable force in a certain passage, which it will be well to quote here in its entirety, long as it is (vol. II of the Continuation of *Divers Thoughts on the Comet*, ch. 152, p. 771 *seqq.*): 'According to the teaching of countless writers of importance', he says, 'there is in nature and in the essence of certain things a moral good or evil that precedes the divine decree. They prove this doctrine principally through the frightful consequences that attend the opposite dogma. Thus from the proposition that to do wrong to no man would be a good action, not in itself but by an arbitrary dispensation of God's will, it would follow that God could have given to man a law directly opposed at all points to the commandments of the Decalogue. That is horrifying. But here is a more direct proof, one derived from metaphysics. One thing is certain, that the existence of God is not an effect of his will. He exists not because he wills his

existence, but through the necessity of his infinite nature. His power and his knowledge exist through the same necessity. He is all-powerful, he knows all things, not because he wills it thus, but because these are attributes necessarily identified with him. The dominion of his will relates only to the exercise of his power, he gives effect outside himself only to that which he wills, and he leaves all the rest in the state of mere possibility. Thence it comes that this dominion extends only over the existence of creatures, and not over their essential being. God was able to create matter, a man, a circle, or leave them in nothingness, but he was not able to produce them without giving them their essential properties. He had of necessity to make man a rational animal and to give the round shape to a circle, since, according to his eternal ideas, independent of the free decrees of his will, the essence of man lay in the properties of being animal and rational, and since the essence of the circle lay in having a circumference equally distant from the centre as to all its parts. This is what has caused the Christian philosophers to acknowledge that the essences of things are eternal, and that there are propositions of eternal truth; consequently that the essences of things and the truth of the first principles are immutable. That is to be understood not only of theoretical but also of practical first principles, and of all the propositions that contain the true definition of creatures. These essences and these truths emanate from the same necessity of nature as the knowledge of God. Since therefore it is by the nature of things that God exists, that he is all-powerful, and that he has perfect knowledge of all things, it is also by the nature of things that matter, the triangle, man and certain actions of man, etc., have such and such properties essentially. God saw from all eternity and in all necessity the essential relations of numbers, and the identity of the subject and predicate in the propositions that contain the essence of each thing. He saw likewise that the term just is included in these propositions: to esteem what is estimable, be grateful to one's benefactor, fulfil the conditions of a contract, and so on, with many others relating to morals. One is therefore justified in saying that the precepts of natural law assume the reasonableness and justice of that which is enjoined, and that it would be man's duty to practise what they contain even though God should have been so indulgent as to ordain nothing in that respect. Pray observe that in going back with our visionary thoughts to that ideal moment when God has yet decreed nothing, we find in the ideas of God the principles of morals under terms that imply an obligation. We understand these maxims as certain, and derived from the eternal and immutable order: it beseems the rational creature to conform to reason; a rational creature conforming to reason is to be commended, but not conforming thereto is blameworthy. You would not dare to deny that these truths impose upon man a duty in relation to all acts which are in conformity with strict reason, such as these: one must esteem all that is estimable; render good for good; do wrong to no man; honour one's father; render to every man that which is his due, etc. Now since by the very nature of things, and before the divine laws, the truths of morality impose upon man certain duties, Thomas Aquinas and Grotius were justified in saying that if there were no God we should nevertheless be obliged to conform to natural law. Others have said that even supposing all rational beings in existence were to perish, true propositions would remain true. Cajetan maintained that if he remained alone in the universe, all other things without any exception having been destroyed, the knowledge that he had of the nature of a rose would nevertheless subsist.'

184. The late Jacob Thomasius, a celebrated Professor at Leipzig, made the apt observation in his elucidations of the philosophic rules of Daniel Stahl, a Jena professor, that it is not advisable to go altogether beyond God, and that one must not say, with some Scotists, that the eternal verities would exist even though there were no understanding, not even that of God. For it is, in my judgement, the divine understanding which gives reality to the eternal verities, albeit God's will have no part therein. All reality must be founded on something existent. It is true that an atheist may be a geometrician: but if there were no God, geometry would have no object. And without God, not only would there be nothing existent, but there would be nothing possible. That, however, does not hinder those who do not see the connexion of all things one with another and with God from being able to understand certain sciences, without knowing their first source, which is in God. Aristotle, although he also scarcely knew that source, nevertheless said something of the same kind which was very apposite. He acknowledged that the principles of individual forms of knowledge depend on a superior knowledge which gives the reason for them; and this superior knowledge must

have being, and consequently God, the source of being, for its object. Herr Dreier of Königsberg has aptly observed that the true metaphysics which Aristotle sought, and which he called τὴν ζητουμένην, his *desideratum*, was theology.

185. Yet the same M. Bayle, who says so much that is admirable in order to prove that the rules of goodness and justice, and the eternal verities in general, exist by their nature, and not by an arbitrary choice of God, has spoken very hesitatingly about them in another passage (Continuation of *Divers Thoughts on the Comet*, vol. II, ch. 114, towards the end). After having given an account of the opinion of M. Descartes and a section of his followers, who maintain that God is the free cause of truths and of essences, he adds (p. 554): 'I have done all that I could to gain true understanding of this dogma and to find the solution of the difficulties surrounding it. I confess to you quite simply that I still cannot properly fathom it. That does not discourage me; I suppose, as other philosophers in other cases have supposed, that time will unfold the meaning of this noble paradox. I wish that Father Malebranche had thought fit to defend it, but he took other measures.' Is it possible that the enjoyment of doubt can have such influence upon a gifted man as to make him wish and hope for the power to believe that two contradictories never exist together for the sole reason that God forbade them to, and, moreover, that God could have issued them an order to ensure that they always walked together? There is indeed a noble paradox! Father Malebranche showed great wisdom in taking other measures.

186. I cannot even imagine that M. Descartes can have been quite seriously of this opinion, although he had adherents who found this easy to believe, and would in all simplicity follow him where he only made pretence to go. It was apparently one of his tricks, one of his philosophic feints: he prepared for himself some loophole, as when for instance he discovered a trick for denying the movement of the earth, while he was a Copernican in the strictest sense. I suspect that he had in mind here another extraordinary manner of speaking, of his own invention, which was to say that affirmations and negations, and acts of inner judgement in general, are operations of the will. Through this artifice the eternal verities, which until the time of Descartes had been named an object of the divine understanding, suddenly became an object of God's will. Now the acts of his will are free, therefore God is the

free cause of the verities. That is the outcome of the matter. *Spectatum admissi*. A slight change in the meaning of terms has caused all this commotion. But if the affirmations of necessary truths were actions of the will of the most perfect mind, these actions would be anything but free, for there is nothing to choose. It seems that M. Descartes did not declare himself sufficiently on the nature of freedom, and that his conception of it was somewhat unusual: for he extended it so far that he even held the affirmations of necessary truths to be free in God. That was preserving only the name of freedom.

187. M. Bayle, who with others conceives this to be a freedom of indifference, that God had had to establish (for instance) the truths of numbers, and to ordain that three times three made nine, whereas he could have commanded them to make ten, imagines in this strange opinion, supposing it were possible to defend it, some kind of advantage gained against the Stratonists. Strato was one of the leaders of the School of Aristotle, and the successor of Theophrastus; he maintained (according to Cicero's account) that this world had been formed such as it is by Nature or by a necessary cause devoid of cognition. I admit that that might be so, if God had so preformed matter as to cause such an effect by the laws of motion alone. But without God there would not even have been any reason for existence, and still less for any particular existence of things: thus Strato's system is not to be feared.

188. Nevertheless M. Bayle is in difficulties over this: he will not admit plastic natures devoid of cognition, which Mr. Cudworth and others had introduced, for fear that the modern Stratonists, that is, the Spinozists, take advantage of it. This has involved him in disputes with M. le Clerc. Under the influence of this error, that a non-intelligent cause can produce nothing where contrivance appears, he is far from conceding to me that *preformation* which produces naturally the organs of animals, and *the system of a harmony pre-established by God* in bodies, to make them respond in accordance with their own laws to the thoughts and the wills of souls. But it ought to have been taken into account that this non-intelligent cause, which produces such beautiful things in the grains and seeds of plants and animals, and effects the actions of bodies as the will ordains them, was formed by the hand of God: and God is infinitely more skilful than a watchmaker, who him-

self makes machines and automata that are capable of producing as wonderful effects as if they possessed intelligence.

189. Now to come to M. Bayle's apprehensions concerning the Stratonists, in case one should admit truths that are not dependent upon the will of God: he seems to fear lest they may take advantage against us of the perfect regularity of the eternal verities. Since this regularity springs only from the nature and necessity of things, without being directed by any cognition, M. Bayle fears that one might with Strato thence infer that the world also could have become regular through a blind necessity. But it is easy to answer that. In the region of the eternal verities are found all the possibles, and consequently the regular as well as the irregular: there must be a reason accounting for the preference for order and regularity, and this reason can only be found in understanding. Moreover these very truths can have no existence without an understanding to take cognizance of them; for they would not exist if there were no divine understanding wherein they are realized, so to speak. Hence Strato does not attain his end, which is to exclude cognition from that which enters into the origin of things.

190. The difficulty that M. Bayle has imagined in connexion with Strato seems a little too subtle and far-fetched. That is termed: *timere, ubi non est timor.* He makes another difficulty, which has just as slight a foundation, namely, that God would be subjected to a kind of *fatum.* Here are his words (p. 555): 'If they are propositions of eternal truth, which are such by their nature and not by God's institution, if they are not true by a free decree of his will, but if on the contrary he has recognized them as true of necessity, because such was their nature, there is a kind of *fatum* to which he is subjected; there is an absolutely insurmountable natural necessity. Thence comes also the result that the divine understanding in the infinity of its ideas has always and at the outset hit upon their perfect conformity with their objects, without the guidance of any cognition; for it would be a contradiction to say that any exemplary cause had served as a plan for the acts of God's understanding. One would never that way find eternal ideas or any first intelligence. One must say, then, that a nature which exists of necessity always finds its way, without any need for it to be shown. How then shall we overcome the obstinacy of a Stratonist?'

191. But again it is easy to answer. This so-called *fatum*, which

binds even the Divinity, is nothing but God's own nature, his own understanding, which furnishes the rules for his wisdom and his goodness; it is a happy necessity, without which he would be neither good nor wise. Is it to be desired that God should not be bound to be perfect and happy? Is our condition, which renders us liable to fail, worth envying? And should we not be well pleased to exchange it for sinlessness, if that depended upon us? One must be indeed weary of life to desire the freedom to destroy oneself and to pity the Divinity for not having that freedom. M. Bayle himself reasons thus elsewhere against those who laud to the skies an extravagant freedom which they assume in the will, when they would make the will independent of reason.

192. Moreover, M. Bayle wonders 'that the divine understanding in the infinity of its ideas always and at the outset hits upon their perfect conformity with their objects, without the guidance of any cognition'. This objection is null and void. Every distinct idea is, through its distinctness, in conformity with its object, and in God there are distinct ideas only. At first, moreover, the object exists nowhere; but when it comes into existence, it will be formed according to this idea. Besides, M. Bayle knows very well that the divine understanding has no need of time for seeing the connexion of things. All trains of reasoning are in God in a transcendent form, and they preserve an order amongst them in his understanding, as well as in ours: but with him it is only an order and a *priority of nature*, whereas with us there is a *priority of time*. It is therefore not to be wondered at that he who penetrates all things at one stroke should always strike true at the outset; and it must not be said that he succeeds without the guidance of any cognition. On the contrary, it is because his knowledge is perfect that his voluntary actions are also perfect.

193. Up to now I have shown that the Will of God is not independent of the rules of Wisdom, although indeed it is a matter for surprise that one should have been constrained to argue about it, and to do battle for a truth so great and so well established. But it is hardly less surprising that there should be people who believe that God only half observes these rules, and does not choose the best, although his wisdom causes him to recognize it; and, in a word, that there should be writers who hold that God could have done better. That is more or less the error of the famous Alfonso, King of Castile, who was elected King of the Romans by certain

Electors, and originated the astronomical tables that bear his name. This prince is reported to have said that if God in making the world had consulted him he would have given God good advice. Apparently the Ptolemaic system, which prevailed at that time, was displeasing to him. He believed therefore that something better planned could have been made, and he was right. But if he had known the system of Copernicus, with the discoveries of Kepler, now extended by knowledge of the gravity of the planets, he would indeed have confessed that the contrivance of the true system is marvellous. We see, therefore, that here the question concerned the more or less only; Alfonso maintained that better could have been done, and his opinion was censured by everyone.

194. Yet philosophers and theologians dare to support dogmatically such a belief; and I have many times wondered that gifted and pious persons should have been capable of setting bounds to the goodness and the perfection of God. For to assert that he knows what is best, that he can do it and that he does it not, is to avow that it rested with his will only to make the world better than it is; but that is what one calls lacking goodness. It is acting against that axiom already quoted: *Minus bonum habet rationem mali.* If some adduce experience to prove that God could have done better, they set themselves up as ridiculous critics of his works. To such will be given the answer given to all those who criticize God's course of action, and who from this same assumption, that is, the alleged defects of the world, would infer that there is an evil God, or at least a God neutral between good and evil. And if we hold the same opinion as King Alfonso, we shall, I say, receive this answer: You have known the world only since the day before yesterday, you see scarce farther than your nose, and you carp at the world. Wait until you know more of the world and consider therein especially the parts which present a complete whole (as do organic bodies); and you will find there a contrivance and a beauty transcending all imagination. Let us thence draw conclusions as to the wisdom and the goodness of the author of things, even in things that we know not. We find in the universe some things which are not pleasing to us; but let us be aware that it is not made for us alone. It is nevertheless made for us if we are wise: it will serve us if we use it for our service; we shall be happy in it if we wish to be.

195. Someone will say that it is impossible to produce the best, because there is no perfect creature, and that it is always possible to produce one which would be more perfect. I answer that what can be said of a creature or of a particular substance, which can always be surpassed by another, is not to be applied to the universe, which, since it must extend through all future eternity, is an infinity. Moreover, there is an infinite number of creatures in the smallest particle of matter, because of the actual division of the *continuum* to infinity. And infinity, that is to say, the accumulation of an infinite number of substances, is, properly speaking, not a whole any more than the infinite number itself, whereof one cannot say whether it is even or uneven. That is just what serves to confute those who make of the world a God, or who think of God as the Soul of the world; for the world or the universe cannot be regarded as an animal or as a substance.

196. It is therefore not a question of a creature, but of the universe; and the adversary will be obliged to maintain that one possible universe may be better than the other, to infinity; but there he would be mistaken, and it is that which he cannot prove. If this opinion were true, it would follow that God had not produced any universe at all: for he is incapable of acting without reason, and that would be even acting against reason. It is as if one were to suppose that God had decreed to make a material sphere, with no reason for making it of any particular size. This decree would be useless, it would carry with it that which would prevent its effect. It would be quite another matter if God decreed to draw from a given point one straight line to another given straight line, without any determination of the angle, either in the decree or in its circumstances. For in this case the determination would spring from the nature of the thing, the line would be perpendicular, and the angle would be right, since that is all that is determined and distinguishable. It is thus one must think of the creation of the best of all possible universes, all the more since God not only decrees to create a universe, but decrees also to create the best of all. For God decrees nothing without knowledge, and he makes no separate decrees, which would be nothing but antecedent acts of will: and these we have sufficiently explained, distinguishing them from genuine decrees.

197. M. Diroys, whom I knew in Rome, theologian to Cardinal d'Estrées, wrote a book entitled *Proofs and Assumptions in Favour of*

the Christian Religion, published in Paris in the year 1683. M. Bayle (*Reply to the Questions of a Provincial,* vol. III, ch. 165, p. 1058) recounts this objection brought up by M. Diroys: 'There is one more difficulty', he says, 'which it is no less important to meet than those given earlier, since it causes more trouble to those who judge goods and evils by considerations founded on the purest and most lofty maxims. This is that God being the supreme wisdom and goodness, it seems to them that he ought to do all things as wise and virtuous persons would wish them to be done, following the rules of wisdom and of goodness which God has imprinted in them, and as they would be obliged themselves to do these things if they depended upon them. Thus, seeing that the affairs of the world do not go so well as, in their opinion, they might go, and as they would go if they interfered themselves, they conclude that God, who is infinitely better and wiser than they, or rather wisdom and goodness itself, does not concern himself with these affairs.'

198. M. Diroys makes some apt remarks concerning this, which I will not repeat, since I have sufficiently answered the objection in more than one passage, and that has been the chief end of all my discourse. But he makes one assertion with which I cannot agree. He claims that the objection proves too much. One must again quote his own words with M. Bayle, p. 1059: 'If it does not behove the supreme Wisdom and Goodness to fail to do what is best and most perfect, it follows that all Beings are eternally, immutably and essentially as perfect and as good as they can be, since nothing can change except by passing either from a state less good to a better, or from a better to a less good. Now that cannot happen if it does not behove God to fail to do that which is best and most perfect, when he can do it. It will therefore be necessary that all beings be eternally and essentially filled with a knowledge and a virtue as perfect as God can give them. Now all that which is eternally and essentially as perfect as God can make it proceeds essentially from him; in a word, is eternally and essentially good as he is, and consequently it is God, as he is. That is the bearing of this maxim, that it is repugnant to supreme justice and goodness not to make things as good and perfect as they can be. For it is essential to essential wisdom and goodness to banish all that is repugnant to it altogether. One must therefore assert as a primary truth concerning the conduct of God in relation to creatures that there is nothing repugnant to this goodness and this wisdom in

making things less perfect than they could be, or in permitting the goods that it has produced either completely to cease to be or to change and deteriorate. For it causes no offence to God that there should be other Beings than he, that is beings who can be not what they are, and do not what they do or do what they do not.'

199. M. Bayle calls this answer paltry, but I find his counter-objection involved. M. Bayle will have those who are for the two principles to take their stand chiefly on the assumption of the supreme freedom of God: for if he were compelled to produce all that which he can, he would produce also sins and sorrows. Thus the Dualists could from the existence of evil conclude nothing contrary to the oneness of the principle, if this principle were as much inclined to evil as to good. There M. Bayle carries the notion of freedom too far: for even though God be supremely free, it does not follow that he maintains an indifference of equipoise: and even though he be inclined to act, it does not follow that he is compelled by this inclination to produce all that which he can. He will produce only that which he wills, for his inclination prompts him to good. I admit the supreme freedom of God, but I do not confuse it with indifference of equipoise, as if he could act without reason. M. Diroys therefore imagines that the Dualists, in their insistence that the single good principle produce no evil, ask too much; for by the same reason, according to M. Diroys, they ought also to ask that he should produce the greatest good, the less good being a kind of evil. I hold that the Dualists are wrong in respect of the first point, and that they would be right in respect of the second, where M. Diroys blames them without cause; or rather that one can reconcile the evil, or the less good, in some parts with the best in the whole. If the Dualists demanded that God should do the best, they would not be demanding too much. They are mistaken rather in claiming that the best in the whole should be free from evil in the parts, and that therefore what God has made is not the best.

200. But M. Diroys maintains that if God always produces the best he will produce other Gods; otherwise each substance that he produced would not be the best nor the most perfect. But he is mistaken, through not taking into account the order and con-nexion of things. If each substance taken separately were perfect, all would be alike; which is neither fitting nor possible. If they

were Gods, it would not have been possible to produce them. The best system of things will therefore not contain Gods; it will always be a system of bodies (that is, things arranged according to time and place) and of souls which represent and are aware of bodies, and in accordance with which bodies are in great measure directed. So, as the design of a building may be the best of all in respect of its purpose, of expense and of circumstances; and as an arrangement of some figured representations of bodies which is given to you may be the best that one can find, it is easy to imagine likewise that a structure of the universe may be the best of all, without becoming a god. The connexion and order of things brings it about that the body of every animal and of every plant is composed of other animals and of other plants, or of other living and organic beings; consequently there is subordination, and one body, one substance serves the other: thus their perfection cannot be equal.

201. M. Bayle thinks (p. 1063) that M. Diroys has confused two different propositions. According to the one, God must do all things as wise and virtuous persons would wish that they should be done, by the rules of wisdom and of goodness that God has imprinted in them, and as they would be obliged themselves to do them if those things depended upon them. The other is that it is not consistent with supreme wisdom and goodness to fail to do what is best and most perfect. M. Diroys (in M. Bayle's opinion) sets up the first proposition as an objection for himself, and replies to the second. But therein he is justified, as it seems to me. For these two propositions are connected, the second is a result of the first: to do less good than one could is to be lacking in wisdom or in goodness. To be the best, and to be desired by those who are most virtuous and wise, comes to the same thing. And it may be said that, if we could understand the structure and the economy of the universe, we should find that it is made and directed as the wisest and most virtuous could wish it, since God cannot fail to do thus. This necessity nevertheless is only of a moral nature: and I admit that if God were forced by a metaphysical necessity to produce that which he makes, he would produce all the possibles, or nothing; and in this sense M. Bayle's conclusion would be fully correct. But as all the possibles are not compatible together in one and the same world-sequence, for that very reason all the possibles cannot be produced, and it must be said that God is not

forced, metaphysically speaking, into the creation of this world. One may say that as soon as God has decreed to create something there is a struggle between all the possibles, all of them laying claim to existence, and that those which, being united, produce most reality, most perfection, most significance carry the day. It is true that all this struggle can only be ideal, that is to say, it can only be a conflict of reasons in the most perfect understanding, which cannot fail to act in the most perfect way, and consequently to choose the best. Yet God is bound by a moral necessity, to make things in such a manner that there can be nothing better: otherwise not only would others have cause to criticize what he makes, but, more than that, he would not himself be satisfied with his work, he would blame himself for its imperfection; and that conflicts with the supreme felicity of the divine nature. This perpetual sense of his own fault or imperfection would be to him an inevitable source of grief, as M. Bayle says on another occasion (p. 953).

202. M. Diroys' argument contains a false assumption, in his statement that nothing can change except by passing from a state less good to a better or from a better to a less good; and that thus, if God makes the best, what he has produced cannot be changed: it would be an eternal substance, a god. But I do not see why a thing cannot change its kind in relation to good or evil, without changing its degree. In the transition from enjoyment of music to enjoyment of painting, or *vice versa* from the pleasure of the eyes to that of the ears, the degree of enjoyment may remain the same, the latter gaining no advantage over the former save that of novelty. If the quadrature of the circle should come to pass or (what is the same thing) the circulature of the square, that is, if the circle were changed into a square of the same size, or the square into a circle, it would be difficult to say, on the whole, without having regard to some special use, whether one would have gained or lost. Thus the best may be changed into another which neither yields to it nor surpasses it: but there will always be an order among them, and that the best order possible. Taking the whole sequence of things, the best has no equal; but one part of the sequence may be equalled by another part of the same sequence. Besides it might be said that the whole sequence of things to infinity may be the best possible, although what exists all through the universe in each portion of time be not the best. It

might be therefore that the universe became even better and better, if the nature of things were such that it was not permitted to attain to the best all at once. But these are problems of which it is hard for us to judge.

203. M. Bayle says (p. 1064) that the question whether God could have made things more perfect than he made them is also very difficult, and that the reasons for and against are very strong. But it is, so it seems to me, as if one were to question whether God's actions are consistent with the most perfect wisdom and the greatest goodness. It is a very strange thing, that by changing the terms a little one throws doubt upon what is, if properly understood, as clear as anything can be. The reasons to the contrary have no force, being founded only on the semblance of defects; and M. Bayle's objection, which tends to prove that the law of the best would impose upon God a true metaphysical necessity, is only an illusion that springs from the misuse of terms. M. Bayle formerly held a different opinion, when he commended that of Father Malebranche, which was akin to mine on this subject. But M. Arnauld having written in opposition to Father Malebranche, M. Bayle altered his opinion; and I suppose that his tendency towards doubt, which increased in him with the years, was conducive to that result. M. Arnauld was doubtless a great man, and his authority has great weight: he made sundry good observations in his writings against Father Malebranche, but he was not justified in contesting those of his statements that were akin to mine on the rule of the best.

204. The excellent author of *The Search for Truth*, having passed from philosophy to theology, published finally an admirable treatise on Nature and Grace. Here he showed in his way (as M. Bayle explained in his *Divers Thoughts on the Comet*, ch. 234) that the events which spring from the enforcement of general laws are not the object of a particular will of God. It is true that when one wills a thing one wills also in a sense everything that is necessarily attached to it, and in consequence God cannot will general laws without also willing in a sense all the particular effects that must of necessity be derived from them. But it is always true that these particular events are not willed for their own sake, and that is what is meant by the expression that they are not willed by a *particular* and direct *will*. There is no doubt that when God resolved to act outside himself, he made choice of a manner of action which

should be worthy of the supremely perfect Being, that is, which should be infinitely simple and uniform, but yet of an infinite productivity. One may even suppose that this manner of action by *general acts of will* appeared to him preferable—although there must thence result some superfluous events (and even bad if they are taken separately, that is my own addition)—to another manner more composed and more regular; such is Father Malebranche's opinion. Nothing is more appropriate than this assumption (according to the opinion of M. Bayle, when he wrote his *Divers Thoughts on the Comet*) to solve a thousand difficulties which are brought up against divine providence: 'To ask God', he says, 'why he has made things which serve to render men more wicked, that would be to ask why God has carried out his plan (which can only be of infinite beauty) by the simplest and most uniform methods, and why, by a complexity of decrees that would unceasingly cut across one another, he has not prevented the wrong use of man's free will.' He adds 'that miracles being particular acts of will must have an end worthy of God'.

205. On these foundations he makes some good reflexions (ch. 231) concerning the injustice of those who complain of the prosperity of the wicked. 'I shall have no scruples', he says, 'about saying that all those who are surprised at the prosperity of the wicked have pondered very little upon the nature of God, and that they have reduced the obligations of a cause which directs all things, to the scope of a providence altogether subordinate; and that is small-minded. What then! Should God, after having made free causes and necessary causes, in a mixture infinitely well fitted to show forth the wonders of his infinite wisdom, have established laws consistent with the nature of free causes, but so lacking in firmness that the slightest trouble that came upon a man would overthrow them entirely, to the ruin of human freedom? A mere city governor will become an object of ridicule if he changes his regulations and orders as often as someone is pleased to murmur against him. And shall God, whose laws concern a good so universal that all of the world that is visible to us perchance enters into it as no more than a trifling accessary, be bound to depart from his laws, because they to-day displease the one and to-morrow the other? Or again because a superstitious person, deeming wrongly that a monstrosity presages something deadly, proceeds from his error to a criminal sacrifice? Or because a good

soul, who yet does not value virtue highly enough to believe that to have none is punishment enough in itself, is shocked that a wicked man should become rich and enjoy vigorous health? Can one form any falser notions of a universal providence? Everyone agrees that this law of nature, the strong prevails over the weak, has been very wisely laid down, and that it would be absurd to maintain that when a stone falls on a fragile vase which is the delight of its owner, God should depart from this law in order to spare that owner vexation. Should one then not confess that it is just as absurd to maintain that God must depart from the same law to prevent a wicked man from growing rich at the expense of a good man? The more the wicked man sets himself above the promptings of conscience and of honour, the more does he exceed the good man in strength, so that if he comes to grips with the good man he must, according to the course of nature, ruin him. If, moreover, they are both engaged in the business of finance, the wicked man must, according to the same course of nature, grow richer than the good man, just as a fierce fire consumes more wood than a fire of straw. Those who would wish sickness for a wicked man are sometimes as unfair as those who would wish that a stone falling on a glass should not break it: for his organs being arranged as they are, neither the food that he takes nor the air that he breathes can, according to natural laws, be detrimental to his health. Therefore those who complain about his health complain of God's failure to violate the laws which he has established. And in this they are all the more unfair because, through combinations and concatenations which were in the power of God alone, it happens often enough that the course of nature brings about the punishment of sin.'

206. It is a thousand pities that M. Bayle so soon quitted the way he had so auspiciously begun, of reasoning on behalf of providence: for his work would have been fruitful, and in saying fine things he would have said good things as well. I agree with Father Malebranche that God does things in the way most worthy of him. But I go a little further than he, with regard to 'general and particular acts of will'. As God can do nothing without reasons, even when he acts miraculously, it follows that he has no will about individual events but what results from some general truth or will. Thus I would say that God never has a *particular will* such as this Father implies, that is to say, *a particular primitive will*.

207. I think even that miracles have nothing to distinguish them from other events in this regard: for reasons of an order superior to that of Nature prompt God to perform them. Thus I would not say, with this Father, that God departs from general laws whenever order requires it: he departs from one law only for another law more applicable, and what order requires cannot fail to be in conformity with the rule of order, which is one of the general laws. The distinguishing mark of miracles (taken in the strictest sense) is that they cannot be accounted for by the natures of created things. That is why, should God make a general law causing bodies to be attracted the one to the other, he could only achieve its operation by perpetual miracles. And likewise, if God willed that the organs of human bodies should conform to the will of the soul, according to the *system of occasional causes*, this law also would come into operation only through perpetual miracles.

208. Thus one must suppose that, among the general rules which are not absolutely necessary, God chooses those which are the most natural, which it is easiest to explain, and which also are of greatest service for the explanation of other things. That is doubtless the conclusion most excellent and most pleasing; and even though the System of Pre-established Harmony were not necessary otherwise, because it banishes superfluous miracles, God would have chosen it as being the most harmonious. The ways of God are those most simple and uniform: for he chooses rules that least restrict one another. They are also the most *productive* in proportion to the *simplicity of ways and means*. It is as if one said that a certain house was the best that could have been constructed at a certain cost. One may, indeed, reduce these two conditions, simplicity and productivity, to a single advantage, which is to produce as much perfection as is possible: thus Father Malebranche's system in this point amounts to the same as mine. Even if the effect were assumed to be greater, but the process less simple, I think one might say that, when all is said and done, the effect itself would be less great, taking into account not only the final effect but also the mediate effect. For the wisest mind so acts, as far as it is possible, that the *means* are also in a sense *ends*, that is, they are desirable not only on account of what they do, but on account of what they are. The more intricate processes take up too much ground, too much space, too much place, too much time that might have been better employed.

209. Now since everything resolves itself into this greatest perfection, we return to my law of the best. For perfection includes not only the *moral good* and the *physical good* of intelligent creatures, but also the good which is purely *metaphysical*, and concerns also creatures devoid of reason. It follows that the evil that is in rational creatures happens only by concomitance, not by antecedent will but by a consequent will, as being involved in the best possible plan; and the metaphysical good which includes everything makes it necessary sometimes to admit physical evil and moral evil, as I have already explained more than once. It so happens that the ancient Stoics were not far removed from this system. M. Bayle remarked upon this himself in his *Dictionary* in the article on 'Chrysippus', rem. T. It is of importance to give his own words, in order sometimes to face him with his own objections and to bring him back to the fine sentiments that he had formerly pronounced: 'Chrysippus', he says (p. 930), 'in his work on Providence examined amongst other questions this one: Did the nature of things, or the providence that made the world and the human kind, make also the diseases to which men are subject? He answers that the chief design of Nature was not to make them sickly, that would not be in keeping with the cause of all good; but Nature, in preparing and producing many great things excellently ordered and of great usefulness, found that some drawbacks came as a result, and thus these were not in conformity with the original design and purpose; they came about as a sequel to the work, they existed only as consequences. For the formation of the human body, Chrysippus said, the finest idea as well as the very utility of the work demanded that the head should be composed of a tissue of thin, fine bones; but because of that it was bound to have the disadvantage of not being able to resist blows. Nature made health, and at the same time it was necessary by a kind of concomitance that the source of diseases should be opened up. The same thing applies with regard to virtue; the direct action of Nature, which brought it forth, produced by a counter stroke the brood of vices. I have not translated literally, for which reason I give here the actual Latin of Aulus Gellius, for the benefit of those who understand that language (Aul. Gellius, lib. 6, cap. 1): "Idem Chrysippus in eod. lib. (quarto, περὶ προνοίας) tractat consideratque, dignumque esse id quaeri putat, εἰ αἱ τῶν ἀνθρώπων νόσοι κατὰ φύσιν γίγνονται. Id est, naturane ipsa rerum, vel

providentia quae compagem hanc mundi et genus hominum fecit, morbos quoque et debilitates et aegritudines corporum, quas patiuntur homines, fecerit. Existimat autem non fuisse hoc principale naturae consilium, ut faceret homines morbis obnoxios. Nunquam enim hoc convenisse naturae auctori parentique rerum omnium bonarum. Sed quum multa, inquit, atque magna gigneret, pareretque aptissima et utilissima, alia quoque simul agnata sunt incommoda iis ipsis, quae faciebat, cohaerentia: eaque non per naturam, sed per sequelas quasdam necessarias facta dicit, quod ipse appellat κατὰ παρακολούθησιν. Sicut, inquit, quum corpora hominum natura fingeret, ratio subtilior et utilitas ipsa operis postulavit ut tenuissimis minutisque ossiculis caput compingeret. Sed hanc utilitatem rei majoris alia quaedam incommoditas extrinsecus consecuta est, ut fieret caput tenuiter munitum et ictibus offensionibusque parvis fragile. Proinde morbi quoque et aegritudines partae sunt, dum salus paritur. Sic Hercle, inquit, dum virtus hominibus per consilium naturae gignitur, vitia ibidem per affinitatem contrariam nata sunt." I do not think that a pagan could have said anything more reasonable, considering his ignorance of the first man's fall, the knowledge of which has only reached us through revelation, and which indeed is the true cause of our miseries. If we had sundry like extracts from the works of Chrysippus, or rather if we had his works, we should have a more favourable idea than we have of the beauty of his genius.'

210. Let us now see the reverse of the medal in the altered M. Bayle. After having quoted in his *Reply to the Questions of a Provincial* (vol. III, ch. 155, p. 962) these words of M. Jacquelot, which are much to my liking: 'To change the order of the universe is something of infinitely greater consequence than the prosperity of a good man,' he adds: 'This thought has something dazzling about it: Father Malebranche has placed it in the best possible light; and he has persuaded some of his readers that a system which is simple and very productive is more consistent with God's wisdom than a system more composite and less productive in proportion, but more capable of averting irregularities. M. Bayle was one of those who believed that Father Malebranche in that way gave a wonderful solution.' (It is M. Bayle himself speaking.) 'But it is almost impossible to be satisfied with it after having read M. Arnauld's books against this system, and after having contemplated the vast and boundless idea of the supremely

perfect Being. This idea shows us that nothing is easier for God than to follow a plan which is simple, productive, regular and opportune for all creatures simultaneously.'

211. While I was in France I showed to M. Arnauld a dialogue I had composed in Latin on the cause of evil and the justice of God; it was not only before his disputes with Father Malebranche, but even before the book on *The Search for Truth* appeared. That principle which I uphold here, namely that sin had been permitted because it had been involved in the best plan for the universe, was already applied there; and M. Arnauld did not seem to be startled by it. But the slight contentions which he has since had with Father Malebranche have given him cause to examine this subject with closer attention, and to be more severe in his judgement thereof. Yet I am not altogether pleased with M. Bayle's manner of expression here on this subject, and I am not of the opinion 'that a more composite and less productive plan might be more capable of averting irregularities'. Rules are the expression of general will: the more one observes rules, the more regularity there is; simplicity and productivity are the aim of rules. I shall be met with the objection that a uniform system will be free from irregularities. I answer that it would be an irregularity to be too uniform, that would offend against the rules of harmony. *Et citharoedus Ridetur chorda qui semper oberrat eadem.* I believe therefore that God can follow a simple, productive, regular plan; but I do not believe that the best and the most regular is always opportune for all creatures simultaneously; and I judge *a posteriori*, for the plan chosen by God is not so. I have, however, also shown this *a priori* in examples taken from mathematics, and I will presently give another here. An Origenist who maintains that all rational creatures become happy in the end will be still easier to satisfy. He will say, in imitation of St. Paul's saying about the sufferings of this life, that those which are finite are not worthy to be compared with eternal bliss.

212. What is deceptive in this subject, as I have already observed, is that one feels an inclination to believe that what is the best in the whole is also the best possible in each part. One reasons thus in geometry, when it is a question *de maximis et minimis*. If the road from A to B that one proposes to take is the shortest possible, and if this road passes by C, then the road from A to C, part of the first, must also be the shortest possible. But the inference from

quantity to *quality* is not always right, any more than that which is drawn from equals to similars. For *equals* are those whose quantity is the same, and *similars* are those not differing according to qualities. The late Herr Sturm, a famous mathematician in Altorf, while in Holland in his youth published there a small book under the title of *Euclides Catholicus*. Here he endeavoured to give exact and general rules in subjects not mathematical, being encouraged in the task by the late Herr Erhard Weigel, who had been his tutor. In this book he transfers to similars what Euclid had said of equals, and he formulates this axiom: *Si similibus addas similia, tota sunt similia*. But so many limitations were necessary to justify this new rule, that it would have been better, in my opinion, to enounce it at the outset with a reservation, by saying, *Si similibus similia addas similiter, tota sunt similia*. Moreover, geometricians often require *non tantum similia, sed et similiter posita*.

213. This difference between quantity and quality appears also in our case. The part of the shortest way between two extreme points is also the shortest way between the extreme points of this part; but the part of the best Whole is not of necessity the best that one could have made of this part. For the part of a beautiful thing is not always beautiful, since it can be extracted from the whole, or marked out within the whole, in an irregular manner. If goodness and beauty always lay in something absolute and uniform, such as extension, matter, gold, water, and other bodies assumed to be homogeneous or similar, one must say that the part of the good and the beautiful would be beautiful and good like the whole, since it would always have resemblance to the whole: but this is not the case in things that have mutual relations. An example taken from geometry will be appropriate to explain my idea.

214. There is a kind of geometry which Herr Jung of Hamburg, one of the most admirable men of his time, called 'empiric'. It makes use of conclusive experiments and proves various propositions of Euclid, but especially those which concern the equality of two figures, by cutting the one in pieces, and putting the pieces together again to make the other. In this manner, by cutting carefully in parts the squares on the two sides of the right-angled triangle, and arranging these parts carefully, one makes from them the square on the hypotenuse; that is demonstrating empirically the 47th proposition of the first book of Euclid. Now supposing that some of these pieces taken from the two smaller

squares are lost, something will be lacking in the large square that is to be formed from them; and this defective combination, far from pleasing, will be disagreeably ugly. If then the pieces that remained, composing the faulty combination, were taken separately without any regard to the large square to whose formation they ought to contribute, one would group them together quite differently to make a tolerably good combination. But as soon as the lost pieces are retrieved and the gap in the faulty combination is filled, there will ensue a beautiful and regular thing, the complete large square: this perfect combination will be far more beautiful than the tolerably good combination which had been made from the pieces one had not mislaid alone. The perfect combination corresponds to the universe in its entirety, and the faulty combination that is a part of the perfect one corresponds to some part of the universe, where we find defects which the Author of things has allowed, because otherwise, if he had wished to re-shape this faulty part and make thereof a tolerably good combination, the whole would not then have been so beautiful. For the parts of the faulty combination, grouped better to make a tolerably good combination, could not have been used properly to form the whole and perfect combination. Thomas Aquinas had an inkling of these things when he said: *ad prudentem gubernatorem pertinet, negligere aliquem defectum bonitatis in parte, ut faciat augmentum bonitatis in toto* (Thom., *Contra Gentiles*, lib. 2, c. 71). Thomas Gatacre, in his Notes on the book of Marcus Aurelius (lib. 5, cap. 8, with M. Bayle), cites also passages from authors who say that the evil of the parts is often the good of the whole.

215. Let us return to M. Bayle's illustrations. He imagines a prince (p. 963) who is having a city built, and who, in bad taste, aims rather at airs of magnificence therein, and a bold and unusual style of architecture, than at the provision of conveniences of all kinds for the inhabitants. But if this prince has true magnanimity he will prefer the convenient to the magnificent architecture. That is M. Bayle's judgement. I consider, however, that there are cases where one will justifiably prefer beauty of construction in a palace to the convenience of a few domestics. But I admit that the construction would be bad, however beautiful it might be, if it were a cause of diseases to the inhabitants; provided it was possible to make one that would be better, taking into account beauty, convenience and health all together. It may be, indeed, that one cannot

have all these advantages at once. Thus, supposing one wished to build on the northern and more bracing side of the mountain, if the castle were then bound to be of an unendurable construction, one would prefer to make it face southward.

216. M. Bayle raises the further objection, that it is true that our legislators can never invent regulations such as are convenient for all individuals, 'Nulla lex satis commoda omnibus est; id modo quaeritur, si majori parti et in summam prodest. (Cato apud Livium, L. 34, circa init.)' But the reason is that the limited condition of their knowledge compels them to cling to laws which, when all is taken into account, are more advantageous than harmful. Nothing of all that can apply to God, who is as infinite in power and understanding as in goodness and true greatness. I answer that since God chooses the best possible, one cannot tax him with any limitation of his perfections; and in the universe not only does the good exceed the evil, but also the evil serves to augment the good.

217. He observes also that the Stoics derived a blasphemy from this principle, saying that evils must be endured with patience, or that they were necessary, not only to the well-being and completeness of the universe, but also to the felicity, perfection and conservation of God, who directs it. The Emperor Marcus Aurelius gave expression to that in the eighth chapter of the fifth book of his *Meditations*. 'Duplici ratione', he says, 'diligas oportet, quidquid evenerit tibi; altera quod tibi natum et tibi coordinatum et ad te quodammodo affectum est; altera quod universi gubernatori prosperitatis et consummationis atque adeo permansionis ipsius procurandae (τῆς εὐοδίας καὶ τῆς συντελείας καὶ τῆς συμμονῆς αὐτῆς) ex parte causa est.' This precept is not the most reasonable of those stated by that great emperor. A *diligas oportet* (στέργειν χρὴ) is of no avail; a thing does not become pleasing just because it is necessary, and because it is destined for or attached to someone: and what for me would be an evil would not cease to be such because it would be my master's good, unless this good reflected back on me. One good thing among others in the universe is that the general good becomes in reality the individual good of those who love the Author of all good. But the principal error of this emperor and of the Stoics was their assumption that the good of the universe must please God himself, because they imagined God as the soul of the world. This error has nothing in

common with my dogma, according to which God is *Intelligentia extramundana*, as Martianus Capella calls him, or rather *supramundana*. Further, he acts to do good, and not to receive it. *Melius est dare quam accipere*; his bliss is ever perfect and can receive no increase, either from within or from without.

218. I come now to the principal objection M. Bayle, after M. Arnauld, brings up against me. It is complicated: they maintain that God would be under compulsion, that he would act of necessity, if he were bound to create the best; or at least that he would have been lacking in power if he could not have found a better expedient for excluding sins and other evils. That is in effect denying that this universe is the best, and that God is bound to insist upon the best. I have met this objection adequately in more than one passage: I have proved that God cannot fail to produce the best; and from that assumption it follows that the evils we experience could not have been reasonably excluded from the universe, since they are there. Let us see, however, what these two excellent men bring up, or rather let us see what M. Bayle's objection is, for he professes to have profited by the arguments of M. Arnauld.

219. 'Would it be possible', he says, *Reply to the Questions of a Provincial*, vol. III, ch. 158, p. 890, 'that a nature whose goodness, holiness, wisdom, knowledge and power are infinite, who loves virtue supremely, and hates vice supremely, as our clear and distinct idea of him shows us, and as well-nigh every page of Scripture assures us, could have found in virtue no means fitting and suited for his ends? Would it be possible that vice alone had offered him this means? One would have thought on the contrary that nothing beseemed this nature more than to establish virtue in his work to the exclusion of all vice.' M. Bayle here exaggerates things. I agree that some vice was connected with the best plan of the universe, but I do not agree with him that God could not find in virtue any means suited for his ends. This objection would have been valid if there were no virtue, if vice took its place everywhere. He will say it suffices that vice prevails and that virtue is trifling in comparison. But I am far from agreeing with him there, and I think that in reality, properly speaking, there is incomparably more moral good than moral evil in rational creatures; and of these we have knowledge of but few.

220. This evil is not even so great in men as it is declared to be.

It is only people of a malicious disposition or those who have become somewhat misanthropic through misfortunes, like Lucian's Timon, who find wickedness everywhere, and who poison the best actions by the interpretations they give to them. I speak of those who do it in all seriousness, to draw thence evil conclusions, by which their conduct is tainted; for there are some who only do it to show off their own acumen. People have found that fault in Tacitus, and that again is the criticism M. Descartes (in one of his letters) makes of Mr. Hobbes's book *De Cive*, of which only a few copies had at that time been printed for distribution among friends, but to which some notes by the author were added in the second edition which we have. For although M. Descartes acknowledges that this book is by a man of talent, he observes therein some very dangerous principles and maxims, in the assumption there made that all men are wicked, or the provision of them with motives for being so. The late Herr Jacob Thomasius said in his admirable *Tables of Practical Philosophy* that the πρῶτον ψεῦδος, the primary cause of errors in this book by Mr. Hobbes, was that he took *statum legalem pro naturali*, that is to say that the corrupt state served him as a gauge and rule, whereas it is the state most befitting human nature which Aristotle had had in view. For according to Aristotle, that is termed *natural* which conforms most closely to the perfection of the nature of the thing; but Mr. Hobbes applies the term *natural state* to that which has least art, perhaps not taking into account that human nature in its perfection carries art with it. But the question of name, that is to say, of what may be called natural, would not be of great importance were it not that Aristotle and Hobbes fastened upon it the notion of natural right, each one following his own signification. I have said here already that I found in the book on the Falsity of human Virtues the same defect as M. Descartes found in Mr. Hobbes's *De Cive*.

221. But even if we assume that vice exceeds virtue in the human kind, as it is assumed the number of the damned exceeds that of the elect, it by no means follows that vice and misery exceed virtue and happiness in the universe: one should rather believe the opposite, because the City of God must be the most perfect of all possible states, since it was formed and is perpetually governed by the greatest and best of all Monarchs. This answer confirms the observation I made earlier, when speaking of the conformity of faith with reason, namely, that one of the greatest

sources of fallacy in the objections is the confusion of the apparent with the real. And here by the apparent I mean not simply such as would result from an exact discussion of facts, but that which has been derived from the small extent of our experiences. It would be senseless to try to bring up appearances so imperfect, and having such slight foundation, in opposition to the proofs of reason and the revelations of faith.

222. Finally, I have already observed that love of virtue and hatred of vice, which tend in an undefined way to bring virtue into existence and to prevent the existence of vice, are only antecedent acts of will, such as is the will to bring about the happiness of all men and to save them from misery. These acts of antecedent will make up only a portion of all the antecedent will of God taken together, whose result forms the consequent will, or the decree to create the best. Through this decree it is that love for virtue and for the happiness of rational creatures, which is undefined in itself and goes as far as is possible, receives some slight limitations, on account of the heed that must be paid to good in general. Thus one must understand that God loves virtue supremely and hates vice supremely, and that nevertheless some vice is to be permitted.

223. M. Arnauld and M. Bayle appear to maintain that this method of explaining things and of establishing a best among all the plans for the universe, one such as may not be surpassed by any other, sets a limit to God's power. 'Have you considered', says M. Arnauld to Father Malebranche (in his *Reflexions on the New System of Nature and Grace*, vol. II, p. 385), 'that in making such assumptions you take it upon yourself to subvert the first article of the creed, whereby we make profession of believing in God the Father Almighty?' He had said already (p. 362): 'Can one maintain, without trying to blind oneself, that a course of action which could not fail to have this grievous result, namely, that the majority of men perish, bears the stamp of God's goodness more than a different course of action, which would have caused, if God had followed it, the salvation of all men?' And, as M. Jacquelot does not differ from the principles I have just laid down, M. Bayle raises like objections in his case (*Reply to the Questions of a Provincial*, vol. III, ch. 151, p. 900): 'If one adopts such explanations', he says, 'one sees oneself constrained to renounce the most obvious notions on the nature of the supremely perfect Being. These teach us that all things not implying contradiction

are possible for him, that consequently it is possible for him to save people whom he does not save: for what contradiction would result supposing the number of the elect were greater than it is? They teach us besides that, since he is supremely happy, he has no will which he cannot carry out. How, then, shall we understand that he wills to save all men and that he cannot do so? We sought some light to help us out of the perplexities we feel in comparing the idea of God with the state of the human kind, and lo! we are given elucidations that cast us into darkness more dense.'

224. All these obstacles vanish before the exposition I have just given. I agree with M. Bayle's principle, and it is also mine, that everything implying no contradiction is possible. But as for me, holding as I do that God did the best that was possible, or that he could not have done better than he has done, deeming also that to pass any other judgement upon his work in its entirety would be to wrong his goodness or his wisdom, I must say that to make something which surpasses in goodness the best itself, that indeed would imply contradiction. That would be as if someone maintained that God could draw from one point to another a line shorter than the straight line, and accused those who deny this of subverting the article of faith whereby we believe in God the Father Almighty.

225. The infinity of possibles, however great it may be, is no greater than that of the wisdom of God, who knows all possibles. One may even say that if this wisdom does not exceed the possibles extensively, since the objects of the understanding cannot go beyond the possible, which in a sense is alone intelligible, it exceeds them intensively, by reason of the infinitely infinite combinations it makes thereof, and its many deliberations concerning them. The wisdom of God, not content with embracing all the possibles, penetrates them, compares them, weighs them one against the other, to estimate their degrees of perfection or imperfection, the strong and the weak, the good and the evil. It goes even beyond the finite combinations, it makes of them an infinity of infinites, that is to say, an infinity of possible sequences of the universe, each of which contains an infinity of creatures. By this means the divine Wisdom distributes all the possibles it had already contemplated separately, into so many universal systems which it further compares the one with the other. The result of all these comparisons and deliberations is the choice of the best from

ESSAYS ON THE JUSTICE OF GOD AND THE

among all these possible systems, which wisdom makes in order to satisfy goodness completely; and such is precisely the plan of the universe as it is. Moreover, all these operations of the divine understanding, although they have among them an order and a priority of nature, always take place together, no priority of time existing among them.

226. The careful consideration of these things will, I hope, induce a different idea of the greatness of the divine perfections, and especially of the wisdom and goodness of God, from any that can exist in the minds of those who make God act at random, without cause or reason. And I do not see how they could avoid falling into an opinion so strange, unless they acknowledged that there are reasons for God's choice, and that these reasons are derived from his goodness: whence it follows of necessity that what was chosen had the advantage of goodness over what was not chosen, and consequently that it is the best of all the possibles. The best cannot be surpassed in goodness, and it is no restriction of the power of God to say that he cannot do the impossible. Is it possible, said M. Bayle, that there is no better plan than that one which God carried out? One answers that it is very possible and indeed necessary, namely that there is none: otherwise God would have preferred it.

227. It seems to me that I have proved sufficiently that among all the possible plans of the universe there is one better than all the rest, and that God has not failed to choose it. But M. Bayle claims to infer thence that God is therefore not free. This is how he speaks on that question (*ubi supra*, ch. 151, p. 899): 'I thought to argue with a man who assumed as I do that the goodness and the power of God are infinite, as well as his wisdom; and now I see that in reality this man assumes that God's goodness and power are enclosed within rather narrow bounds.' As to that, the objection has already been met: I set no bounds to God's power, since I recognize that it extends *ad maximum, ad omnia,* to all that implies no contradiction; and I set none to his goodness, since it attains to the best, *ad optimum.* But M. Bayle goes on: 'There is therefore no freedom in God; he is compelled by his wisdom to create, and then to create precisely such a work, and finally to create it precisely in such ways. These are three servitudes which form a more than Stoic *fatum,* and which render impossible all that is not within their sphere. It seems that, according to this system, God could

have said, even before shaping his decrees: I cannot save such and such a man, nor condemn such and such another, *quippe vetor fatis*, my wisdom permits it not.'

228. I answer that it is goodness which prompts God to create with the purpose of communicating himself; and this same goodness combined with wisdom prompts him to create the best: a best that includes the whole sequence, the effect and the process. It prompts him thereto without compelling him, for it does not render impossible that which it does not cause him to choose. To call that *fatum* is taking it in a good sense, which is not contrary to freedom: *fatum* comes from *fari*, to speak, to pronounce; it signifies a judgement, a decree of God, the award of his wisdom. To say that one cannot do a thing, simply because one does not will it, is to misuse terms. The wise mind wills only the good: is it then a servitude when the will acts in accordance with wisdom? And can one be less a slave than to act by one's own choice in accordance with the most perfect reason? Aristotle used to say that that man is in a natural servitude (*natura servus*) who lacks guidance, who has need of being directed. Slavery comes from without, it leads to that which offends, and especially to that which offends with reason: the force of others and our own passions enslave us. God is never moved by anything outside himself, nor is he subject to inward passions, and he is never led to that which can cause him offence. It appears, therefore, that M. Bayle gives odious names to the best things in the world, and turns our ideas upside-down, applying the term slavery to the state of the greatest and most perfect freedom.

229. He had also said not long before (ch. 151, p. 891): 'If virtue, or any other good at all, had been as appropriate as vice for the Creator's ends, vice would not have been given preference; it must therefore have been the only means that the Creator could have used; it was therefore employed purely of necessity. As therefore he loves his glory, not with a freedom of indifference, but by necessity, he must by necessity love all the means without which he could not manifest his glory. Now if vice, as vice, was the only means of attaining to this end, it will follow that God of necessity loves vice as vice, a thought which can only inspire us with horror; and he has revealed quite the contrary to us.' He observes at the same time that certain doctors among the Supralapsarians (like Rutherford, for example) denied that God wills sin as sin, whilst

they admitted that he wills sin permissively in so far as it is punishable and pardonable. But he urges in objection, that an action is only punishable and pardonable in so far as it is vicious.

230. M. Bayle makes a false assumption in these words that we have just read, and draws from them false conclusions. It is not true that God loves his glory by necessity, if thereby it is understood that he is led by necessity to acquire his glory through his creatures. For if that were so, he would acquire his glory always and everywhere. The decree to create is free: God is prompted to all good; the good, and even the best, inclines him to act; but it does not compel him, for his choice creates no impossibility in that which is distinct from the best; it causes no implication of contradiction in that which God refrains from doing. There is therefore in God a freedom that is exempt not only from constraint but also from necessity. I mean this in respect of metaphysical necessity; for it is a moral necessity that the wisest should be bound to choose the best. It is the same with the means which God chooses to attain his glory. And as for vice, it has been shown in preceding pages that it is not an object of God's decree as *means*, but as *conditio sine qua non*, and that for that reason alone it is permitted. One is even less justified in saying that vice is *the only means*; it would be at most one of the means, but one of the least among innumerable others.

231. 'Another frightful consequence,' M. Bayle goes on, 'the fatality of all things, ensues: God will not have been free to arrange events in a different way, since the means he chose to show forth his glory was the only means befitting his wisdom.' This so-called fatality or necessity is only moral, as I have just shown: it does not affect freedom; on the contrary, it assumes the best use thereof; it does not render impossible the objects set aside by God's choice. 'What, then, will become', he adds, 'of man's free will? Will there not have been necessity and fatality for Adam to sin? For if he had not sinned, he would have overthrown the sole plan that God had of necessity created.' That is again a misuse of terms. Adam sinning freely was seen of God among the ideas of the possibles, and God decreed to admit him into existence as he saw him. This decree does not change the nature of the objects: it does not render necessary that which was contingent in itself, or impossible that which was possible.

270

232. M. Bayle goes on (p. 892): 'The subtle Scotus asserts with much discernment that if God had no freedom of indifference no creature could have this kind of freedom.' I agree provided it is not meant as an indifference of equipoise, where there is no reason inclining more to one side than the other. M. Bayle acknowledges (farther on in chapter 168, p. 1111) that what is termed indifference does not exclude prevenient inclinations and pleasures. It suffices therefore that there be no metaphysical necessity in the action which is termed free, that is to say, it suffices that a choice be made between several courses possible.

233. He goes on again in the said chapter 157, p. 893: 'If God is not determined to create the world by a free motion of his goodness, but by the interests of his glory, which he loves by necessity, and which is the only thing he loves, for it is not different from his substance; and if the love that he has for himself has compelled him to show forth his glory through the most fitting means, and if the fall of man was this same means, it is evident that this fall happened entirely by necessity and that the obedience of Eve and Adam to God's commands was impossible.' Still the same error. The love that God bears to himself is essential to him, but the love for his glory, or the will to acquire his glory, is not so by any means: the love he has for himself did not impel him by necessity to actions without; they were free; and since there were possible plans whereby the first parents should not sin, their sin was therefore not necessary. Finally, I say in effect what M. Bayle acknowledges here, 'that God resolved to create the world by a free motion of his goodness'; and I add that this same motion prompted him to the best.

234. The same answer holds good against this statement of M. Bayle's (ch. 165, p. 1071): 'The means most appropriate for attaining an end is of necessity one alone' (that is very well said, at least for the cases where God has chosen). 'Therefore if God was prompted irresistibly to employ this means, he employed it by necessity.' (He was certainly prompted thereto, he was determined, or rather he determined himself thereto: but that which is certain is not always necessary, or altogether irresistible; the thing might have gone otherwise, but that did not happen, and with good reason. God chose between different courses all possible: thus, metaphysically speaking, he could have chosen or done what was not the best; but he could not morally speaking have done so.

Let us make use of a comparison from geometry. The best way from one point to another (leaving out of account obstacles and other considerations accidental to the medium) is one alone: it is that one which passes by the shortest line, which is the straight line. Yet there are innumerable ways from one point to another. There is therefore no necessity which binds me to go by the straight line; but as soon as I choose the best, I am determined to go that way, although this is only a moral necessity in the wise. That is why the following conclusions fail.) 'Therefore he could only do that which he did. Therefore that which has not happened or will never happen is absolutely impossible.' (These conclusions fail, I say: for since there are many things which have never happened and never will happen, and which nevertheless are clearly conceivable, and imply no contradiction, how can one say they are altogether impossible? M. Bayle has refuted that himself in a passage opposing the Spinozists, which I have already quoted here, and he has frequently acknowledged that there is nothing impossible except that which implies contradiction: now he changes style and terminology.) 'Therefore Adam's perseverance in innocence was always impossible; therefore his fall was altogether inevitable, and even antecedently to God's decree, for it implied contradiction that God should be able to will a thing opposed to his wisdom: it is, after all, the same thing to say, that it is impossible for God, as to say, God could do it, if he so willed, but he cannot will it.' (It is misusing terms in a sense to say here: one can will, one will will; 'can' here concerns the actions that one does will. Nevertheless it implies no contradiction that God should will—directly or permissively—a thing not implying contradiction, and in this sense it is permitted to say that God can will it.)

235. In a word, when one speaks of the *possibility* of a thing it is not a question of the causes that can bring about or prevent its actual existence: otherwise one would change the nature of the terms, and render useless the distinction between the possible and the actual. This Abélard did, and Wyclif appears to have done after him, in consequence of which they fell needlessly into unsuitable and disagreeable expressions. That is why, when one asks if a thing is possible or necessary, and brings in the consideration of what God wills or chooses, one alters the issue. For God chooses among the possibles, and for that very reason he chooses freely,

and is not compelled; there would be neither choice nor freedom if there were but one course possible.

236. One must also answer M. Bayle's syllogisms, so as to neglect none of the objections of a man so gifted: they occur in Chapter 151 of his *Reply to the Questions of a Provincial* (vol. III, pp. 900, 901).

FIRST SYLLOGISM

'God can will nothing that is opposed to the necessary love which he has for his wisdom.

'Now the salvation of all men is opposed to the necessary love which God has for his wisdom.

'Therefore God cannot will the salvation of all men.'

The major is self-evident, for one can do nothing whereof the opposite is necessary. But the minor cannot be accepted, for, albeit God loves his wisdom of necessity, the actions whereto his wisdom prompts him cannot but be free, and the objects whereto his wisdom does not prompt him do not cease to be possible. Moreover, his wisdom has prompted him to will the salvation of all men, but not by a consequent and decretory will. Yet this consequent will, being only a result of free antecedent acts of will, cannot fail to be free also.

SECOND SYLLOGISM

'The work most worthy of God's wisdom involves amongst other things the sin of all men and the eternal damnation of the majority of men.

'Now God wills of necessity the work most worthy of his wisdom.

'He wills therefore of necessity the work that involves amongst other things the sin of all men and the eternal damnation of the majority of men.'

The major holds good, but the minor I deny. The decrees of God are always free, even though God be always prompted thereto by reasons which lie in the intention towards good: for to be morally compelled by wisdom, to be bound by the consideration of good, is to be free; it is not compulsion in the metaphysical sense. And metaphysical necessity alone, as I have observed so many times, is opposed to freedom.

238. I shall not examine the syllogisms that M. Bayle urges in objection in the following chapter (Ch. 152), against the system of the Supralapsarians, and particularly against the oration made by

Theodore de Bèze at the Conference of Montbéliard in the year 1586. This conference also only served to increase the acrimony of the parties. 'God created the World to his glory: his glory is not known (according to Bèze), if his mercy and his justice are not declared; for this cause simply by his grace he decreed for some men life eternal, and for others by a just judgement eternal damnation. Mercy presupposes misery, justice presupposes guilt.' (He might have added that misery also supposes guilt.) 'Nevertheless God being good, indeed goodness itself, he created man good and righteous, but unstable, and capable of sinning of his own free will. Man did not fall at random or rashly, or through causes ordained by some other God, as the Manichaeans hold, but by the providence of God; in such a way notwithstanding, that God was not involved in the fault, inasmuch as man was not constrained to sin.'

239. This system is not of the best conceived: it is not well fitted to show forth the wisdom, the goodness and the justice of God; and happily it is almost abandoned to-day. If there were not other more profound reasons capable of inducing God to permit guilt, the source of misery, there would be neither guilt nor misery in the world, for the reasons alleged here do not suffice. He would declare his mercy better in preventing misery, and he would declare his justice better in preventing guilt, in advancing virtue, in recompensing it. Besides, one does not see how he who not only causes a man to be capable of falling, but who so disposes circumstances that they contribute towards causing his fall, is not culpable, if there are no other reasons compelling him thereto. But when one considers that God, altogether good and wise, must have produced all the virtue, goodness, happiness whereof the best plan of the universe is capable, and that often an evil in some parts may serve the greater good of the whole, one readily concludes that God may have given room for unhappiness, and even permitted guilt, as he has done, without deserving to be blamed. It is the only remedy that supplies what all systems lack, however they arrange the decrees. These thoughts have already been favoured by St. Augustine, and one may say of Eve what the poet said of the hand of Mucius Scaevola:

Si non errasset, fecerat illa minus.

240. I find that the famous English prelate who wrote an ingenious book on the origin of evil, some passages of which were

disputed by M. Bayle in the second volume of his *Reply to the Questions of a Provincial*, while disagreeing with some of the opinions that I have upheld here and appearing to resort sometimes to a despotic power, as if the will of God did not follow the rules of wisdom in relation to good or evil, but decreed arbitrarily that such and such a thing must be considered good or evil; and as if even the will of the creature, in so far as it is free, did not choose because the object appears good to him, but by a purely arbitrary determination, independent of the representation of the object; this bishop, I say, in other passages nevertheless says things which seem more in favour of my doctrine than of what appears contrary thereto in his own. He says that what an infinitely wise and free cause has chosen is better than what it has not chosen. Is not that recognizing that goodness is the object and the reason of his choice? In this sense one will here aptly say:

Sic placuit superis; quaerere plura, nefas.

ESSAYS

ON THE JUSTICE OF GOD
AND THE FREEDOM OF MAN
IN THE ORIGIN OF EVIL

PART THREE

241. Now at last I have disposed of the cause of moral evil; *physical evil*, that is, sorrows, sufferings, miseries, will be less troublesome to explain, since these are results of moral evil. *Poena est malum passionis, quod infligitur ob malum actionis*, according to Grotius. One suffers because one has acted; one suffers evil because one does evil.

> *Nostrorum causa malorum*
> *Nos sumus.*

It is true that one often suffers through the evil actions of others; but when one has no part in the offence one must look upon it as a certainty that these sufferings prepare for us a greater happiness. The question of *physical evil*, that is, of the origin of sufferings, has difficulties in common with that of the origin of *metaphysical evil*, examples whereof are furnished by the monstrosities and other apparent irregularities of the universe. But one must believe that even sufferings and monstrosities are part of order; and it is well to bear in mind not only that it was better to admit these defects and these monstrosities than to violate general laws, as Father Malebranche sometimes argues, but also that these very monstrosities are in the rules, and are in conformity with general acts of will, though we be not capable of discerning this conformity.

276

THE JUSTICE OF GOD AND THE FREEDOM OF MAN

It is just as sometimes there are appearances of irregularity in mathematics which issue finally in a great order when one has finally got to the bottom of them: that is why I have already in this work observed that according to my principles all individual events, without exception, are consequences of general acts of will.

242. It should be no cause for astonishment that I endeavour to elucidate these things by comparisons taken from pure mathematics, where everything proceeds in order, and where it is possible to fathom them by a close contemplation which grants us an enjoyment, so to speak, of the vision of the ideas of God. One may propose a succession or series of numbers perfectly irregular to all appearance, where the numbers increase and diminish variably without the emergence of any order; and yet he who knows the key to the formula, and who understands the origin and the structure of this succession of numbers, will be able to give a rule which, being properly understood, will show that the series is perfectly regular, and that it even has excellent properties. One may make this still more evident in lines. A line may have twists and turns, ups and downs, points of reflexion and points of inflexion, interruptions and other variations, so that one sees neither rhyme nor reason therein, especially when taking into account only a portion of the line; and yet it may be that one can give its equation and construction, wherein a geometrician would find the reason and the fittingness of all these so-called irregularities. That is how we must look upon the irregularities constituted by monstrosities and other so-called defects in the universe.

243. In this sense one may apply that fine adage of St. Bernard (Ep. 276, Ad Eugen., 111): 'Ordinatissimum est, minus interdum ordinate fieri aliquid.' It belongs to the great order that there should be some small disorder. One may even say that this small disorder is apparent only in the whole, and it is not even apparent when one considers the happiness of those who walk in the ways of order.

244. When I mention monstrosities I include numerous other apparent defects besides. We are acquainted with hardly anything but the surface of our globe; we scarce penetrate into its interior beyond a few hundred fathoms. That which we find in this crust of the globe appears to be the effect of some great upheavals. It seems that this globe was once on fire, and that the rocks forming the base of this crust of the earth are scoria remaining from a great

fusion. In their entrails are found metal and mineral products, which closely resemble those emanating from our furnaces: and the entire sea may be a kind of *oleum per deliquium*, just as tartaric oil forms in a damp place. For when the earth's surface cooled after the great conflagration the moisture that the fire had driven into the air fell back upon the earth, washed its surface and dissolved and absorbed the solid salt that was left in the cinders, finally filling up this great cavity in the surface of our globe, to form the ocean filled with salt water.

245. But, after the fire, one must conclude that earth and water made ravages no less. It may be that the crust formed by the cooling, having below it great cavities, fell in, so that we live only on ruins, as among others Thomas Burnet, Chaplain to the late King of Great Britain, aptly observed. Sundry deluges and inundations have left deposits, whereof traces and remains are found which show that the sea was in places that to-day are most remote from it. But these upheavals ceased at last, and the globe assumed the shape that we see. Moses hints at these changes in few words: the separation of light from darkness indicates the melting caused by the fire; and the separation of the moist from the dry marks the effects of inundations. But who does not see that these disorders have served to bring things to the point where they now are, that we owe to them our riches and our comforts, and that through their agency this globe became fit for cultivation by us. These disorders passed into order. The disorders, real or apparent, that we see from afar are sunspots and comets; but we do not know what uses they supply, nor the rules prevailing therein. Time was when the planets were held to be wandering stars: now their motion is found to be regular. Peradventure it is the same with the comets: posterity will know.

246. One does not include among the disorders inequality of conditions, and M. Jacquelot is justified in asking those who would have everything equally perfect, why rocks are not crowned with leaves and flowers? why ants are not peacocks? And if there must needs be equality everywhere, the poor man would serve notice of appeal against the rich, the servant against the master. The pipes of an organ must not be of equal size. M. Bayle will say that there is a difference between a privation of good and a disorder; between a disorder in inanimate things, which is purely metaphysical, and a disorder in rational creatures, which is composed of crime and

sufferings. He is right in making a distinction between them, and I am right in combining them. God does not neglect inanimate things: they do not feel, but God feels for them. He does not neglect animals: they have not intelligence, but God has it for them. He would reproach himself for the slightest actual defect there were in the universe, even though it were perceived of none.

247. It seems M. Bayle does not approve any comparison between the disorders which may exist in inanimate things and those which trouble the peace and happiness of rational creatures; nor would he agree to our justifying the permission of vice on the pretext of the care that must be taken to avoid disturbing the laws of motion. One might thence conclude, according to him (posthumous Reply to M. Jacquelot, p. 183), 'that God created the world only to display his infinite skill in architecture and mechanics, whilst his property of goodness and love of virtue took no part in the construction of this great work. This God would pride himself only on skill; he would prefer to let the whole human kind perish rather than suffer some atoms to go faster or more slowly than general laws require.' M. Bayle would not have made this antithesis if he had been informed on the system of general harmony which I assume, which states that the realm of efficient causes and that of final causes are parallel to each other; that God has no less the quality of the best monarch than that of the greatest architect; that matter is so disposed that the laws of motion serve as the best guidance for spirits; and that consequently it will prove that he has attained the utmost good possible, provided one reckon the metaphysical, physical and moral goods together.

248. But (M. Bayle will say) God having power to avert innumerable evils by one small miracle, why did he not employ it? He gives so much extraordinary help to fallen men; but slight help of such a kind given to Eve would have prevented her fall and rendered the temptation of the serpent ineffective. I have sufficiently met objections of this sort with this general answer, that God ought not to make choice of another universe since he has chosen the best, and has only made use of the miracles necessary thereto. I had answered M. Bayle that miracles change the natural order of the universe. He replies, that that is an illusion, and that the miracle of the wedding at Cana (for instance) made no change in the air of the room, except that instead of receiving

into its pores some corpuscles of water, it received corpuscles of wine. But one must bear in mind that once the best plan of things has been chosen nothing can be changed therein.

249. As for miracles (concerning which I have already said something in this work), they are perhaps not all of one and the same kind: there are many, to all appearances, which God brings about through the ministry of invisible substances, such as the angels, as Father Malebranche also believes. These angels or these substances act according to the ordinary laws of their nature, being combined with bodies more rarefied and more vigorous than those we have at our command. And such miracles are only so by comparison, and in relation to us; just as our works would be considered miraculous amongst animals if they were capable of remarking upon them. The changing of water into wine might be a miracle of this kind. But the Creation, the Incarnation and some other actions of God exceed all the power of creatures and are truly miracles, or indeed Mysteries. If, nevertheless, the changing of water into wine at Cana was a miracle of the highest kind, God would have thereby changed the whole course of the universe, because of the connexion of bodies; or else he would have been bound to prevent this connexion miraculously also, and cause the bodies not concerned in the miracle to act as if no miracle had happened. After the miracle was over, it would have been necessary to restore all things in those very bodies concerned to the state they would have reached without the miracle: whereafter all would have returned to its original course. Thus this miracle demanded more than at first appears.

250. As for physical evil in creatures, to wit their sufferings, M. Bayle contends vigorously against those who endeavour to justify by means of particular reasons the course of action pursued by God in regard to this. Here I set aside the sufferings of animals, and I see that M. Bayle insists chiefly on those of men, perhaps because he thinks that brute beasts have no feeling. It is on account of the injustice there would be in the sufferings of beasts that divers Cartesians wished to prove that they are only machines, *quoniam sub Deo justo nemo innocens miser est*: it is impossible that an innocent creature should be unhappy under such a master as God. The principle is good, but I do not think it warrants the inference that beasts have no feeling, because I think that, properly speaking, perception is not sufficient to cause misery if it is not accompanied

by reflexion. It is the same with happiness: without reflexion there is none.

O fortunatos nimium, sua qui bona norint!

One cannot reasonably doubt the existence of pain among animals; but it seems as if their pleasures and their pains are not so keen as they are in man: for animals, since they do not reflect, are susceptible neither to the grief that accompanies pain, nor to the joy that accompanies pleasure. Men are sometimes in a state approaching that of the beasts, when they act almost on instinct alone and simply on the impressions made by the experience of the senses: and, in this state, their pleasures and their pains are very slight.

251. But let us pass from the beasts and return to rational creatures. It is with regard to them that M. Bayle discusses this question: whether there is more physical evil than physical good in the world? (*Reply to the Questions of a Provincial*, vol. II, ch. 75.) To settle it aright, one must explain wherein these goods and evils lie. We are agreed that physical evil is simply displeasure and under that heading I include pain, grief, and every other kind of discomfort. But does physical good lie solely in pleasure? M. Bayle appears to be of this opinion; but I consider that it lies also in a middle state, such as that of health. One is well enough when one has no ill; it is a degree of wisdom to have no folly:

Sapientia prima est,
Stultitia caruisse.

In the same way one is worthy of praise when one cannot with justice be blamed:

Si non culpabor, sat mihi laudis erit.

That being the case, all the sensations not unpleasing to us, all the exercises of our powers that do not incommode us, and whose prevention would incommode us, are physical goods, even when they cause us no pleasure; for privation of them is a physical evil. Besides we only perceive the good of health, and other like goods, when we are deprived of them. On those terms I would dare to maintain that even in this life goods exceed evils, that our comforts exceed our discomforts, and that M. Descartes was justified in writing (vol. I, Letter 9) 'that natural reason teaches us that we have more goods than evils in this life'.

252. It must be added that pleasures enjoyed too often and to excess would be a very great evil. There are some which Hippocrates compared to the falling sickness, and Scioppius doubtless only made pretence of envying the sparrows in order to be agreeably playful in a learned and far from playful work. Highly seasoned foods are injurious to health and impair the niceness of a delicate sense; and in general bodily pleasures are a kind of expenditure of the spirit, though they be made good in some better than in others.

253. As proof, however, that the evil exceeds the good is quoted the instance of M. de la Motte le Vayer (Letter 134), who would not have been willing to return to the world, supposing he had had to play the same part as providence had already assigned to him. But I have already said that I think one would accept the proposal of him who could re-knot the thread of Fate if a new part were promised to us, even though it should not be better than the first. Thus from M. de la Motte le Vayer's saying it does not follow that he would not have wished for the part he had already played, provided it had been new, as M. Bayle seems to take it.

254. The pleasures of the mind are the purest, and of greatest service in making joy endure. Cardan, when already an old man, was so content with his state that he protested solemnly that he would not exchange it for the state of the richest of young men who at the same time was ignorant. M. de la Motte le Vayer quotes the saying himself without criticizing it. Knowledge has doubtless charms which cannot be conceived by those who have not tasted them. I do not mean a mere knowledge of facts without that of reasons, but knowledge like that of Cardan, who with all his faults was a great man, and would have been incomparable without those faults.

> *Felix, qui potuit rerum cognoscere causas* !
> *Ille metus omnes et inexorabile fatum*
> *Subjecit pedibus.*

It is no small thing to be content with God and with the universe, not to fear what destiny has in store for us, nor to complain of what befalls us. Acquaintance with true principles gives us this advantage, quite other than that the Stoics and the Epicureans derived from their philosophy. There is as much difference between true morality and theirs as there is between joy and patience: for their tranquillity was founded only on necessity, while ours must rest upon the perfection and beauty of things, upon our own happiness.

255. What, then, shall we say of bodily sufferings? May they not be sufficiently acute to disturb the sage's tranquillity? Aristotle assents; the Stoics were of a different opinion, and even the Epicureans likewise. M. Descartes revived the doctrine of these philosophers; he says in the letter just quoted: 'that even amid the worst misfortunes and the most overwhelming sufferings one may always be content, if only one knows how to exercise reason'. M. Bayle says concerning this (*Reply to the Questions of a Provincial*, vol. III, ch. 157, p. 991) 'that it is saying nothing, that it is prescribing for us a remedy whose preparation hardly anyone understands'. I hold that the thing is not impossible, and that men could attain it by dint of meditation and practice. For apart from the true martyrs and those who have been aided in wonderful wise from on high, there have been counterfeits who imitated them. That Spanish slave who killed the Carthaginian governor in order to avenge his master and who evinced great joy in his deed, even in the greatest tortures, may shame the philosophers. Why should not one go as far as he? One may say of an advantage, as of a disadvantage:

Cuivis potest accidere, quod cuiquam potest.

256. But even to-day entire tribes, such as the Hurons, the Iroquois, the Galibis and other peoples of America teach us a great lesson on this matter: one cannot read without astonishment of the intrepidity and well-nigh insensibility wherewith they brave their enemies, who roast them over a slow fire and eat them by slices. If such people could retain their physical superiority and their courage, and combine them with our acquirements, they would surpass us in every way,

Extat ut in mediis turris aprica casis.

They would be, in comparison with us, as a giant to a dwarf, a mountain to a hill:

*Quantus Eryx, et quantus Athos, gaudetque nivali
Vertice se attollens pater Apenninus ad auras.*

ESSAYS ON THE JUSTICE OF GOD AND THE

257. All that which is effected by a wonderful vigour of body and mind in these savages, who persist obstinately in the strangest point of honour, might be acquired in our case by training, by well-seasoned mortifications, by an overmastering joy founded on reason, by great practice in preserving a certain presence of mind in the midst of the distractions and impressions most liable to disturb it. Something of this kind is related of the ancient Assassins, subjects and pupils of the Old Man or rather the Seigneur (*Senior*) of the Mountain. Such a school (for a better purpose) would be good for missionaries who would wish to return to Japan. The Gymnosophists of the ancient Indians had perhaps something resembling this, and that Calanus, who provided for Alexander the Great the spectacle of his burning alive, had doubtless been encouraged by the great examples of his masters and trained by great sufferings not to fear pain. The wives of these same Indians, who even to-day ask to be burned with the bodies of their husbands, seem still to keep something of the courage of those ancient philosophers of their country. I do not expect that there should straightway be founded a religious order whose purpose would be to exalt man to that high pitch of perfection: such people would be too much above the rest, and too formidable for the authorities. As it rarely happens that people are exposed to extremes where such great strength of mind would be needed, one will scarce think of providing for it at the expense of our usual comforts, albeit incomparably more would be gained than lost thereby.

258. Nevertheless the very fact that one has no need of that great remedy is a proof that the good already exceeds the evil. Euripides also said:

πλείω τὰ χρηστὰ τῶν κακῶν εἶναι βροτοῖς.
Mala nostra longe judico vinci a bonis.

Homer and divers other poets were of another mind, and men in general agree with them. The reason for this is that the evil arouses our attention rather than the good: but this same reason proves that the evil is more rare. One must therefore not credit the petulant expressions of Pliny, who would have it that Nature is a stepmother, and who maintains that man is the most unhappy and most vain of all creatures. These two epithets do not agree: one is not so very unhappy, when one is full of oneself. It is true that men hold human nature only too much in contempt, apparently because they see no other creatures capable of arousing their emulation; but they have all too much self-esteem, and individually are but too easily satisfied. I therefore agree with Meric Casaubon, who in his notes on the Xenophanes of Diogenes Laertius praises exceedingly the admirable sentiments of Euripides, going so far as to credit him with having said things *quae spirant θεόπνευστον pectus*. Seneca (Lib. 4, c. 5, *De Benefic.*) speaks eloquently of the blessings Nature has heaped upon us. M. Bayle in his *Dictionary*, article 'Xenophanes', brings up sundry authorities against this, and among others that of the poet Diphilus in the Collections of Stobaeus, whose Greek might be thus expressed in Latin:

> *Fortuna cyathis bibere nos datis jubens,*
> *Infundit uno terna pro bono mala.*

259. M. Bayle believes that if it were a question only of the evil of guilt, or of moral evil among men, the case would soon be terminated to the advantage of Pliny, and Euripides would lose his action. To that I am not opposed; our vices doubtless exceed our virtues, and this is the effect of original sin. It is nevertheless true that also on that point men in general exaggerate things, and that even some theologians disparage man so much that they wrong the providence of the Author of mankind. That is why I am not in favour of those who thought to do great honour to our religion by saying that the virtues of the pagans were only *splendida peccata*, splendid vices. It is a sally of St. Augustine's which has no foundation in holy Scripture, and which offends reason. But here we are only discussing a physical good and evil, and one must compare in detail the prosperities and the adversities of this life. M. Bayle would wish almost to set aside the consideration of health; he likens it to the rarefied bodies, which are scarcely felt, like air, for example; but he likens pain to the bodies that have much density and much weight in slight volume. But pain itself makes us aware of the importance of health when we are bereft of it. I have already observed that excess of physical pleasures would be a real evil, and the matter ought not to be otherwise; it is too important for the spirit to be free. Lactantius (*Divin. Instit.*, lib. 3, cap. 18) had said that men are so squeamish that they complain of the slightest ill, as if it swallowed up all the goods they have enjoyed. M. Bayle says, concerning this, that the very fact that

men have this feeling warrants the judgement that they are in evil case, since it is feeling which measures the extent of good or evil. But I answer that present feeling is anything rather than the true measure of good and evil past and future. I grant that one is in evil case while one makes these peevish reflexions; but that does not exclude a previous state of well-being, nor imply that, everything reckoned in and all allowance made, the good does not exceed the evil.

260. I do not wonder that the pagans, dissatisfied with their gods, made complaints against Prometheus and Epimetheus for having forged so weak an animal as man. Nor do I wonder that they acclaimed the fable of old Silenus, foster-father of Bacchus, who was seized by King Midas, and as the price of his deliverance taught him that ostensibly fine maxim that the first and the greatest of goods was not to be born, and the second, to depart from this life with dispatch (Cic., *Tuscul.*, lib. 1). Plato believed that souls had been in a happier state, and many of the ancients, amongst others Cicero in his Consolation (according to the account of Lactantius), believed that for their sins they were confined in bodies as in a prison. They rendered thus a reason for our ills, and asserted their prejudices against human life: for there is no such thing as a beautiful prison. But quite apart from the consideration that, even according to these same pagans, the evils of this life would be counterbalanced and exceeded by the goods of past and future lives, I make bold to say that we shall find, upon unbiassed scrutiny of the facts, that taking all in all human life is in general tolerable. And adding thereto the motives of religion, we shall be content with the order God has set therein. Moreover, for a better judgement of our goods and our evils, it will be well to read Cardan, *De Utilitate ex Adversis Capienda*, and Novarini, *De Occultis Dei Beneficiis*.

261. M. Bayle dilates upon the misfortunes of the great, who are thought to be the most fortunate: the constant experience of the fair aspect of their condition renders them unaware of good, but greatly aware of evil. Someone will say: so much the worse for them; if they know not how to enjoy the advantages of nature and fortune, is that the fault of either? There are nevertheless great men possessed of more wisdom, who know how to profit by the favours God has shown them, who are easily consoled for their misfortunes, and who even turn their own faults to account. M.

Bayle pays no heed to that: he prefers to listen to Pliny, who thinks that Augustus, one of the princes most favoured by fortune, experienced at least as much evil as good. I admit that he found great causes of trouble in his family and that remorse for having crushed the Republic may have tormented him; but I think that he was too wise to grieve over the former, and that Maecenas apparently made him understand that Rome had need of a master. Had not Augustus been converted on this point, Vergil would never have said of a lost soul:

> *Vendidit hic auro patriam Dominumque potentem*
> *Imposuit, fixit leges pretio atque refixit.*

Augustus would have thought that he and Caesar were alluded to in these lines, which speak of a master given to a free state. But there is every indication that he applied it just as little to his dominion, which he regarded as compatible with liberty and as a necessary remedy for public evils, as the princes of to-day apply to themselves the words used of the kings censured in M. de Cambray's *Telemachus*. Each one considers himself within his rights. Tacitus, an unbiassed writer, justifies Augustus in two words, at the beginning of his *Annals*. But Augustus was better able than anyone to judge of his good fortune. He appears to have died content, as may be inferred from a proof he gave of contentedness with his life: for in dying he repeated to his friends a line in Greek, which has the signification of that *Plaudite* that was wont to be spoken at the conclusion of a well-acted play. Suetonius quotes it:

> Δότε κρότον καὶ πάντες ὑμεῖς μετὰ χαρᾶς κτυπήσατε.

262. But even though there should have fallen to the lot of the human kind more evil than good, it is enough where God is concerned that there is incomparably more good than evil in the universe. Rabbi Maimonides (whose merit is not sufficiently recognized in the statement that he is the first of the Rabbis to have ceased talking nonsense) also gave wise judgement on this question of the predominance of good over evil in the world. Here is what he says in his *Doctor Perplexorum* (cap. 12, p. 3): 'There arise often in the hearts of ill-instructed persons thoughts which persuade them there is more evil than good in the world: and one often finds in the poems and songs of the pagans that it is as it were a miracle when something good comes to pass, whereas

evils are usual and constant. This error has taken hold not of the common herd only, those very persons who wish to be considered wise have been beguiled thereby. A celebrated writer named Alrasi, in his *Sepher Elohuth,* or Theosophy, amongst other absurdities has stated that there are more evils than goods, and that upon comparison of the recreations and the pleasures man enjoys in times of tranquillity with the pains, the torments, the troubles, faults, cares, griefs and afflictions whereby he is overwhelmed our life would prove to be a great evil, and an actual penalty inflicted upon us to punish us.' Maimonides adds that the cause of their extravagant error is their supposition that Nature was made for them only, and that they hold of no account what is separate from their person; whence they infer that when something unpleasing to them occurs all goes ill in the universe.

263. M. Bayle says that this observation of Maimonides is not to the point, because the question is whether among men evil exceeds good. But, upon consideration of the Rabbi's words, I find that the question he formulates is general, and that he wished to refute those who decide it on one particular motive derived from the evils of the human race, as if all had been made for man ; and it seems as though the author whom he refutes spoke also of good and evil in general. Maimonides is right in saying that if one took into account the littleness of man in relation to the universe one would comprehend clearly that the predominance of evil, even though it prevailed among men, need not on that account occur among the angels, nor among the heavenly bodies, nor among the elements and inanimate compounds, nor among many kinds of animals. I have shown elsewhere that in supposing that the number of the damned exceeds that of the saved (a supposition which is nevertheless not altogether certain) one might admit that there is more evil than good in respect of the human kind known to us. But I pointed out that that neither precludes the existence of incomparably more good than evil, both moral and physical, in rational creatures in general, nor prevents the city of God, which contains all creatures, from being the most perfect state. So also on consideration of the metaphysical good and evil which is in all substances, whether endowed with or devoid of intelligence, and which taken in such scope would include physical good and moral good, one must say that the universe, such as it actually is, must be the best of all systems.

264. Moreover, M. Bayle will not have it that our transgression should have anything to do with the consideration of our sufferings. He is right when it is simply a matter of appraising these sufferings; but the case is not the same when one asks whether they should be ascribed to God, this indeed being the principal cause of M. Bayle's difficulties when he places reason or experience in opposition to religion. I know that he is wont to say that it is of no avail to resort to our free will, since his objections tend also to prove that the misuse of free will must no less be laid to the account of God, who has permitted it and who has co-operated therein. He states it as a maxim that for one difficulty more or less one must not abandon a system. This he advances especially in favour of the methods of the strict and the dogma of the Supralapsarians. For he supposes that one can subscribe to their opinion, although he leaves all the difficulties in their entirety, because the other systems, albeit they put an end to some of the difficulties, cannot meet them all. I hold that the true system I have expounded satisfies all. Nevertheless, even were that not so, I confess that I cannot relish this maxim of M. Bayle's, and I should prefer a system which would remove a great portion of the difficulties, to one which would meet none of them. And the consideration of the wickedness of men, which brings upon them well-nigh all their misfortunes, shows at least that they have no right to complain. No justice need trouble itself over the origin of a scoundrel's wickedness when it is only a question of punishing him: it is quite another matter when it is a question of prevention. One knows well that disposition, upbringing, conversation, and often chance itself, have much share in that origin: is the man any the less deserving of punishment?

265. I confess that there still remains another difficulty. If God is not bound to account to the wicked for their wickedness, it seems as if he owes to himself, and to those who honour him and love him, justification for his course of action with regard to the permission of vice and crime. But God has already given that satisfaction, as far as it is needed here on earth: by granting us the light of reason he has bestowed upon us the means whereby we may meet all difficulties. I hope that I have made it plain in this discourse, and have elucidated the matter in the preceding portion of these Essays, almost as far as it can be done through general arguments. Thereafter, the permission of sin being justified, the

other evils that are a consequence thereof present no further difficulty. Thus also I am justified in restricting myself here to the evil of guilt to account for the evil of punishment, as Holy Scripture does, and likewise well-nigh all the Fathers of the Church and the Preachers. And, to the end that none may say that is only good *per la predica*, it is enough to consider that, after the solutions I have given, nothing must seem more right or more exact than this method. For God, having found already among things possible, before his actual decrees, man misusing his freedom and bringing upon himself his misfortune, yet could not avoid admitting him into existence, because the general plan required this. Wherefore it will no longer be necessary to say with M. Jurieu that one must dogmatize like St. Augustine and preach like Pelagius.

266. This method, deriving the evil of punishment from the evil of guilt, cannot be open to censure, and serves especially to account for the greatest physical evil, which is damnation. Ernst Sonner, sometime Professor of Philosophy at Altorf (a university established in the territory of the free city of Nuremberg), who was considered an excellent Aristotelian, but was finally recognized as being secretly a Socinian, had composed a little discourse entitled: *Demonstration against the Eternity of Punishment*. It was founded on this somewhat trite principle, that there is no proportion between an infinite punishment and a finite guilt. It was conveyed to me, printed (so it seemed) in Holland; and I replied that there was one thing to be considered which had escaped the late Herr Sonner: namely that it was enough to say that the duration of the guilt caused the duration of the penalty. Since the damned remained wicked they could not be withdrawn from their misery; and thus one need not, in order to justify the continuation of their sufferings, assume that sin has become of infinite weight through the infinite nature of the object offended, who is God. This thesis I had not explored enough to pass judgement thereon. I know that the general opinion of the Schoolmen, according to the Master of the Sentences, is that in the other life there is neither merit nor demerit; but I do not think that, taken literally, it can pass for an article of faith. Herr Fecht, a famous theologian at Rostock, well refuted that in his book on *The State of the Damned*. It is quite wrong, he says (§ 59); God cannot change his nature; justice is essential to him; death has closed the door of grace, but not that of justice.

267. I have observed that sundry able theologians have accounted for the duration of the pains of the damned as I have just done. Johann Gerhard, a famous theologian of the Augsburg Confession (in *Locis Theol.*, loco de Inferno, § 60), brings forward amongst other arguments that the damned have still an evil will and lack the grace that could render it good. Zacharias Ursinus, a theologian of Heidelberg, who follows Calvin, having formulated this question (in his treatise *De Fide*) why sin merits an eternal punishment, advances first the common reason, that the person offended is infinite, and then also this second reason, *quod non cessante peccato non potest cessare poena*. And the Jesuit Father Drexler says in his book entitled *Nicetas, or Incontinence Overcome* (book 2, ch. 11, § 9): 'Nec mirum damnatos semper torqueri, continue blasphemant, et sic quasi semper peccant, semper ergo plectuntur.' He declares and approves the same reason in his work on *Eternity* (book 2, ch. 15) saying: 'Sunt qui dicant, nec displicet responsum: scelerati in locis infernis semper peccant, ideo semper puniuntur.' And he indicates thereby that this opinion is very common among learned men in the Roman Church. He alleges, it is true, another more subtle reason, derived from Pope Gregory the Great (lib. 4, Dial. c. 44), that the damned are punished eternally because God foresaw by a kind of *mediate knowledge* that they would always have sinned if they had always lived upon earth. But it is a hypothesis very much open to question. Herr Fecht quotes also various eminent Protestant theologians for Herr Gerhard's opinion, although he mentions also some who think differently.

268. M. Bayle himself in various places has supplied me with passages from two able theologians of his party, which have some reference to these statements of mine. M. Jurieu in his book on the *Unity of the Church*, in opposition to that written by M. Nicole on the same subject, gives the opinion (p. 379) 'that reason tells us that a creature which cannot cease to be criminal can also not cease to be miserable'. M. Jacquelot in his book on *The Conformity of Faith with Reason* (p. 220) is of opinion 'that the damned must remain eternally deprived of the glory of the blessed, and that this deprivation might well be the origin and the cause of all their pains, through the reflexions these unhappy creatures make upon their crimes which have deprived them of an eternal bliss. One knows what burning regrets, what pain envy causes to those who see themselves deprived of a good, of a notable honour which had

been offered to them, and which they rejected, especially when they see others invested with it.' This position is a little different from that of M. Jurieu, but both agree in this sentiment, that the damned are themselves the cause of the continuation of their torments. M. le Clerc's Origenist does not entirely differ from this opinion when he says in the *Select Library* (vol. 7, p. 341): 'God, who foresaw that man would fall, does not condemn him on that account, but only because, although he has the power to recover himself, he yet does not do so, that is, he freely retains his evil ways to the end of his life.' If he carries this reasoning on beyond this life, he will ascribe the continuation of the pains of the wicked to the continuation of their guilt.

269. M. Bayle says (*Reply to the Questions of a Provincial*, ch. 175, p. 1188) 'that this dogma of the Origenist is heretical, in that it teaches that damnation is not founded simply on sin, but on voluntary impenitence': but is not this voluntary impenitence a continuation of sin? I would not simply say, however, that it is because man, having the power to recover himself, does not; and would wish to add that it is because man does not take advantage of the succour of grace to aid him to recover himself. But after this life, though one assume that the succour ceases, there is always in the man who sins, even when he is damned, a freedom which renders him culpable, and a power, albeit remote, of recovering himself, even though it should never pass into action. And there is no reason why one may not say that this degree of freedom, exempt from necessity, but not exempt from certainty, remains in the damned as well as in the blessed. Moreover, the damned have no need of a succour that is needed in this life, for they know only too well what one must believe here.

270. The illustrious prelate of the Anglican Church who published recently a book on the origin of evil, concerning which M. Bayle made some observations in the second volume of his *Reply*, speaks with much subtlety about the pains of the damned. This prelate's opinion is presented (according to the author of the *Nouvelles de la République des Lettres*, June 1703) as if he made 'of the damned just so many madmen who will feel their miseries acutely, but who will nevertheless congratulate themselves on their own behaviour, and who will rather choose to be, and to be that which they are, than not to be at all. They will love their state, unhappy as it will be, even as angry people, lovers, the ambitious,

the envious take pleasure in the very things that only augment their misery. Furthermore the ungodly will have so accustomed their mind to wrong judgements that they will henceforth never make any other kind, and will perpetually pass from one error into another. They will not be able to refrain from desiring perpetually things whose enjoyment will be denied them, and, being deprived of which, they will fall into inconceivable despair, while experience can never make them wiser for the future. For by their own fault they will have altogether corrupted their understanding, and will have rendered it incapable of passing a sound judgement on any matter.'

271. The ancients already imagined that the Devil dwells remote from God voluntarily, in the midst of his torments, and that he is unwilling to redeem himself by an act of submission. They invented a tale that an anchorite in a vision received a promise from God that he would receive into grace the Prince of the bad angels if he would acknowledge his fault; but that the devil rebuffed this mediator in a strange manner. At the least, the theologians usually agree that the devils and the damned hate God and blaspheme him; and such a state cannot but be followed by continuation of misery. Concerning that, one may read the learned treatise of Herr Fecht on the *State of the Damned*.

272. There were times when the belief was held that it was not impossible for a lost soul to be delivered. The story told of Pope Gregory the Great is well known, how by his prayers he had withdrawn from hell the soul of the Emperor Trajan, whose goodness was so renowned that to new emperors the wish was offered that they should surpass Augustus in good fortune and Trajan in goodness. It was this that won for the latter the pity of the Holy Father. God acceded to his prayers (it is said), but he forbade him to make the like prayers in future. According to this fable, the prayers of St. Gregory had the force of the remedies of Aesculapius, who recalled Hippolytus from Hades; and, if he had continued to make such prayers, God would have waxed wroth, like Jupiter in Vergil:

> *At pater omnipotens aliquem indignatus ab umbris*
> *Mortalem infernis ad lumina surgere vitae,*
> *Ipse repertorem medicinae talis et artis*
> *Fulmine Phoebigenam Stygias detrusit ad undas.*

Godescalc, a monk of the ninth century, who set at variance the theologians of his day, and even those of our day, maintained that the reprobate should pray God to render their pains more bearable; but one is never justified in believing oneself reprobate so long as one is alive. The passage in the Mass for the dead is more reasonable: it asks for the abatement of the torments of the damned, and, according to the hypothesis that I have just stated, one must wish for them *meliorem mentem*. Origen having applied the passage from Psalm lxxvii, verse 10: God will not forget to be gracious, neither will he shut up his loving-kindness in displeasure, St. Augustine replies (*Enchirid.*, c. 112) that it is possible that the pains of the damned last eternally, and that they may nevertheless be mitigated. If the text implied that, the abatement would, as regards its duration, go on to infinity; and yet that abatement would, as regards its extent, have a *non plus ultra*. Even so there are asymptote figures in geometry where an infinite length makes only a finite progress in breadth. If the parable of the wicked rich man represented the state of a definitely lost soul, the hypothesis which makes these souls so mad and so wicked would be groundless. But the charity towards his brothers attributed to him in the parable does not seem to be consistent with that degree of wickedness which is ascribed to the damned. St. Gregory the Great (IX *Mor.*, 39) thinks that the rich man was afraid lest their damnation should increase his: but it seems as though this fear is not sufficiently consistent with the disposition of a perfectly wicked will. Bonaventura, on the Master of the Sentences, says that the wicked rich man would have desired to see everyone damned; but since that was not to be, he desired the salvation of his brothers rather than that of the rest. This reply is by no means sound. On the contrary, the mission of Lazarus that he desired would have served to save many people; and he who takes so much pleasure in the damnation of others that he desires it for everyone will perhaps desire that damnation for some more than others; but, generally speaking, he will have no inclination to gain salvation for anyone. However that may be, one must admit that all this detail is problematical, God having revealed to us all that is needed to put us in fear of the greatest of misfortunes, and not what is needed for our understanding thereof.

273. Now since it is henceforth permitted to have recourse to the misuse of free will, and to evil will, in order to account for other

evils, since the divine permission of this misuse is plainly enough justified, the ordinary system of the theologians meets with justification at the same time. Now we can seek with confidence *the origin of evil in the freedom of creatures*. The first wickedness is well known to us, it is that of the Devil and his angels: the Devil sinneth from the beginning, and for this purpose the Son of God was manifested, that he might destroy the works of the Devil (1 John iii. 8). The Devil is the father of wickedness, he was a murderer from the beginning, and abode not in the truth (John viii. 44). And therefore God spared not the angels that sinned, but cast them down to Hell, and delivered them into chains of darkness, to be reserved unto judgement (2 Pet. ii. 4). And the angels which kept not their own habitation, he hath reserved in *eternal* (that is to say everlasting) chains under darkness unto the judgement of the great day (Jude i. 6). Whence it is easy to observe that one of these two letters must have been seen by the author of the other.

274. It seems as if the author of the Apocalypse wished to throw light upon what the other canonical writers had left obscure: he gives us an account of a battle that took place in Heaven. Michael and his angels fought against the Dragon, and the Dragon fought and his angels. 'But they prevailed not, neither was their place found any more in heaven. And the great Dragon was cast out, that old serpent, called the Devil, and Satan, which deceiveth the whole world: and he was cast out into the earth, and his angels were cast out with him' (Rev. xii. 7, 8, 9). For although this account is placed after the flight of the woman into the wilderness, and it may have been intended to indicate thereby some revulsion favourable to the Church, it appears as though the author's design was to show simultaneously the old fall of the first enemy and a new fall of a new enemy.

275. Lying or wickedness springs from the Devil's own nature, ἐκ τῶν ἰδίων, from his will, because it was written in the book of the eternal verities, which contains the things possible before any decree of God, that this creature would freely turn toward evil if it were created. It is the same with Eve and Adam; they sinned freely, albeit the Devil tempted them. God gives the wicked over to a reprobate mind (Rom. i. 28), abandoning them to themselves and denying them a grace which he owes them not, and indeed ought to deny to them.

276. It is said in the Scriptures that God hardeneth (Exod. iv.

21 and vii. 3; Isa. lxiii. 17); that God sendeth a lying spirit (1 Kings xxii. 23); strong delusion that they should believe a lie (2 Thess. ii. 11); that he deceived the prophet (Ezek. xiv. 9); that he commanded Shimei to curse (2 Sam xvi. 10); that the children of Eli hearkened not unto the voice of their father, because the Lord would slay them (1 Sam. ii. 25); that the Lord took away Job's substance, even although that was done through the malice of brigands (Job i. 21); that he raised up Pharaoh, to show his power in him (Exod. ix. 19; Rom. ix. 17) that he is like a potter who maketh a vessel unto dishonour (Rom. ix. 21); that he hideth the truth from the wise and prudent (Matt. xi. 25); that he speaketh in parables unto them that are without, that seeing they may see and not perceive, and hearing they may hear and not understand, lest at any time they might be converted, and their sins might be forgiven them (Mark iv. 12; Luke viii. 10); that Jesus was delivered by the determinate counsel and foreknowledge of God (Acts ii. 23); that Pontius Pilate and Herod with the Gentiles and the people of Israel did that which the hand and the counsel of God had determined before to be done (Acts iv. 27, 28); that it was of the Lord to harden the hearts of the enemy, that they should come against Israel in battle, that he might destroy them utterly, and that they might have no favour (Joshua xi. 20); that the Lord mingled a perverse spirit in the midst of Egypt, and caused it to err in all its works, like a drunken man (Isa. xix. 14); that Rehoboam hearkened not unto the word of the people, for the cause was from the Lord (1 Kings xii. 15); that he turned the hearts of the Egyptians to hate his people (Ps. cv. 25). But all these and other like expressions suggest only that the things God has done are used as occasion for ignorance, error, malice and evil deeds, and contribute thereto, God indeed foreseeing this, and intending to use it for his ends, since superior reasons of perfect wisdom have determined him to permit these evils, and even to co-operate therein. 'Sed non sineret bonus fieri male, nisi omnipotens etiam de malo posset facere bene', in St. Augustine's words. But this has been expounded more fully in the preceding part.

277. God made man in his image (Gen. i. 26); he made him upright (Eccles. vii. 29). But also he made him free. Man has behaved badly, he has fallen; but there remains still a certain freedom after the fall. Moses said as from God: 'I call heaven and earth to record this day against you, that I have set before you life

and death, blessing and cursing; therefore choose life' (Deut. xxx. 19). 'Thus saith the Lord: Behold, I set before you the way of life, and the way of death' (Jer. xxi. 8). He has left man in the power of his counsel, giving him his ordinances and his commandments. 'If thou wilt, thou shalt keep the commandments' (or they shall keep thee). 'He hath set before thee fire and water, to stretch forth thine hand to whichever thou wilt' (Sirach xv. 14, 15, 16). Fallen and unregenerate man is under the domination of sin and of Satan, because it pleases him so to be; he is a voluntary slave through his evil lust. Thus it is that free will and will in bondage are one and the same thing.

278. 'Let no man say, I am tempted of God'; 'but every man is tempted, when he is drawn away of his own lust and enticed' (Jas. i. 13, 14). And Satan contributes thereto. He 'blindeth the minds of them which believe not' (2 Cor. iv. 4). But man is delivered up to the Devil by his covetous desire: the pleasure he finds in evil is the bait that hooks him. Plato has said so already, and Cicero repeats it: 'Plato voluptatem dicebat escam malorum.' Grace sets over against it a greater pleasure, as St. Augustine observed. All *pleasure* is a feeling of some perfection; one *loves* an object in proportion as one feels its perfections; nothing surpasses the divine perfections. Whence it follows that charity and love of God give the greatest pleasure that can be conceived, in that proportion in which one is penetrated by these feelings, which are not common among men, busied and taken up as men are with the objects that are concerned with their passions.

279. Now as our corruption is not altogether invincible and as we do not necessarily sin even when we are under the bondage of sin, it must likewise be said that we are not aided invincibly; and, however efficacious divine grace may be, there is justification for saying that one can resist it. But when it indeed proves victorious, it is certain and infallible beforehand that one will yield to its allurements, whether it have its strength of itself or whether it find a way to triumph through the congruity of circumstances. Thus one must always distinguish between the infallible and the necessary.

280. The system of those who call themselves Disciples of St. Augustine is not far removed from this, provided one exclude certain obnoxious things, whether in the expressions or in the dogmas themselves. In the *expressions* I find that it is principally the

use of terms like 'necessary' or 'contingent', 'possible' or 'impossible', which sometimes gives a handle and causes much ado. That is why, as Herr Löscher the younger aptly observed in a learned dissertation on the *Paroxysms of the Absolute Decree*, Luther desired, in his book *On the Will in Bondage*, to find a word more fitting for that which he wished to express than the word necessity Speaking generally, it appears more reasonable and more fitting to say that obedience to God's precepts is always *possible*, even for the unregenerate; that the grace of God is always *resistible*, even in those most holy, and that *freedom* is exempt not only from *constraint* but also from *necessity*, although it be never without infallible *certainty* or without inclining *determination*.

281. Nevertheless there is on the other hand a sense wherein it would be permitted to say, in certain conjunctures, that the *power* to do good is often lacking, even in the just; that sins are often *necessary*, even in the regenerate; that it is *impossible* sometimes for one not to sin; that grace is *irresistible*; that freedom is not exempt from *necessity*. But these expressions are less exact and less pleasing in the circumstances that prevail about us to-day. They are also in general more open to misuse; and moreover they savour somewhat of the speech of the people, where terms are employed with great latitude. There are, however, circumstances which render them acceptable and even serviceable. It is the case that sacred and orthodox writers, and even the holy Scriptures, have made use of expressions on both sides, and no real contradiction has arisen, any more than between St. Paul and St. James, or any error on either side that might be attributable to the ambiguity of the terms. One is so well accustomed to these various ways of speaking that often one is put to it to say precisely which sense is the more ordinary and the more natural, and even that more intended by the author (*quis sensus magis naturalis, obvius, intentus*). For the same writer has different aims in different passages, and the same ways of speaking are more or less accepted or acceptable before or after the decision of some great man or of some authority that one respects and follows. As a result of this one may well authorize or ban, as opportunity arises and at certain times, certain expressions; but it makes no difference to the sense, or to the content of faith, if sufficient explanations of the terms are not added.

282. It is therefore only necessary to understand fully some distinctions, such as that I have very often urged between the

necessary and the certain, and between metaphysical necessity
and moral necessity. It is the same with possibility and impossibility, since the event whose opposite is possible is contingent,
even as that whose opposite is impossible is necessary. A distinction is rightly drawn also between a proximate potency and a
remote potency; and, according to these different senses, one
says now that a thing may be and now that it may not be. It may
be said in a certain sense that it is necessary that the blessed should
not sin; that the devils and the damned should sin; that God himself should choose the best; that man should follow the course
which after all attracts him most. But this necessity is not opposed
to contingency; it is not of the kind called logical, geometrical or
metaphysical, whose opposite implies contradiction. M. Nicole
has made use somewhere of a comparison which is not amiss. It
is considered impossible that a wise and serious magistrate, who
has not taken leave of his senses, should publicly commit some
outrageous action, as it would be, for instance, to run about the
streets naked in order to make people laugh. It is the same, in a
sense, with the blessed; they are still less capable of sinning, and
the necessity that forbids them to sin is of the same kind. Finally I
also hold that 'will' is a term as equivocal as potency and necessity. For I have already observed that those who employ this
axiom, that one does not fail to do what one wills when one can,
and who thence infer that God therefore does not will the salvation of all, imply a *decretory will*. Only in that sense can one support
this proposition, that wisdom never wills what it knows to be
among the things that shall not happen. On the other hand, one
may say, taking will in a sense more general and more in conformity with customary use, that the wise will is *inclined* antecedently to all good, although it *decrees* finally to do that which is
most fitting. Thus one would be very wrong to deny to God the
serious and strong inclination to save all men, which Holy
Scripture attributes to him; or even to attribute to him an original
distaste which diverts him from the salvation of a number of
persons, *odium antecedaneum*. One should rather maintain that the
wise mind tends towards all good, as good, in proportion to his
knowledge and his power, but that he only produces the best that
can be achieved. Those who admit that, and yet deny to God the
antecedent will to save all men, are wrong only in their misuse of
the term, provided that they acknowledge, besides, that God gives

to all help sufficient to enable them to win salvation if only they have the will to avail themselves thereof.

283. In the *dogmas* themselves held by the Disciples of St. Augustine I cannot approve the damnation of unregenerate children, nor in general damnation resulting from original sin alone. Nor can I believe that God condemns those who are without the necessary light. One may believe, with many theologians, that men receive more aid than we are aware of, were it only when they are at the point of death. It does not appear necessary either that all those who are saved should always be saved through a grace efficacious of itself, independently of circumstances. Also I consider it unnecessary to say that all the virtues of the pagans were false or that all their actions were sins; though it be true that what does not spring from faith, or from the uprightness of the soul before God, is infected with sin, at least virtually. Finally I hold that God cannot act as if at random by an absolutely absolute decree, or by a will independent of reasonable motives. And I am persuaded that he is always actuated, in the dispensation of his grace, by reasons wherein the nature of the objects participates. Otherwise he would not act in accordance with wisdom. I grant nevertheless that these reasons are not of necessity bound up with the good or the less evil natural qualities of men, as if God gave his grace only according to these good qualities. Yet I hold, as I have explained already here, that these qualities are taken into consideration like all the other circumstances, since nothing can be neglected in the designs of supreme wisdom.

284. Save for these points, and some few others, where St. Augustine appears obscure or even repellent, it seems as though one can conform to his system. He states that from the substance of God only a God can proceed, and that thus the creature is derived from nothingness (Augustine *De Lib. Arb.*, lib. 1, c. 2). That is what makes the creature imperfect, faulty and corruptible (*De Genesi ad Lit.*, c. 15, *Contra Epistolam Manichaei*, c. 36). Evil comes not from nature, but from evil will (Augustine, in the whole book *On the Nature of Good*). God can command nothing that would be impossible. 'Firmissime creditur Deum justum et bonum impossibilia non potuisse praecipere' (*Lib. de Nat. et Grat.*, c. 43, p. 69). Nemo peccat in eo, quod caveri non potest (lib. 3, *De Lib. Arb.*, c. 16, 17, *lib.* 1 *Retract.* c. 11, 13, 15). Under a just God, none can be unhappy who deserves not so to be, 'neque sub Deo justo

miser esse quisquam, nisi mereatur, potest' (lib. 1, c. 39). Free will cannot carry out God's commands without the aid of grace (*Ep. ad Hilar. Caesaraugustan.*). We know that grace is not given according to deserts (Ep. 106, 107, 120). Man in the state of innocence had the aid necessary to enable him to do good if he wished; but the wish depended on free will, 'habebat adjutorium, per quod posset, et sine quo non vellet, sed non adjutorium quo vellet' (*Lib. de Corrept.*, c. 11 et c. 10, 12). God let angels and men try what they could do by their free will, and after that what his grace and his justice could achieve (ibid., c. 10, 11, 12). Sin turned man away from God, to turn him towards creatures (lib. 1, qu. 2, *Ad Simplicium*). To take pleasure in sinning is the freedom of a slave (*Enchirid.*, c. 103). 'Liberum arbitrium usque adeo in peccatore non periit, ut per illud peccent maxime omnes, qui cum delectatione peccant' (lib. 1, *Ad Bonifac.*, c. 2, 3).

285. God said to Moses: 'I will be gracious to whom I will be gracious, and will shew mercy on whom I will shew mercy' (Exod. xxxiii. 19). 'So then it is not of him that willeth, nor of him that runneth, but of God that sheweth mercy' (Rom. ix. 15, 16). That does not prevent all those who have good will, and who persevere therein, from being saved. But God gives them the willing and the doing. 'Therefore hath he mercy on whom he will have mercy, and whom he will he hardeneth' (Rom. ix. 18). And yet the same Apostle says that God willeth that all men should be saved, and come to the knowledge of the truth; which I would not interpret in accordance with some passages of St. Augustine, as if it signified that no men are saved except those whose salvation he wills, or as if he would save *non singulos generum, sed genera singulorum*. But I would rather say that there is none whose salvation he willeth not, in so far as this is permitted by greater reasons. For these bring it about that God only saves those who accept the faith he has offered to them and who surrender themselves thereto by the grace he has given them, in accordance with what was consistent with the plan of his works in its entirety, than which none can be better conceived.

286. As for predestination to salvation, it includes also, according to St. Augustine, the ordinance of the means that shall lead to salvation. 'Praedestinatio sanctorum nihil aliud est, quam praescientia et praeparatio beneficiorum Dei, quibus certissime liberantur quicunque liberantur' (*Lib. de Persev.*, c. 14). He does

not then understand it there as an absolute decree; he maintains that there is a grace which is not rejected by any hardened heart, because it is given in order to remove especially the hardness of hearts (*Lib. de Praedest.*, c. 8; *Lib. de Grat.*, c. 13, 14). I do not find, however, that St. Augustine conveys sufficiently that this grace, which subdues the heart, is always efficacious of itself. And one might perhaps have asserted without offence to him that the same degree of inward grace is victorious in the one, where it is aided by outward circumstances, but not in the other.

287. Will is proportionate to the sense we have of the good, and follows the sense which prevails. 'Si utrumque tantundem diligimus, nihil horum dabimus. Item: Quod amplius nos delectat, secundum id operemur necesse est' (in c. 5, *Ad Gal.*). I have explained already how, despite all that, we have indeed a great power over our will. St. Augustine takes it somewhat differently, and in a way that does not go far, when he says that nothing is so much within our power as the action of our will. And he gives a reason which is almost tautological: for (he says) this action is ready at the moment when we will. 'Nihil tam in nostra potestate est, quam ipsa voluntas, ea enim mox ut volumus praesto est' (lib. 3, *De Lib. Arb.*, c. 3; lib. 5, *De Civ. Dei*, c. 10). But that only means that we will when we will, and not that we will that which we wish to will. There is more reason for saying with him: '*aut voluntas non est, aut libera dicenda est*' (d. 1, 3, c. 3); and that what inclines the will towards good infallibly, or certainly, does not prevent it from being free. 'Perquam absurdum est, ut ideo dicamus non pertinere ad voluntatem [libertatem] nostram, quod beati esse volumus, quia id omnino nolle non possumus, nescio qua bona constrictione naturae. Nec dicere audemus ideo Deum non voluntatem [libertatem], sed necessitatem habere justitiae, quia non potest velle peccare. Certe Deus ipse numquid quia peccare non potest, ideo liberum arbitrium habere negandus est?' (*De Nat. et Grat.*, c. 46, 47, 48, 49). He also says aptly, that God gives the first good impulse, but that afterwards man acts also. 'Aguntur ut agant, non ut ipsi nihil agant' (*De Corrept.*, c. 2).

288. I have proved that free will is the proximate cause of the evil of guilt, and consequently of the evil of punishment; although it is true that the original imperfection of creatures, which is already presented in the eternal ideas, is the first and most remote

cause. M. Bayle nevertheless always disputes this use of the notion of free will; he will not have the cause of evil ascribed to it. One must listen to his objections, but first it will be well to throw further light on the nature of freedom. I have shown that freedom, according to the definition required in the schools of theology, consists in intelligence, which involves a clear knowledge of the object of deliberation, in spontaneity, whereby we determine, and in contingency, that is, in the exclusion of logical or metaphysical necessity. Intelligence is, as it were, the soul of freedom, and the rest is as its body and foundation. The free substance is self-determining and that according to the motive of good perceived by the understanding, which inclines it without compelling it: and all the conditions of freedom are comprised in these few words. It is nevertheless well to point out that the imperfection present in our knowledge and our spontaneity, and the infallible determination that is involved in our contingency, destroy neither freedom nor contingency.

289. Our knowledge is of two kinds, distinct or confused. Distinct knowledge, or *intelligence*, occurs in the actual use of reason; but the senses supply us with confused thoughts. And we may say that we are immune from bondage in so far as we act with a distinct knowledge, but that we are the slaves of passion in so far as our perceptions are confused. In this sense we have not all the freedom of spirit that were to be desired, and we may say with St. Augustine that being subject to sin we have the freedom of a slave. Yet a slave, slave as he is, nevertheless has freedom to choose according to the state wherein he is, although more often than not he is under the stern necessity of choosing between two evils, because a superior force prevents him from attaining the goods whereto he aspires. That which in a slave is effected by bonds and constraint in us is effected by passions, whose violence is sweet, but none the less pernicious. In truth we will only that which pleases us: but unhappily what pleases us now is often a real evil, which would displease us if we had the eyes of the understanding open. Nevertheless that evil state of the slave, which is also our own, does not prevent us, any more than him, from making a free choice of that which pleases us most, in the state to which we are reduced, in proportion to our present strength and knowledge.

290. As for spontaneity, it belongs to us in so far as we have within us the source of our actions, as Aristotle rightly conceived.

The impressions of external things often, indeed, divert us from our path, and it was commonly believed that, at least in this respect, some of the sources of our actions were outside ourselves. I admit that one is bound to speak thus, adapting oneself to the popular mode of expression, as one may, in a certain sense, without doing violence to truth. But when it is a question of expressing oneself accurately I maintain that our spontaneity suffers no exception and that external things have no physical influence upon us, I mean in the strictly philosophical sense.

291. For better understanding of this point, one must know that true spontaneity is common to us and all simple substances, and that in the intelligent or free substance this becomes a mastery over its actions. That cannot be better explained than by the System of Pre-established Harmony, which I indeed propounded some years ago. There I pointed out that by nature every simple substance has perception, and that its individuality consists in the perpetual law which brings about the sequence of perceptions that are assigned to it, springing naturally from one another, to represent the body that is allotted to it, and through its instrumentality the entire universe, in accordance with the point of view proper to this simple substance and without its needing to receive any physical influence from the body. Even so the body also for its part adapts itself to the wishes of the soul by its own laws, and consequently only obeys it according to the promptings of these laws. Whence it follows that the soul has in itself a perfect spontaneity, so that it depends only upon God and upon itself in its actions.

292. As this system was not known formerly, other ways were sought for emerging from this labyrinth, and the Cartesians themselves were in difficulties over the subject of free will. They were no longer satisfied by the 'faculties' of the Schoolmen, and they considered that all the actions of the soul appear to be determined by what comes from without, according to the impressions of the senses, and that, ultimately, all is controlled in the universe by the providence of God. Thence arose naturally the objection that there is therefore no freedom. To that M. Descartes replied that we are assured of God's providence by reason; but that we are likewise assured of our freedom by experience thereof within ourselves; and that we must believe in both, even though we see not how it is possible to reconcile them.

293. That was cutting the Gordian knot, and answering the conclusion of an argument not by refuting it but by opposing thereto a contrary argument. Which procedure does not conform to the laws for philosophical disputes. Notwithstanding, most of the Cartesians contented themselves with this, albeit the inward experience they adduce does not prove their assertion, as M. Bayle has clearly shown. M. Regis (*Philos.*, vol. 1, Metaph., book 2, part 2, c. 22) thus paraphrases M. Descartes' doctrine: 'Most philosophers', he says, 'have fallen into error. Some, not being able to understand the relation existing between free actions and the providence of God, have denied that God was the first efficient cause of free will: but that is sacrilegious. The others, not being able to apprehend the relation between God's efficacy and free actions, have denied that man was endowed with freedom: and that is a blasphemy. The mean to be found between these two extremes is to say' (id. ibid., p. 485) 'that, even though we were not able to understand all the relations existing between freedom and God's providence, we should nevertheless be bound to acknowledge that we are free and dependent upon God. For both these truths are equally known, the one through experience, and the other through reason; and prudence forbids one to abandon truths whereof one is assured, under the pretext that one cannot apprehend all the relations existing between them and other truths well known.'

294. M. Bayle here remarks pertinently in the margin, 'that these expressions of M. Regis fail to point out that we are aware of relations between man's actions and God's providence, such as appear to us to be incompatible with our freedom.' He adds that these expressions are over-circumspect, weakening the statement of the problem. 'Authors assume', he says, 'that the difficulty arises solely from our lack of enlightenment; whereas they ought to say that it arises in the main from the enlightenment which we have, and cannot reconcile' (in M. Bayle's opinion) 'with our Mysteries.' That is exactly what I said at the beginning of this work, that if the Mysteries were irreconcilable with reason, and if there were unanswerable objections, far from finding the mystery incomprehensible, we should comprehend that it was false. It is true that here there is no question of a mystery, but only of natural religion.

295. This is how M. Bayle combats those inward experiences,

whereon the Cartesians make freedom rest: but he begins by reflexions with which I cannot agree. 'Those who do not make profound examination', he says (*Dictionary*, art. 'Helen.', lit. *TΔ*), 'of that which passes within them easily persuade themselves that they are free, and that, if their will prompts them to evil, it is their fault, it is through a choice whereof they are the masters. Those who judge otherwise are persons who have studied with care the springs and the circumstances of their actions, and who have thought over the progress of their soul's impulses. Those persons usually have doubts about their free will, and even come to persuade themselves that their reason and mind are slaves, without power to resist the force that carries them along where they would not go. It was principally persons of this kind who ascribed to the gods the cause of their evil deeds.'

296. These words remind me of those of Chancellor Bacon, who says that a little philosophy inclineth us away from God, but that depth in philosophy bringeth men's minds about to him. It is the same with those who reflect upon their actions: it appears to them at first that all we do is only impulsion from others, and that all we apprehend comes from without through the senses, and is traced upon the void of our mind *tanquam in tabula rasa*. But more profound meditation shows us that all (even perceptions and passions) comes to us from our own inner being, with complete spontaneity.

297. Yet M. Bayle cites poets who pretend to exonerate men by laying the blame upon the gods. Medea in Ovid speaks thus:

> *Frustra, Medea, repugnas,*
> *Nescio quid Deus obstat, ait.*

And a little later Ovid makes her add:

> *Sed trahit invitam nova vis, aliudque Cupido,*
> *Mens aliud suadet; video meliora proboque,*
> *Deteriora sequor.*

But one could set against that a passage from Vergil, who makes Nisus say with far more reason:

> *Di ne hunc ardorem mentibus addunt,*
> *Euryale, an sua cuique Deus fit dira cupido?*

298. Herr Wittich seems to have thought that in reality our independence is only apparent. For in his *Diss. de providentia Dei*

actuali (n. 61) he makes free will consist in our being inclined towards the objects that present themselves to our soul for affirmation or denial, love or hate, in such a way that we *do not feel* we
are being determined by any outward force. He adds that it is
when God himself causes our volitions that we act with most
freedom; and that the more efficacious and powerful God's
action is upon us, the more we are masters of our actions. 'Quia
enim Deus operatur ipsum velle, quo efficacius operatur, eo
magis volumus; quod autem, cum volumus, facimus, id maxime
habemus in nostra potestate.' It is true that when God causes a
volition in us he causes a free action. But it seems to me that the
question here is not of the universal cause or of that production of
our will which is proper to it in so far as it is a created effect, whose
positive elements are actually created continually through God's
co-operation, like all other absolute reality of things. We are concerned here with the reasons for willing, and the means God uses
when he gives us a good will or permits us to have an evil will. It
is always we who produce it, good or evil, for it is our action: but
there are always reasons that make us act, without impairing
either our spontaneity or our freedom. Grace does no more than
give impressions which are conducive to making will operate
through fitting motives, such as would be an attention, *a dic cur hic*,
a prevenient pleasure. And it is quite evident that that does not
interfere with freedom, any more than could a friend who gives
counsel and furnishes motives. Thus Herr Wittich has not supplied
an answer to the question, any more than M. Bayle, and recourse
to God is of no avail here.

299. But let me give another much more reasonable passage
from the same M. Bayle, where he disputes with greater force the
so-called lively sense of freedom, which according to the Cartesians
is a proof of freedom. His words are indeed full of wit, and worthy
of consideration, and occur in the *Reply to the Questions of a Provincial* (vol. III, ch. 140, p. 761 *seqq.*). Here they are: 'By the clear
and distinct sense we have of our existence we do not discern
whether we exist through ourselves or derive our being from
another. We discern that only by reflexion, that is, through meditation upon our powerlessness in the matter of conserving ourselves
as much as we would, and of freeing ourselves from dependence
upon the beings that surround us, etc. It is indeed certain that the
pagans (the same must be said of the Socinians, since they deny

the creation) never attained to the knowledge of that true dogma that we were created from nothing, and that we are derived from nothingness at every moment of our continuance. They therefore thought erroneously that all substances in the universe exist of themselves and can never be reduced to nothing, and that thus they depend upon no other thing save in respect of their modifications, which are liable to be destroyed by the action of an external cause. Does not this error spring from the fact that we are unconscious of the creative action which conserves us, and that we are only conscious of our existence? That we are conscious of it, I say, in such a way that we should for ever remain ignorant of the cause of our being if other knowledge did not aid us? Let us say also, that the clear and distinct sense we have of the acts of our will cannot make us discern whether we give them ourselves to ourselves or receive them from that same cause which gives us existence. We must have recourse to reflexion or to meditation in order to effect this discrimination. Now I assert that one can never by purely philosophical meditations arrive at an established certainty that we are the efficient cause of our volitions: for every person who makes due investigation will recognize clearly, that if we were only passive subjects with regard to will we should have the same sensations of experience as we have when we think that we are free. Assume, for the sake of argument, that God so ordered the laws of the union between soul and body that all the modalities of the soul, without a single exception, are of necessity linked together with the interposition of the modalities of the brain. You will then understand that nothing will happen to us except that of which we are conscious: there will be in our soul the same sequence of thoughts from the perception of objects of the senses, which is its first step, up to the most definite volitions, which are its final step. There will be in this sequence the consciousness of ideas, that of affirmations, that of irresolutions, that of velleities and that of volitions. For whether the act of willing be impressed upon us by an external cause or we bring it about ourselves, it will be equally true that we will, and that we feel that we will. Moreover, as this external cause can blend as much pleasure as it will with the volition which it impresses upon us, we shall be able to feel at times that the acts of our will please us infinitely, and that they lead us according to the bent of our strongest inclinations. We shall feel no constraint; you know the maxim: *voluntas non potest cogi.* Do you not clearly understand that a weather-vane, always having communicated to it simultaneously (in such a way, however, that priority of nature or, if one will, a real momentary priority, should attach to the desire for motion) movement towards a certain point on the horizon, and the wish to turn in that direction, would be persuaded that it moved of itself to fulfil the desires which it conceived? I assume that it would not know that there were winds, or that an external cause changed everything simultaneously, both its situation and its desires. That is the state we are in by our nature: we know not whether an invisible cause makes us pass sufficiently from one thought to another. It is therefore natural that men are persuaded that they determine their own acts. But it remains to be discovered whether they are mistaken in that, as in countless other things they affirm by a kind of instinct and without having made use of philosophic meditation. Since therefore there are two hypotheses as to what takes place in man: the one that he is only a passive subject, the other that he has active virtues, one cannot in reason prefer the second to the first, so long as one can only adduce proofs of feeling. For we should feel with an equal force that we wish this or that, whether all our volitions were imprinted upon our soul by an exterior and invisible cause, or we formed them ourselves.'

300. There are here excellent arguments, which are valid against the usual systems; but they fail in respect of the System of Pre-established Harmony, which takes us further than we were able to go formerly. M. Bayle asserts, for instance, 'that by purely philosophical meditations one can never attain to an established certainty that we are the efficient cause of our volitions'. But this is a point which I do not concede to him: for the establishment of this system demonstrates beyond a doubt that in the course of nature each substance is the sole cause of all its actions, and that it is free of all physical influence from every other substance, save the customary co-operation of God. And this system shows that our spontaneity is real, and not only apparent, as Herr Wittich believed it to be. M. Bayle asserts also on the same reasons (ch. 170, p. 1132) that if there were a *fatum Astrologicum* this would not destroy freedom; and I would concede that to him, if freedom consisted only in an apparent spontaneity.

301. The spontaneity of our actions can therefore no longer be questioned; and Aristotle has defined it well, saying that an

action is *spontaneous* when its source is in him who acts. 'Spontaneum est, cujus principium est in agente.' Thus it is that our actions and our wills depend entirely upon us. It is true that we are not directly the masters of our will, although we be its cause; for we do not choose volitions, as we choose our actions by our volitions. Yet we have a certain power also over our will, because we can contribute indirectly towards willing another time that which we would fain will now, as I have here already shown: that, however, is no *velleity*, properly speaking. There also we have a mastery, individual and even perceptible, over our actions and our wills, resulting from a combination of spontaneity with intelligence.

302. Up to this point I have expounded the two conditions of freedom mentioned by Aristotle, that is, *spontaneity* and *intelligence*, which are found united in us in deliberation, whereas beasts lack the second condition. But the Schoolmen demand yet a third, which they call *indifference*. And indeed one must admit it, if indifference signifies as much as 'contingency'; for I have already said here that freedom must exclude an absolute and metaphysical or logical necessity. But, as I have declared more than once, this indifference, this contingency, this non-necessity, if I may venture so to speak, which is a characteristic attribute of freedom, does not prevent one from having stronger inclinations towards the course one chooses; nor does it by any means require that one be absolutely and equally indifferent towards the two opposing courses.

303. I therefore admit indifference only in the one sense, implying the same as contingency, or non-necessity. But, as I have declared more than once, I do not admit an indifference of equipoise, and I do not think that one ever chooses when one is absolutely indifferent. Such a choice would be, as it were, mere chance, without determining reason, whether apparent or hidden. But such a chance, such an absolute and actual fortuity, is a chimera which never occurs in nature. All wise men are agreed that chance is only an apparent thing, like fortune: only ignorance of causes gives rise to it. But if there were such a vague indifference, or rather if we were to choose without having anything to prompt us to the choice, chance would then be something actual, resembling what, according to Epicurus, took place in that little deviation of the atoms, occurring without cause or reason. Epicurus had

introduced it in order to evade necessity, and Cicero with good reason ridiculed it.

304. This deviation had a final cause in the mind of Epicurus, his aim being to free us from fate; but it can have no efficient cause in the nature of things, it is one of the most impossible of chimeras. M. Bayle himself refutes it admirably, as we shall see presently. And yet it is surprising that he appears to admit elsewhere himself something of like nature with this supposed deviation: here is what he says, when speaking of Buridan's ass (*Dictionary*, art. 'Buridan', lit. 13): 'Those who advocate free will properly so called admit in man a power of determining, either to the right hand or the left, even when the motives are perfectly uniform on the side of each of the two opposing objects. For they maintain that our soul can say, without having any reason other than that of using its freedom: "I prefer this to that, although I see nothing more worthy of my choice in the one than the other".'

305. All those who admit a free will properly so called will not for that reason concede to M. Bayle this determination springing from an indeterminate cause. St. Augustine and the Thomists believe that all is determined. And one sees that their opponents resort also to the circumstances which contribute to our choice. Experience by no means approves the chimera of an indifference of equipoise; and one can employ here the argument that M. Bayle himself employed against the Cartesians' manner of proving freedom by the lively sense of our independence. For although I do not always see the reason for an inclination which makes me choose between two apparently uniform courses, there will always be some impression, however imperceptible, that determines us. The mere desire to make use of one's freedom has no effect of specifying, or determining us to the choice of one course or the other.

306. M. Bayle goes on: 'There are at the very least two ways whereby man can extricate himself from the snares of equipoise. One, which I have already mentioned, is for a man to flatter himself with the pleasing fancy that he is master in his own house, and that he does not depend upon objects.' This way is blocked: for all that one might wish to play master in one's own house, that has no determining effect, nor does it favour one course more than the other. M. Bayle goes on: 'He would make this Act: I will prefer

this to that, because it pleases me to behave thus.' But these words, 'because it pleases me', 'because such is my pleasure', imply already a leaning towards 'the object that pleases'.

307. There is therefore no justification for continuing thus: 'And so that which determined him would not be taken from the object; the motive would be derived only from the ideas men have of their own perfections, or of their natural faculties. The other way is that of the lot or chance: the short straw would decide.' This way has an outlet, but it does not reach the goal: it would alter the issue, for in such a case it is not man who decides. Or again if one maintains that it is still the man who decides by lot, man himself is no longer in equipoise, because the lot is not, and the man has attached himself to it. There are always reasons in Nature which cause that which happens by chance or through the lot. I am somewhat surprised that a mind so shrewd as M. Bayle's could have allowed itself to be so misled on this point. I have set out elsewhere the true rejoinder to the Buridan sophism: it is that the case of perfect equipoise is impossible, since the universe can never be halved, so as to make all impressions equivalent on both sides.

308. Let us see what M. Bayle himself says elsewhere against the chimerical or absolutely undefined indifference. Cicero had said (in his book *De Fato*) that Carneades had found something more subtle than the deviation of atoms, attributing the cause of a so-called absolutely undefined indifference to the voluntary motions of souls, because these motions have no need of an external cause, coming as they do from our nature. But M. Bayle (*Dictionary*, art. 'Epicurus', p. 1143) aptly replies that all that which springs from the nature of a thing is determined: thus determination always remains, and Carneades' evasion is of no avail.

309. He shows elsewhere (*Reply to the Questions of a Provincial*, ch. 90, l. 2, p. 229) 'that a freedom far removed from this so-called equipoise is incomparably more beneficial. I mean', he says, 'a freedom such as may always follow the judgements of the mind, and such as cannot resist objects clearly recognized as good. I know of no people who do not agree that truth clearly recognized necessitates' (determines rather, unless one speak of a moral necessity) 'the assent of the soul; experience teaches us that. In the schools they teach constantly that as the true is the object of

the understanding, so the good is the object of the will. So like-wise they teach that as the understanding can never affirm any-thing save that which is shown to it under the semblance of truth, the will can never love anything which to it does not appear to be good. One never believes the false as such, and one never loves evil as evil. There is in the understanding a natural determination towards the true in general, and towards each individual truth clearly recognized. There is in the will a natural determination towards good in general; whence many philosophers conclude that from the moment when individual goods are clearly recog-nized by us we are of necessity compelled to love them. The under-standing suspends its actions only when its objects show themselves obscurely, so that there is cause for doubt as to whether they are false or true. That leads many persons to the conclusion that the will remains in equipoise only when the soul is uncertain whether the object presented to it is a good with regard to it; but that also, the moment the soul decides in the affirmative, it of necessity clings to that object until other judgements of the mind determine it otherwise. Those who expound freedom in this fashion think to find therein plentiful enough material for merit or demerit. For they assume that these judgements of the mind proceed from a free attention of the soul in examining the objects, comparing them together, and discriminating between them. I must not forget that there are very learned men' (such as Bellarmine, lib. 3, *De Gratia et Libero Arbitrio*, c. 8, et 9, and Cameron, in *Responsione ad Episto-lam Viri Docti, id est Episcopii*) 'who maintain with very cogent reasons that the will always of necessity follows the last practical act of the understanding.'

310. One must make some observations on this discourse. A very clear recognition of the best *determines* the will; but it does not necessitate it, properly speaking. One must always distinguish between the necessary and the certain or infallible, as I have already observed more than once, and distinguish metaphysical necessity from moral necessity. I think also that it is only God's will which always follows the judgements of the understanding: all intelligent creatures are subject to some passions, or to per-ceptions at least, that are not composed entirely of what I call *adequate ideas*. And although in the blessed these passions always tend towards the true good, by virtue of the laws of Nature and the system of things pre-established in relation to them, yet this

does not always happen in such a way that they have a perfect knowledge of that good. It is the same with them as with us, who do not always understand the reason for our instincts. The angels and the blessed are created beings, even as we are, in whom there is always some confused perception mingled with distinct knowledge. Suarez said something similar concerning them. He thinks (*Treatise on Prayer*, book I, ch. 11) that God has so ordered things beforehand that their prayers, when they are made with a full will, always succeed: that is an example of a pre-established harmony. As for us, in addition to the judgement of the understanding, of which we have an express knowledge, there are mingled therewith confused perceptions of the senses, and these beget passions and even imperceptible inclinations, of which we are not always aware. These movements often thwart the judgement of the practical understanding.

311. As for the parallel between the relation of the understanding to the true and that of the will to the good, one must know that a clear and distinct perception of a truth contains within it actually the affirmation of this truth: thus the understanding is necessitated in that direction. But whatever perception one may have of the good, the effort to act in accordance with the judgement, which in my opinion forms the essence of the will, is distinct from it. Thus, since there is need of time to raise this effort to its climax, it may be suspended, and even changed, by a new perception or inclination which passes athwart it, which diverts the mind from it, and which even causes it sometimes to make a contrary judgement. Hence it comes that our soul has so many means of resisting the truth which it knows, and that the passage from mind to heart is so long. Especially is this so when the understanding to a great extent proceeds only by faint *thoughts*, which have only slight power to affect, as I have explained elsewhere. Thus the connexion between judgement and will is not so necessary as one might think.

312. M. Bayle goes on to say, with truth (p. 221): 'Indeed, it cannot be a fault in man's soul that it has no freedom of indifference as regards good in general. It would be rather a disorder, an inordinate imperfection, if one could say truthfully: It is all one to me whether I am happy or unhappy; I have no more determination to love the good than to hate it; I can do both equally. Now if it is a praiseworthy and advantageous quality to be determinate

as regards good in general, it cannot be a fault if one is necessitated as regards each individual good recognized plainly as for our good. It seems even as though it were a necessary conclusion, that if the soul has no freedom of indifference as regards good in general, it also has none in respect of particular goods which after due examination it judges to be goods in relation to it. What should we think of a soul which, having formed that judgement, had, and prided itself on having, the power not to love these goods, and even to hate them, and which said: I recognize clearly that these are goods for me, I have all the enlightenment necessary on that point; nevertheless I will not love them, I will hate them; my decision is made, I act upon it; it is not that any reason' (that is, any other reason than that which is founded upon 'Such is my good pleasure') 'urges me thereto, but it pleases me so to behave: what should we think, I say, of such a soul? Should we not find it more imperfect and more unhappy than if it had not this freedom of indifference?

313. 'Not only does the doctrine that subjects the will to the final acts of the understanding give a more favourable idea of the state of the soul, but it shows also that it is easier to lead man to happiness along that road than along the road of indifference. It will suffice to enlighten his mind upon his true interests, and straightway his will will comply with the judgements that reason shall have pronounced. But if he has a freedom independent of reason and of the quality of objects clearly recognized, he will be the most intractable of all animals, and it will never be possible to rely upon making him choose the right course. All the counsels, all the arguments in the world may prove unavailing; you will give him explanations, you will convince his mind, and yet his will will play the haughty madam and remain motionless as a rock. Vergil, *Aen.*, lib. 6, v. 470:

> *Non magis incepto vultum sermone movetur,*
> *Quam si dura silex, aut stet Marpesia cautes.*

A caprice, an empty whim will make her stiffen against reasons of all kinds; it will not please her to love her clearly recognized good, it will please her to hate it. Do you consider such a faculty, sir, to be the richest present God can have made to man, and the sole instrument of our happiness? Is it not rather an obstacle to our felicity? Is there cause for boasting in being able to say: "I have scorned all the judgements of my reason, and I have followed an altogether different path, simply from considerations of my own good pleasure?" With what regrets would one not be torn, in that case, if the determination made had an ill result? Such a freedom would therefore be more harmful than profitable to men, because the understanding would not present all the goodness of the objects clearly enough to deprive the will of the power of rejection. It would be therefore infinitely better for man to be always of necessity determined by the judgement of the understanding, than to permit the will to suspend its action. For by this means it would achieve its aim with greater ease and certainty.'

314. Upon this discourse I make the further observation, that it is very true that a freedom of indifference, undefined and without any determining reason, would be as harmful, and even objectionable, as it is impracticable and chimerical. The man who wished to behave thus, or at the least appear to be acting without due cause, would most certainly be looked upon as irrational. But it is very true also that the thing is impossible, when it is taken strictly in accordance with the assumption. As soon as one tries to give an example of it one misses one's aim and stumbles upon the case of a man who, while he does not come to a decision without cause, does so rather under the influence of inclination or passion than of judgement. As soon as one says: 'I scorn the judgements of my reason simply from considerations of my own good pleasure, it pleases me to behave thus', it is as if one were to say: I prefer my inclination to my interest, my pleasure to my profit.

315. Even so some capricious man, fancying that it is ignominious for him to follow the advice of his friends or his servants, might prefer the satisfaction of contradicting them to the profit he could derive from their counsel. It may happen, however, that in a matter of small moment a wise man acts irregularly and against his own interest in order to thwart another who tries to restrain him or direct him, or that he may disconcert those who watch his steps. It is even well at times to imitate Brutus by concealing one's wit, and even to feign madness, as David did before the King of the Philistines.

316. M. Bayle admirably supplements his remarks with the object of showing that to act against the judgement of the understanding would be a great imperfection. He observes (p. 225) that,

even according to the Molinists, 'the understanding which does its DUTY well indicates that which is THE BEST'. He introduces God (ch. 91, p. 227) saying to our first parents in the Garden of Eden: 'I have given you my knowledge, the faculty of judging things, and full power to dispose your wills. I shall give you instructions and orders; but the free will that I have bestowed upon you is of such a nature that you have equal power (according to circumstances) to obey me and to disobey me. You will be tempted: if you make a good use of your freedom you will be happy; and if you use it ill you will be unhappy. It is for you to see if you wish to ask of me, as a new grace, either that I permit you to abuse your freedom when you shall make resolve to do so, or that I prevent you from doing so. Consider carefully, I give you four and twenty hours. Do you not clearly understand' (adds M. Bayle) 'that their reason, which had not yet been obscured by sin, would have made them conclude that they must ask God, as the crowning point of the favours wherewith he had honoured them, not to permit them to destroy themselves by an ill use of their powers? And must one not admit that if Adam, through wrongly making it a point of honour to order his own goings, had refused a divine direction that would have safeguarded his happiness, he would have been the prototype of all such as Phaeton and Icarus? He would have been well-nigh as ungodly as the Ajax of Sophocles, who wished to conquer without the aid of the gods, and who said that the most craven would put their enemies to flight with such aid.'

317. M. Bayle also shows (ch. 80) that one congratulates oneself no less, or even takes more credit to oneself, for having been aided from above, than for owing one's happiness to one's own choice. And if one does well through having preferred a tumultuous instinct, which arose suddenly, to reasons maturely considered, one feels an extraordinary joy in this; for one assumes that either God, or our Guardian Angel, or something or other which one pictures to oneself under the vague name of *good luck* has impelled us thereto. Indeed, Sulla and Caesar boasted more of their good luck than of their prudence. The pagans, and particularly the poets (Homer especially), determined their heroes' acts by divine promptings. The hero of the *Aeneid* proceeds only under the direction of a God. It was very great praise offered to the Emperors if one said that they were victorious both through their

troops and through their gods whom they lent to their generals: 'Te copias, te consilium et tuos praebente Divos,' said Horace. The generals fought under the auspices of the Emperors, as if trusting to the Emperor's good luck, for subordinate officers had no rights regarding the auspices. One takes credit to oneself for being a favourite of heaven, one rates oneself more highly for the possession of good fortune than of talent. There are no people that think themselves more fortunate than the mystics, who imagine that they keep still while God acts within them.

318. 'On the other hand', M. Bayle adds (ch. 83), 'a Stoic philosopher, who attaches to everything an inevitable necessity, is as susceptible as another man to the pleasure of having chosen well. And every man of sense will find that, far from taking pleasure in the thought of having deliberated long and finally chosen the most honourable course, one feels incredible satisfaction in persuading oneself that one is so firmly rooted in the love of virtue that without the slightest resistance one would repel a temptation. A man to whom is suggested the doing of a deed contrary to his duty, his honour and his conscience, who answers forthwith that he is incapable of such a crime, and who is certainly not capable of it, is far more contented with himself than if he asked for time to consider it, and were for some hours in a state of indecision as to which course to take. One is on many occasions regretful over not being able to make up one's mind between two courses, and one would be well pleased that the counsel of a good friend, or some succour from above, should impel us to make a good choice.' All that demonstrates for us the advantage a determinate judgement has over that vague indifference which leaves us in uncertainty. But indeed I have proved sufficiently that only ignorance or passion has power to keep us in doubt, and have thus given the reason why God is never in doubt. The nearer one comes to him, the more perfect is freedom, and the more it is determined by the good and by reason. The character of Cato, of whom Velleius said that it was impossible for him to perform a dishonourable action, will always be preferred to that of a man who is capable of wavering.

319. I have been well pleased to present and to support these arguments of M. Bayle against vague indifference, as much for the elucidation of the subject as to confront him with himself, and to demonstrate that he ought therefore not to complain of the

alleged necessity imposed upon God, of choosing the best way that is possible. For either God will act through a vague indifference and at random, or again he will act on caprice or through some other passion, or finally he must act through a prevailing inclination of reason which prompts him to the best. But passions, which come from the confused perception of an apparent good, cannot occur in God; and vague indifference is something chimerical. It is therefore only the strongest reason that can regulate God's choice. It is an imperfection in our freedom that makes us capable of choosing evil instead of good, a greater evil instead of the lesser evil, the lesser good instead of the greater good. That arises from the appearances of good and evil, which deceive us; whereas God is always prompted to the true and the greatest good, that is, to the absolutely true good, which he cannot fail to know.

320. This false idea of freedom, conceived by those who, not content with exempting it, I do not say from constraint, but from necessity itself, would also exempt it from certainty and determination, that is, from reason and perfection, nevertheless pleased some Schoolmen, people who often become entangled in their own subtleties, and take the straw of terms for the grain of things. They assume some chimerical notion, whence they think to derive some use, and which they endeavour to maintain by quibblings. Complete indifference is of this nature: to concede it to the will is to grant it a privilege of the kind that some Cartesians and some mystics find in the divine nature, of being able to do the impossible, to produce absurdities, to cause two contradictory propositions to be true simultaneously. To claim that a determination comes from a complete indifference absolutely indeterminate is to claim that it comes naturally from nothing. Let it be assumed that God does not give this determination: it has accordingly no fountain-head in the soul, nor in the body, nor in circumstances, since all is assumed to be indeterminate; and yet there it is, appearing and existing without preparation, nothing making ready for it, no angel, not even God himself, being able to see or to show how it exists. That would be not only the emergence of something from nothing, but its emergence thence *of itself*. This doctrine introduces something as preposterous as the theory already mentioned, of the deviation of atoms, whereby Epicurus asserted that one of these small bodies, going in a straight line, would turn aside all at

once from its path, without any reason, simply because the will so commands. Take note moreover that he resorted to that only to justify this alleged freedom of complete indifference, a chimerical notion which appears to be of very ancient origin; and one may with good reason say : *Chimaera Chimaeram parit*.

321. This is the way Signor Marchetti has expressed it in his admirable translation of Lucretius into Italian verse, which has not yet been published (Book 2) :

> *Mà ch'i principii poi non corran punto*
> *Della lor dritta via, chi veder puote?*
> *Sì finalmente ogni lor moto sempre*
> *Insieme s'aggruppa, e dall' antico*
> *Sempre con ordin certo il nuovo nasce;*
> *Ne tracciando i primi semi, fanno*
> *Di moto un tal principio, il qual poi rompa*
> *I decreti del fato, acciò non segua*
> *L'una causa dell' altra in infinito;*
> *Onde han questa, dich' io,* del fato sciolta
> Libera voluntà, *per cui ciascuno*
> *Va dove piu l'agrada? I moti ancora*
> *Si declinan sovente, e non in tempo*
> *Certo, ne certa region, mà solo*
> *Quando e dove commanda il nostro arbitrio;*
> *Poiche senz' alcun dubbio à queste cose*
> *Dà sol principio il voler proprio, e quindi*
> *Van poi scorrendo per le membra i moti.*

It is comical that a man like Epicurus, after having discarded the gods and all incorporeal substances, could have supposed that the will, which he himself takes as composed of atoms, could have had control over the atoms, and diverted them from their path, without its being possible for one to say how.

322. Carneades, not going so far back as to the atoms, claimed to find at once in the soul of man the reason for the so-called vague indifference, assuming as reason for the thing just that for which Epicurus sought a reason. Carneades gained nothing thereby, except that he more easily deceived careless people, in transferring the absurdity from one subject, where it is somewhat too evident, to another subject where it is easier to confuse matters, that is to say, from the body to the soul. For most philosophers

had not very distinct notions of the nature of the soul. Epicurus, who composed it of atoms, was at least right in seeking the origin of its determination in that which he believed to be the origin of the soul itself. That is why Cicero and M. Bayle were wrong to find so much fault with him, and to be indulgent towards, and even praise, Carneades, who is no less irrational. I do not understand how M. Bayle, who was so clear-sighted, was thus satisfied by a disguised absurdity, even to the extent of calling it the greatest effort the human mind can make on this matter. It is as if the soul, which is the seat of reason, were more capable than the body of acting without being determined by some reason or cause, internal or external; or as if the great principle which states that nothing comes to pass without cause only related to the body.

323. It is true that the Form or the Soul has this advantage over matter, that it is the source of action, having within itself the principle of motion or of change, in a word, τὸ αὐτοκίνητον, as Plato calls it; whereas matter is simply passive, and has need of being impelled to act, *agitur, ut agat*. But if the soul is active of itself (as it indeed is), for that very reason it is not of itself absolutely indifferent to the action, like matter, and it must find in itself a ground of determination. According to the System of Pre-established Harmony the soul finds in itself, and in its ideal nature anterior to existence, the reasons for its determinations, adjusted to all that shall surround it. That way it was determined from all eternity in its state of mere possibility to act freely, as it does, when it attains to existence.

324. M. Bayle himself remarks aptly that freedom of indifference (such as must be admitted) does not exclude inclinations and does not demand equipoise. He demonstrates amply enough (*Reply to the Questions of a Provincial*, ch. 139, p. 748 *seqq.*) that the soul may be compared to a balance, where reasons and inclinations take the place of weights. According to him, one can explain what passes in our resolutions by the hypothesis that the will of man is like a balance which is at rest when the weights of its two pans are equal, and which always inclines either to one side or the other according to which of the pans is the more heavily laden. A new reason makes a heavier weight, a new idea shines more brightly than the old; the fear of a heavy penalty prevails over some pleasure; when two passions dispute the ground, it is always the stronger which gains the mastery, unless the other be

assisted by reason or by some other contributing passion. When one flings away merchandise in order to save oneself, the action, which the Schoolmen call mixed, is voluntary and free; and yet love of life indubitably prevails over love of possessions. Grief arises from remembrance of lost possessions, and one has all the greater difficulty in making one's resolve, the nearer the approach to even weight in the opposing reasons, as also we see that the balance is determined more promptly when there is a great difference between the weights.

325. Nevertheless, as very often there are divers courses to choose from, one might, instead of the balance, compare the soul with a force which puts forth effort on various sides simultaneously, but which acts only at the spot where action is easiest or there is least resistance. For instance, air if it is compressed too firmly in a glass vessel will break it in order to escape. It puts forth effort at every part, but finally flings itself upon the weakest. Thus do the inclinations of the soul extend over all the goods that present themselves: they are antecedent acts of will; but the consequent will, which is their result, is determined in the direction of that which touches most closely.

326. This ascendancy of inclinations, however, does not prevent man from being master in his own domain, provided that he knows how to make use of his power. His dominion is that of reason: he has only to prepare himself in good time to resist the passions, and he will be capable of checking the vehemence of the most furious. Let us assume that Augustus, about to give orders for putting to death Fabius Maximus, acts, as is his wont, upon the advice a philosopher had given him, to recite the Greek alphabet before doing anything in the first heat of his anger: this reflexion will be capable of saving the life of Fabius and the glory of Augustus. But without some fortunate reflexion, which one owes sometimes to a special divine mercy, or without some skill acquired beforehand, like that of Augustus, calculated to make us reflect fittingly as to time and place, passion will prevail over reason. The driver is master over the horses if he controls them as he should, and as he can; but there are occasions when he becomes negligent, and then for a time he will have to let go the reins:

Fertur equis auriga, nec audit currus habenas.

327. One must admit that there is always within us enough

power over our will, but we do not always bethink ourselves of employing it. That shows, as I have observed more than once, that the power of the soul over its inclinations is a control which can only be exercised in an *indirect* manner, almost as Bellarmine would have had the Popes exercise rights over the temporal power of kings. In truth, the external actions that do not exceed our powers depend absolutely upon our will; but our volitions depend upon our will only through certain artful twists which give us means of suspending our resolutions, or of changing them. We are masters in our own house, not as God is in the world, he having but to speak, but as a wise prince is in his dominions or as a good father of a family is in his home. M. Bayle sometimes takes the matter differently, as though we must have, in order to boast of a free will, an absolute power over ourselves, independent of reasons and of means. But even God has not such a power, and must not have in this sense, in relation to his will: he cannot change his nature, nor act otherwise than according to method; and how could man transform himself all of a sudden? I have already said God's dominion, the dominion of wisdom, is that of reason. It is only God, however, who always wills what is most to be desired, and consequently he has no need of the power to change his will.

328. If the soul is mistress in its own house (says M. Bayle, p. 753) it has only to will, and straightway that vexation and pain which is attendant upon victory over the passions will vanish away. For this effect it would suffice, in his opinion, to give oneself indifference to the objects of the passions (p. 758). Why, then, do men not give themselves this indifference (he says), if they are masters in their own house? But this objection is exactly as if I were to ask why a father of a family does not give himself gold when he has need thereof? He can acquire some, but through skill, and not, as in the age of the fairies, or of King Midas, through a mere command of the will or by his touch. It would not suffice to be master in one's own house; one must be master of all things in order to give oneself all that one wishes; for one does not find everything in one's own house. Working thus upon oneself, one must do as in working upon something else; one must have knowledge of the constitution and the qualities of one's object, and adapt one's operations thereto. It is therefore not in a moment and by a mere act of the will that one corrects oneself, and that one acquires a better will.

ESSAYS ON THE JUSTICE OF GOD AND THE

329. Nevertheless it is well to observe that the vexations and pains attendant upon victory over the passions in some people turn into pleasure, through the great satisfaction they find in the lively sense of the force of their mind, and of the divine grace. Ascetics and true mystics can speak of this from experience; and even a true philosopher can say something thereof. One can attain to that happy state, and it is one of the principal means the soul can use to strengthen its dominion.

330. If the Scotists and the Molinists appear to favour vague indifference (appear, I say, for I doubt whether they do so in reality, once they have learnt to know it), the Thomists and the disciples of Augustine are for predetermination. For one must have either the one or the other. Thomas Aquinas is a writer who is accustomed to reason on sound principles, and the subtle Scotus, seeking to contradict him, often obscures matters instead of throwing light upon them. The Thomists as a general rule follow their master, and do not admit that the soul makes its resolve without the existence of some predetermination which contributes thereto. But the predetermination of the new Thomists is not perhaps exactly that which one needs. Durand de Saint-Pourçain, who often enough formed a party of his own, and who opposed the idea of the special co-operation of God, was nevertheless in favour of a certain predetermination. He believed that God saw in the state of the soul, and of its surroundings, the reason for his determinations.

331. The ancient Stoics were in that almost of the same opinion as the Thomists. They were at the same time in favour of determination and against necessity, although they have been accused of attaching necessity to everything. Cicero says in his book *De Fato* that Democritus, Heraclitus, Empedocles and Aristotle believed that fate implied necessity; that others were opposed to that (he means perhaps Epicurus and the Academicians); and that Chrysippus sought a middle course. I think that Cicero is mistaken as regards Aristotle, who fully recognized contingency and freedom, and went even too far, saying (inadvertently, as I think) that propositions on contingent futurities had no determinate truth; on which point he was justifiably abandoned by most of the Schoolmen. Even Cleanthes, the teacher of Chrysippus, although he upheld the determinate truth of future events, denied their necessity. Had the Schoolmen, so fully convinced of this

324

determination of contingent futurities (as were for instance the Fathers of Coimbra, authors of a famous Course of Philosophy), seen the connexion between things in the form wherein the System of General Harmony proclaims it, they would have judged that one cannot admit preliminary certainty, or determination of futurition, without admitting a predetermination of the thing in its causes and in its reasons.

332. Cicero has endeavoured to expound for us the middle course taken by Chrysippus; but Justus Lipsius observed, in his *Stoic Philosophy*, that the passage from Cicero was mutilated, and that Aulus Gellius has preserved for us the whole argument of the Stoic philosopher (*Noct. Att.*, lib. 6, c. 2). Here it is in epitome. Fate is the inevitable and eternal connexion of all events. Against this is urged in objection, that it follows that the acts of the will would be necessary, and that criminals, being coerced into evil, should not be punished. Chrysippus answers that evil springs from the original constitution of souls, which forms part of the destined sequence; that souls which are of a good natural disposition offer stronger resistance to the impressions of external causes; but that those whose natural defects had not been corrected by discipline allowed themselves to be perverted. Next he distinguishes (according to Cicero) between principal causes and accessary causes, and uses the comparison of a cylinder, whose rotatory force and speed or ease in motion comes chiefly from its shape, whereas it would be retarded by any roughness in formation. Nevertheless it has need of impulsion, even as the soul needs to be acted upon by the objects of the senses, and receives this impression according to its own constitution.

333. Cicero considers that Chrysippus becomes so confused that, whether he will or no, he confirms the necessity of fate. M. Bayle is almost of the same opinion (*Dictionary*, art. 'Chrysippus', lit. H). He says that this philosopher does not get out of the bog, since the cylinder is regular or uneven according to what the craftsman has made it; and thus God, providence, fate will be the causes of evil in such a way as to render it necessary. Justus Lipsius answers that, according to the Stoics, evil came from matter. That is (to my mind) as if he had said that the stone on which the craftsman worked was sometimes too rough and too irregular to produce a good cylinder. M. Bayle cites against Chrysippus the fragments of Onomaus and Diogenianus that

325

Eusebius has preserved for us in the *Praeparatio Evangelica* (lib. 6, c. 7, 8); and above all he relies upon Plutarch's refutation in his book against the Stoics, quoted art. 'Paulicians', lit. G. But this refutation does not amount to very much. Plutarch maintains that it would be better to deny power to God than to impute to him the permission of evils; and he will not admit that evil may serve a greater good. I have already shown, on the contrary, that God cannot but be all-powerful, even though he can do no better than produce the best, which includes the permission of evil. Moreover, I have pointed out repeatedly that what is to the disadvantage of a part taken separately may serve the perfection of the whole.

334. Chrysippus had already made an observation to this effect, not only in his fourth book on Providence, as given by Aulus Gellius (lib. 6, c. 1) where he asserts that evil serves to bring the good to notice (a reason which is not sufficient here), but still better when he applies the comparison of a stage play, in his second book on Nature (as Plutarch quotes it himself). There he says that there are sometimes portions in a comedy which are of no worth in themselves and which nevertheless lend grace to the whole poem. He calls these portions epigrams or inscriptions. We have not enough acquaintance with the nature of the ancient comedy for full understanding of this passage from Chrysippus; but since Plutarch assents to the fact, there is reason to believe that this comparison was not a poor one. Plutarch replies in the first place that the world is not like a play to provide entertainment. But that is a poor answer: the comparison lies in this point alone, that one bad part may make the whole better. He replies secondly that this bad passage is only a small part of the comedy, whereas human life swarms with evils. This reply is of no value either: for he ought to have taken into account that what we know is also a very small part of the universe.

335. But let us return to the cylinder of Chrysippus. He is right in saying that vice springs from the original constitution of some minds. He was met with the objection that God formed them, and he could only reply by pointing to the imperfection of matter, which did not permit God to do better. This reply is of no value, for matter in itself is indifferent to all forms, and God made it. Evil springs rather from the *Forms* themselves in their detached state, that is, from the ideas that God has not produced by an act

326

of his will, any more than he thus produced numbers and figures, and all possible essences which one must regard as eternal and necessary; for they are in the ideal region of the possibles, that is, in the divine understanding. God is therefore not the author of essences in so far as they are only possibilities. But there is nothing actual to which he has not decreed and given existence; and he has permitted evil because it is involved in the best plan existing in the region of possibles, a plan which supreme wisdom could not fail to choose. This notion satisfies at once the wisdom, the power and the goodness of God, and yet leaves a way open for the entrance of evil. God gives perfection to creatures in so far as it is possible in the universe. One gives a turn to the cylinder, but any roughness in its shape restricts the swiftness of its motion. This comparison made by Chrysippus does not greatly differ from mine, which was taken from a laden boat that is carried along by the river current, its pace becoming slower as the load grows heavier. These comparisons tend towards the same end; and that shows that if we were sufficiently informed concerning the opinions of ancient philosophers, we should find therein more reason than is supposed.

336. M. Bayle himself commends the passage from Chrysippus (art. 'Chrysippus', lit. T) that Aulus Gellius quotes in the same place, where this philosopher maintains that evil has come *by concomitance*. That also is made clear by my system. For I have demonstrated that the evil which God permitted was not an object of his will, as an end or a means, but simply as a condition, since it had to be involved in the best. Yet one must confess that the cylinder of Chrysippus does not answer the objection of necessity. He ought to have added, in the first place, that it is by the free choice of God that some of the possibles exist; secondly, that rational creatures act freely also, in accordance with their original nature, which existed already in the eternal ideas; and lastly, that the motive power of good inclines the will without compelling it.

337. The advantage of freedom which is in the creature without doubt exists to an eminent degree in God. That must be understood in so far as it is genuinely an advantage and in so far as it presupposes no imperfection. For to be able to make a mistake and go astray is a disadvantage, and to have control over the passions is in truth an advantage, but one that presupposes an imperfection,

namely passion itself, of which God is incapable. Scotus was justified in saying that if God were not free and exempt from necessity, no creature would be so. But God is incapable of being indeterminate in anything whatsoever: he cannot be ignorant, he cannot doubt, he cannot suspend his judgement; his will is always decided, and it can only be decided by the best. God can never have a primitive particular will, that is, independent of laws or general acts of will; such a thing would be unreasonable. He cannot determine upon Adam, Peter, Judas or any individual without the existence of a reason for this determination; and this reason leads of necessity to some general enunciation. The wise mind always acts *according to principles*; always *according to rules*, and never *according to exceptions*, save when the rules come into collision through opposing tendencies, where the strongest carries the day: or else, either they will stop one another or some third course will emerge as a result. In all these cases one rule serves as an exception to the other, and there are never any *original exceptions* with one who always acts in a regular way.

338. If there are people who believe that election and reprobation are accomplished on God's part by a despotic absolute power, not only without any apparent reason but actually without any reason, even a concealed one, they maintain an opinion that destroys alike the nature of things and the divine perfections. Such an *absolutely absolute decree* (so to speak) would be without doubt insupportable. But Luther and Calvin were far from such a belief: the former hopes that the life to come will make us comprehend the just reasons of God's choice; and the latter protests explicitly that these reasons are just and holy, although they be unknown to us. I have already in that connexion quoted Calvin's treatise on predestination, and here are the actual words: 'God before the fall of Adam had reflected upon what he had to do, and that for causes concealed from us. . . . It is evident therefore that he had just causes for the reprobation of some of mankind, but causes to us UNKNOWN.'

339. This truth, that all God does is reasonable and cannot be better done, strikes at the outset every man of good sense, and extorts, so to speak, his approbation. And yet the most subtle of philosophers have a fatal propensity for offending sometimes without observing it, during the course and in the heat of disputes, against the first principles of good sense, when these are shrouded

in terms that disguise them. We have here already seen how the excellent M. Bayle, with all his shrewdness, has nevertheless combated this principle which I have just indicated, and which is a sure consequence of the supreme perfection of God. He thought to defend in that way the cause of God and to exempt him from an imaginary necessity, by leaving him the freedom to choose from among various goods the least. I have already spoken of M. Diroys and others who have also been deluded by this strange opinion, one that is far too commonly accepted. Those who uphold it do not observe that it implies a wish to preserve for, or rather bestow upon, God a false freedom, which is the freedom to act unreasonably. That is rendering his works subject to correction, and making it impossible for us to say or even to hope that anything reasonable can be said upon the permission of evil.

340. This error has much impaired M. Bayle's arguments, and has barred his way of escape from many perplexities. That appears again in relation to the laws of the realm of Nature: he believes them to be arbitrary and indifferent, and he objects that God could better have attained his end in the realm of grace if he had not clung to these laws, if he had more often dispensed with their observance, or even if he had made others. He believed this especially with regard to the law of the union between the soul and the body. For he is persuaded, with the modern Cartesians, that the ideas of the perceptible qualities that God gives (according to them) to the soul, occasioned by movements of the body, have nothing representing these movements or resembling them. Accordingly it was a purely arbitrary act on God's part to give us the ideas of heat, cold, light and other qualities which we experience, rather than to give us quite different ideas occasioned in the same way. I have often wondered that people so talented should have been capable of relishing notions so unphilosophic and so contrary to the fundamental maxims of reason. For nothing gives clearer indication of the imperfection of a philosophy than the necessity experienced by the philosopher to confess that something comes to pass, in accordance with his system, for which there is no reason. That applies to the idea of Epicurus on the deviation of atoms. Whether it be God or Nature that operates, the operation will always have its reasons. In the operations of Nature, these reasons will depend either upon necessary truths or upon the laws that God has found the most reasonable; and in the operations of

God, they will depend upon the choice of the supreme reason which causes them to act.

341. M. Regis, a famous Cartesian, had asserted in his 'Metaphysics' (part 2, book 2, c. 29) that the faculties God has given to men are the most excellent that they were capable of in conformity with the general order of nature. 'Considering only', he says, 'the power of God and the nature of man by themselves, it is very easy to conceive that God could have made man more perfect: but if one will consider man, not in himself and separately from all other creatures, but as a member of the universe and a portion which is subject to the general laws of motions, one will be bound to acknowledge that man is as perfect as he could have been.' He adds 'that we cannot conceive that God could have employed any other means more appropriate than pain for the conservation of our bodies'. M. Regis is right in a general way in saying that God cannot do better than he has done in relation to all. And although there be apparently in some places in the universe rational animals more perfect than man, one may say that God was right to create every kind of species, some more perfect than others. It is perhaps not impossible that there be somewhere a species of animals much resembling man and more perfect than we are. It may be even that the human race will attain in time to a greater perfection than that which we can now envisage. Thus the laws of motions do not prevent man from being more perfect: but the place God has assigned to man in space and in time limits the perfections he was able to receive.

342. I also doubt, with M. Bayle, whether pain be necessary in order to warn men of peril. But this writer goes too far (*Reply to the Questions of a Provincial*, vol. II, ch. 77, p. 104): he seems to think that a feeling of pleasure could have the same effect, and that, in order to prevent a child from going too near the fire, God could give him ideas of pleasure in proportion to the distance he kept from it. This expedient does not appear very practicable with regard to all evils, unless a miracle were involved. It is more natural that what if it were too near would cause an evil should cause some foreboding of evil when it is a little less near. Yet I admit that it is possible such a foreboding will be something less than pain, and usually this is the case. Thus it indeed appears that pain is not necessary for causing one to shun present peril; it is wont rather to serve as a penalty for having actually plunged into

evil, and a warning against further lapse. There are also many painful evils the avoidance whereof rests not with us. As a dissolution of the continuity of our body is a consequence of many accidents that may happen to us, it was natural that this imperfection of the body should be represented by some sense of imperfection in the soul. Nevertheless I would not guarantee that there were no animals in the universe whose structure was cunning enough to cause a sense of indifference as accompaniment to this dissolution of continuity, as for instance when a gangrenous limb is cut off; or even a sense of pleasure, as if one were only scratching oneself. For the imperfection that attends the dissolution of the body might lead to the sense of a greater perfection, which was suspended or checked by the continuity which is now broken: and in this respect the body would be as it were a prison.

343. There is also nothing to preclude the existence in the universe of animals resembling that one which Cyrano de Bergerac encountered in the sun. The body of this animal being a sort of fluid composed of innumerable small animals, that were capable of ranging themselves in accordance with the desires of the great animal, by this means it transformed itself in a moment, just as it pleased; and the dissolution of continuity caused it no more hurt than the stroke of an oar can cause to the sea. But, after all, these animals are not men, they are not in our globe or in our present century; and God's plan ensured that there should not be lacking here on earth a rational animal clothed in flesh and bones, whose structure involves susceptibility to pain.

344. But M. Bayle further opposes this on another principle, one which I have already mentioned. It seems that he thinks the ideas which the soul conceives in relation to the feelings of the body are arbitrary. Thus God might have caused the dissolution of continuity to give us pleasure. He even maintains that the laws of motion are entirely arbitrary. 'I would wish to know', he says (vol. III, ch. 166, p. 1080), 'whether God established by an act of his freedom of indifference general laws on the communication of movements, and the particular laws on the union of the human soul with an organic body? In this case, he could have established quite different laws, and adopted a system whose results involved neither moral evil nor physical evil. But if the answer is given that God was constrained by supreme wisdom to establish the laws that he has established, there we have neither more nor

less than the *Fatum* of the Stoics. Wisdom will have marked out a way for God, the abandonment whereof will have been as impossible to him as his own self-destruction.' This objection has been sufficiently overthrown: it is only a moral necessity; and it is always a happy necessity to be bound to act in accordance with the rules of perfect wisdom.

345. Moreover, it appears to me that the reason for the belief held by many that the laws of motion are arbitrary comes from the fact that few people have properly examined them. It is known now that M. Descartes was much mistaken in his statement of them. I have proved conclusively that conservation of the same quantity of motion cannot occur, but I consider that the same quantity of force is conserved, whether absolute or directive and respective, whether total or partial. My principles, which carry this subject as far as it can go, have not yet been published in full; but I have communicated them to friends competent to judge of them, who have approved them, and have converted some other persons of acknowledged erudition and ability. I discovered at the same time that the laws of motion actually existing in Nature, and confirmed by experiments, are not in reality absolutely demonstrable, as a geometrical proposition would be; but neither is it necessary that they be so. They do not spring entirely from the principle of necessity, but rather from the principle of perfection and order; they are an effect of the choice and the wisdom of God. I can demonstrate these laws in divers ways, but must always assume something that is not of an absolutely geometrical necessity. Thus these admirable laws are wonderful evidence of an intelligent and free being, as opposed to the system of absolute and brute necessity, advocated by Strato or Spinoza.

346. I have found that one may account for these laws by assuming that the effect is always equal in force to its cause, or, which amounts to the same thing, that the same force is conserved always: but this axiom of higher philosophy cannot be demonstrated geometrically. One may again apply other principles of like nature, for instance the principle that action is always equal to reaction, one which assumes in things a distaste for external change, and cannot be derived either from extension or impenetrability; and that other principle, that a simple movement has the same properties as those which might belong to a compound

movement such as would produce the same phenomena of loco-motion. These assumptions are very plausible, and are successful as an explanation of the laws of motion : nothing is so appropriate, all the more since they are in accord with each other. But there is to be found in them no absolute necessity, such as may compel us to admit them, in the way one is compelled to admit the rules of logic, of arithmetic and geometry.

347. It seems, when one considers the indifference of matter to motion and to rest, that the largest body at rest could be carried along without any resistance by the smallest body in motion, in which case there would be action without reaction and an effect greater than its cause. There is also no necessity to say of the motion of a ball which runs freely on an even, horizontal plane, with a certain degree of speed, termed A, that this motion must have the properties of that motion which it would have if it were going with lesser speed in a boat, itself moving in the same direc-tion with the residue of the speed, to ensure that the ball, seen from the bank, advance with the same degree A. For, although the same appearance of speed and of direction results through this medium of the boat, it is not because it is the same thing. Never-theless it happens that the effects of the collision of the balls in the boat, the motion in each one separately combined with that of the boat giving the appearance of that which goes on outside the boat, also give the appearance of the effects that these same balls colliding would have outside the boat. All that is admirable, but one does not see its absolute necessity. A movement on the two sides of the right-angled triangle composes a movement on the hypotenuse ; but it does not follow that a ball moving on the hypo-tenuse must produce the effect of two balls of its own size moving on the two sides : yet that is true. Nothing is so appropriate as this result, and God has chosen the laws that produce it : but one sees no geometrical necessity therein. Yet it is this very lack of necessity which enhances the beauty of the laws that God has chosen, wherein divers admirable axioms exist in conjunction, and it is impossible for one to say which of them is the primary.

348. I have also shown that therein is observed that excellent law of continuity, which I have perhaps been the first to state, and which is a kind of touchstone whose test the rules of M. Descartes, of Father Fabry, Father Pardies, Father de Malebranche and others cannot pass. In virtue of this law, one must be able to

regard rest as a movement vanishing after having continually diminished, and likewise equality as an inequality that vanishes also, as would happen through the continual diminution of the greater of two unequal bodies, while the smaller retains its size. As a consequence of this consideration, the general rule for unequal bodies, or bodies in motion, must apply also to equal bodies or to bodies one of which is at rest, as to a particular case of the rule. This does result in the true laws of motion, and does not result in certain laws invented by M. Descartes and by some other men of talent, which already on that score alone prove to be illconcerted, so that one may predict that experiment will not favour them.

349. These considerations make it plain that the laws of Nature regulating movements are neither entirely necessary nor entirely arbitrary. The middle course to be taken is that they are a choice of the most perfect wisdom. And this great example of the laws of motion shows with the utmost clarity how much difference there is between these three cases, to wit, firstly *an absolute necessity*, metaphysical or geometrical, which may be called blind, and which does not depend upon any but efficient causes; in the second place, *a moral necessity*, which comes from the free choice of wisdom in relation to final causes; and finally in the third place, *something absolutely arbitrary*, depending upon an indifference of equipoise, which is imagined, but which cannot exist, where there is no sufficient reason either in the efficient or in the final cause. Consequently one must conclude how mistaken it is to confuse either that which is absolutely necessary with that which is determined by the reason of the best, or the freedom that is determined by reason with a vague indifference.

350. This also settles M. Bayle's difficulty, for he fears that, if God is always determinate, Nature could dispense with him and bring about that same effect which is attributed to him, through the necessity of the order of things. That would be true if the laws of motion for instance, and all the rest, had their source in a geometrical necessity of efficient causes; but in the last analysis one is obliged to resort to something depending upon final causes and upon what is fitting. This also utterly destroys the most plausible reasoning of the Naturalists. Dr. Johann Joachim Becher, a German physician, well known for his books on chemistry, had composed a prayer which looked like getting him into trouble. It

began: 'O sancta mater natura, aeterne rerum ordo'. And it ended by saying that this Nature must forgive him his errors, since she herself was their cause. But the nature of things, if taken as without intelligence and without choice, has in it nothing sufficiently determinant. Herr Becher did not sufficiently take into account that the Author of things (*natura naturans*) must be good and wise, and that we can be evil without complicity on his part in our acts of wickedness. When a wicked man exists, God must have found in the region of possibles the idea of such a man forming part of that sequence of things, the choice of which was demanded by the greatest perfection of the universe, and in which errors and sins are not only punished but even repaired to greater advantage, so that they contribute to the greatest good.

351. M. Bayle, however, has extended the free choice of God a little too far. Speaking of the Peripatetic Strato (*Reply to the Questions of a Provincial*, vol. III, ch. 180, p. 1239), who asserted that everything had been brought forth by the necessity of a nature devoid of intelligence, he maintains that this philosopher, on being asked why a tree has not the power to form bones and veins, might have asked in his turn: Why has matter precisely three dimensions? why should not two have sufficed for it? why has it not four? 'If one had answered that there can be neither more nor less than three dimensions he would have demanded the cause of this impossibility.' These words lead one to believe that M. Bayle suspected that the number of the dimensions of matter depended upon God's choice, even as it depended upon him to cause or not to cause trees to produce animals. Indeed, how do we know whether there are not planetary globes or earths situated in some more remote place in the universe where the fable of the Barnacle-geese of Scotland (birds that were said to be born of trees) proves true, and even whether there are not countries where one could say:

> ... *populos umbrosa creavit*
> *Fraxinus, et foeta viridis puer excidit alno?*

But with the dimensions of matter it is not thus: the ternary number is determined for it not by the reason of the best, but by a geometrical necessity, because the geometricians have been able to prove that there are only three straight lines perpendicular to one another which can intersect at one and the same point.

Nothing more appropriate could have been chosen to show the difference there is between the moral necessity that accounts for the choice of wisdom and the brute necessity of Strato and the adherents of Spinoza, who deny to God understanding and will, than a consideration of the difference existing between the reason for the laws of motion and the reason for the ternary number of the dimensions: for the first lies in the choice of the best and the second in a geometrical and blind necessity.

352. Having spoken of the laws of bodies, that is, of the rules of motion, let us come to the laws of the union between body and soul, where M. Bayle believes that he finds again some vague indifference, something absolutely arbitrary. Here is the way he speaks of it in his *Reply* (vol. II, ch. 84, p. 163): 'It is a puzzling question whether bodies have some natural property of doing harm or good to man's soul. If one answers yes, one plunges into an insane labyrinth: for, as man's soul is an immaterial substance, one will be bound to say that the local movement of certain bodies is an efficient cause of the thoughts in a mind, a statement contrary to the most obvious notions that philosophy imparts to us. If one answers no, one will be constrained to admit that the influence of our organs upon our thoughts depends neither upon the internal qualities of matter, nor upon the laws of motion, but upon an *arbitrary institution* of the creator. One must then admit that it depended altogether upon God's freedom to combine particular thoughts of our soul with particular modifications of our body, even when he had once established all the laws for the action of bodies one upon another. Whence it results that there is in the universe no portion of matter which by its proximity can harm us, save when God wills it; and consequently, that the earth is as capable as any other place of being the abode of the happy man. . . . In short it is evident that there is no need, in order to prevent the wrong choices of freedom, to transport man outside the earth. God could do on earth with regard to all the acts of the will what he does in respect of the good works of the predestined when he settles their outcome, whether by efficacious or by sufficient grace: and that grace, without in any way impairing freedom, is always followed by the assent of the soul. It would be as easy for him on earth as in heaven to bring about the determination of our souls to a good choice.'

353. I agree with M. Bayle that God could have so ordered

bodies and souls on this globe of earth, whether by ways of nature or by extraordinary graces, that it would have been a perpetual paradise and a foretaste of the celestial state of the blessed. There is no reason why there should not be worlds happier than ours; but God had good reasons for willing that ours should be such as it is. Nevertheless, in order to prove that a better state would have been possible here, M. Bayle had no need to resort to the system of occasional causes: it abounds in miracles and in hypotheses for which their very originators confess there is no justification; and these are two defects such as will most of all estrange a system from true philosophy. It is a cause for surprise, in the first place, that M. Bayle did not bethink himself of the System of Pre-established Harmony which he had examined before, and which for this matter was so opportune. But as in this system all is connected and harmonious, all following from reasons and nothing being left incomplete or exposed to the rash discretion of perfect indifference, it seems that it was not pleasing to M. Bayle: for he was here somewhat biassed in favour of such indifference, which, notwithstanding, he contested so strongly on other occasions. He was much given to passing from one extreme to the other, not with an ill intention or against his own conviction, but because there was as yet nothing settled in his mind on the question concerned. He contented himself with whatever suited him for frustrating the opponent he had in mind, his aim being only to perplex philosophers, and show the weakness of our reason; and never, in my opinion, did either Arcesilaus or Carneades argue for and against with more eloquence and more wit. But, after all, one must not doubt for the sake of doubting: doubts must serve us as a gangway to the truth. That is what I often said to the late Abbé Foucher, a few specimens of whose work prove that he designed to do with regard to the Academicians what Lipsius and Scioppius had done for the Stoics, and M. Gassendi for Epicurus, and what M. Dacier has so well begun for Plato. It must not be possible for us to offer true philosophers such a reproach as that implied in the celebrated Casaubon's answer to those who, in showing him the hall of the Sorbonne, told him that debate had been carried on there for some centuries. What conclusions have been reached? he said to them.

354. M. Bayle goes on (p. 166): 'It is true that since the laws of motion were instituted in such forms as we see now in the world, it is an inevitable necessity that a hammer striking a nut should

break it, and that a stone falling on a man's foot should cause some bruise or some derangement of its parts. But that is all that can follow the action of this stone upon the human body. If you want it in addition to cause a feeling of pain, then one must assume the institution of a code other than that one which regulates the action and reaction of bodies one upon another; one must, I say, have recourse to the particular system of the laws of union between the soul and certain bodies. Now as this system is not of necessity connected with the other, the indifference of God does not cease in relation to the one immediately upon his choice of the other. He therefore combined these two systems with a complete freedom, like two things which did not follow naturally the one from the other. Thus it is by an arbitrary institution he has ordained that wounds in the body should cause pain in the soul which is united to this body. It therefore only rested with him to have chosen another system of union between soul and body: he was therefore able to choose one in accordance wherewith wounds only evoke the idea of the remedy and an intense but agreeable desire to apply it. He was able to arrange that all bodies which were on the point of breaking a man's head or piercing his heart should evoke a lively sense of danger, and that this sense should cause the body to remove itself promptly out of reach of the blow. All that would have come to pass without miracles, since there would have been general laws on this subject. The system which we know by experience teaches us that the determination of the movement of certain bodies changes in pursuance of our desires. It was therefore possible for a combination to be effected between our desires and the movement of certain bodies, whereby the nutritive juices were so modified that the good arrangement of our organs was never affected.'

355. It is evident that M. Bayle believes that everything accomplished through general laws is accomplished without miracles. But I have shown sufficiently that if the law is not founded on reasons and does not serve to explain the event through the nature of things, it can only be put into execution by a miracle. If, for example, God had ordained that bodies must have a circular motion, he would have needed perpetual miracles, or the ministry of angels, to put this order into execution: for that is contrary to the nature of motion, whereby the body naturally abandons the circular line to continue in the tangent straight line if nothing

holds it back. Therefore it is not enough for God to ordain simply that a wound should excite an agreeable sensation : natural means must be found for that purpose. The real means whereby God causes the soul to be conscious of what happens in the body have their origin in the nature of the soul, which represents the bodies, and is so made beforehand that the representations which are to spring up one from another within it, by a natural sequence of thoughts, correspond to the changes in the body.

356. The representation has a natural relation to that which is to be represented. If God should have the round shape of a body represented by the idea of a square, that would be an unsuitable representation : for there would be angles or projections in the representation, while all would be even and smooth in the original. The representation often suppresses something in the objects when it is imperfect; but it can add nothing: that would render it, not more than perfect, but false. Moreover, the suppression is never complete in our perceptions, and there is in the representation, confused as it is, more than we see there. Thus there is reason for supposing that the ideas of heat, cold, colours, etc., also only represent the small movements carried out in the organs, when one is conscious of these qualities, although the multiplicity and the diminutive character of these movements prevents their clear representation. Almost in the same way it happens that we do not distinguish the blue and the yellow which play their part in the representation as well as in the composition of the green, when the microscope shows that what appears to be green is composed of yellow and blue parts.

357. It is true that the same thing may be represented in different ways ; but there must always be an exact relation between the representation and the thing, and consequently between the different representations of one and the same thing. The projections in perspective of the conic sections of the circle show that one and the same circle may be represented by an ellipse, a parabola and a hyperbola, and even by another circle, a straight line and a point. Nothing appears so different nor so dissimilar as these figures ; and yet there is an exact relation between each point and every other point. Thus one must allow that each soul represents the universe to itself according to its point of view, and through a relation which is peculiar to it ; but a perfect harmony always subsists therein. God, if he wished to effect representation

of the dissolution of continuity of the body by an agreeable sensation in the soul, would not have neglected to ensure that this very dissolution should serve some perfection in the body, by giving it some new relief, as when one is freed of some burden or loosed from some bond. But organic bodies of such kinds, although possible, do not exist upon our globe, which doubtless lacks innumerable inventions that God may have put to use elsewhere. Nevertheless it is enough that, due allowance being made for the place our world holds in the universe, nothing can be done for it better than what God does. He makes the best possible use of the laws of nature which he has established and (as M. Regis also acknowledged in the same passage) 'the laws that God has established in nature are the most excellent it is possible to conceive'.

358. I will add to that the remark from the *Journal des Savants* of the 16th March 1705, which M. Bayle has inserted in chapter 162 of the *Reply to the Questions of a Provincial* (vol. III, p. 1030). The matter in question is the extract from a very ingenious modern book on the Origin of Evil, to which I have already referred here. It is stated: 'that the general solution in respect of physical evil which this book gives is that the universe must be regarded as a work composed of various pieces which form a whole; that, according to the laws established in nature, some parts cannot be better unless others become worse, whence would result a system less perfect as a whole. This principle', the writer goes on, 'is good; but if nothing is added to it, it does not appear sufficient. Why has God established laws that give rise to so many difficulties? philosophers who are somewhat precise will say. Could he not have established others of a kind not subject to any defects? And to cut the matter short, how comes it that he has prescribed laws for himself? Why does he not act without general laws, in accordance with all his power and all his goodness? The writer has not carried the difficulty as far as that. By disentangling his ideas one might indeed possibly find means of solving the difficulty, but there is no development of the subject in his work.'

359. I suppose that the gifted author of this extract, when he thought the difficulty could be solved, had in mind something akin to my principles on this matter. If he had vouchsafed to declare himself in this passage, he would to all appearance have replied, like M. Regis, that the laws God established were the most excellent that could be established. He would have acknowledged,

at the same time, that God could not have refrained from establishing laws and following rules, because laws and rules are what makes order and beauty; that to act without rules would be to act without reason; and that because God *called into action all his goodness* the exercise of his omnipotence was consistent with the laws of wisdom, to secure as much good as was possible of attainment. Finally, he would have said, the existence of certain particular disadvantages which strike us is a sure indication that the best plan did not permit of their avoidance, and that they assist in the achievement of the total good, an argument wherewith M. Bayle in more than one place expresses agreement.

360. Now that I have proved sufficiently that everything comes to pass according to determinate reasons, there cannot be any more difficulty over these principles of God's foreknowledge. Although these determinations do not compel, they cannot but be certain, and they foreshadow what shall happen. It is true that God sees all at once the whole sequence of this universe, when he chooses it, and that thus he has no need of the connexion of effects and causes in order to foresee these effects. But since his wisdom causes him to choose a sequence in perfect connexion, he cannot but see one part of the sequence in the other. It is one of the rules of my system of general harmony, *that the present is big with the future*, and that he who sees all sees in that which is that which shall be. What is more, I have proved conclusively that God sees in each portion of the universe the whole universe, owing to the perfect connexion of things. He is infinitely more discerning than Pythagoras, who judged the height of Hercules by the size of his footprint. There must therefore be no doubt that effects follow their causes determinately, in spite of contingency and even of freedom, which nevertheless exist together with certainty or determination.

361. Durand de Saint-Pourçain, among others, has indicated this clearly in saying that contingent futurities are seen determinately in their causes, and that God, who knows all, seeing all that shall have power to tempt or repel the will, will see therein the course it shall take. I could cite many other authors who have said the same thing, and reason does not allow the possibility of thinking otherwise. M. Jacquelot implies also (*Conformity of Faith with Reason*, p. 318 *et seqq.*), as M. Bayle observes (*Reply to the Questions of a Provincial*, vol. III, ch. 142, p. 796), that the dispositions of the human heart and those of circumstances acquaint God

unerringly with the choice that man shall make. M. Bayle adds that some Molinists say the same, and refers us to those who are quoted in the *Suavis Concordia* of Pierre de S. Joseph, the Feuillant (pp. 579, 580).

362. Those who have confused this determination with necessity have fabricated monsters in order to fight them. To avoid a reasonable thing which they had disguised under a hideous shape, they have fallen into great absurdities. For fear of being obliged to admit an imaginary necessity, or at least one different from that in question, they have admitted something which happens without the existence of any cause or reason for it. This amounts to the same as the absurd deviation of atoms, which according to Epicurus happened without any cause. Cicero, in his book on Divination, saw clearly that if the cause could produce an effect towards which it was entirely indifferent there would be a true chance, a genuine luck, an actual fortuitous case, that is, one which would be so not merely in relation to us and our ignorance, according to which one may say:

> *Sed Te*
> *Nos facimus, Fortuna, Deam, caeloque locamus,*

but even in relation to God and to the nature of things. Consequently it would be impossible to foresee events by judging of the future by the past. He adds fittingly in the same passage: 'Qui potest provideri, quicquam futurum esse, quod neque causam habet ullam, neque notam cur futurum sit?' and soon after: 'Nihil est tam contrarium rationi et constantiae, quam fortuna; ut mihi ne in Deum quidem cadere videatur, ut sciat quid casu et fortuito futurum sit. Si enim scit, certe illud eveniet: sin certe eveniet, nulla fortuna est.' If the future is certain, there is no such thing as luck. But he wrongly adds: 'Est autum fortuna; rerum igitur fortuitarum nulla praesensio est.' There is luck, therefore future events cannot be foreseen. He ought rather to have concluded that, events being predetermined and foreseen, there is no luck. But he was then speaking against the Stoics, in the character of an Academician.

363. The Stoics already derived from the decrees of God the prevision of events. For, as Cicero says in the same book: 'Sequitur porro nihil Deos ignorare, quod omnia ab iis sint constituta.' And, according to my system, God, having seen the possible world that

he desired to create, foresaw everything therein. Thus one may say that the *divine knowledge of vision differs from the knowledge of simple intelligence* only in that it adds to the latter the acquaintance with the actual decree to choose this sequence of things which simple intelligence had already presented, but only as possible; and this decree now makes the present universe.

364. Thus the Socinians cannot be excused for denying to God the certain knowledge of future events, and above all of the future resolves of a free creature. For even though they had supposed that there is a freedom of complete indifference, so that the will can choose without cause, and that thus this effect could not be seen in its cause (which is a great absurdity), they ought always to take into account that God was able to foresee this event in the idea of the possible world that he resolved to create. But the idea which they have of God is unworthy of the Author of things, and is not commensurate with the skill and wit which the writers of this party often display in certain particular discussions. The author of the *Reflexion on the Picture of Socinianism* was not altogether mistaken in saying that the God of the Socinians would be ignorant and powerless, like the God of Epicurus, every day confounded by events and living from one day to the next, if he only knows by conjecture what the will of men is to be.

365. The whole difficulty here has therefore only come from a wrong idea of contingency and of freedom, which was thought to have need of a complete indifference or equipoise, an imaginary thing, of which neither a notion nor an example exists, nor ever can exist. Apparently M. Descartes had been imbued with the idea in his youth, at the College of la Flèche. That caused him to say (part I of his *Principles*, art. 41): 'Our thought is finite, and the knowledge and omnipotence of God, whereby he has not only known from all eternity everything that is, or that can be, but also has willed it, is infinite. Thus we have enough intelligence to recognize clearly and distinctly that this power and this knowledge are in God; but we have not enough so to comprehend their extent that we can know how they leave the actions of men entirely free and indeterminate.' The continuation has already been quoted above. 'Entirely free', that is right; but one spoils everything by adding 'entirely indeterminate'. One has no need of infinite knowledge in order to see that the foreknowledge and the providence of God allow freedom to our actions, since God has foreseen those

actions in his ideas, just as they are, that is, free. Laurentius Valla indeed, in his *Dialogue against Boethius* (which I will presently quote in epitome) ably undertakes to reconcile freedom with foreknowledge, but does not venture to hope that he can reconcile it with providence. Yet there is no more difficulty in the one than the other, because the decree to give existence to this action no more changes its nature than does one's mere consciousness thereof. But there is no knowledge, however infinite it be, which can reconcile the knowledge and providence of God with actions of an indeterminate cause, that is to say, with a chimerical and impossible being. The actions of the will are determined in two ways, by the foreknowledge or providence of God, and also by the dispositions of the particular immediate cause, which lie in the inclinations of the soul. M. Descartes followed the Thomists on this point; but he wrote with his usual circumspection, so as not to come into conflict with some other theologians.

366. M. Bayle relates (*Reply to the Questions of a Provincial*, vol. III, ch. 142, p. 804) that Father Gibieuf of the Oratory published a Latin treatise on the freedom of God and of the creature, in the year 1639; that he was met with protests, and was shown a collection of seventy contradictions taken from the first book of his work; and that, twenty years after, Father Annat, Confessor to the King of France, reproached him in his book *De Incoacta Libertate* (ed. Rome, 1654, in 4to.), for the silence he still maintained. Who would not think (adds M. Bayle), after the uproar of the *de Auxiliis* Congregations, that the Thomists taught things touching the nature of free will which were entirely opposed to the opinion of the Jesuits? When, however, one considers the passages that Father Annat quoted from the works of the Thomists (in a pamphlet entitled: *Jansenius a Thomistis, gratiae per se ipsam efficacis defensoribus, condemnatus*, printed in Paris in the year 1654 in 4to.) one can in reality only see verbal controversies between the two sects. The grace efficacious of itself, according to the one side, leaves to free will quite as much power of resistance as the congruent grace of the others. M. Bayle thinks one can say almost as much of Jansenius himself. He was (so he says) an able man, of a methodical mind and of great assiduity. He worked for twenty-two years at his *Augustinus*. One of his aims was to refute the Jesuits on the dogma of free will; yet no decision has yet been reached as to whether he rejects or adopts freedom of indifference.

From his work innumerable passages are quoted for and against this opinion, as Father Annat has himself shown in the work that has just been mentioned, *De Incoacta Libertate*. So easy is it to render this subject obscure, as M. Bayle says at the conclusion of this discourse. As for Father Gibieuf, it must be admitted that he often alters the meaning of his terms, and that consequently he does not answer the question in the main, albeit he often writes with good sense.

367. Indeed, confusion springs, more often than not, from ambiguity in terms, and from one's failure to take trouble over gaining clear ideas about them. That gives rise to these eternal, and usually mistaken, contentions on necessity and contingency, on the possible and the impossible. But provided that it is understood that necessity and possibility, taken metaphysically and strictly, depend solely upon this question, whether the object in itself or that which is opposed to it implies contradiction or not; and that one takes into account that contingency is consistent with the inclinations, or reasons which contribute towards causing determination by the will; provided also that one knows how to distinguish clearly between necessity and determination or certainty, between metaphysical necessity, which admits of no choice, presenting only one single object as possible, and moral necessity, which constrains the wisest to choose the best; finally, provided that one is rid of the chimera of complete indifference, which can only be found in the books of philosophers, and on paper (for they cannot even conceive the notion in their heads, or prove its reality by an example in things) one will easily escape from a labyrinth whose unhappy Daedalus was the human mind. That labyrinth has caused infinite confusion, as much with the ancients as with those of later times, even so far as to lead men into the absurd error of the Lazy Sophism, which closely resembles fate after the Turkish fashion. I do not wonder if in reality the Thomists and the Jesuits, and even the Molinists and the Jansenists, agree together on this matter more than is supposed. A Thomist and even a wise Jansenist will content himself with certain determination, without going on to necessity: and if someone goes so far, the error mayhap will lie only in the word. A wise Molinist will be content with an indifference opposed to necessity, but such as shall not exclude prevalent inclinations.

368. These difficulties, however, have greatly impressed M. Bayle,

who was more inclined to dwell on them than to solve them, although he might perhaps have had better success than anyone if he had thought fit to turn his mind in that direction. Here is what he says of them in his *Dictionary*, art. 'Jansenius', lit. G, p. 1626: 'Someone has said that the subject of Grace is an ocean which has neither shore nor bottom. Perhaps he would have spoken more correctly if he had compared it to the Strait of Messina, where one is always in danger of striking one reef while endeavouring to avoid another.

> *Dextrum Scylla latus, laevum implacata Charybdis*
> *Obsidet.*

Everything comes back in the end to this: Did Adam sin freely? If you answer yes, then you will be told, his fall was not foreseen. If you answer no, then you will be told, he is not guilty. You may write a hundred volumes against the one or the other of these conclusions, and yet you will confess, either that the infallible prevision of a contingent event is a mystery impossible to conceive, or that the way in which a creature which acts without freedom sins nevertheless is altogether incomprehensible.'

369. Either I am greatly mistaken or these two alleged incomprehensibilities are ended altogether by my solutions. Would to God it were as easy to answer the question how to cure fevers, and how to avoid the perils of two chronic sicknesses that may originate, the one from not curing the fever, the other from curing it wrongly. When one asserts that a free event cannot be foreseen, one is confusing freedom with indetermination, or with indifference that is complete and in equipoise; and when one maintains that the lack of freedom would prevent man from being guilty, one means a freedom exempt, not from determination or from certainty, but from necessity and from constraint. This shows that the dilemma is not well expressed, and that there is a wide passage between the two perilous reefs. One will reply, therefore, that Adam sinned freely, and that God saw him sinning in the possible state of Adam, which became actual in accordance with the decree of the divine permission. It is true that Adam was determined to sin in consequence of certain prevailing inclinations: but this determination destroys neither contingency nor freedom. Moreover, the certain determination to sin which exists in man does not deprive him of the power to avoid sinning (speaking generally) or,

since he does sin, prevent him from being guilty and deserving punishment. This is more especially so since the punishment may be of service to him or others, to contribute towards determining them another time not to sin. There is besides punitive justice, which goes beyond compensation and amendment, and wherein also there is nothing liable to be shaken by the certain determination of the contingent resolutions of the will. It may be said, on the contrary, that the penalties and rewards would be to some extent unavailing, and would fail in one of their aims, that of amendment, if they could not contribute towards determining the will to do better another time.

370. M. Bayle continues: 'Where freedom is concerned there are only two courses to take: one is to say that all the causes distinct from the soul, and co-operating with it, leave it the power to act or not to act; the other is to say that they so determine it to act that it cannot forbear to do so. The first course is that taken by the Molinists, the other is that of the Thomists and Jansenists and the Protestants of the Geneva Confession. Yet the Thomists have clamorously maintained that they were not Jansenists; and the latter have maintained with equal warmth that where freedom was concerned they were not Calvinists. On the other hand, the Molinists have maintained that St. Augustine did not teach Jansenism. Thus the one side not wishing to admit that they were in conformity with people who were considered heretics, and the other side not wishing to admit that they were in opposition to a learned saint whose opinions were always considered orthodox, have both performed a hundred feats of contortion, etc.'

371. The two courses which M. Bayle distinguishes here do not exclude a third course, according to which the determination of the soul does not come solely from the co-operation of all the causes distinct from the soul, but also from the state of the soul itself and its inclinations which mingle with the impressions of the senses, strengthening or weakening them. Now all the internal and external causes taken together bring it about that the soul is determined certainly, but not of necessity: for no contradiction would be implied if the soul were to be determined differently, it being possible for the will to be inclined, but not possible for it to be compelled by necessity. I will not venture upon a discussion of the difference existing between the Jansenists and the Reformed on this matter. They are not perhaps always fully in accord with

themselves as regards things, or as regards expressions, on a matter where one often loses one's way in bewildering subtleties. Father Theophile Raynaud, in his book entitled *Calvinismus Religio Bestiarum*, wished to strike at the Dominicans, without naming them. On the other hand, those who professed to be followers of St. Augustine reproached the Molinists with Pelagianism or at the least semi-Pelagianism. Things were carried to excess at times by both sides, whether in their defence of a vague indifference and the granting of too much to man, or in their teaching *determinationem ad unum secundum qualitatem actus licet non quoad ejus substantiam*, that is to say, a determination to evil in the non-regenerate, as if they did nothing but sin. After all, I think one must not reproach any but the adherents of Hobbes and Spinoza with destroying freedom and contingency; for they think that that which happens is alone possible, and must happen by a brute geometrical necessity. Hobbes made everything material and subjected it to mathematical laws alone; Spinoza also divested God of intelligence and choice, leaving him a blind power, whence all emanates of necessity. The theologians of the two Protestant parties are equally zealous in refuting an unendurable necessity. Although those who follow the Synod of Dordrecht teach sometimes that it suffices for freedom to be exempt from constraint, it seems that the necessity they leave in it is only hypothetical, or rather that which is more appropriately termed certainty and infallibility. Thus it results that very often the difficulties only lie in the terms. I say as much with regard to the Jansenists, although I do not wish to make excuse for those people in everything.

372. With the Hebrew Cabalists, *Malcuth* or the Kingdom, the last of the Sephiroth, signified that God controls everything irresistibly, but gently and without violence, so that man thinks he is following his own will while he carries out God's. They said that Adam's sin had been *truncatio Malcuth a caeteris plantis*, that is to say, that Adam had cut back the last of the Sephiroth, by making a dominion for himself within God's dominion, and by assuming for himself a freedom independent of God, but that his fall had taught him that he could not subsist of himself, and that men must needs be redeemed by the Messiah. This doctrine may receive a good interpretation. But Spinoza, who was versed in the Cabala of the writers of his race, and who says (*Tractatus Politicus*, c. 2, n. 6) that men, conceiving of freedom as they do, establish a

dominion within God's dominion, has gone too far. The dominion of God is with Spinoza nothing but the dominion of necessity, and of a blind necessity (as with Strato), whereby everything emanates from the divine nature, while no choice is left to God, and man's choice does not exempt him from necessity. He adds that men, in order to establish what is termed *Imperium in Imperio*, supposed that their soul was a direct creation of God, something which could not be produced by natural causes, furthermore that it had an absolute power of determination, a state of things contrary to experience. Spinoza is right in opposing an absolute power of determination, that is, one without any grounds; it does not belong even to God. But he is wrong in thinking that a soul, that a simple substance, can be produced naturally. It seems, indeed, that the soul to him was only a transient modification; and when he pretends to make it lasting, and even perpetual, he substitutes for it the idea of the body, which is purely a notion and not a real and actual thing.

373. The story M. Bayle relates of Johan Bredenburg, a citizen of Rotterdam (*Dictionary*, art. 'Spinoza', lit. H, p. 2774) is curious. He published a book against Spinoza, entitled: *Enervatio Tractatus Theologico-politici, una cum demonstratione geometrico ordine disposita, Naturam non esse Deum, cujus effati contrario praedictus Tractatus unice innititur.* One was surprised to see that a man who did not follow the profession of letters, and who had but slight education (having written his book in Flemish, and had it translated into Latin), had been able to penetrate with such subtlety all the principles of Spinoza, and succeed in overthrowing them, after having reduced them by a candid analysis to a state wherein they could appear in their full force. I have been told (adds M. Bayle) that this writer after copious reflexion upon his answer, and upon the principle of his opponent, finally found that this principle could be reduced to the form of a demonstration. He undertook therefore to prove that there is no cause of all things other than a nature which exists necessarily, and which acts according to an immutable, inevitable and irrevocable necessity. He examined the whole system of the geometricians, and after having constructed his demonstration he scrutinized it from every imaginable angle, he endeavoured to find its weak spot and was never able to discover any means of destroying it, or even of weakening it. That caused him real distress: he groaned over it and begged

the most talented of his friends to help him in searching out the defects of this demonstration. For all that, he was not well pleased that copies of the book were made. Franz Cuper, a Socinian (who had written *Arcana Atheismi Revelata* against Spinoza, Rotterdam, 1676, in 4to.), having obtained a copy, published it just as it was, that is, in Flemish, with some reflexions, and accused the author of being an atheist. The accused made his defence in the same tongue. Orobio, a very able Jewish physician (that one who was refuted by M. Limbourg, and who replied, so I have heard say, in a work posthumously circulated, but unpublished), brought out a book opposing Bredenburg's demonstration, entitled: *Certamen Philosophicum Propugnatae Veritatis Divinae ac Naturalis, adversus J.B. principia, Amsterdam*, 1684. M. Aubert de Versé also wrote in opposition to him the same year under the name of Latinus Serbattus Sartensis. Bredenburg protested that he was convinced of free will and of religion, and that he wished he might be shown a possibility of refuting his own demonstration.

374. I would desire to see this alleged demonstration, and to know whether it tended to prove that primitive Nature, which produces all, acts without choice and without knowledge. In this case, I admit that his proof was Spinozistic and dangerous. But if he meant perhaps that the divine nature is determined toward that which it produces, by its choice and through the motive of the best, there was no need for him to grieve about this so-called immutable, inevitable, irrevocable necessity. It is only moral, it is a happy necessity; and instead of destroying religion it shows divine perfection to the best advantage.

375. I take this opportunity to add that M. Bayle quotes (p. 2773) the opinion of those who believe that the book entitled *Lucii Antistii Constantis de Jure Ecclesiasticorum Liber Singularis*, published in 1665, is by Spinoza. But I have reason for doubting this, despite that M. Colerus, who has passed on to me an account he wrote of the life of that famous Jew, is also of that opinion. The initial letters L.A.C. lead me to believe that the author of this book was M. de la Cour or Van den Hoof, famous for works on the *Interest of Holland, Political Equipoise*, and numerous other books that he published (some of them under the signature V.D.H.) attacking the power of the Governor of Holland, which was at that time considered a danger to the Republic; for the memory of Prince William the Second's attempt upon the city of Amsterdam

was still quite fresh. Most of the ecclesiastics of Holland were on the side of this prince's son, who was then a minor, and they suspected M. de Witt and what was called the Lowenstein faction of favouring the Arminians, the Cartesians, and other sects that were feared still more, endeavouring to rouse the populace against them, and not without success, as the event proved. It was thus very natural that M. de la Cour should publish this book. It is true that people seldom keep to the happy mean in works published to further party interests. I will say in passing that a French version of the *Interest of Holland* by M. de la Cour has just been published, under the deceptive title of *Mémoires de M. le Grand-Pensionnaire de Witt*; as if the thoughts of a private individual, who was, to be sure, of de Witt's party, and a man of talent, but who had not enough acquaintance with public affairs or enough ability to write as that great Minister of State might have written, could pass for the production of one of the first men of his time.

376. I saw M. de la Cour as well as Spinoza on my return from France by way of England and Holland, and I learnt from them a few good anecdotes on the affairs of that time. M. Bayle says, p. 2770, that Spinoza studied Latin under a physician named Franz van den Ende. He tells at the same time, on the authority of Sebastian Kortholt (who refers to it in the preface to the second edition of the book by his late father, *De Tribus Impostoribus, Herberto L. B. de Cherbury, Hobbio et Spinoza*) that a girl instructed Spinoza in Latin, and that she afterwards married M. Kerkering, who was her pupil at the same time as Spinoza. In connexion with that I note that this young lady was a daughter of M. van den Ende, and that she assisted her father in the work of teaching. Van den Ende, who was also called A. Finibus, later went to Paris, and there kept a boarding-school in the Faubourg St. Antoine. He was considered excellent as an instructor, and he told me, when I called upon him there, that he would wager that his audiences would always pay attention to his words. He had with him as well at that time a young girl who also spoke Latin, and worked upon geometrical demonstrations. He had insinuated himself into M. Arnauld's good graces, and the Jesuits began to be jealous of his reputation. But he disappeared shortly afterwards, having been mixed up in the Chevalier de Rohan's conspiracy.

377. I think I have sufficiently proved that neither the fore-knowledge nor the providence of God can impair either his justice

or his goodness, or our freedom. There remains only the difficulty arising from God's co-operation with the actions of the creature, which seems to concern more closely both his goodness, in relation to our evil actions, and our freedom, in relation to good actions as well as to others. M. Bayle has brought out this also with his usual acuteness. I will endeavour to throw light upon the difficulties he puts forward, and then I shall be in a position to conclude this work. I have already proved that the co-operation of God consists in giving us continually all that is real in us and in our actions, in so far as it involves perfection; but that all that is limited and imperfect therein is a consequence of the previous limitations which are originally in the creature. Since, moreover, every action of the creature is a change of its modifications, it is obvious that action arises in the creature in relation to the limitations or negations which it has within itself, and which are diversified by this change.

378. I have already pointed out more than once in this work that evil is a consequence of privation, and I think that I have explained that intelligibly enough. St. Augustine has already put forward this idea, and St. Basil said something of the same kind in his *Hexaëmeron*, Homil. 2, 'that vice is not a living and animate substance, but an affection of the soul contrary to virtue, which arises from one's abandoning the good; and there is therefore no need to look for an original evil'. M. Bayle, quoting this passage in his *Dictionary* (art. 'Paulicians', lit. D, p. 2325) commends a remark by Herr Pfanner (whom he calls a German theologian, but he is a jurist by profession, Counsellor to the Dukes of Saxony), who censures St. Basil for not being willing to admit that God is the author of physical evil. Doubtless God is its author, when the moral evil is assumed to be already in existence; but speaking generally, one might assert that God permitted physical evil by implication, in permitting moral evil which is its source. It appears that the Stoics knew also how slender is the entity of evil. These words of Epictetus are an indication: 'Sicut aberrandi causa meta non ponitur, sic nec natura mali in mundo existit.'

379. There was therefore no need to have recourse to a principle of evil, as St. Basil aptly observes. Nor is it necessary either to seek the origin of evil in matter. Those who believed that there was a chaos before God laid his hand upon it sought therein the source of disorder. It was an opinion which Plato introduced into his *Timaeus*. Aristotle found fault with him for that (in his third book

on Heaven, ch. 2) because, according to this doctrine, disorder would be original and natural, and order would have been introduced against nature. This Anaxagoras avoided by making matter remain at rest until it was stirred by God; and Aristotle in the same passage commends him for it. According to Plutarch (*De Iside et Osiride*, and *Tr. de Animae Procreatione ex Timaeo*) Plato recognized in matter a certain maleficent soul or force, rebellious against God: it was an actual blemish, an obstacle to God's plans. The Stoics also believed that matter was the source of defects, as Justus Lipsius showed in the first book of the Physiology of the Stoics.

380. Aristotle was right in rejecting chaos: but it is not always easy to disentangle the conceptions of Plato, and such a task would be still less easy in respect of some ancient authors whose works are lost. Kepler, one of the most excellent of modern mathematicians, recognized a species of imperfection in matter, even when there is no irregular motion: he calls it its 'natural inertia', which gives it a resistance to motion, whereby a greater mass receives less speed from one and the same force. There is soundness in this observation, and I have used it to advantage in this work, in order to have a comparison such as should illustrate how the original imperfection of the creatures sets bounds to the action of the Creator, which tends towards good. But as matter is itself of God's creation, it only furnishes a comparison and an example, and cannot be the very source of evil and of imperfection. I have already shown that this source lies in the forms or ideas of the possibles, for it must be eternal, and matter is not so. Now since God made all positive reality that is not eternal, he would have made the source of evil, if that did not rather lie in the possibility of things or forms, that which alone God did not make, since he is not the author of his own understanding.

381. Yet even though the source of evil lies in the possible forms, anterior to the acts of God's will, it is nevertheless true that God co-operates in evil in the actual performance of introducing these forms into matter: and this is what causes the difficulty in question here. Durand de Saint-Pourçain, Cardinal Aureolus, Nicolas Taurel, Father Louis de Dole, M. Bernier and some others, speaking of this co-operation, would have it only general, for fear of impairing the freedom of man and the holiness of God. They seem to maintain that God, having given to creatures the power

to act, contents himself with conserving this power. On the other hand, M. Bayle, according to some modern writers, carries the co-operation of God too far: he seems to fear lest the creature be not sufficiently dependent upon God. He goes so far as to deny action to creatures; he does not even acknowledge any real distinction between accident and substance.

382. He places great reliance especially on that doctrine accepted of the Schoolmen, that conservation is a continued creation. The conclusion to be drawn from this doctrine would seem to be that the creature never exists, that it is ever new-born and ever dying, like time, movement and other transient beings. Plato believed this of material and tangible things, saying that they are in a perpetual flux, *semper fluunt, nunquam sunt.* But of immaterial substances he judged quite differently, regarding them alone as real: nor was he in that altogether mistaken. Yet continued creation applies to all creatures without distinction. Sundry good philosophers have been opposed to this dogma, and M. Bayle tells that David de Rodon, a philosopher renowned among those of the French who have adhered to Geneva, deliberately refuted it. The Arminians also do not approve of it; they are not much in favour of these metaphysical subtleties. I will say nothing of the Socinians, who relish them even less.

383. For a proper enquiry as to *whether conservation is a continued creation*, it would be necessary to consider the reasons whereon this dogma is founded. The Cartesians, after the example of their master, employ in order to prove it a principle which is not conclusive enough. They say that 'the moments of time having no necessary connexion with one another, it does not follow that because I am at this moment I shall exist at the moment which shall follow, if the same cause which gives me being for this moment does not also give it to me for the instant following.' The author of the *Reflexion on the Picture of Socinianism* has made use of this argument, and M. Bayle (perhaps the author of this same *Reflexion*) quotes it (*Reply to the Questions of a Provincial*, vol. III, ch. 141, p. 771). One may answer that in fact it does not follow *of necessity* that, because I am, I shall be; but this follows *naturally*, nevertheless, that is, of itself, *per se*, if nothing prevents it. It is the distinction that can be drawn between the essential and the natural. For the same movement endures naturally unless some new cause prevents it or changes it, because the reason which makes it cease

at this instant, if it is no new reason, would have already made it cease sooner.

384. The late Herr Erhard Weigel, a celebrated mathematician and philosopher at Jena, well known for his *Analysis Euclidea*, his mathematical philosophy, some neat mechanical inventions, and finally the trouble he took to induce the Protestant princes of the Empire to undertake the last reform of the Almanac, whose success, notwithstanding, he did not witness; Herr Weigel, I say, communicated to his friends a certain demonstration of the existence of God, which indeed amounted to this idea of continued creation. As he was wont to draw parallels between reckoning and reasoning—witness his Arithmetical Ethics (*rechenschaftliche Sittenlehre*)—he said that the foundation of the demonstration was this beginning of the Pythagorean Table, *once one is one*. These repeated unities were the moments of the existence of things, each one of them depending upon God, who resuscitates, as it were, all things outside himself at each moment: falling away as they do at each moment, they must ever have one who shall resuscitate them, and that cannot be any other than God. But there would be need of a more exact proof if that is to be called a demonstration. It would be necessary to prove that the creature always emerges from nothingness and relapses thither forthwith. In particular it must be shown that the privilege of enduring more than a moment by its nature belongs to the necessary being alone. The difficulties on the composition of the *continuum* enter also into this matter. This dogma appears to resolve time into moments, whereas others regard moments and points as mere modalities of the *continuum*, that is, as extremities of the parts that can be assigned to it, and not as constituent parts. But this is not the place for entering into that labyrinth.

385. What can be said for certain on the present subject is that the creature depends continually upon divine operation, and that it depends upon that no less after the time of its beginning than when it first begins. This dependence implies that it would not continue to exist if God did not continue to act; in short, that this action of God is free. For if it were a necessary emanation, like that of the properties of the circle, which issue from its essence, it must then be said that God in the beginning produced the creature by necessity; or else it must be shown how, in creating it once, he imposed upon himself the necessity of conserving it. Now there is

no reason why this conserving action should not be called production, and even creation, if one will: for the dependence being as great afterwards as at the beginning, the extrinsic designation of being new or not does not change the nature of that action.

386. Let us then admit in such a sense that conservation is a continued creation, and let us see what M. Bayle seems to infer thence (p. 771) after the author of the *Reflexion on the Picture of Socinianism*, in opposition to M. Jurieu. 'It seems to me', this writer says, 'that one must conclude that God does all, and that in all creation there are no first or second or even occasional causes, as can be easily proved. At this moment when I speak, I am such as I am, with all my circumstances, with such thought, such action, whether I sit or stand, that if God creates me in this moment such as I am, as one must of necessity say in this system, he creates me with such thought, such action, such movement and such determination. One cannot say that God creates me in the first place, and that once I am created he produces with me my movements and my determinations. That is indefensible for two reasons. The first is, that when God creates me or conserves me at this instant, he does not conserve me as a being without form, like a species, or another of the Universals of Logic. I am an individual; he creates me and conserves me as such, and as being all that I am in this instant, with all my attendant circumstances. The second reason is that if God creates me in this instant, and one says that afterwards he produces with me my actions, it will be necessary to imagine another instant for action: for before acting one must exist. Now that would be two instants where we only assume one. It is therefore certain in this hypothesis that creatures have neither more connexion nor more relation with their actions than they had with their production at the first moment of the first creation.' The author of this *Reflexion* draws thence very harsh conclusions which one can picture to oneself; and he testifies at the end that one would be deeply indebted to any man that should teach those who approve this system how to extricate themselves from these frightful absurdities.

387. M. Bayle carries this still further. 'You know', he says (p. 775), 'that it is demonstrated in the Scholastic writings' (he cites Arriaga, *Disp.* 9, Phys., sect. 6 et praesertim, sub-sect. 3) 'that the creature cannot be either the total cause or the partial cause of its conservation: for if it were, it would exist before existing,

which is contradictory. You know that the argument proceeds like this: that which conserves itself acts; now that which acts exists, and nothing can act before it has attained complete existence; therefore, if a creature conserved itself, it would act before being. This argument is not founded upon probabilities, but upon the first principles of Metaphysics, *non entis nulla sunt accidentia, operari sequitur esse*, axioms as clear as daylight. Let us go further. If creatures co-operated with God (here is meant an active co-operation, and not co-operation by a passive instrument) to conserve themselves they would act before being: that has been demonstrated. Now if they co-operated with God for the production of any other thing, they would also act before being; it is therefore as impossible for them to co-operate with God for the production of any other thing (such as local movement, an affirmation, volition, entities actually distinct from their substance, so it is asserted) as for their own conservation. Since their conservation is a continued creation, and since all human creatures in the world must confess that they cannot co-operate with God at the first moment of their existence, either to produce themselves or to give themselves any modality, since that would be to act before being (observe that Thomas Aquinas and sundry other Schoolmen teach that if the angels had sinned at the first moment of their creation God would be the author of the sin: see the Feuillant Pierre de St. Joseph, p. 318, *et seqq.*, of the *Suavis Concordia Humanae Libertatis*; it is a sign that they acknowledge that at the first instant the creature cannot act in anything whatsoever), it follows manifestly that they cannot co-operate with God in any one of the subsequent moments, either to produce themselves or to produce any other thing. If they could co-operate therein at the second moment of their existence, nothing would prevent their being able to co-operate at the first moment.'

388. This is the way it will be necessary to answer these arguments. Let us assume that the creature is produced anew at each instant; let us grant also that the instant excludes all priority of time, being indivisible; but let us point out that it does not exclude priority of nature, or what is called anteriority *in signo rationis*, and that this is sufficient. The production, or action whereby God produces, is anterior by nature to the existence of the creature that is produced; the creature taken in itself, with its nature and its necessary properties, is anterior to its accidental affections and

to its actions; and yet all these things are in being in the same moment. God produces the creature in conformity with the exigency of the preceding instants, according to the laws of his wisdom; and the creature operates in conformity with that nature which God conveys to it in creating it always. The limitations and imperfections arise therein through the nature of the subject, which sets bounds to God's production; this is the consequence of the original imperfection of creatures. Vice and crime, on the other hand, arise there through the free inward operation of the creature, in so far as this can occur within the instant, repetition afterwards rendering it discernible.

389. This anteriority of nature is a commonplace in philosophy: thus one says that the decrees of God have an order among themselves. When one ascribes to God (and rightly so) understanding of the arguments and conclusions of creatures, in such sort that all their demonstrations and syllogisms are known to him, and are found in him in a transcendent way, one sees that there is in the propositions or truths a natural order; but there is no order of time or interval, to cause him to advance in knowledge and pass from the premises to the conclusion.

390. I find in the arguments that have just been quoted nothing which these reflexions fail to satisfy. When God produces the thing he produces it as an individual and not as a universal of logic (I admit); but he produces its essence before its accidents, its nature before its operations, following the priority of their nature, and *in signo anteriore rationis*. Thus one sees how the creature can be the true cause of the sin, while conservation by God does not prevent the sin; God disposes in accordance with the preceding state of the same creature, in order to follow the laws of his wisdom notwithstanding the sin, which in the first place will be produced by the creature. But it is true that God would not in the beginning have created the soul in a state wherein it would have sinned from the first moment, as the Schoolmen have justly observed: for there is nothing in the laws of his wisdom that could have induced him so to do.

391. This law of wisdom brings it about also that God reproduces the same substance, the same soul. Such was the answer that could have been given by the Abbé whom M. Bayle introduces in his *Dictionary* (art. 'Pyrrhon.' lit. B, p. 2432). This wisdom effects the connexion of things. I concede therefore that the creature

does not co-operate with God to conserve himself (in the sense in which I have just explained conservation). But I see nothing to prevent the creature's co-operation with God for the production of any other thing: and especially might this concern its inward operation, as in the case of a thought or a volition, things really distinct from the substance.

392. But there I am once more at grips with M. Bayle. He maintains that there are no such accidents distinct from the substance. 'The reasons', he says, 'which our modern philosophers have employed to demonstrate that the accidents are not beings in reality distinct from the substance are not mere difficulties; they are arguments which overwhelm one, and which cannot be refuted. Take the trouble', he adds, 'to look for them in the writings of Father Maignan, or Father Malebranche or M. Calli' (Professor of Philosophy at Caen) 'or in the *Accidentia profligata* of Father Saguens, disciple of Father Maignan, the extract from which is to be found in the *Nouvelles de la République des Lettres*, June 1702. Or if you wish one author only to suffice you, choose Dom François Lami, a Benedictine monk, and one of the strongest Cartesians to be found in France. You will find among his *Philosophical Letters*, printed at Trévoux in 1703, that one wherein by the geometricians' method he demonstrates "that God is the sole true cause of all that which is real."' I would wish to see all these books; and as for this last proposition, it may be true in a very good sense: God is the one principal cause of pure and absolute realities, or of perfections. *Causae secundae agunt in virtute primae.* But when one comprises limitations and privations under the term realities one may say that the second causes co-operate in the production of that which is limited; otherwise God would be the cause of sin, and even the sole cause,

393. It is well to beware, moreover, lest in confusing substances with accidents, in depriving created substances of action, one fall into Spinozism, which is an exaggerated Cartesianism. That which does not act does not merit the name of substance. If the accidents are not distinct from the substances; if the created substance is a successive being, like movement; if it does not endure beyond a moment, and does not remain the same (during some stated portion of time) any more than its accidents; if it does not operate any more than a mathematical figure or a number: why shall one not say, with Spinoza, that God is the

only substance, and that creatures are only accidents or modifications? Hitherto it has been supposed that the substance remains, and that the accidents change; and I think one ought still to abide by this ancient doctrine, for the arguments I remember having read do not prove the contrary, and prove more than is needed.

394. 'One of the absurdities', says M. Bayle (p. 779), 'that arise from the so-called distinction which is alleged to exist between substances and their accidents is that creatures, if they produce the accidents, would possess a power of creation and annihilation. Accordingly one could not perform the slightest action without creating an innumerable number of real beings, and without reducing to nothingness an endless multitude of them. Merely by moving the tongue to cry out or to eat, one creates as many accidents as there are movements of the parts of the tongue, and one destroys as many accidents as there are parts of that which one eats, which lose their form, which become chyle, blood, etc.' This argument is only a kind of bugbear. What harm would be done, supposing that an infinity of movements, an infinity of figures spring up and disappear at every moment in the universe, and even in each part of the universe? It can be demonstrated, moreover, that that must be so.

395. As for the so-called creation of the accidents, who does not see that one needs no creative power in order to change place or shape, to form a square or a column, or some other parade-ground figure, by the movement of the soldiers who are drilling; or again to fashion a statue by removing a few pieces from a block of marble; or to make some figure in relief, by changing, decreasing or increasing a piece of wax? The production of modifications has never been called *creation*, and it is an abuse of terms to scare the world thus. God produces substances from nothing, and the substances produce accidents by the changes of their limits.

396. As for the souls or substantial forms, M. Bayle is right in adding: 'that there is nothing more inconvenient for those who admit substantial forms than the objection which is made that they could not be produced save by an actual creation, and that the Schoolmen are pitiable in their endeavours to answer this.' But there is nothing more convenient for me and for my system than this same objection. For I maintain that all the Souls, Entelechies or primitive forces, substantial forms, simple substances, or Monads, whatever name one may apply to them, can neither

spring up naturally nor perish. And the qualities or derivative forces, or what are called accidental forms, I take to be modifications of the primitive Entelechy, even as shapes are modifications of matter. That is why these modifications are perpetually changing, while the simple substance remains.

397. I have shown already (part I, § 86 *seqq.*) that souls cannot spring up naturally, or be derived from one another, and that it is necessary that ours either be created or be pre-existent. I have even pointed out a certain middle way between a creation and an entire pre-existence. I find it appropriate to say that the soul pre-existing in the seeds from the beginning of things was only sentient, but that it was elevated to the superior degree, which is that of reason, when the man to whom this soul should belong was conceived, and when the organic body, always accompanying this soul from the beginning, but under many changes, was determined for forming the human body. I considered also that one might attribute this elevation of the sentient soul (which makes it reach a more sublime degree of being, namely reason) to the extraordinary operation of God. Nevertheless it will be well to add that I would dispense with miracles in the generating of man, as in that of the other animals. It will be possible to explain that, if one imagines that in this great number of souls and of animals, or at least of living organic bodies which are in the seeds, those souls alone which are destined to attain one day to human nature contain the reason that shall appear therein one day, and the organic bodies of these souls alone are preformed and predisposed to assume one day the human shape, while the other small animals or seminal living beings, in which no such thing is pre-established, are essentially different from them and possessed only of an inferior nature. This production is a kind of *traduction*, but more manageable than that kind which is commonly taught: it does not derive the soul from a soul, but only the animate from an animate, and it avoids the repeated miracles of a new creation, which would cause a new and pure soul to enter a body that must corrupt it.

398. I am, however, of the same opinion as Father Malebranche, that, in general, creation properly understood is not so difficult to admit as might be supposed, and that it is in a sense involved in the notion of the dependence of creatures. 'How stupid and ridiculous are the Philosophers!' (he exclaims, in his *Christian Meditations*, 9, No. 3). 'They assume that Creation is

impossible, because they cannot conceive how God's power is great enough to make something from nothing. But can they any better conceive how the power of God is capable of stirring a straw?' He adds, again with great truth (No. 5), 'If matter were uncreate, God could not move it or form anything from it. For God cannot move matter, or arrange it wisely, if he does not know it. Now God cannot know it, if he does not give it being: he can derive his knowledge only from himself. Nothing can act on him or enlighten him.'

399. M. Bayle, not content with saying that we are created continually, insists also on this other doctrine which he would fain derive thence: that our soul cannot act. This is the way he speaks on that matter (ch. 141, p. 765): 'He has too much acquaintance with Cartesianism' (it is of an able opponent he is speaking) 'not to know with what force it has been maintained in our day that there is no creature capable of producing motion, and that our soul is a purely passive subject in relation to sensations and ideas, and feelings of pain and of pleasure, etc. If this has not been carried as far as the volitions, that is on account of the existence of revealed truths; otherwise the acts of the will would have been found as passive as those of the understanding. The same reasons which prove that our soul does not form our ideas, and does not stir our organs, would prove also that it cannot form our acts of love and our volitions, etc.' He might add: our vicious actions, our crimes.

400. The force of these proofs, which he praises, must not be so great as he thinks, for if it were they would prove too much. They would make God the author of sin. I admit that the soul cannot stir the organs by a physical influence; for I think that the body must have been so formed beforehand that it would do in time and place that which responds to the volitions of the soul, although it be true nevertheless that the soul is the principle of the operation. But if it be said that the soul does not produce its thoughts, its sensations, its feelings of pain and of pleasure, that is something for which I see no reason. In my system every simple substance (that is, every true substance) must be the true immediate cause of all its actions and inward passions; and, speaking strictly in a metaphysical sense, it has none other than those which it produces. Those who hold a different opinion, and who make God the sole agent, are needlessly becoming involved in expressions whence they will only with difficulty extricate themselves without offence

against religion; moreover, they unquestionably offend against reason.

401. Here is, however, the foundation of M. Bayle's argument. He says that we do not do that of which we know not the way it is done. But it is a principle which I do not conecde to him. Let us listen to his dissertation (p. 767 *seqq.*): 'It is an astonishing thing that almost all philosophers (with the exception of those who expounded Aristotle, and who admitted a universal intelligence distinct from our soul, and cause of our perceptions: see in the *Historical and Critical Dictionary*, Note E of the article "Averroes") have shared the popular belief that we form our ideas actively. Yet where is the man who knows not on the one hand that he is in absolute ignorance as to how ideas are made, and on the other hand, that he could not sew two stitches if he were ignorant of how to sew? Is the sewing of two stitches in itself a work more difficult than the painting in one's mind of a rose, the very first time one's eyes rest upon it, and although one has never learnt this kind of painting? Does it not appear on the contrary that this mental portrait is in itself a work more difficult than tracing on canvas the shape of a flower, a thing we cannot do without having learnt it? We are all convinced that a key would be of no use to us for opening a chest if we were ignorant as to how to use the key, and yet we imagine that our soul is the efficient cause of the movement of our arms, despite that it knows neither where the nerves are which must be used for this movement, nor whence to obtain the animal spirits that are to flow into these nerves. We have the experience every day that the ideas we would fain recall do not come, and that they appear of themselves when we are no longer thinking of them. If that does not prevent us from thinking that we are their efficient cause, what reliance shall one place on the proof of feeling, which to M. Jacquelot appears so conclusive? Does our authority over our ideas more often fall short than our authority over our volitions? If we were to count up carefully, we should find in the course of our life more velleities than volitions, that is, more evidences of the servitude of our will than of its dominion. How many times does one and the same man not experience an inability to do a certain act of will (for example, an act of love for a man who had just injured him; an act of scorn for a fine sonnet that he had composed; an act of hatred for a mistress; an act of approval of an absurd epigram. Take note that I speak

only of inward acts, expressed by an "I will", such as "I will scorn", "approve", etc.) even if there were a hundred pistoles to be gained forthwith, and he ardently desired to gain these hundred pistoles, and he were fired with the ambition to convince himself by an experimental proof that he is master in his own domain?

402. 'To put together in few words the whole force of what I have just said to you, I will observe that it is evident to all those who go deeply into things, that the true efficient cause of an effect must know the effect, and be aware also of the way in which it must be produced. That is not necessary when one is only the instrument of the cause, or only the passive subject of its action; but one cannot conceive of it as not necessary to a true agent. Now if we examine ourselves well we shall be strongly convinced, (1) that, independently of experience, our soul is just as little aware of what a volition is as of what an idea is; (2) that after a long experience it is no more fully aware of how volitions are formed than it was before having willed anything. What is one to conclude from that, save that the soul cannot be the efficient cause of its volitions, any more than of its ideas, and of the motion of the spirits which cause our arms to move? (Take note that no pretence is made of deciding the point here absolutely, it is only being considered in relation to the principles of the objection.)'

403. That is indeed a strange way of reasoning! What necessity is there for one always to be aware how that which is done is done? Are salts, metals, plants, animals and a thousand other animate or inanimate bodies aware how that which they do is done, and need they be aware? Must a drop of oil or of fat understand geometry in order to become round on the surface of water? Sewing stitches is another matter: one acts for an end, one must be aware of the means. But we do not form our ideas because we will to do so, they form themselves within us, they form themselves through us, not in consequence of our will, but in accordance with our nature and that of things. The foetus forms itself in the animal, and a thousand other wonders of nature are produced by a certain *instinct* that God has placed there, that is by virtue of *divine preformation*, which has made these admirable automata, adapted to produce mechanically such beautiful effects. Even so it is easy to believe that the soul is a spiritual automaton still more admirable, and that it is through divine preformation that it produces these

beautiful ideas, wherein our will has no part and to which our art cannot attain. The operation of spiritual automata, that is of souls, is not mechanical, but it contains in the highest degree all that is beautiful in mechanism. The movements which are developed in bodies are concentrated in the soul by representation as in an ideal world, which expresses the laws of the actual world and their consequences, but with this difference from the perfect ideal world which is in God, that most of the perceptions in the other substances are only confused. For it is plain that every simple substance embraces the whole universe in its confused perceptions or sensations, and that the succession of these perceptions is regulated by the particular nature of this substance, but in a manner which always expresses all the nature in the universe; and every present perception leads to a new perception, just as every movement that it represents leads to another movement. But it is impossible that the soul can know clearly its whole nature, and perceive how this innumerable number of small perceptions, piled up or rather concentrated together, shapes itself there: to that end it must needs know completely the whole universe which is embraced by them, that is, it must needs be a God.

404. As regards *velleities*, they are only a very imperfect kind of conditional will. I would, if I could: *liberet si liceret*; and in the case of a velleity, we do not will, properly speaking, to will, but to be able. That explains why there are none in God; and they must not be confused with antecedent will. I have explained sufficiently elsewhere that our control over volitions can be exercised only indirectly, and that one would be unhappy if one were sufficiently master in one's own domain to be able to will without cause, without rhyme or reason. To complain of not having such a control would be to argue like Pliny, who carps at the power of God because God cannot destroy himself.

405. I intended to finish here after having met (as it seems to me) all the objections of M. Bayle on this matter that I could find in his works. But remembering Laurentius Valla's *Dialogue on Free Will*, in opposition to Boethius, which I have already mentioned, I thought it would be opportune to quote it in abstract, retaining the dialogue form, and then to continue from where it ends, keeping up the fiction it initiated; and that less with the purpose of enlivening the subject, than in order to explain myself towards the end of my dissertation as clearly as I can, and in a way most

likely to be generally understood. This Dialogue of Valla and his books on Pleasure and the True Good make it plain that he was no less a philosopher than a humanist. These four books were opposed to the four books on the *Consolation of Philosophy* by Boethius, and the Dialogue to the fifth book. A certain Spaniard named Antonio Glarea requests of him elucidation on the difficulty of free will, whereof little is known as it is worthy to be known, for upon it depend justice and injustice, punishment and reward in this life and in the life to come. Laurentius Valla answers him that we must console ourselves for an ignorance which we share with the whole world, just as one consoles oneself for not having the wings of birds.

406. ANTONIO–I know that you can give me those wings, like another Daedalus, so that I may emerge from the prison of ignorance, and rise to the very region of truth, which is the homeland of souls. The books that I have seen have not satisfied me, not even the famous Boethius, who meets with general approval. I know not whether he fully understood himself what he says of God's understanding, and of eternity superior to time; and I ask for your opinion on his way of reconciling foreknowledge with freedom. LAURENT–I am fearful of giving offence to many people, if I confute this great man; yet I will give preference over this fear to the consideration I have for the entreaties of a friend, provided that you make me a promise. ANT.–What? LAUR.–It is, that when you have dined with me you do not ask me to give you supper, that is to say, I desire that you be content with the answer to the question you have put to me, and do not put a further question.

407. ANT.–I promise you. Here is the heart of the difficulty. If God foresaw the treason of Judas, it was necessary that he should betray, it was impossible for him not to betray. There is no obligation to do the impossible. He therefore did not sin, he did not deserve to be punished. That destroys justice and religion, and the fear of God. LAUR.–God foresaw sin; but he did not compel man to commit it; sin is voluntary. ANT.–That will was necessary, since it was foreseen. LAUR.–If my knowledge does not cause things past or present to exist, neither will my foreknowledge cause future things to exist.

408. ANT.–That comparison is deceptive: neither the present nor the past can be changed, they are already necessary; but the future, movable in itself, becomes fixed and necessary through

foreknowledge. Let us pretend that a god of the heathen boasts of knowing the future: I will ask him if he knows which foot I shall put foremost, then I will do the opposite of that which he shall have foretold. LAUR.–This God knows what you are about to do. ANT.–How does he know it, since I will do the opposite of what he shall have said, and I suppose that he will say what he thinks? LAUR.–Your supposition is false: God will not answer you; or again, if he were to answer you, the veneration you would have for him would make you hasten to do what he had said; his prediction would be to you an order. But we have changed the question. We are not concerned with what God will foretell but with what he foresees. Let us therefore return to foreknowledge, and distinguish between the necessary and the certain. It is not impossible for what is foreseen not to happen; but it is infallibly sure that it will happen. I can become a Soldier or Priest, but I shall not become one.

409. ANT.–Here I have you firmly held. The philosophers' rule maintains that all that which is possible can be considered as existing. But if that which you affirm to be possible, namely an event different from what has been foreseen, actually happened, God would have been mistaken. LAUR.–The rules of the philosophers are not oracles for me. This one in particular is not correct. Two contradictories are often both possible. Can they also both exist? But, for your further enlightenment, let us pretend that Sextus Tarquinius, coming to Delphi to consult the Oracle of Apollo, receives the answer:

> *Exul inopsque cades irata pulsus ab urbe.*
> A beggared outcast of the city's rage,
> Beside a foreign shore cut short thy age.

The young man will complain: I have brought you a royal gift, O Apollo, and you proclaim for me a lot so unhappy? Apollo will say to him: Your gift is pleasing to me, and I will do that which you ask of me, I will tell you what will happen. I know the future, but I do not bring it about. Go make your complaint to Jupiter and the Parcae. Sextus would be ridiculous if he continued thereafter to complain about Apollo. Is not that true? ANT.–He will say: I thank you, O holy Apollo, for not having repaid me with silence, for having revealed to me the Truth. But whence comes it that Jupiter is so cruel towards me, that he prepares so hard a fate for an innocent man, for a devout worshipper of the Gods? LAUR.–You innocent? Apollo will say. Know that you will be proud, that you will commit adulteries, that you will be a traitor to your country. Could Sextus reply: It is you who are the cause, O Apollo; you compel me to do it, by foreseeing it? ANT.–I admit that he would have taken leave of his senses if he were to make this reply. LAUR.–Therefore neither can the traitor Judas complain of God's foreknowledge. And there is the answer to your question.

410. ANT.–You have satisfied me beyond my hopes, you have done what Boethius was not able to do: I shall be beholden to you all my life long. LAUR.–Yet let us carry our tale a little further. Sextus will say: No, Apollo, I will not do what you say. ANT.– What! the God will say, do you mean then that I am a liar? I repeat to you once more, you will do all that I have just said. LAUR.–Sextus, mayhap, would pray the Gods to alter fate, to give him a better heart. ANT.–He would receive the answer:

Desine fata Deum flecti sperare precando.

He cannot cause divine foreknowledge to lie. But what then will Sextus say? Will he not break forth into complaints against the Gods? Will he not say? What? I am then not free? It is not in my power to follow virtue? LAUR.–Apollo will say to him perhaps: Know, my poor Sextus, that the Gods make each one as he is. Jupiter made the wolf ravening, the hare timid, the ass stupid, and the lion courageous. He gave you a soul that is wicked and irreclaimable; you will act in conformity with your natural disposition, and Jupiter will treat you as your actions shall deserve; he has sworn it by the Styx.

411. ANT.–I confess to you, it seems to me that Apollo in excusing himself accuses Jupiter more than he accuses Sextus, and Sextus would answer him: Jupiter therefore condemns in me his own crime; it is he who is the only guilty one. He could have made me altogether different: but, made as I am, I must act as he has willed. Why then does he punish me? Could I have resisted his will? LAUR.–I confess that I am brought to a pause here as you are. I have made the Gods appear on the scene, Apollo and Jupiter, to make you distinguish between divine foreknowledge and providence. I have shown that Apollo and foreknowledge do not impair freedom; but I cannot satisfy you on the decrees of Jupiter's will, that is to say, on the orders of providence. ANT.–You have

dragged me out of one abyss, and you plunge me back into another and greater abyss. LAUR.–Remember our contract: I have given you dinner, and you ask me to give you supper also.

412. ANT.–Now I discover your cunning: You have caught me, this is not an honest contract. LAUR.–What would you have me do? I have given you wine and meats from my home produce, such as my small estate can provide; as for nectar and ambrosia, you will ask the Gods for them: that divine nurture is not found among men. Let us hearken to St. Paul, that chosen vessel who was carried even to the third heaven, who heard there unutterable words: he will answer you with the comparison of the potter, with the incomprehensibility of the ways of God, and wonder at the depth of his wisdom. Nevertheless it is well to observe that one does not ask why God foresees the thing, for that is understood, it is because it will be: but one asks why he ordains thus, why he hardens such an one, why he has compassion on another. We do not know the reasons which he may have for this; but *since he is very good and very wise that is enough to make us deem that his reasons are good*. As he is just also, it follows that his decrees and his operation do not destroy our freedom. Some men have sought some reason therein. They have said that we are made from a corrupt and impure mass, indeed of mud. But Adam and the Angels were made of silver and gold, and they sinned notwithstanding. One sometimes becomes hardened again after regeneration. We must therefore seek another cause for evil, and I doubt whether even the Angels are aware of it; yet they cease not to be happy and to praise God. Boethius hearkened more to the answer of philosophy than to that of St. Paul; that was the cause of his failure. Let us believe in Jesus Christ, he is the virtue and the wisdom of God: he teaches us that God willeth the salvation of all, that he willeth not the death of the sinner. Let us therefore put our trust in the divine mercy, and let us not by our vanity and our malice disqualify ourselves to receive it.

413. This dialogue of Valla's is excellent, even though one must take exception to some points in it: but its chief defect is that it cuts the knot and that it seems to condemn providence under the name of Jupiter, making him almost the author of sin. Let us therefore carry the little fable still further. Sextus, quitting Apollo and Delphi, seeks out Jupiter at Dodona. He makes sacrifices and then he exhibits his complaints. Why have you condemned me, O

great God, to be wicked and unhappy? Change my lot and my heart, or acknowledge your error. Jupiter answers him: If you will renounce Rome, the Parcae shall spin for you different fates, you shall become wise, you shall be happy. SEXTUS–Why must I renounce the hope of a crown? Can I not come to be a good king? JUPITER–No, Sextus; I know better what is needful for you. If you go to Rome, you are lost. Sextus, not being able to resolve upon so great a sacrifice, went forth from the temple, and abandoned himself to his fate. Theodorus, the High Priest, who had been present at the dialogue between God and Sextus, addressed these words to Jupiter: Your wisdom is to be revered, O great Ruler of the Gods. You have convinced this man of his error; he must henceforth impute his unhappiness to his evil will; he has not a word to say. But your faithful worshippers are astonished; they would fain wonder at your goodness as well as at your greatness: it rested with you to give him a different will. JUPITER–Go to my daughter Pallas, she will inform you what I was bound to do.

414. Theodorus journeyed to Athens: he was bidden to lie down to sleep in the temple of the Goddess. Dreaming, he found himself transported into an unknown country. There stood a palace of unimaginable splendour and prodigious size. The Goddess Pallas appeared at the gate, surrounded by rays of dazzling majesty.

Qualisque videri
Coelicolis et quanta solet.

She touched the face of Theodorus with an olive-branch, which she was holding in her hand. And lo! he had become able to confront the divine radiancy of the daughter of Jupiter, and of all that she should show him. Jupiter who loves you (she said to him) has commended you to me to be instructed. You see here the palace of the fates, where I keep watch and ward. Here are representations not only of that which happens but also of all that which is possible. Jupiter, having surveyed them before the beginning of the existing world, classified the possibilities into worlds, and chose the best of all. He comes sometimes to visit these places, to enjoy the pleasure of recapitulating things and of renewing his own choice, which cannot fail to please him. I have only to speak, and we shall see a whole world that my father might have produced, wherein will be represented anything that can be asked of him; and in this way one may know also what would happen if any particular possibility should attain unto existence. And whenever the conditions are not determinate enough, there will be as many such worlds differing from one another as one shall wish, which will answer differently the same question, in as many ways as possible. You learnt geometry in your youth, like all well-instructed Greeks. You know therefore that when the conditions of a required point do not sufficiently determine it, and there is an infinite number of them, they all fall into what the geometricians call a locus, and this locus at least (which is often a line) will be determinate. Thus you can picture to yourself an ordered succession of worlds, which shall contain each and every one the case that is in question, and shall vary its circumstances and its consequences. But if you put a case that differs from the actual world only in one single definite thing and in its results, a certain one of those determinate worlds will answer you. These worlds are all here, that is, in ideas. I will show you some, wherein shall be found, not absolutely the same Sextus as you have seen (that is not possible, he carries with him always that which he shall be) but several Sextuses resembling him, possessing all that you know already of the true Sextus, but not all that is already in him imperceptibly, nor in consequence all that shall yet happen to him. You will find in one world a very happy and noble Sextus, in another a Sextus content with a mediocre state, a Sextus, indeed, of every kind and endless diversity of forms.

415. Thereupon the Goddess led Theodorus into one of the halls of the palace: when he was within, it was no longer a hall, it was a world,

Solemque suum, sua sidera norat.

At the command of Pallas there came within view Dodona with the temple of Jupiter, and Sextus issuing thence; he could be heard saying that he would obey the God. And lo! he goes to a city lying between two seas, resembling Corinth. He buys there a small garden; cultivating it, he finds a treasure; he becomes a rich man, enjoying affection and esteem; he dies at a great age, beloved of the whole city. Theodorus saw the whole life of Sextus as at one glance, and as in a stage presentation. There was a great volume of writings in this hall: Theodorus could not refrain from asking what that meant. It is the history of this world which we are now visiting, the Goddess told him; it is the book of its fates. You have seen a number on the forehead of Sextus. Look in this book for the place which it indicates. Theodorus looked for it, and found there the history of Sextus in a form more ample than the outline he had seen. Put your finger on any line you please, Pallas said to him, and you will see represented actually in all its detail that which the line broadly indicates. He obeyed, and he saw coming into view all the characteristics of a portion of the life of that Sextus. They passed into another hall, and lo! another world, another Sextus, who, issuing from the temple, and having resolved to obey Jupiter, goes to Thrace. There he marries the daughter of the king, who had no other children; he succeeds him, and he is adored by his subjects. They went into other rooms, and always they saw new scenes.

416. The halls rose in a pyramid, becoming even more beautiful as one mounted towards the apex, and representing more beautiful worlds. Finally they reached the highest one which completed the pyramid, and which was the most beautiful of all: for the pyramid had a beginning, but one could not see its end; it had an apex, but no base; it went on increasing to infinity. That is (as the Goddess explained) because amongst an endless number of possible worlds there is the best of all, else would God not have determined to create any; but there is not any one which has not also less perfect worlds below it: that is why the pyramid goes on descending to infinity. Theodorus, entering this highest hall, became entranced in ecstasy; he had to receive succour from the Goddess, a drop of a divine liquid placed on his tongue restored him; he was beside himself for joy. We are in the real true world (said the Goddess) and you are at the source of happiness. Behold what Jupiter makes ready for you, if you continue to serve him faithfully. Here is Sextus as he is, and as he will be in reality. He issues from the temple in a rage, he scorns the counsel of the Gods. You see him going to Rome, bringing confusion everywhere, violating the wife of his friend. There he is driven out with his father, beaten, unhappy. If Jupiter had placed here a Sextus happy at Corinth or King in Thrace, it would be no longer this world. And nevertheless he could not have failed to choose this world, which surpasses in perfection all the others, and which forms the apex of the pyramid. Else would Jupiter have renounced his wisdom, he would have banished me, me his daughter. You see that my father did not make Sextus wicked; he was so from all

372

eternity, he was so always and freely. My father only granted him the existence which his wisdom could not refuse to the world where he is included: he made him pass from the region of the possible to that of the actual beings. The crime of Sextus serves for great things: it renders Rome free; thence will arise a great empire, which will show noble examples to mankind. But that is nothing in comparison with the worth of this whole world, at whose beauty you will marvel, when, after a happy passage from this mortal state to another and better one, the Gods shall have fitted you to know it.

417. At this moment Theodorus wakes up, he gives thanks to the Goddess, he owns the justice of Jupiter. His spirit pervaded by what he has seen and heard, he carries on the office of High Priest, with all the zeal of a true servant of his God, and with all the joy whereof a mortal is capable. It seems to me that this continuation of the tale may elucidate the difficulty which Valla did not wish to treat. If Apollo has represented aright God's knowledge of vision (that which concerns beings in existence), I hope that Pallas will have not discreditably filled the rôle of what is called knowledge of simple intelligence (that which embraces all that is possible), wherein at last the source of things must be sought.

APPENDICES

SUMMARY OF THE CONTROVERSY
REDUCED TO FORMAL ARGUMENTS

SOME persons of discernment have wished me to make this addition. I have the more readily deferred to their opinion, because of the opportunity thereby gained for meeting certain difficulties, and for making observations on certain matters which were not treated in sufficient detail in the work itself.

OBJECTION I

Whoever does not choose the best course is lacking either in power, or knowledge, or goodness.

God did not choose the best course in creating this world.

Therefore God was lacking in power, or knowledge, or goodness.

ANSWER

I deny the minor, that is to say, the second premiss of this syllogism, and the opponent proves it by this

PROSYLLOGISM

Whoever makes things in which there is evil, and which could have been made without any evil, or need not have been made at all, does not choose the best course.

God made a world wherein there is evil; a world, I say, which could have been made without any evil or which need not have been made at all.

Therefore God did not choose the best course.

ANSWER

I admit the minor of this prosyllogism: for one must confess that there is evil in this world which God has made, and that it would have been possible to make a world without evil or even not to create any world, since its creation depended upon the free will of God. But I deny the major, that is, the first of the two premises of the prosyllogism, and I might content myself with asking for its proof. In order, however, to give a clearer exposition of the matter, I would justify this denial by pointing out that the best course is not always that one which tends towards avoiding evil, since it is possible that the evil may be accompanied by a greater good. For example, the general of an army will prefer a great victory with a slight wound to a state of affairs without wound and without victory. I have proved this in further detail in this work by pointing out, through instances taken from mathematics and elsewhere, that an imperfection in the part may be required for a greater perfection in the whole. I have followed therein the opinion of St. Augustine, who said a hundred times that God permitted evil in order to derive from it a good, that is to say, a greater good; and Thomas Aquinas says (in libr. 2, *Sent. Dist.* 32, qu. 1, art. 1) that the permission of evil tends towards the good of the universe. I have shown that among older writers the fall of Adam was termed *felix culpa*, a fortunate sin, because it had been expiated with immense benefit by the incarnation of the Son of God: for he gave to the universe something more noble than anything there would otherwise have been amongst created beings. For the better understanding of the matter I added, following the example of many good authors, that it was consistent with order and the general good for God to grant to certain of his creatures the opportunity to exercise their freedom, even when he foresaw that they would turn to evil: for God could easily correct the evil, and it was not fitting that in order to prevent sin he should always act in an extraordinary way. It will therefore sufficiently refute the objection to show that a world with evil may be better than a world without evil. But I have gone still further in the work, and have even shown that this universe must be indeed better than every other possible universe.

OBJECTION II

If there is more evil than good in intelligent creatures, there is more evil than good in all God's work.

Now there is more evil than good in intelligent creatures.

Therefore there is more evil than good in all God's work.

ANSWER

I deny the major and the minor of this conditional syllogism. As for the major, I do not admit it because this supposed inference from the part to the whole, from intelligent creatures to all creatures, assumes tacitly and without proof that creatures devoid of reason cannot be compared or taken into account with those that have reason. But why might not the surplus of good in the non-intelligent creatures that fill the world compensate for and even exceed incomparably the surplus of evil in rational creatures? It is true that the value of the latter is greater; but by way of compensation the others are incomparably greater in number; and it may be that the proportion of number and quantity surpasses that of value and quality.

The minor also I cannot admit, namely, that there is more evil than good in intelligent creatures. One need not even agree that there is more evil than good in the human kind. For it is possible, and even a very reasonable thing, that the glory and the perfection of the blessed may be incomparably greater than the misery and imperfection of the damned, and that here the excellence of the total good in the smaller number may exceed the total evil which is in the greater number. The blessed draw near to divinity through a divine Mediator, so far as can belong to these created beings, and make such progress in good as is impossible for the damned to make in evil, even though they should approach as nearly as may be the nature of demons. God is infinite, and the Devil is finite; good can and does go on *ad infinitum*, whereas evil has its bounds. It may be therefore, and it is probable, that there happens in the comparison between the blessed and the damned the opposite of what I said could happen in the comparison between the happy and the unhappy, namely that in the latter the proportion of degrees surpasses that of numbers, while in the comparison between intelligent and non-intelligent the proportion of numbers is greater than that of values. One is justified in assuming that a thing may be so as long as one does not prove that it is impossible, and indeed what is here put forward goes beyond assumption.

But secondly, even should one admit that there is more evil than good in the human kind, one still has every reason for not admitting that there is more evil than good in all intelligent creatures. For there is an inconceivable number of Spirits, and perhaps of other rational creatures besides: and an opponent cannot prove that in the whole City of God, composed as much of Spirits as of rational animals without number and of endless different kinds, the evil exceeds the good. Although one need not, in order to answer an objection, prove that a thing is, when its mere possibility suffices, I have nevertheless shown in this present work that it is a result of the supreme perfection of the Sovereign of the Universe that the kingdom of God should be the most perfect of all states or governments possible, and that in consequence what little evil there is should be required to provide the full measure of the vast good existing there.

OBJECTION III

If it is always impossible not to sin, it is always unjust to punish.

Now it is always impossible not to sin, or rather all sin is necessary.

Therefore it is always unjust to punish.

The minor of this is proved as follows.

FIRST PROSYLLOGISM

Everything predetermined is necessary.

Every event is predetermined.

Therefore every event (and consequently sin also) is necessary.

Again this second minor is proved thus.

SECOND PROSYLLOGISM

That which is future, that which is foreseen, that which is involved in causes is predetermined.

Every event is of this kind.

Therefore every event is predetermined.

ANSWER

I admit in a certain sense the conclusion of the second prosyllogism, which is the minor of the first; but I shall deny the

380

major of the first prosyllogism, namely that everything pre-determined is necessary; taking 'necessity', say the necessity to sin, or the impossibility of not sinning, or of not doing some action, in the sense relevant to the argument, that is, as a necessity essential and absolute, which destroys the morality of action and the justice of punishment. If anyone meant a different necessity or impossibility (that is, a necessity only moral or hypo-thetical, which will be explained presently) it is plain that we would deny him the major stated in the objection. We might con-tent ourselves with this answer, and demand the proof of the proposition denied: but I am well pleased to justify my manner of procedure in the present work, in order to make the matter clear and to throw more light on this whole subject, by explaining the necessity that must be rejected and the determination that must be allowed. The truth is that the necessity contrary to morality, which must be avoided and which would render punish-ment unjust, is an insuperable necessity, which would render all opposition unavailing, even though one should wish with all one's heart to avoid the necessary action, and though one should make all possible efforts to that end. Now it is plain that this is not applicable to voluntary actions, since one would not do them if one did not so desire. Thus their prevision and predetermination is not absolute, but it presupposes will: if it is certain that one will do them, it is no less certain that one will will to do them. These voluntary actions and their results will not happen whatever one may do and whether one will them or not; but they will happen because one will do, and because one will will to do, that which leads to them. That is involved in prevision and predetermination, and forms the reason thereof. The necessity of such events is called conditional or hypothetical, or again necessity of consequence, because it presupposes the will and the other requisites. But the necessity which destroys morality, and renders punishment un-just and reward unavailing, is found in the things that will be whatever one may do and whatever one may will to do: in a word, it exists in that which is essential. This it is which is called an absolute necessity. Thus it avails nothing with regard to what is necessary absolutely to ordain interdicts or commandments, to propose penalties or prizes, to blame or to praise; it will come to pass no more and no less. In voluntary actions, on the contrary, and in what depends upon them, precepts, armed with power to punish and to reward, very often serve, and are included in the order of causes that make action exist. Thus it comes about that not only pains and effort but also prayers are effective, God having had even these prayers in mind before he ordered things, and having made due allowance for them. That is why the precept *Ora et labora* (Pray and work) remains intact. Thus not only those who (under the empty pretext of the necessity of events) maintain that one can spare oneself the pains demanded by affairs, but also those who argue against prayers, fall into that which the ancients even in their time called 'the Lazy Sophism'. So the predetermination of events by their causes is precisely what contributes to morality instead of destroying it, and the causes incline the will without necessitating it. For this reason the determination we are concerned with is not a necessitation. It is certain (to him who knows all) that the effect will follow this inclination; but this effect does not follow thence by a consequence which is necessary, that is, whose contrary implies contradiction; and it is also by such an inward inclination that the will is determined, without the presence of necessity. Suppose that one has the greatest possible passion (for example, a great thirst), you will admit that the soul can find some reason for resisting it, even if it were only that of displaying its power. Thus though one may never have complete indifference of equipoise, and there is always a predominance of inclination for the course adopted, that predominance does not render absolutely necessary the resolution taken.

OBJECTION IV

Whoever can prevent the sin of others and does not so, but rather contributes to it, although he be fully apprised of it, is accessary thereto.

God can prevent the sin of intelligent creatures; but he does not so, and he rather contributes to it by his co-operation and by the opportunities he causes, although he is fully cognizant of it.

Therefore, etc.

ANSWER

I deny the major of this syllogism. It may be that one can prevent the sin, but that one ought not to do so, because one could not do so without committing a sin oneself, or (when God is concerned) without acting unreasonably. I have given instances of that, and have applied them to God himself. It may be also that one contributes to the evil, and that one even opens the way to it sometimes, in doing things one is bound to do. And when one does one's duty, or (speaking of God) when, after full consideration, one does that which reason demands, one is not responsible for events, even when one foresees them. One does not will these evils; but one is willing to permit them for a greater good, which one cannot in reason help preferring to other considerations. This is a *consequent* will, resulting from acts of *antecedent* will, in which one wills the good. I know that some persons, in speaking of the antecedent and consequent will of God, have meant by the antecedent that which wills that all men be saved, and by the consequent that which wills, in consequence of persistent sin, that there be some damned, damnation being a result of sin. But these are only examples of a more general notion, and one may say with the same reason, that God wills by his antecedent will that men sin not, and that by his consequent or final and decretory will (which is always followed by its effect) he wills to permit that they sin, this permission being a result of superior reasons. One has indeed justification for saying, in general, that the antecedent will of God tends towards the production of good and the prevention of evil, each taken in itself, and as it were detached (*particulariter et secundum quid*: Thom., I, qu. 19, art. 6) according to the measure of the degree of each good or of each evil. Likewise one may say that the consequent, or final and total, divine will tends towards the production of as many goods as can be put together, whose combination thereby becomes determined, and involves also the permission of some evils and the exclusion of some goods, as the best possible plan of the universe demands. Arminius, in his *Antiperkinsus*, explained very well that the will of God can be called consequent not only in relation to the action of the creature considered beforehand in the divine understanding, but also in relation to other anterior acts of divine will. But it is enough to consider the passage cited from Thomas Aquinas, and that from Scotus (I, dist. 46, qu. 11), to see that they make this distinction as I have made it here. Nevertheless if anyone will not suffer this use of the terms, let him put 'previous' in place of 'antecedent' will, and 'final' or 'decretory' in place of 'consequent' will. For I do not wish to wrangle about words.

OBJECTION V

Whoever produces all that is real in a thing is its cause.
God produces all that is real in sin.
Therefore God is the cause of sin.

ANSWER

I might content myself with denying the major or the minor, because the term 'real' admits of interpretations capable of rendering these propositions false. But in order to give a better explanation I will make a distinction. 'Real' either signifies that which is positive only, or else it includes also privative beings: in the first case, I deny the major and I admit the minor; in the second case, I do the opposite. I might have confined myself to that; but I was willing to go further, in order to account for this distinction. I have therefore been well pleased to point out that every purely positive or absolute reality is a perfection, and that every imperfection comes from limitation, that is, from the privative: for to limit is to withhold extension, or the more beyond. Now God is the cause of all perfections, and consequently of all realities, when they are regarded as purely positive. But limitations or privations result from the original imperfection of creatures which restricts their receptivity. It is as with a laden boat, which the river carries along more slowly or less slowly in proportion to the weight that it bears: thus the speed comes from the river, but the retardation which restricts this speed comes from the load. Also I have shown in the present work how the creature, in causing sin, is a deficient cause; how errors and evil inclinations spring from privation; and how privation is efficacious accidentally. And I have justified the opinion of St. Augustine (lib. I, *Ad. Simpl.*, qu. 2) who explains (for example) how God hardens the soul, not in giving it something evil, but because the effect of the good he imprints is restricted by the resistance of the soul, and by the circumstances contributing to this resistance, so that he does not give it all the good that would overcome its evil. 'Nec (*inquit*) ab illo erogatur aliquid quo homo fit deterior, sed tantum quo fit melior non erogatur.' But if God had willed to do more here he must needs have produced either fresh natures in his creatures or fresh miracles to change their natures, and this the best plan did not allow. It is just as if the current of the river must needs be more rapid than its slope permits or the boats themselves be less laden, if they had to be impelled at a greater speed. So the limitation or original imperfection of creatures brings it about that even the best plan of the universe cannot admit more good, and cannot be exempted from certain evils, these, however, being only of such a kind as may tend towards a greater good. There are some disorders in the parts which wonderfully enhance the beauty of the whole, just as certain dissonances, appropriately used, render harmony more beautiful. But that depends upon the answer which I have already given to the first objection.

OBJECTION VI

Whoever punishes those who have done as well as it was in their power to do is unjust.

God does so.

Therefore, etc.

ANSWER

I deny the minor of this argument. And I believe that God always gives sufficient aid and grace to those who have good will, that is to say, who do not reject this grace by a fresh sin. Thus I do not admit the damnation of children dying unbaptized or outside the Church, or the damnation of adult persons who have acted according to the light that God has given them. And I believe that, *if anyone has followed the light he had*, he will undoubtedly receive thereof in greater measure as he has need, even as the late Herr Hulsemann, who was celebrated as a profound theologian at Leipzig, has somewhere observed; and if such a man had failed to receive light during his life, he would receive it at least in the hour of death.

OBJECTION VII

Whoever gives only to some, and not to all, the means of producing effectively in them good will and final saving faith has not enough goodness.

God does so.

Therefore, etc.

ANSWER

I deny the major. It is true that God could overcome the greatest resistance of the human heart, and indeed he sometimes

does so, whether by an inward grace or by the outward circumstances that can greatly influence souls; but he does not always
do so. Whence comes this distinction, someone will say, and
wherefore does his goodness appear to be restricted? The truth is
that it would not have been in order always to act in an extraordinary way and to derange the connexion of things, as I have
observed already in answering the first objection. The reasons for
this connexion, whereby the one is placed in more favourable
circumstances than the other, are hidden in the depths of God's
wisdom: they depend upon the universal harmony. The best plan
of the universe, which God could not fail to choose, required
this. One concludes thus from the event itself; since God made the
universe, it was not possible to do better. Such management, far
from being contrary to goodness, has rather been prompted by
supreme goodness itself. This objection with its solution might
have been inferred from what was said with regard to the first
objection; but it seemed advisable to touch upon it separately.

OBJECTION VIII

Whoever cannot fail to choose the best is not free.
God cannot fail to choose the best.
Therefore God is not free.

ANSWER

I deny the major of this argument. Rather is it true freedom,
and the most perfect, to be able to make the best use of one's free
will, and always to exercise this power, without being turned aside
either by outward force or by inward passions, whereof the one
enslaves our bodies and the other our souls. There is nothing less
servile and more befitting the highest degree of freedom than to be
always led towards the good, and always by one's own inclination,
without any constraint and without any displeasure. And to
object that God therefore had need of external things is only a
sophism. He creates them freely: but when he had set before him
an end, that of exercising his goodness, his wisdom determined
him to choose the means most appropriate for obtaining this end.
To call that a *need* is to take the term in a sense not usual, which
clears it of all imperfection, somewhat as one does when speaking
of the wrath of God.

Seneca says somewhere, that God commanded only once, but

that he obeys always, because he obeys the laws that he willed to ordain for himself: *semel jussit, semper paret*. But he had better have said, that God always commands and that he is always obeyed: for in willing he always follows the tendency of his own nature, and all other things always follow his will. And as this will is always the same one cannot say that he obeys that will only which he formerly had. Nevertheless, although his will is always indefectible and always tends towards the best, the evil or the lesser good which he rejects will still be possible in itself. Otherwise the necessity of good would be geometrical (so to speak) or metaphysical, and altogether absolute; the contingency of things would be destroyed, and there would be no choice. But necessity of this kind, which does not destroy the possibility of the contrary, has the name by analogy only: it becomes effective not through the mere essence of things, but through that which is outside them and above them, that is, through the will of God. This necessity is called moral, because for the wise what is necessary and what is owing are equivalent things; and when it is always followed by its effect, as it indeed is in the perfectly wise, that is, in God, one can say that it is a happy necessity. The more nearly creatures approach this, the closer do they come to perfect felicity. Moreover, necessity of this kind is not the necessity one endeavours to avoid, and which destroys morality, reward and commendation. For that which it brings to pass does not happen whatever one may do and whatever one may will, but because one desires it. A will to which it is natural to choose well deserves most to be commended; and it carries with it its own reward, which is supreme happiness. And as this constitution of the divine nature gives an entire satisfaction to him who possesses it, it is also the best and the most desirable from the point of view of the creatures who are all dependent upon God. If the will of God had not as its rule the principle of the best, it would tend towards evil, which would be worst of all; or else it would be indifferent somehow to good and to evil, and guided by chance. But a will that would always drift along at random would scarcely be any better for the government of the universe than the fortuitous concourse of corpuscles, without the existence of divinity. And even though God should abandon himself to chance only in some cases, and in a certain way (as he would if he did not always tend entirely towards the best, and if he were capable of preferring a lesser good to a greater good, that is, an evil to a good, since that which prevents a greater good is an evil) he would be no less imperfect than the object of his choice. Then he would not deserve absolute trust; he would act without reason in such a case, and the government of the universe would be like certain games equally divided between reason and luck. This all proves that this objection which is made against the choice of the best perverts the notions of free and necessary, and represents the best to us actually as evil: but that is either malicious or absurd.

EXCURSUS ON THEODICY

§ 392

published by the author in Mémoires de Trévoux

July 1712

<hr/>

February 1712

I said in my essays, § 392, that I wished to see the demonstrations mentioned by M. Bayle and contained in the sixth letter printed at Trévoux in 1703. Father des Bosses has shown me this letter, in which the writer essays to demonstrate by the geometrical method that God is the sole true cause of all that is real. My perusal of it has confirmed me in the opinion which I indicated in the same passage, namely, that this proposition can be true in a very good sense, God being the only cause of pure and absolute realities, or perfections; but when one includes limitations or privations under the name of realities one can say that second causes co-operate in the production of what is limited, and that otherwise God would be the cause of sin, and even its sole cause. And I am somewhat inclined to think that the gifted author of the letter does not greatly differ in opinion from me, although he seems to include all modalities among the realities of which he declares God to be the sole cause. For in actual fact I think he will not admit that God is the cause and the author of sin. Indeed, he explains himself in a manner which seems to overthrow his thesis and to grant real action to creatures. For in the proof of the eighth corollary of his second proposition these words occur: 'The natural motion of the soul, although determinate in itself, is indeterminate in respect of its objects. For it is love of good in general. It is through the ideas of good appearing in individual objects that this motion becomes individual and determinate in relation to those objects. And thus as the mind has the power of varying its own ideas it can also change the determinations of its love. And for that purpose it is not necessary that it overcome the power of God or oppose his action. These determinations of motion towards individual objects are not invincible. It is this non-invincibility which causes the mind to be free and capable of changing them; but after all the mind makes these changes only through the motion which God gives to it and conserves for it.' In my own style I would have said that the perfection which is in the action of the creature comes from God, but that the limitations to be found there are a consequence of the original limitation and the preceding limitations that occurred in the creature. Further, this is so not only in minds but also in all other substances, which thereby are causes co-operating in the change which comes to pass in themselves; for this determination of which the author speaks is nothing but a limitation.

Now if after that one reviews all the demonstrations or corollaries of the letter, one will be able to admit or reject the majority of its assertions, in accordance with the interpretation one may make of them. If by 'reality' one means only perfections or positive realities, God is the only true cause; but if that which involves limitations is included under the realities, one will deny a considerable portion of the theses, and the author himself will have shown us the example. It is in order to render the matter more comprehensible that I used in the Essays the example of a laden boat, which, the more laden it is, is the more slowly carried along by the stream. There one sees clearly that the stream is the cause of what is positive in this motion, of the perfection, the force, the speed of the boat, but that the load is the cause of the restriction of this force, and that it brings about the retardation.

It is praiseworthy in anyone to attempt to apply the geometrical method to metaphysical matters. But it must be admitted that hitherto success has seldom been attained: and M. Descartes himself, with all that very great skill which one cannot deny in him, never perhaps had less success than when he essayed to do this in one of his answers to objections. For in mathematics it is easier to succeed, because numbers, figures and calculations make good the defects concealed in words; but in metaphysics, where one is deprived of this aid (at least in ordinary argumentation), the strictness employed in the form of the argument and in the exact definitions of the terms must needs supply this lack. But in neither argument nor definition is that strictness here to be seen.

The author of the letter, who undoubtedly displays much ardour and penetration, sometimes goes a little too far, as when he claims to prove that there is as much reality and force in rest as in motion, according to the fifth corollary of the second proposition. He asserts that the will of God is no less positive in rest than in motion, and that it is not less invincible. Be it so, but does it follow that there is as much reality and force in each of the two? I do not see this conclusion, and with the same argument one would prove that there is as much force in a strong motion as in a weak motion. God in willing rest wills that the body be at the place A, where it was immediately before, and for that it suffices that there be no reason to prompt God to the change. But when God wills that afterwards the body be at the place B, there must needs be a new reason, of such a kind as to determine God to will that it be in B and not in C or in any other place, and that it be there more or less promptly. It is upon these reasons, the volitions of God, that we must assess the force and the reality existent in things. The author speaks much of the will of God, but he does not speak much in this letter of the reasons which prompt God to will, and upon which all depends. And these reasons are taken from the objects.

I observe first, indeed, with regard to the second corollary of the first proposition, that it is very true, but that it is not very well proven. The writer affirms that if God only ceased to will the existence of a being, that being would no longer exist; and here is the proof given word for word:

'Demonstration. That which exists only by the will of God no longer exists once that will has ceased.' (But that is what must be proved. The writer endeavours to prove it by adding:) 'Remove the cause, you remove the effect.' (This maxim ought to have been placed among the axioms which are stated at the beginning. But unhappily this axiom may be reckoned among those rules of philosophy which are subject to many exceptions.) 'Now by the preceding proposition and by its first corollary no being exists save by the will of God. Therefore, etc.' There is ambiguity in this expression, that nothing exists save by the will of God. If one means that things begin to exist only through this will, one is justified in referring to the preceding propositions; but if one means that the existence of things is at all times a consequence of the will of God, one assumes more or less what is in question. Therefore it was necessary to prove first that the existence of things depends upon the will of God, and that it is not only a mere effect of that will, but a dependence, in proportion to the perfection which things contain; and once that is assumed, they will depend upon God's will no less afterwards than at the beginning. That is the way I have taken the matter in my Essays.

Nevertheless I recognize that the letter upon which I have just made observations is admirable and well deserving of perusal, and that it contains noble and true sentiments, provided it be taken in the sense I have just indicated. And arguments in this form may serve as an introduction to meditations somewhat more advanced.

REFLEXIONS ON THE WORK THAT MR. HOBBES PUBLISHED IN ENGLISH ON 'FREEDOM, NECESSITY AND CHANCE'

1. As the question of Necessity and Freedom, with other questions depending thereon, was at one time debated between the famous Mr. Hobbes and Dr. John Bramhall, Bishop of Derry, in books published by each of them, I have deemed it appropriate to give a clear account of them (although I have already mentioned them more than once); and this all the more since these writings of Mr. Hobbes have hitherto only appeared in English, and since the works of this author usually contain something good and ingenious. The Bishop of Derry and Mr. Hobbes, having met in Paris at the house of the Marquis, afterwards Duke, of Newcastle in the year 1646, entered into a discussion on this subject. The dispute was conducted with extreme restraint; but the bishop shortly afterwards sent a note to My Lord Newcastle, desiring him to induce Mr. Hobbes to answer it. He answered; but at the same time he expressed a wish that his answer should not be published, because he believed it possible for ill-instructed persons to abuse dogmas such as his, however true they might be. It so happened, however, that Mr. Hobbes himself passed it to a French friend, and allowed a young Englishman to translate it into French for the benefit of this friend. This young man kept a copy of the English original, and published it later in England without the author's knowledge. Thus the bishop was obliged to reply to it,

and Mr. Hobbes to make a rejoinder, and to publish all the pieces together in a book of 348 pages printed in London in the year 1656, in 4to., entitled, *Questions concerning Freedom, Necessity and Chance, elucidated and discussed between Doctor Bramhall, Bishop of Derry, and Thomas Hobbes of Malmesbury*. There is a later edition, of the year 1684, in a work entitled *Hobbes's Tripos*, where are to be found his book on human nature, his treatise on the body politic and his treatise on freedom and necessity; but the latter does not contain the bishop's reply, nor the author's rejoinder. Mr. Hobbes argues on this subject with his usual wit and subtlety; but it is a pity that in both the one and the other we stumble upon petty tricks, such as arise in excitement over the game. The bishop speaks with much vehemence and behaves somewhat arrogantly. Mr. Hobbes for his part is not disposed to spare the other, and manifests rather too much scorn for theology, and for the terminology of the Schoolmen, which is apparently favoured by the bishop.

2. One must confess that there is something strange and indefensible in the opinions of Mr. Hobbes. He maintains that doctrines touching the divinity depend entirely upon the determination of the sovereign, and that God is no more the cause of the good than of the bad actions of creatures. He maintains that all that which God does is just, because there is none above him with power to punish and constrain him. Yet he speaks sometimes as if what is said about God were only compliments, that is to say expressions proper for paying him honour, but not for knowing him. He testifies also that it seems to him that the pains of the wicked must end in their destruction: this opinion closely approaches that of the Socinians, but it seems that Mr. Hobbes goes much further. His philosophy, which asserts that bodies alone are substances, hardly appears favourable to the providence of God and the immortality of the soul. On other subjects nevertheless he says very reasonable things. He shows clearly that nothing comes about by chance, or rather that chance only signifies the ignorance of causes that produce the effect, and that for each effect there must be a concurrence of all the sufficient conditions anterior to the event, not one of which, manifestly, can be lacking when the event is to follow, because they are conditions: the event, moreover, does not fail to follow when these conditions exist all together, because they are sufficient conditions. All which amounts to the same as I have said so many times, that everything comes to pass

as a result of determining reasons, the knowledge whereof, if we had it, would make us know at the same time why the thing has happened and why it did not go otherwise.

3. But this author's humour, which prompts him to paradoxes and makes him seek to contradict others, has made him draw out exaggerated and odious conclusions and expressions, as if everything happened through an absolute necessity. The Bishop of Derry, on the other hand, has aptly observed in the answer to article 35, page 327, that there results only a hypothetical necessity, such as we all grant to events in relation to the foreknowledge of God, while Mr. Hobbes maintains that even divine foreknowledge alone would be sufficient to establish an absolute necessity of events. This was also the opinion of Wyclif, and even of Luther, when he wrote *De Servo Arbitrio*; or at least they spoke so. But it is sufficiently acknowledged to-day that this kind of necessity which is termed hypothetical, and springs from foreknowledge or from other anterior reasons, has nothing in it to arouse one's alarm: whereas it would be quite otherwise if the thing were necessary of itself, in such a way that the contrary implied contradiction. Mr. Hobbes refuses to listen to anything about a moral necessity either, on the ground that everything really happens through physical causes. But one is nevertheless justified in making a great difference between the necessity which constrains the wise to do good, and which is termed moral, existing even in relation to God, and that blind necessity whereby according to Epicurus, Strato, Spinoza, and perhaps Mr. Hobbes, things exist without intelligence and without choice, and consequently without God. Indeed, there would according to them be no need of God, since in consequence of this necessity all would have existence through its own essence, just as necessarily as two and three make five. And this necessity is absolute, because everything it carries with it must happen, whatever one may do; whereas what happens by a hypothetical necessity happens as a result of the supposition that this or that has been foreseen or resolved, or done beforehand; and moral necessity contains an obligation imposed by reason, which is always followed by its effect in the wise. This kind of necessity is happy and desirable, when one is prompted by good reasons to act as one does; but necessity blind and absolute would subvert piety and morality.

4. There is more reason in Mr. Hobbes's discourse when he

admits that our actions are in our power, so that we do that which we will when we have the power to do it, and when there is no hindrance. He asserts notwithstanding that our volitions themselves are not so within our power that we can give ourselves, without difficulty and according to our good pleasure, inclinations and wills which we might desire. The bishop does not appear to have taken notice of this reflexion, which Mr. Hobbes also does not develop enough. The truth is that we have some power also over our volitions, but obliquely, and not absolutely and indifferently. This has been explained in some passages of this work. Finally Mr. Hobbes shows, like others before him, that the certainty of events, and necessity itself, if there were any in the way our actions depend upon causes, would not prevent us from employing deliberations, exhortations, blame and praise, punishments and rewards: for these are of service and prompt men to produce actions or to refrain from them. Thus, if human actions were necessary, they would be so through these means. But the truth is, that since these actions are not necessary absolutely whatever one may do, these means contribute only to render the actions determinate and certain, as they are indeed; for their nature shows that they are not subject to an absolute necessity. He gives also a good enough notion of *freedom*, in so far as it is taken in a general sense, common to intelligent and non-intelligent substances: he states that a thing is deemed free when the power which it has is not impeded by an external thing. Thus the water that is dammed by a dyke has the power to spread, but not the freedom. On the other hand, it has not the power to rise above the dyke, although nothing would prevent it then from spreading, and although nothing from outside prevents it from rising so high. To that end it would be necessary that the water itself should come from a higher point or that the water-level should be raised by an increased flow. Thus a prisoner lacks the freedom, while a sick man lacks the power, to go his way.

5. There is in Mr. Hobbes's preface an abstract of the disputed points, which I will give here, adding some expression of opinion. *On one side* (he says) the assertion is made, (1) 'that it is not in the present power of man to choose for himself the will that he should have'. That is *well* said, especially in relation to present will: men choose the objects through will, but they do not choose their present wills, which spring from reasons and dispositions. It is

true, however, that one can seek new reasons for oneself, and with time give oneself new dispositions; and by this means one can also obtain for oneself a will which one had not and could not have given oneself forthwith. It is (to use the comparison Mr. Hobbes himself uses) as with hunger or with thirst. At the present it does not rest with my will to be hungry or not; but it rests with my will to eat or not to eat; yet, for the time to come, it rests with me to be hungry, or to prevent myself from being so at such and such an hour of day, by eating beforehand. In this way it is possible often to avoid an evil will. Even though Mr. Hobbes states in his reply (No. 14, p. 138) that it is the manner of laws to say, you must do or you must not do this, but that there is no law saying, you must will, or you must not will it, yet it is clear that he is mistaken in regard to the Law of God, which says *non concupisces*, thou shalt not covet; it is true that this prohibition does not concern the first motions, which are involuntary. It is asserted (2) 'That hazard' (*chance* in English, *casus* in Latin) 'produces nothing', that is, that nothing is produced without cause or reason. Very *right*, I admit it, if one thereby intends a real hazard. For fortune and hazard are only appearances, which spring from ignorance of causes or from disregard of them. (3) 'That all events have their necessary causes.' *Wrong*: they have their determining causes, whereby one can account for them; but these are not necessary causes. The contrary might have happened, without implying contradiction. (4) 'That the will of God makes the necessity of all things.' *Wrong*: the will of God produces only contingent things, which could have gone differently, since time, space and matter are indifferent with regard to all kinds of shape and movement.

6. *On the other side* (according to Mr. Hobbes) it is asserted, (1) 'That man is free' (absolutely) not only 'to choose what he wills to do, but also to choose what he wills to will.' That is *ill* said: one is not absolute master of one's will, to change it forthwith, without making use of some means or skill for that purpose. (2) 'When man wills a good action, the will of God co-operates with his, otherwise not.' That is *well* said, provided one means that God does not will evil actions, although he wills to permit them, to prevent the occurrence of something which would be worse than these sins. (3) 'That the will can choose whether it wills to will or not.' *Wrong*, with regard to present volition. (4) 'That things happen without necessity by chance.' *Wrong*: what

happens without necessity does not because of that happen by chance, that is to say, without causes and reasons. (5) 'Notwithstanding that God may foresee that an event will happen, it is not necessary that it happen, since God foresees things, not as futurities and as in their causes, but as present.' That begins *well*, and finishes *ill*. One is justified in admitting the necessity of the consequence, but one has no reason to resort to the question how the future is present to God: for the necessity of the consequence does not prevent the event or consequent from being contingent in itself.

7. Our author thinks that since the doctrine revived by Arminius had been favoured in England by Archbishop Laud and by the Court, and important ecclesiastical promotions had been only for those of that party, this contributed to the revolt which caused the bishop and him to meet in their exile in Paris at the house of Lord Newcastle, and to enter into a discussion. I would not approve all the measures of Archbishop Laud, who had merit and perhaps also good will, but who appears to have goaded the Presbyterians excessively. Nevertheless one may say that the revolutions, as much in the Low Countries as in Great Britain, in part arose from the extreme intolerance of the strict party. One may say also that the defenders of the absolute decree were at least as strict as the others, having oppressed their opponents in Holland with the authority of Prince Maurice and having fomented the revolts in England against King Charles I. But these are the faults of men, and not of dogmas. Their opponents do not spare them either, witness the severity used in Saxony against Nicolas Krell and the proceedings of the Jesuits against the Bishop of Ypres's party.

8. Mr. Hobbes observes, after Aristotle, that there are two sources for proofs: reason and authority. As for reason, he says that he admits the reasons derived from the attributes of God, which he calls argumentative, and the notions whereof are conceivable; but he maintains that there are others wherein one conceives nothing, and which are only expressions by which we aspire to honour God. But I do not see how one can honour God by expressions that have no meaning. It may be that with Mr. Hobbes, as with Spinoza, wisdom, goodness, justice are only fictions in relation to God and the universe, since the prime cause, according to them, acts through the necessity of its power, and

not by the choice of its wisdom. That is an opinion whose falsity I have sufficiently proved. It appears that Mr. Hobbes did not wish to declare himself enough, for fear of causing offence to people; on which point he is to be commended. It was also on that account, as he says himself, that he had desired that what had passed between the bishop and him in Paris should not be published. He adds that it is not good to say that an action which God does not will happens, since that is to say in effect that God is lacking in power. But he adds also at the same time that it is not good either to say the opposite, and to attribute to God that he wills the evil; because that is not seemly, and would appear to accuse God of lack of goodness. He believes, therefore, that in these matters telling the truth is not advisable. He would be right if the truth were in the paradoxical opinions that he maintains. For indeed it appears that according to the opinion of this writer God has no goodness, or rather that that which he calls God is nothing but the blind nature of the mass of material things, which acts according to mathematical laws, following an absolute necessity, as the atoms do in the system of Epicurus. If God were as the great are sometimes here on earth, it would not be fitting to utter all the truths concerning him. But God is not as a man, whose designs and actions often must be concealed; rather it is always permissible and reasonable to publish the counsels and the actions of God, because they are always glorious and worthy of praise. Thus it is always right to utter truths concerning the divinity; one need not anyhow refrain from fear of giving offence. And I have explained, so it seems to me, in a way which satisfies reason, and does not wound piety, how it is to be understood that God's will takes effect, and concurs with sin, without compromising his wisdom and his goodness.

9. As to the authorities derived from Holy Scripture, Mr. Hobbes divides them into three kinds; some, he says, are for me, the second kind are neutral, and the third seem to be for my opponent. The passages which he thinks favourable to his opinion are those which ascribe to God the cause of our will. Thus Gen. xlv. 5, where Joseph says to his brethren, 'Be not grieved, nor angry with yourselves, that you sold me hither: for God did send me before you to preserve life'; and verse 8, 'it was not you that sent me hither, but God.' And God said (Exod. vii. 3), 'I will harden Pharaoh's heart.' And Moses said (Deut. ii. 30),

'But Sihon King of Heshbon would not let us pass by him: for the Lord thy God hardened his spirit, and made his heart obstinate, that he might deliver him into thy hand.' And David said of Shimei (2 Sam. xvi. 10), 'Let him curse, because the Lord hath said unto him: Curse David. Who shall then say, wherefore hast thou done so?' And (1 Kings xii. 15), 'The King [Rehoboam] hearkened not unto the people; for the cause was from the Lord.' Job xii. 16: 'The deceived and the deceiver are his.' v. 17: 'He maketh the judges fools'; v. 24: 'He taketh away the heart of the chief of the people of the earth, and causeth them to wander in a wilderness'; v. 25: 'He maketh them to stagger like a drunken man.' God said of the King of Assyria (Isa. x. 6), 'Against the people will I give him a charge, to take the spoil, and to take the prey, and to tread them down like the mire of the streets.' And Jeremiah said (Jer. x. 23), 'O Lord, I know that the way of man is not in himself: it is not in man that walketh to direct his steps.' And God said (Ezek. iii. 20), 'When a righteous man doth turn from his righteousness, and commit iniquity, and I lay a stumbling-block before him, he shall die.' And the Saviour said (John vi. 44), 'No man can come to me, except the Father which hath sent me draw him.' And St. Peter (Acts ii. 23), 'Jesus having been delivered by the determinate counsel and foreknowledge of God, ye have taken.' And Acts iv. 27, 28, 'Both Herod and Pontius Pilate, with the Gentiles and the people of Israel, were gathered together, for to do whatsoever thy hand and thy counsel determined before to be done.' And St. Paul (Rom. ix. 16), 'It is not of him that willeth, nor of him that runneth, but of God that showeth mercy.' And v. 18: 'Therefore hath he mercy on whom he will have mercy, and whom he will he hardeneth'; v. 19: 'Thou wilt say then unto me, why doth he yet find fault? For who hath resisted his will?'; v. 20: 'Nay but, O man, who art thou that repliest against God? Shall the thing formed say to him that formed it, why hast thou made me thus?' And 1 Cor. iv. 7: 'For who maketh thee to differ from another? and what hast thou that thou didst not receive?' And 1 Cor. xii. 6: 'There are diversities of operations, but it is the same God which worketh all in all.' And Eph. ii. 10: 'We are his workmanship, created in Christ Jesus unto good works, which God hath before ordained that we should walk in them.' And Phil. ii. 13: 'It is God which worketh in you both to will and to do of his good pleasure.' One may add to these passages all those which make God the author of all grace and of all good inclinations, and all those which say that we are as dead in sin.

10. Here now are the neutral passages, according to Mr. Hobbes. These are those where Holy Scripture says that man has the choice to act if he wills, or not to act if he wills not. For example Deut. xxx. 19: 'I call heaven and earth to record this day against you, that I have set before you life and death, blessing and cursing: therefore choose life, that both thou and thy seed may live.' And Joshua xxiv. 15: 'Choose you this day whom ye will serve.' And God said to Gad the prophet (2 Sam. xxiv. 12), 'Go and say unto David: Thus saith the Lord, I offer thee three things; choose thee one of them, that I may do it unto thee.' And Isa. vii. 16: 'Until the child shall know to refuse the evil and choose the good.' Finally the passages which Mr. Hobbes acknowledges to be apparently contrary to his opinion are all those where it is indicated that the will of man is not in conformity with that of God. Thus Isa. v. 4: 'What could have been done more to my vineyard, that I have not done in it? Wherefore, when I looked that it should bring forth grapes, brought it forth wild grapes?' And Jer. xix. 5: 'They have built also the high places of Baal, to burn their sons with fire for burnt offerings unto Baal; which I commanded not, nor spake it, neither came it into my mind.' And Hos. xiii. 9: 'O Israel, thou hast destroyed thyself; but in me is thine help.' And 1 Tim. ii. 4: 'God will have all men to be saved, and to come unto the knowledge of the truth.' He avows that he could quote very many other passages, such as those which indicate that God willeth not iniquity, that he willeth the salvation of the sinner, and generally all those which declare that God commands good and forbids evil.

11. Mr. Hobbes makes answer to these passages that God does not always will that which he commands, as for example when he commanded Abraham to sacrifice his son, and that God's revealed will is not always his full will or his decree, as when he revealed to Jonah that Nineveh would perish in forty days. He adds also, that when it is said that God wills the salvation of all, that means simply that God commands that all do that which is necessary for salvation; when, moreover, the Scripture says that God wills not sin, that means that he wills to punish it. And as for the rest, Mr. Hobbes ascribes it to the forms of expression used among men. But one will answer him that it would be to God's discredit that

his revealed will should be opposed to his real will: that what he bade Jonah say to the Ninevites was rather a threat than a prediction, and that thus the condition of impenitence was implied therein; moreover the Ninevites took it in this sense. One will say also, that it is quite true that God in commanding Abraham to sacrifice his son willed obedience, but did not will action, which he prevented after having obtained obedience; for that was not an action deserving in itself to be willed. And it is not the same in the case of actions where he exerts his will positively, and which are in fact worthy to be the object of his will. Of such are piety, charity and every virtuous action that God commands; of such is omission of sin, a thing more alien to divine perfection than any other. It is therefore incomparably better to explain the will of God as I have explained it in this work. Thus I shall say that God, by virtue of his supreme goodness, has in the beginning a serious inclination to produce, or to see and cause to be produced, all good and every laudable action, and to prevent, or to see and cause to fail, all evil and every bad action. But he is determined by this same goodness, united to an infinite wisdom, and by the very concourse of all the previous and particular inclinations towards each good, and towards the preventing of each evil, to produce the best possible design of things. This is his final and decretory will. And this design of the best being of such a nature that the good must be enhanced therein, as light is enhanced by shade, by some evil which is incomparably less than this good, God could not have excluded this evil, nor introduced certain goods that were excluded from this plan, without wronging his supreme perfection. So for that reason one must say that he permitted the sins of others, because otherwise he would have himself performed an action worse than all the sin of creatures.

12. I find that the Bishop of Derry is at least justified in saying, article XV, in his Reply, p. 153, that the opinion of his opponents is contrary to piety, when they ascribe all to God's power only, and that Mr. Hobbes ought not to have said that honour or worship is only a sign of the power of him whom one honours: for one may also, and one must, acknowledge and honour wisdom, goodness, justice and other perfections. *Magnos facile laudamus, bonos libenter.* This opinion, which despoils God of all goodness and of all true justice, which represents him as a Tyrant, wielding an absolute power, independent of all right and of all equity, and

creating millions of creatures to be eternally unhappy, and this without any other aim than that of displaying his power, this opinion, I say, is capable of rendering men very evil; and if it were accepted no other Devil would be needed in the world to set men at variance among themselves and with God; as the Serpent did in making Eve believe that God, when he forbade her the fruit of the tree, did not will her good. Mr. Hobbes endeavours to parry this thrust in his Rejoinder (p. 160) by saying that goodness is a part of the power of God, that is to say, the power of making himself worthy of love. But that is an abuse of terms by an evasion, and confounds things that must be kept distinct. After all, if God does not intend the good of intelligent creatures, if he has no other principles of justice than his power alone, which makes him produce either arbitrarily that which chance presents to him, or by necessity all that which is possible, without the intervention of choice founded on good, how can he make himself worthy of love? It is therefore the doctrine either of blind power or of arbitrary power, which destroys piety: for the one destroys the intelligent principle or the providence of God, the other attributes to him actions which are appropriate to the evil principle. Justice in God, says Mr. Hobbes (p. 161), is nothing but the power he has, which he exercises in distributing blessings and afflictions. This definition surprises me: it is not the power to distribute them, but the will to distribute them reasonably, that is, goodness guided by wisdom, which makes the justice of God. But, says he, justice is not in God as in a man, who is only just through the observance of laws made by his superior. Mr. Hobbes is mistaken also in that, as well as Herr Pufendorf, who followed him. Justice does not depend upon arbitrary laws of superiors, but on the eternal rules of wisdom and of goodness, in men as well as in God. Mr. Hobbes asserts in the same passage that the wisdom which is attributed to God does not lie in a logical consideration of the relation of means to ends, but in an incomprehensible attribute, attributed to an incomprehensible nature to honour it. It seems as if he means that it is an indescribable something attributed to an indescribable something, and even a chimerical quality given to a chimerical substance, to intimidate and to deceive the nations through the worship which they render to it. After all, it is difficult for Mr. Hobbes to have a different opinion of God and of wisdom, since he admits only material substances. If Mr. Hobbes were still alive, I would beware of ascribing to him opinions which might do him injury; but it is difficult to exempt him from this. He may have changed his mind subsequently, for he attained to a great age; thus I hope that his errors may not have been deleterious to him. But as they might be so to others, it is expedient to give warnings to those who shall read the writings of one who otherwise is of great merit, and from whom one may profit in many ways. It is true that God does not reason, properly speaking, using time as we do, to pass from one truth to the other: but as he understands at one and the same time all the truths and all their connexions, he knows all the conclusions, and he contains in the highest degree within himself all the reasonings that we can develop. And just because of that his wisdom is perfect.

OBSERVATIONS ON THE BOOK
CONCERNING 'THE ORIGIN OF EVIL'
PUBLISHED RECENTLY IN LONDON

1. IT is a pity that M. Bayle should have seen only the reviews of this admirable work, which are to be found in the journals. If he had read it himself and examined it properly, he would have provided us with a good opportunity of throwing light on many difficulties, which spring again and again like the head of the hydra, in a matter where it is easy to become confused when one has not seen the whole system or does not take the trouble to reason according to a strict plan. For strictness of reasoning performs in subjects that transcend imagination the same function as figures do in geometry: there must always be something capable of fixing our attention and forming a connexion between our thoughts. That is why when this Latin book, so learned and so elegant of style, printed originally in London and then reprinted in Bremen, fell into my hands, I judged that the seriousness of the matter and the author's merit required an attention which readers might fairly expect of me, since we are agreed only in regard to half of the subject. Indeed, as the work contains five chapters, and the fifth with the appendix equals the rest in size, I have observed that the first four, where it is a question of evil in general and of physical evil in particular, are in harmony with my principles (save for a few individual passages), and that they sometimes even develop with force and eloquence some points I had treated but

slightly because M. Bayle had not placed emphasis upon them. But the fifth chapter, with its sections (of which some are equal to entire chapters) speaking of freedom and of the moral evil dependent upon it, is constructed upon principles opposed to mine, and often, indeed, to those of M. Bayle; that is, if it were possible to credit him with any fixed principles. For this fifth chapter tends to show (if that were possible) that true freedom depends upon an indifference of equipoise, vague, complete and absolute; so that, until the will has determined itself, there would be no reason for its determination, either in him who chooses or in the object; and one would not choose what pleases, but in choosing without reason one would cause what one chooses to be pleasing.

2. This principle of choice without cause or reason, of a choice, I say, divested of the aim of wisdom and goodness, is regarded by many as the great privilege of God and of intelligent substances, and as the source of their freedom, their satisfaction, their morality and their good or evil. The fantasy of a power to declare one's independence, not only of inclination, but of reason itself within and of good and evil without, is sometimes painted in such fine colours that one might take it to be the most excellent thing in the world. Nevertheless it is only a hollow fantasy, a suppression of the reasons for the caprice of which one boasts. What is asserted is impossible, but if it came to pass it would be harmful. This fantastic character might be attributed to some Don Juan in a St. Peter's Feast, and a man of romantic disposition might even affect the outward appearances of it and persuade himself that he has it in reality. But in Nature there will never be any choice to which one is not prompted by the previous representation of good or evil, by inclinations or by reasons: and I have always challenged the supporters of this absolute indifference to show an example thereof. Nevertheless if I call fantastic this choice whereto one is determined by nothing, I am far from calling visionaries the supporters of that hypothesis, especially our gifted author. The Peripatetics teach some beliefs of this nature; but it would be the greatest injustice in the world to be ready to despise on that account an Occam, a Suisset, a Cesalpino, a Conringius, men who still advocated certain scholastic opinions which have been improved upon to-day.

3. One of these opinions, revived, however, and introduced by

degenerate scholasticism, and in the Age of Chimeras, is vague indifference of choice, or real chance, assumed in our souls; as if nothing gave us any inclination unless we perceived it distinctly, and as if an effect could be without causes, when these causes are imperceptible. It is much as some have denied the existence of insensible corpuscles because they do not see them. Modern philosophers have improved upon the opinions of the Schoolmen by showing that, according to the laws of corporeal nature, a body can only be set in motion by the movement of another body propelling it. Even so we must believe that our souls (by virtue of the laws of spiritual nature) can only be moved by some reason of good or evil: and this even when no distinct knowledge can be extracted from our mental state, on account of a concourse of innumerable little perceptions which make us now joyful and now sad, or again of some other humour, and cause us to like one thing more than another without its being possible to say why. Plato, Aristotle and even Thomas Aquinas, Durand and other Schoolmen of the sounder sort reason on that question like the generality of men, and as unprejudiced people always have reasoned. They assume that freedom lies in the use of reason and the inclinations, which cause the choice or rejection of objects. But finally some rather too subtle philosophers have extracted from their alembic an inexplicable notion of choice independent of anything whatsoever, which is said to do wonders in solving all difficulties. But the notion is caught up at the outset in one of the greatest difficulties, by offending against the grand principle of reasoning which makes us always assume that nothing is done without some sufficient cause or reason. As the Schoolmen often forgot to apply this great principle, admitting certain prime occult qualities, one need not wonder if this fiction of vague indifference met with applause amongst them, and if even most worthy men have been imbued therewith. Our author, who is otherwise rid of many of the errors of the ordinary Schoolmen, is still deluded by this fiction: but he is without doubt one of the most skilful of those who have supported it.

Si Pergama dextra
Defendi possent, etiam hac defensa fuissent.

He gives it the best possible turn, and only shows it on its good side. He knows how to strip spontaneity and reason of their advantages, transferring all these to vague indifference: only through this indifference is one active, resisting the passions, taking pleasure in one's choice, or being happy; it appears indeed that one would be miserable if some happy necessity should oblige us to choose aright. Our author had said admirable things on the origin and reasons of natural evils: he only had to apply the same principles to moral evil; indeed, he believes himself that moral evil becomes an evil through the physical evils that it causes or tends to cause. But somehow or other he thinks that it would be a degradation of God and men if they were to be made subject to reason; that thus they would all be rendered passive to it and would no longer be satisfied with themselves; in short that men would have nothing wherewith to oppose the misfortunes that come to them from without, if they had not within them this admirable privilege of rendering things good or tolerable by choosing them, and of changing all into gold by the touch of this wondrous faculty.

4. We will examine it in closer detail presently; but it will be well to profit beforehand by the excellent ideas of our author on the nature of things and on natural evils, particularly since there are some points in which we shall be able to go a little further: by this means also we shall gain a better understanding of the whole arrangement of his system. The first chapter contains the principles. The writer calls substance a being the idea of which does not involve the existence of another. I do not know if there are any such among created beings, by reason of the connexion existing between all things; and the example of a wax torch is not the example of a substance, any more than that of a swarm of bees would be. But one may take the terms in an extended sense. He observes aptly that after all the changes of matter and after all the qualities of which it may be divested, there remain extension, mobility, divisibility and resistance. He explains also the nature of notions, and leaves it to be understood that *universals* indicate only the resemblances which exist between *individuals*; that we understand by *ideas* only that which is known through an immediate sensation, and that the rest is known to us only through relations with these ideas. But when he admits that we have no idea of God, of spirit, of substance, he does not appear to have observed sufficiently that we have immediate apperception of substance and of spirit in our apperception of ourselves, and that

the idea of God is found in the idea of ourselves through a suppression of the limits of our perfections, as extension taken in an absolute sense is comprised in the idea of a globe. He is right also in asserting that our simple ideas at least are innate, and in rejecting the *Tabula rasa* of Aristotle and of Mr. Locke. But I cannot agree with him that our ideas have scarce any more relation to things than words uttered into the air or writings traced upon paper have to our ideas, and that the bearing of our sensations is arbitrary and *ex instituto*, like the signification of words. I have already indicated elsewhere why I am not in agreement with our Cartesians on that point.

5. For the purpose of advancing to the first Cause, the author seeks a criterion, a distinguishing mark of truth; and he finds it in the force whereby our inward assertions, when they are evident, compel the understanding to give them its consent. It is by such a process, he says, that we credit the senses. He points out that the distinguishing mark in the Cartesian scheme, to wit, a clear and distinct perception, has need of a new mark to indicate what is clear and distinct, and that the congruity or non-congruity of ideas (or rather of terms, as one spoke formerly) may still be deceptive, because there are congruities real and apparent. He appears to recognize even that the inward force which constrains us to give our assent is still a matter for caution, and may come from deeprooted prejudices. That is why he confesses that he who should furnish another criterion would have found something very advantageous to the human race. I have endeavoured to explain this criterion in a little *Discourse on Truth and Ideas*, published in 1684; and although I do not boast of having given therein a new discovery I hope that I have expounded things which were only confusedly recognized. I distinguish between truths of fact and truths of reason. Truths of fact can only be verified by confronting them with truths of reason, and by tracing them back to immediate perceptions within us, such as St. Augustine and M. Descartes very promptly acknowledged to be indubitable; that is to say, we cannot doubt that we think, nor indeed that we think this thing or that. But in order to judge whether our inward notions have any reality in things, and to pass from thoughts to objects, my opinion is that it is necessary to consider whether our perceptions are firmly connected among themselves and with others that we have had, in such fashion as to manifest the rules of mathematics and

other truths of reason. In this case one must regard them as real; and I think that it is the only means of distinguishing them from imaginations, dreams and visions. Thus the truth of things outside us can be recognized only through the connexion of phenomena. The criterion of the truths of reason, or those which spring from conceptions, is found in an exact use of the rules of logic. As for ideas or notions, I call *real* all those the possibility of which is certain; and the *definitions* which do not mark this possibility are only *nominal*. Geometricians well versed in analysis are aware what difference there is in this respect between several properties by which some line or figure might be defined. Our gifted author has not gone so far, perhaps; one may see, however, from the account I have given of him already, and from what follows, that he is by no means lacking in profundity or reflexion.

6. Thereafter he proceeds to examine whether motion, matter and space spring from themselves; and to that end he considers whether it is possible to conceive that they do not exist. He remarks upon this privilege of God, that as soon as it is assumed that he exists it must be admitted that he exists of necessity. This is a corollary to a remark which I made in the little discourse mentioned above, namely that as soon as one admits that God is possible, one must admit that he exists of necessity. Now, as soon as one admits that God exists, one admits that he is possible. Therefore as soon as one admits that God exists, one must admit that he exists of necessity. Now this privilege does not belong to the three things of which we have just spoken. The author believes also especially concerning motion, that it is not sufficient to say, with Mr. Hobbes, that the present movement comes from an anterior movement, and this one again from another, and so on to infinity. For, however far back you may go, you will not be one whit nearer to finding the reason which causes the presence of motion in matter. Therefore this reason must be outside the sequence; and even if there were an eternal motion, it would require an eternal motive power. So the rays of the sun, even though they were eternal with the sun, would nevertheless have their eternal cause in the sun. I am well pleased to recount these arguments of our gifted author, that it may be seen how important, according to him, is the principle of sufficient reason. For, if it is permitted to admit something for which it is acknowledged there is no reason, it will be easy for an atheist to overthrow this argu-

ment, by saying that it is not necessary that there be a sufficient reason for the existence of motion. I will not enter into the discussion of the reality and the eternity of space, for fear of straying too far from our subject. It is enough to state that the author believes that space can be annihilated by the divine power, but in entirety and not in portions, and that we could exist alone with God even if there were neither space nor matter, since we do not contain within ourselves the notion of the existence of external things. He also puts forward the consideration that in the sensations of sounds, of odours and of savours the idea of space is not included. But whatever the opinion formed as to space, it suffices that there is a God, the cause of matter and of motion, and in short of all things. The author believes that we can reason about God, as one born blind would reason about light. But I hold that there is something more in us, for our light is a ray from God's light. After having spoken of some attributes of God, the author acknowledges that God acts for an end, which is the communication of his goodness, and that his works are ordered aright. Finally he concludes this chapter very properly, by saying that God in creating the world was at pains to give it the greatest harmony amongst things, the greatest comfort of beings endowed with reason, and the greatest compatibility in desires that an infinite power, wisdom and goodness combined could produce. He adds that, if some evil has remained notwithstanding, one must believe that these infinite divine perfections could not have (I would rather say ought not to have) taken it away.

7. Chapter II anatomizes evil, dividing it as we do into metaphysical, physical and moral. Metaphysical evil consists in imperfections, physical evil in suffering and other like troubles, and moral evil in sin. All these evils exist in God's work; Lucretius thence inferred that there is no providence, and he denied that the world can be an effect of divinity:

Naturam rerum divinitus esse creatam;

because there are so many faults in the nature of things,

quoniam tanta stat praedita culpa.

Others have admitted two principles, the one good, the other evil. There have also been people who thought the difficulty insurmountable, and among these our author appears to have had

M. Bayle in mind. He hopes to show in his work that it is not a Gordian knot, which needs to be cut; and he says rightly that the power, the wisdom and the goodness of God would not be infinite and perfect in their exercise if these evils had been banished. He begins with the evil of imperfection in Chapter III and observes, as St. Augustine does, that creatures are imperfect, since they are derived from nothingness, whereas God producing a perfect substance from his own essence would have made thereof a God. This gives him occasion for making a little digression against the Socinians. But someone will say, why did not God refrain from producing things, rather than make imperfect things? The author answers appositely that the abundance of the goodness of God is the cause. He wished to communicate himself at the expense of a certain fastidiousness which we assume in God, imagining that imperfections offend him. Thus he preferred that there should be the imperfect rather than nothing. But one might have added that God has produced indeed the most perfect whole that was possible, one wherewith he had full cause for satisfaction, the imperfections of the parts serving a greater perfection in the whole. Also the observation is made soon afterwards, that certain things might have been made better, but not without other new and *perhaps* greater disadvantages. This *perhaps* could have been omitted: for the author also states as a certainty, and rightly so, at the end of the chapter, *that it appertains to infinite goodness to choose the best*; and thus he was able to draw this conclusion a little earlier, that imperfect things will be added to those more perfect, so long as they do not preclude the existence of the more perfect in as great a number as possible. Thus bodies were created as well as spirits, since the one does not offer any obstacle to the other; and the creation of matter was not unworthy of the great God, as some heretics of old believed, attributing this work to a certain Demogorgon.

8. Let us now proceed to physical evil, which is treated of in Chapter IV. Our famous author, having observed that metaphysical evil, or imperfection, springs from nothingness, concludes that physical evil, or discomfort, springs from matter, or rather from its movement; for without movement matter would be useless. Moreover there must be contrariety in these movements; otherwise, if all went together in the same direction, there would be neither variety nor generation. But the movements that cause

generations cause also corruptions, since from the variety of movements comes concussion between bodies, by which they are often dissipated and destroyed. The Author of Nature however, in order to render bodies more enduring, distributed them into *systems*, those which we know being composed of luminous and opaque balls, in a manner so excellent and so fitting for the display of that which they contain, and for arousing wonder thereat, that we can conceive of nothing more beautiful. But the crowning point of the work was the construction of animals, to the end that everywhere there should be creatures capable of cognition,

Ne regio foret ulla suis animalibus orba.

Our sagacious author believes that the air and even the purest aether have their denizens as well as the water and the earth. But supposing that there were places without animals, these places might have uses necessary for other places which are inhabited. So for example the mountains, which render the surface of our globe unequal and sometimes desert and barren, are of use for the production of rivers and of winds; and we have no cause to complain of sands and marshes, since there are so many places still remaining to be cultivated. Moreover, it must not be supposed that all is made for man alone: and the author is persuaded that there are not only pure spirits but also immortal animals of a nature akin to these spirits, that is, animals whose souls are united to an ethereal and incorruptible matter. But it is not the same with animals whose body is terrestrial, composed of tubes and fluids which circulate therein, and whose motion is terminated by the breaking of the vessels. Thence the author is led to believe that the immortality granted to Adam, if he had been obedient, would not have been an effect of his nature, but of the grace of God.

9. Now it was necessary for the conservation of corruptible animals that they should have indications causing them to recognize a present danger, and giving them the inclination to avoid it. That is why what is about to cause a great injury must beforehand cause pain such as may force the animal to efforts capable of repulsing or shunning the cause of this discomfort, and of forestalling a greater evil. The dread of death helps also to cause its avoidance: for it if were not so ugly and if the dissolution of continuity were not so painful, very often animals would take no precautions against perishing, or allowing the parts of their body

to perish, and the strongest would have difficulty in subsisting for a whole day.

God has also given hunger and thirst to animals, to compel them to feed and maintain themselves by replacing that which is used up and which disappears imperceptibly. These appetites are of use also to prompt them to work, in order to procure a nourishment meet for their constitution, and which may avail to invigorate them. It was even found necessary by the Author of things that one animal very often should serve as food for another. This hardly renders the victim more unhappy, since death caused by diseases is generally just as painful as a violent death, if not more so; and animals subject to being preyed upon by others, having neither foresight nor anxiety for the future, have a life no less tranquil when they are not in danger. It is the same with inundations, earthquakes, thunderbolts and other disorders, which brute beasts do not fear, and which men have ordinarily no cause to fear, since there are few that suffer thereby.

10. The Author of Nature has compensated for these evils and others, wnich happen only seldom, with a thousand advantages that are ordinary and constant. Hunger and thirst augment the pleasure experienced in the taking of nourishment. Moderate work is an agreeable exercise of the animal's powers; and sleep is also agreeable in an altogether opposite way, restoring the forces through repose. But one of the pleasures most intense is that which prompts animals to propagation. God, having taken care to ensure that the species should be immortal, since the individual cannot be so here on earth, also willed that animals should have a great tenderness for their little ones, even to the point of endangering themselves for their preservation. From pain and from sensual pleasure spring fear, cupidity and the other passions that are ordinarily serviceable, although it may accidentally happen that they sometimes turn towards ill: one must say as much of poisons, epidemic diseases and other hurtful things, namely that these are indispensable consequences of a well-conceived system. As for ignorance and errors, it must be taken into account that the most perfect creatures are doubtless ignorant of much, and that knowledge is wont to be proportionate to needs. Nevertheless it is necessary that one be exposed to hazards which cannot be foreseen, and accidents of such kinds are inevitable. One must often be mistaken in one's judgement, because it is not always permitted

to suspend it long enough for exact consideration. These disadvantages are inseparable from the system of things: for things must very often resemble one another in a certain situation, the one being taken for the other. But the inevitable errors are not the most usual, nor the most pernicious. Those which cause us the most harm are wont to arise through our fault; and consequently one would be wrong to make natural evils a pretext for taking one's own life, since one finds that those who have done so have generally been prompted to such action by voluntary evils.

11. After all, one finds that all these evils of which we have spoken come accidentally from good causes; and there is reason to infer concerning all we do not know, from all we do know, that one could not have done away with them without falling into greater troubles. For the better understanding of this the author counsels us to picture the world as a great building. There must be not only apartments, halls, galleries, gardens, grottoes, but also the kitchen, the cellar, the poultry-yard, stables, drainage. Thus it would not have been proper to make only suns in the world, or to make an earth all of gold and of diamonds, but not habitable. If man had been all eye or all ear, he would not have been fitted for feeding himself. If God had made him without passions, he would have made him stupid; and if he had wished to make man free from error he would have had to deprive him of senses, or give him powers of sensation through some other means than organs, that is to say, there would not have been any man. Our learned author remarks here upon an idea which histories both sacred and profane appear to inculcate, namely that wild beasts, poisonous plants and other natures that are injurious to us have been armed against us by sin. But as he argues here only in accordance with the principles of reason he sets aside what Revelation can teach. He believes, however, that Adam would have been exempted from natural evils (if he had been obedient) only by virtue of divine grace and of a covenant made with God, and that Moses expressly indicates only about seven effects of the first sin. These effects are:

1. The revocation of the gracious gift of immortality.
2. The sterility of the earth, which was no longer to be fertile of itself, save in evil or useless herbs.
3. The rude toil one must exercise in order to gain sustenance.
4. The subjection of the woman to the will of the husband.

5. The pains of childbirth.

6. The enmity between man and the serpent.

7. The banishment of man from the place of delight wherein God had placed him.

But our author thinks that many of our evils spring from the necessity of matter, especially since the withdrawal of grace. Moreover, it seems to him that after our banishment immortality would be only a burden to us, and that it is perhaps more for our good than to punish us that the tree of life has become inaccessible to us. On one point or another one might have something to say in objection, but the body of the discourse by our author on the origin of evils is full of good and sound reflexions, which I have judged it advisable to turn to advantage. Now I must pass on to the subject of our controversy, that is, the explanation of the nature of freedom.

12. The learned author of this work on the origin of evil, proposing to explain the origin of moral evil in the fifth chapter, which makes up half of the whole book, considers that it is altogether different from that of physical evil, which lies in the inevitable imperfection of creatures. For, as we shall see presently, it appears to him that moral evil comes rather from that which he calls a perfection, which the creature has in common, according to him, with the Creator, that is to say, in the power of choosing without any motive and without any final or impelling cause. It is a very great paradox to assert that the greatest imperfection, namely sin, springs from perfection itself. But it is no less a paradox to present as a perfection the thing which is the least reasonable in the world, the advantage whereof would consist in being privileged against reason. And that, after all, rather than pointing out the source of the evil, would be to contend that it has none. For if the will makes its resolve without the existence of anything, either in the person who chooses or in the object which is chosen, to prompt it to the choice, there will be neither cause nor reason for this election; and as moral evil consists in the wrong choice, that is admitting that moral evil has no source at all. Thus in the rules of good metaphysics there would have to be no moral evil in Nature; and also for the same reason there would be no moral good either, and all morality would be destroyed. But we must listen to our gifted author, from whom the subtlety of an opinion maintained by famous philosophers among the Schoolmen, and

the adornments that he has added thereto himself by his wit and his eloquence, have hidden the great disadvantages contained therein. In setting forth the position reached in the controversy, he divides the writers into two parties. The one sort, he says, are content to say that the freedom of the will is exempt from outward constraint; and the other sort maintain that it is also exempt from inward necessity. But this exposition does not suffice, unless one distinguish the necessity that is absolute and contrary to morality from hypothetical necessity and moral necessity, as I have already explained in many places.

13. The first section of this chapter is to indicate the nature of choice. The author sets forth in the first place the opinion of those who believe that the will is prompted by the judgement of the understanding, or by anterior inclinations of the desires, to resolve upon the course that it adopts. But he confuses these authors with those who assert that the will is prompted to its resolution by an absolute necessity, and who maintain that the person who wills has no power over his volitions: that is, he confuses a Thomist with a Spinozist. He makes use of the admissions and the odious declarations of Mr. Hobbes and his like, to lay them to the charge of those who are infinitely far removed from them, and who take great care to refute them. He lays these things to their charge because they believe, as Mr. Hobbes believes, like everyone else (save for some doctors who are enveloped in their own subtleties), that the will is moved by the representation of good and evil. Thence he imputes to them the opinion that there is therefore no such thing as contingency, and that all is connected by an absolute necessity. That is a very speedy manner of reasoning; yet he adds also, that properly speaking there will be no evil will, since if there were, all one could object to therein would be the evil which it can cause. That, he says, is different from the common notion, since the world censures the wicked not because they do harm, but because they do harm without necessity. He holds also that the wicked would be only unfortunate and by no means culpable; that there would be no difference between physical evil and moral evil, since man himself would not be the true cause of an action which he could not avoid; that evil-doers would not be either blamed or maltreated because they deserve it, but because that action may serve to turn people away from evil; again, for this reason only one would find fault with a rogue, but

not with a sick man, that reproaches and threats can correct the one, and cannot cure the other. And further, according to this doctrine, chastisements would have no object save the prevention of future evil, without which the mere consideration of the evil already done would not be sufficient for punishment. Likewise gratitude would have as its sole aim that of procuring a fresh benefit, without which the mere consideration of the past benefit would not furnish a sufficient reason. Finally the author thinks that if this doctrine, which derives the resolution of the will from the representation of good and evil, were true, one must despair of human felicity, since it would not be in our power, and would depend upon things which are outside us. Now as there is no ground for hoping that things from outside will order themselves and agree together in accordance with our wishes, there will always lack something to us, and there will always be something too much. All these conclusions hold, according to him, against those also who think that the will makes its resolve in accordance with the final judgement of the understanding, an opinion which, as he considers, strips the will of its right and renders the soul quite passive. This accusation is also directed against countless serious writers, of accepted authority, who are here placed in the same class with Mr. Hobbes and Spinoza, and with some other discredited authors, whose doctrine is considered odious and insupportable. As for me, I do not require the will always to follow the judgement of the understanding, because I distinguish this judgement from the motives that spring from insensible perceptions and inclinations. But I hold that the will always follows the most advantageous representation, whether distinct or confused, of the good or the evil resulting from reasons, passions and inclinations, although it may also find motives for suspending its judgement. But it is always upon motives that it acts.

14. It will be necessary to answer these objections to my opinion before proceeding to establish that of our author. The misapprehension of my opponents originates in their confusing a consequence which is necessary absolutely, whose contrary implies contradiction, with a consequence which is founded only upon truths of fitness, and nevertheless has its effect. To put it otherwise, there is a confusion between what depends upon the principle of contradiction, which makes necessary and indispensable truths, and what depends upon the principle of the sufficient

reason, which applies also to contingent truths. I have already elsewhere stated this proposition, which is one of the most important in philosophy, pointing out that there are two great principles, namely, *that of identicals or of contradiction*, which states that of two contradictory enunciations the one is true and the other false, and *that of the sufficient reason*, which states that there is no true enunciation whose reason could not be seen by one possessing all the knowledge necessary for its complete understanding. Both principles must hold not only in necessary but also in contingent truths; and it is even necessary that that which has no sufficient reason should not exist. For one may say in a sense that these two principles are contained in the definition of the true and the false. Nevertheless, when in making the analysis of the truth submitted one sees it depending upon truths whose contrary implies contradiction, one may say that it is absolutely necessary. But when, while pressing the analysis to the furthest extent, one can never attain to such elements of the given truth, one must say that it is contingent, and that it originates from a prevailing reason which inclines without necessitating. Once that is granted, it is seen how we can say with sundry famous philosophers and theologians, that the thinking substance is prompted to its resolution by the prevailing representation of good or of evil, and this certainly and infallibly, but not necessarily, that is, by reasons which incline it without necessitating it. That is why contingent futurities, foreseen both in themselves and through their reasons, remain contingent. God was led infallibly by his wisdom and by his goodness to create the world through his power, and to give it the best possible form; but he was not led thereto of necessity, and the whole took place without any diminution of his perfect and supreme wisdom. And I do not know if it would be easy, apart from the reflexions we have just entertained, to untie the Gordian knot of contingency and freedom.

15. This explanation dismisses all the objections of our gifted opponent. In the first place, it is seen that contingency exists together with freedom. Secondly, evil wills are evil not only because they do harm, but also because they are a source of harmful things, or of physical evils, a wicked spirit being, in the sphere of its activity, what the evil principle of the Manichaeans would be in the universe. Moreover, the author has observed (ch. 4, sect. 4, § 8) that divine wisdom has usually forbidden actions

which would cause discomforts, that is to say, physical evils. It is agreed that he who causes evil by necessity is not culpable. But there is neither legislator nor lawyer who by this necessity means the force of the considerations of good or evil, real or apparent, that have prompted man to do ill: else anyone stealing a great sum of money or killing a powerful man in order to attain to high office would be less deserving of punishment than one who should steal a few halfpence for a mug of beer or wantonly kill his neighbour's dog, since these latter were tempted less. But it is quite the opposite in the administration of justice which is authorized in the world: for the greater is the temptation to sin, the more does it need to be repressed by the fear of a great chastisement. Besides, the greater the calculation evident in the design of an evil-doer, the more will it be found that the wickedness has been deliberate, and the more readily will one decide that it is great and deserving of punishment. Thus a too artful fraud causes the aggravating crime called *stellionate*, and a cheat becomes a forger when he has the cunning to sap the very foundations of our security in written documents. But one will have greater indulgence for a great passion, because it is nearer to madness. The Romans punished with the utmost severity the priests of the God Apis, when these had prostituted the chastity of a noble lady to a knight who loved her to distraction, making him pass as their god; while it was found enough to send the lover into exile. But if someone had done evil deeds without apparent reason and without appearance of passion the judge would be tempted to take him for a madman, especially if it proved that he was given to committing such extravagances often: this might tend towards reduction of the penalty, rather than supplying the true grounds of wickedness and punishment. So far removed are the principles of our opponents from the practice of the tribunals and from the general opinion of men.

16. Thirdly, the distinction between physical evil and moral evil will still remain, although there be this in common between them, that they have their reasons and causes. And why manufacture new difficulties for oneself concerning the origin of moral evil, since the principle followed in the solution of those which natural evils have raised suffices also to account for voluntary evils? That is to say, it suffices to show that one could not have prevented men from being prone to errors, without changing the

constitution of the best of systems or without employing miracles
at every turn. It is true that sin makes up a large portion of human
wretchedness, and even the largest; but that does not prevent one
from being able to say that men are wicked and deserving of
punishment: else one must needs say that the actual sins of the
non-regenerate are excusable, because they spring from the first
cause of our wretchedness, which is original sin. Fourthly, to say
that the soul becomes passive and that man is not the true cause
of sin, if he is prompted to his voluntary actions by their objects,
as our author asserts in many passages, and particularly ch. 5,
sect. 1, sub-sect. 3, § 18, is to create for oneself new senses for
terms. When the ancients spoke of that which is ἐφ' ἡμῖν, or when
we speak of that which depends upon us, of spontaneity, of the
inward principle of our actions, we do not exclude the representation of external things; for these representations are in our souls,
they are a portion of the modifications of this active principle
which is within us. No agent is capable of acting without being
predisposed to what the action demands; and the reasons or
inclinations derived from good or evil are the dispositions that
enable the soul to decide between various courses. One will have it
that the will is alone active and supreme, and one is wont to
imagine it to be like a queen seated on her throne, whose minister
of state is the understanding, while the passions are her courtiers
or favourite ladies, who by their influence often prevail over the
counsel of her ministers. One will have it that the understanding
speaks only at this queen's order; that she can vacillate between
the arguments of the minister and the suggestions of the favourites,
even rejecting both, making them keep silence or speak, and giving
them audience or not as seems good to her. But it is a personifica-
tion or mythology somewhat ill-conceived. If the will is to judge,
or take cognizance of the reasons and inclinations which the
understanding or the senses offer it, it will need another understanding in itself, to understand what it is offered. The truth is
that the soul, or the thinking substance, understands the reasons
and feels the inclinations, and decides according to the predominance of the representations modifying its active force, in
order to shape the action. I have no need here to apply my system
of Pre-established Harmony, which shows our independence to
the best advantage and frees us from the physical influence of
objects. For what I have just said is sufficient to answer the

objection. Our author, even though he admits with people in general this physical influence of objects upon us, observes nevertheless with much perspicacity that the body or the objects of the senses do not even give us our ideas, much less the active force of our soul, and that they serve only to draw out that which is within us. This is much in the spirit of M. Descartes' belief that the soul, not being able to give force to the body, gives it at least some direction. It is a mean between one side and the other, between physical influence and Pre-established Harmony.

17. Fifthly, the objection is made that, according to my opinion, sin would neither be censured nor punished because of its deserts, but because the censure and the chastisement serve to prevent it another time; whereas men demand something more, namely, satisfaction for the crime, even though it should serve neither for amendment nor for example. So do men with reason demand that true gratitude should come from a true recognition of the past benefit, and not from the interested aim of extorting a fresh benefit. This objection contains noble and sound considerations, but it does not strike at me. I require a man to be virtuous, grateful, just, not only from the motive of interest, of hope or of fear, but also of the pleasure that he should find in good actions: else one has not yet reached the degree of virtue that one must endeavour to attain. That is what one means by saying that justice and virtue must be loved for their own sake; and it is also what I explained in justifying 'disinterested love', shortly before the opening of the controversy which caused so much stir. Likewise I consider that wickedness is all the greater when its practice becomes a pleasure, as when a highwayman, after having killed men because they resist, or because he fears their vengeance, finally grows cruel and takes pleasure in killing them, and even in making them suffer beforehand. Such a degree of wickedness is taken to be diabolical, even though the man affected with it finds in this execrable indulgence a stronger reason for his homicides than he had when he killed simply under the influence of hope or of fear. I have also observed in answering the difficulties of M. Bayle that, according to the celebrated Conringius, justice which punishes by means of *medicinal* penalties, so to speak, that is, in order to correct the criminal or at least to provide an example for others, might exist in the opinion of those who do away with the freedom that is exempt from necessity.

True retributive justice, on the other hand, going beyond the medicinal, assumes something more, namely, intelligence and freedom in him who sins, because the harmony of things demands a satisfaction, or evil in the form of suffering, to make the mind feel its error after the voluntary active evil whereto it has consented. Mr. Hobbes also, who does away with freedom, has rejected retributive justice, as do the Socinians, drawing on themselves the condemnation of our theologians; although the writers of the Socinian party are wont to exaggerate the idea of freedom.

18. Sixthly, the objection is finally made that men cannot hope for felicity if the will can only be actuated by the representation of good and evil. But this objection seems to me completely null and void, and I think it would be hard to guess how any tolerable interpretation was ever put upon it. Moreover, the line of reasoning adopted to prove it is of a most astounding nature: it is that our felicity depends upon external things, if it is true that it depends upon the representation of good or evil. It is therefore not in our own power, so it is said, for we have no ground for hoping that outward things will arrange themselves for our pleasure. This argument is halting from every aspect. *There is no force in the inference: one might grant the conclusion: the argument may be retorted upon the author.* Let us begin with the retort, which is easy. For are men any happier or more independent of the accidents of fortune upon this argument, or because they are credited with the advantage of choosing without reason? Have they less bodily suffering? Have they less tendency toward true or apparent goods, less fear of true or imaginary evils? Are they any less enslaved by sensual pleasure, by ambition, by avarice? less apprehensive? less envious? Yes, our gifted author will say; I will prove it by a method of counting or assessment. I would rather he had proved it by experience; but let us see this proof by counting. Suppose that by my choice, which enables me to give goodness-for-me to that which I choose, I give to the object chosen six degrees of goodness, when previously there were two degrees of evil in my condition; I shall become happy all at once, and with perfect ease, for I should have four degrees surplus, or net good. Doubtless that is all very well; but unfortunately it is impossible. For what possibility is there of giving these six degrees of goodness to the object? To that end we must needs have the power to change our taste, or the things, as we please. That

would be almost as if I could say to lead, Thou shalt be gold, and make it so; to the pebble, Thou shalt be diamond; or at the least, Thou shalt look like it. Or it would be like the common explanation of the Mosaical passage which seems to say that the desert manna assumed any taste the Israelites desired to give to it. They only had to say to their homerful, Thou shalt be a capon, thou shalt be a partridge. But if I am free to give these six degrees of goodness to the object, am I not permitted to give it more goodness? I think that I am. But if that is so, why shall we not give to the object all the goodness conceivable? Why shall we not even go as far as twenty-four carats of goodness? By this means behold us completely happy, despite the accidents of fortune; it may blow, hail or snow, and we shall not mind: by means of this splendid secret we shall be always shielded against fortuitous events. The author agrees (in this first section of the fifth chapter, sub-sect. 3, § 12) that this power overcomes all the natural appetites and cannot be overcome by any of them; and he regards it (§§ 20, 21, 22) as the soundest foundation for happiness. Indeed, since there is nothing capable of limiting a power so indeterminate as that of choosing without any reason, and of giving goodness to the object through the choice, either this goodness must exceed infinitely that which the natural appetites seek in objects, these appetites and objects being limited while this power is independent or at the least this goodness, given by the will to the chosen object, must be arbitrary and of such a kind as the will desires. For whence would one derive the reason for limits if the object is possible, if it is within reach of him who wills, and if the will can give it the goodness it desires to give, independently of reality and of appearances? It seems to me that may suffice to overthrow a hypothesis so precarious, which contains something of a fairy-tale kind, *optantis ista sunt, non invenientis*. It therefore remains only too true that this handsome fiction cannot render us more immune from evils. And we shall see presently that when men place themselves above certain desires or certain aversions they do so through other desires, which always have their foundation in the representation of good and evil. I said also 'that one might grant the conclusion of the argument', which states that our happiness does not depend absolutely upon ourselves, at least in the present state of human life: for who would question the fact that we are liable to meet a thousand accidents which human prudence cannot evade? How, for example, can I avoid being swallowed up, together with a town where I take up my abode, by an earthquake, if such is the order of things? But finally I can also deny the inference in the argument, which states that if the will is only actuated by the representation of good and evil our happiness does not depend upon ourselves. The inference would be valid if there were no God, if everything were ruled by brute causes; but God's ordinance is that for the attainment of happiness it suffices that one be virtuous. Thus, if the soul follows reason and the orders that God has given it, it is assured of its happiness, even though one may not find a sufficiency thereof in this life.

19. Having thus endeavoured to point out the disadvantages of my hypothesis, our gifted author sets forth the advantages of his own. He believes that it alone is capable of saving our freedom, that all our felicity rests therein, that it increases our goods and lessens our evils, and that an agent possessing this power is so much the more complete. These advantages have almost all been already disproved. We have shown that for the securing of our freedom it is enough that the representations of goods and of evils, and other inward or outward dispositions, should incline us without constraining us. Moreover one does not see how pure indifference can contribute to felicity; on the contrary, the more indifferent one is, the more insensitive and the less capable of enjoying what is good will one prove to be. Besides the hypothesis proves too much. For if an indifferent power could give itself the consciousness of good it could also give itself the most perfect happiness, as has been already shown. And it is manifest that there is nothing which would set limits to that power, since limits would withdraw it from its pure indifference, whence, so our author alleges, it only emerges of itself, or rather wherein it has never been. Finally one does not see wherein the perfection of pure indifference lies: on the contrary, there is nothing more imperfect; it would render knowledge and goodness futile, and would reduce everything to chance, with no rules, and no measures that could be taken. There are, however, still some advantages adduced by our author which have not been discussed. He considers then that by this power alone are we the true cause to which our actions can be imputed, since otherwise we should be under the compulsion of external objects; likewise that by this power alone can one ascribe to oneself the merit of one's own felicity, and feel pleased with oneself.

But the exact opposite is the case: for when one happens upon the action through an absolutely indifferent movement, and not as a result of one's good or bad qualities, is it not just as though one were to happen upon it blindly by chance or hazard? Why then should one boast of a good action, or why should one be censured for an evil one, if the thanks or blame redounds to fortune or hazard? I think that one is more worthy of praise when one owes the action to one's good qualities, and the more culpable in proportion as one has been impelled to it by one's evil qualities. To attempt to assess actions without weighing the qualities whence they spring is to talk at random and to put an imaginary indefinable something in the place of causes. Thus, if this chance or this indefinable something were the cause of our actions, to the exclusion of our natural or acquired qualities, of our inclinations, of our habits, it would not be possible to set one's hopes upon anything depending upon the resolve of others, since it would not be possible to fix something indefinite, or to conjecture into what roadstead the uncertain weather of an extravagant indifference will drive the vessel of the will.

20. But setting aside advantages and disadvantages, let us see how our learned author will justify the hypothesis from which he promises us so much good. He imagines that it is only God and the free creatures who are active in the true sense, and that in order to be active one must be determined by oneself only. Now that which is determined by itself must not be determined by objects, and consequently the free substance, in so far as it is free, must be indifferent with regard to objects, and emerge from this indifference only by its own choice, which shall render the object pleasing to it. But almost all the stages of this argument have their stumbling-blocks. Not only the free creatures, but also all the other substances and natures composed of substances, are active. Beasts are not free, and yet all the same they have active souls, unless one assume, with the Cartesians, that they are mere machines. Moreover, it is not necessary that in order to be active one should be determined only by oneself, since a thing may receive direction without receiving force. So it is that the horse is controlled by the rider and the vessel is steered by the helm; and M. Descartes' belief was that our body, having force in itself, receives only some direction from the soul. Thus an active thing may receive from outside some determination or direction, capable of changing

that direction which it would take of itself. Finally, even though an active substance is determined only by itself, it does not follow that it is not moved by objects: for it is the representation of the object within it which contributes towards the determination. Now the representation does not come from without, and consequently there is complete spontaneity. Objects do not act upon intelligent substances as efficient and physical causes, but as final and moral causes. When God acts in accordance with his wisdom, he is guided by the ideas of the possibles which are his objects, but which have no reality outside him before their actual creation. Thus this kind of spiritual and moral motion is not contrary to the activity of the substance, nor to the spontaneity of its action. Finally, even though free power were not determined by the objects, it can never be indifferent to the action when it is on the point of acting, since the action must have its origin in a disposition to act: otherwise one will do anything from anything, *quidvis ex quovis*, and there will be nothing too absurd for us to imagine. But this disposition will have already broken the charm of mere indifference, and if the soul gives itself this disposition there must needs be another predisposition for this act of giving it. Consequently, however far back one may go, one will never meet with a mere indifference in the soul towards the actions which it is to perform. It is true that these dispositions incline it without constraining it. They relate usually to the objects; but there are some, notwithstanding, which arise variously *a subjecto* or from the soul itself, and which bring it about that one object is more acceptable than the other, or that the same is more acceptable at one time than at another.

21. Our author continually assures us that his hypothesis is true, and he undertakes to show that this indifferent power is indeed found in God, and even that it must be attributed to him of necessity. For (he says) nothing is to God either good or bad in creatures. He has no natural appetite, to be satisfied by the enjoyment of anything outside him. He is therefore absolutely indifferent to all external things, since by them he can neither be helped nor hindered; and he must determine himself and create as it were an appetite in making his choice. And having once chosen, he will wish to abide by his choice, just as if he had been prompted thereto by a natural inclination. Thus will the divine will be the cause of goodness in beings. That is to say, there will

be goodness in the objects, not by their nature, but by the will of God: whereas if that will be excluded neither good nor evil can exist in things. It is difficult to imagine how writers of merit could have been misled by so strange an opinion, for the reason which appears to be advanced here has not the slightest force. It seems to me as though an attempt is being made to justify this opinion by the consideration that all creatures have their whole being from God, so that they cannot act upon him or determine him. But this is clearly an instance of self-deception. When we say that an intelligent substance is actuated by the goodness of its object, we do not assert that this object is necessarily a being existing outside the substance, and it is enough for us that it be conceivable: for its representation acts in the substance, or rather the substance acts upon itself, in so far as it is disposed and influenced by this representation. With God, it is plain that his understanding contains the ideas of all possible things, and that is how everything is in him in a transcendent manner. These ideas represent to him the good and evil, the perfection and imperfection, the order and disorder, the congruity and incongruity of possibles; and his superabundant goodness makes him choose the most advantageous. God therefore determines himself by himself; his will acts by virtue of his goodness, but it is particularized and directed in action by understanding filled with wisdom. And since his understanding is perfect, since his thoughts are always clear, his inclinations always good, he never fails to do the best; whereas we may be deceived by the mere semblances of truth and goodness. But how is it possible for it to be said that there is no good or evil in the ideas before the operation of God's will? Does the will of God form the ideas which are in his understanding? I dare not ascribe to our learned author so strange a sentiment, which would confuse understanding and will, and would subvert the current use of our notions. Now if ideas are independent of will, the perfection or imperfection which is represented in them will be independent also. Indeed, is it by the will of God, for example, or is it not rather by the nature of numbers, that certain numbers allow more than others of various exact divisions? that some are more fitted than others for forming battalions, composing polygons and other regular figures? that the number six has the advantage of being the least of all the numbers that are called perfect? that in a plane six equal circles may touch a seventh? that of all equal bodies, the sphere has the least surface? that certain lines are incommensurable, and consequently ill-adapted for harmony? Do we not see that all these advantages or disadvantages spring from the idea of the thing, and that the contrary would imply contradiction? Can it be thought that the pain and discomfort of sentient creatures, and above all the happiness and unhappiness of intelligent substances, are a matter of indifference to God? And what shall be said of his justice? Is it also something arbitrary, and would he have acted wisely and justly if he had resolved to condemn the innocent? I know that there have been writers so ill-advised as to maintain an opinion so dangerous and so liable to overthrow religion. But I am assured that our illustrious author is far from holding it. Nevertheless, it seems as though this hypothesis tends in that direction, if there is nothing in objects save what is indifferent to the divine will before its choice. It is true that God has need of nothing; but the author has himself shown clearly that God's goodness, and not his need, prompted him to produce creatures. There was therefore in him a reason anterior to the resolution; and, as I have said so many times, it was neither by chance nor without cause, nor even by necessity, that God created this world, but rather as a result of his inclination, which always prompts him to the best. Thus it is surprising that our author should assert here (ch. 5, sect. 1, sub-sect. 4, § 5) that there is no reason which could have induced God, absolutely perfect and happy in himself, to create anything outside him, although, according to the author's previous declarations (ch. 1, sect. 3, §§ 8, 9), God acts for an end, and his aim is to communicate his goodness. It was therefore not altogether a matter of indifference to him whether he should create or not create, and creation is notwithstanding a free act. Nor was it a matter of indifference to him either, whether he should create one world rather than another; a perpetual chaos, or a completely ordered system. Thus the qualities of objects, included in their ideas, formed the reason for God's choice.

22. Our author, having already spoken so admirably about the beauty and fittingness of the works of God, has tried to search out phrases that would reconcile them with his hypothesis, which appears to deprive God of all consideration for the good or the advantage of creatures. The indifference of God prevails (he says) only in his first elections, but as soon as God has chosen something

he has virtually chosen, at the same time, all that which is of necessity connected therewith. There were innumerable possible men equally perfect: the election of some from among them is purely arbitrary (in the judgement of our author). But God, once having chosen them, could not have willed in them anything contrary to human nature. Up to this point the author's words are consistent with his hypothesis; but those that follow go further. He advances the proposition that when God resolved to produce certain creatures he resolved at the same time, by virtue of his infinite goodness, to give them every possible advantage. Nothing, indeed, could be so reasonable, but also nothing could be so contrary to the hypothesis he has put forward, and he does right to overthrow it, rather than prolong the existence of anything so charged with incongruities incompatible with the goodness and wisdom of God. Here is the way to see plainly that this hypothesis cannot harmonize with what has just been said. The first question will be: Will God create something or not, and wherefore? The author has answered that he will create something in order to communicate his goodness. It is therefore no matter of indifference to him whether he shall create or not. Next the question is asked: Will God create such and such a thing, and wherefore? One must needs answer (to speak consistently) that the same goodness makes him choose the best, and indeed the author falls back on that subsequently. But, following his own hypothesis, he answers that God will create such a thing, but that there is no *wherefore*, because God is absolutely indifferent towards creatures, who have their goodness only from his choice. It is true that our author varies somewhat on this point, for he says here (ch. 5, sect. 5, sub-sect. 4, § 12) that God is indifferent to the choice between men of equal perfection, or between equally perfect kinds of rational creatures. Thus, according to this form of expression, he would choose rather the more perfect kind: and as kinds that are of equal perfection harmonize more or less with others, God will choose those that agree best together; there will therefore be no pure and absolute indifference, and the author thus comes back to my principles. But let us speak, as he speaks, in accordance with his hypothesis, and let us assume with him that God chooses certain creatures even though he be absolutely indifferent towards them. He will then just as soon choose creatures that are irregular, ill-shapen, mischievous, unhappy, chaos everlasting, monsters everywhere, scoundrels as sole inhabitants of the earth, devils filling the whole universe, all this rather than excellent systems, shapely forms, upright persons, good angels! No, the author will say, God, when once he had resolved to create men, resolved at the same time to give them all the advantages possible in the world, and it is the same with regard to creatures of other kinds. I answer, that if this advantage were connected of necessity with their nature, the author would be speaking in accordance with his hypothesis. That not being so, however, he must admit that God's resolve to give every possible advantage to men arises from a new election independent of that one which prompted God to make men. But whence comes this new election? Does it also come from mere indifference? If such is the case, nothing prompts God to seek the good of men, and if he sometimes comes to do it, it will be merely by accident. But the author maintains that God was prompted to the choice by his goodness; therefore the good and ill of creatures is no matter of indifference to him, and there are in him primary choices to which the goodness of the object prompts him. He chooses not only to create men, but also to create men as happy as it is possible to be in this system. After that not the least vestige of mere indifference will be left, for we can reason concerning the entire world just as we have reasoned concerning the human race. God resolved to create a world, but he was bound by his goodness at the same time to make choice of such a world as should contain the greatest possible amount of order, regularity, virtue, happiness. For I can see no excuse for saying that whereas God was prompted by his goodness to make the men he has resolved to create as perfect as is possible within this system, he had not the same good intention towards the whole universe. There we have come back again to the goodness of the objects; and pure indifference, where God would act without cause, is altogether destroyed by the very procedure of our gifted author, with whom the force of truth, once the heart of the matter was reached, prevailed over a speculative hypothesis, which cannot admit of any application to the reality of things.

23. Since, therefore, nothing is altogether indifferent to God, who knows all degrees, all effects, all relations of things, and who penetrates at one and the same time all their possible connexions, let us see whether at least the ignorance and insensibility of man can make him absolutely indifferent in his choice. The author

regales us with this pure indifference as with a handsome present. Here are the proofs of it which he gives: (1) We feel it within us. (2) We have experience within ourselves of its marks and its properties. (3) We can show that other causes which might determine our will are insufficient. As for the first point, he asserts that in feeling freedom within us we feel within us at the same time pure indifference. But I do not agree that we feel such indifference, or that this alleged feeling follows upon that of freedom. We feel usually within us something which inclines us to our choice. At times it happens, however, that we cannot account for all our dispositions. If we give our mind to the question, we shall recognize that the constitution of our body and of bodies in our environment, the present or previous temper of our soul, together with countless small things included under these comprehensive headings, may contribute towards our greater or lesser predilection for certain objects, and the variation of our opinions from one time to another. At the same time we shall recognize that none would attribute this to mere indifference, or to some indefinable force of the soul which has the same effect upon objects as colours are said to have upon the chameleon. Thus the author has no cause here to appeal to the judgement of the people: he does so, saying that in many things the people reason better than the philosophers. It is true that certain philosophers have been misled by chimeras, and it would seem that mere indifference is numbered among chimerical notions. But when someone maintains that a thing does not exist because the common herd does not perceive it, here the populace cannot be regarded as a good judge, being, as it is, only guided by the senses. Many people think that air is nothing when it is not stirred by the wind. The majority do not know of imperceptible bodies, the fluid which causes weight or elasticity, magnetic matter, to say nothing of atoms and other indivisible substances. Do we say then that these things are not because the common herd does not know of them? If so, we shall be able to say also that the soul acts sometimes without any disposition or inclination contributing towards the production of its act, because there are many dispositions and inclinations which are not sufficiently perceived by the common herd, for lack of attention and thought. Secondly, as to the marks of the power in question, I have already refuted the claim advanced for it, that it possesses the advantage of making one active, the real cause of one's action, and subject to responsibility and morality: these are not genuine marks of its existence. Here is one the author adduces, which is not genuine either, namely, that we have within us a power of resisting natural appetites, that is to say of resisting not only the senses, but also the reason. But I have already stated this fact: one resists natural appetites through other natural appetites. One sometimes endures inconveniences, and is happy to do so; but that is on account of some hope or of some satisfaction which is combined with the ill and exceeds it: either one anticipates good from it, or one finds good in it. The author asserts that it is through that power to transform appearances which he has introduced on the scene, that we render agreeable what at first displeased us. But who cannot see that the true reason is, that application and attention to the object and custom change our disposition and consequently our natural appetites? Once we become used to a rather high degree of cold or heat, it no longer incommodes us as it formerly did, and yet no one would ascribe this effect to our power of choice. Time is needed, for instance, to bring about that hardening, or rather that callosity, which enables the hands of certain workmen to resist a degree of heat that would burn our hands. The populace, whom the author invokes, guess correctly the cause of this effect, although they sometimes apply it in a laughable manner. Two serving-maids being close to the fire in the kitchen, one who has burnt herself says to the other: Oh, my dear, who will be able to endure the fire of purgatory? The other answers: Don't be absurd, my good woman, one grows used to everything.

24. But (the author will say) this wonderful power which causes us to be indifferent to everything, or inclined towards everything, simply at our own free will, prevails over reason itself. And this is his third proof, namely, that one cannot sufficiently explain our actions without having recourse to this power. One sees numbers of people despising the entreaties of their friends, the counsels of their neighbours, the reproaches of their conscience, discomforts, tortures, death, the wrath of God, hell itself, for the sake of running after follies which have no claim to be good or tolerable, save as being freely chosen by such people. All is well in this argument, with the exception of the last words only. For when one takes an actual instance one will find that there were reasons or causes which led the man to his choice, and that there are very

strong bonds to fasten him thereto. A love-affair, for example, will never have arisen from mere indifference: inclination or passion will have played its part; but habit and stubbornness will cause certain natures to face ruin rather than separation from the beloved. Here is another example cited by the author: an atheist, a man like Lucilio Vanini (that is what many people call him, whereas he himself adopts the magnificent name of Giulio Cesare Vanini in his works), will suffer a preposterous martyrdom for his chimera rather than renounce his impiety. The author does not name Vanini; and the truth is that this man repudiated his wrong opinions, until he was convicted of having published atheistical dogmas and acted as an apostle of atheism. When he was asked whether there was a God, he plucked some grass, saying:

Et levis est cespes qui probet esse Deum.

But since the Attorney General to the Parliament of Toulouse desired to cause annoyance to the First President (so it is said), to whom Vanini was granted considerable access, teaching his children philosophy, if indeed he was not altogether in the service of that magistrate, the inquisition was carried through rigorously. Vanini, seeing that there was no chance of pardon, declared himself, when at the point of death, for what he was, an atheist; and there was nothing very extraordinary in that. But supposing there were an atheist who gave himself up for torture, vanity might be in his case a strong enough motive, as in that of the Gymnosophist, Calanus, and of the Sophist who, according to Lucian's account, was burnt to death of his own will. But the author thinks that that very vanity, that stubbornness, those other wild intentions of persons who otherwise seem to have quite good sense, cannot be explained by the appetites that arise from the representation of good and evil, and that they compel us to have recourse to that transcendent power which transforms good into evil, and evil into good, and the indifferent into good or into evil. But we do not need to go so far, and the causes of our errors are only too visible. Indeed, we can make these transformations, but it is not as with the Fairies, by a mere act of this magic power, but by obscuring and suppressing in one's mind the representations of good or bad qualities which are naturally attached to certain objects, and by contemplating only such representations as conform to our taste or our prejudices; or again, because one attaches to the objects, by dint of thinking of them, certain qualities which are connected with them only accidentally or through our habitual contemplation of them. For example, all my life long I detest a certain kind of good food, because in my childhood I found in it something distasteful, which made a strong impression upon me. On the other hand, a certain natural defect will be pleasing to me, because it will revive within me to some extent the thought of a person I used to esteem or love. A young man will have been delighted by the applause which has been showered upon him after some successful public action; the impression of this great pleasure will have made him remarkably sensitive to reputation; he will think day and night of nothing save what nourishes this passion, and that will cause him to scorn death itself in order to attain his end. For although he may know very well that he will not feel what is said of him after his death, the representation he makes of it for himself beforehand creates a strong impression on his mind. And there are always motives of the same kind in actions which appear most useless and absurd to those who do not enter into these motives. In a word, a strong or oft-repeated impression may alter considerably our organs, our imagination, our memory, and even our reasoning. It happens that a man, by dint of having often related something untrue, which he has perhaps invented, finally comes to believe in it himself. And as one often represents to oneself something pleasing, one makes it easy to imagine, and one thinks it also easy to put into effect, whence it comes that one persuades oneself easily of what one wishes.

Et qui amant ipsi sibi somnia fingunt.

25. Errors are therefore, absolutely speaking, never voluntary, although the will very often contributes towards them indirectly, owing to the pleasure one takes in giving oneself up to certain thoughts, or owing to the aversion one feels for others. Beautiful print in a book will help towards making it persuasive to the reader. The air and manner of a speaker will win the audience for him. One will be inclined to despise doctrines coming from a man one despises or hates, or from another who resembles him in some point that strikes us. I have already said why one is readily disposed to believe what is advantageous or agreeable, and I have known people who at first had changed their religion for worldly

considerations, but who have been persuaded (and well persuaded) afterwards that they had taken the right course. One sees also that stubbornness is not simply wrong choice persevering, but also a disposition to persevere therein, which is due to some good supposed to be inherent in the choice, or some evil imagined as arising from a change. The first choice has perchance been made in mere levity, but the intention to abide by it springs from certain stronger reasons or impressions. There are even some writers on ethics who lay it down that one ought to abide by one's choice so as not to be inconstant or appear so. Yet perseverance is wrong when one despises the warnings of reason, especially when the subject is important enough to be examined carefully; but when the thought of change is unpleasant, one readily averts one's attention from it, and that is the way which most frequently leads one to stubbornness. The author wished to connect stubbornness with his so-called pure indifference. He might then have taken into account that to make us cling to a choice there would be need of more than the mere choice itself or a pure indifference, especially if this choice has been made lightly, and all the more lightly in proportion to the indifference shown. In such a case we shall be readily inclined to reverse the choice, unless vanity, habit, interest or some other motive makes us persevere therein. It must not be supposed either that vengeance pleases without cause. Persons of intense feeling ponder upon it day and night, and it is hard for them to efface the impression of the wrong or the affront they have sustained. They picture for themselves a very great pleasure in being freed from the thought of scorn which comes upon them every moment, and which causes some to find vengeance sweeter than life itself.

Quis vindicta bonum vita jucundius ipsa.

The author would wish to persuade us that usually, when our desire or our aversion is for some object which does not sufficiently deserve it, we have given to it the surplus of good or evil which has affected us, through the alleged power of choice which makes things appear good or evil as we wish. One has had two degrees of natural evil, one gives oneself six degrees of artificial good through the power that can choose without cause. Thus one will have four degrees of net good (ch. 5, sect. 2, § 7). If that could be carried out it would take us far, as I have already said here. The author even thinks that ambition, avarice, the gambling mania and other frivolous passions derive all their force from this power (ch. 5, sect. 5, sub-sect. 6). But there are besides so many false appearances in things, so many imaginations capable of enlarging or diminishing objects, so many unjustified connexions in our arguments, that there is no need of this little Fairy, that is, of this inward power operating as it were by enchantment, to whom the author attributes all these disorders. Indeed, I have already said repeatedly that when we resolve upon some course contrary to acknowledged reason, we are prompted to it by another reason stronger to outward appearance, such as, for instance, is the pleasure of appearing independent and of performing an extraordinary action. There was in days past at the Court of Osnabrück a tutor to the pages, who, like a second Mucius Scaevola, held out his arm into the flame and looked like getting a gangrene, in order to show that the strength of his mind was greater than a very acute pain. Few people will follow his example; and I do not even know if a writer could easily be found who, having once affirmed the existence of a power capable of choosing without cause, or even contrary to reason, would be willing to prove his case by his own example, in renouncing some good benefice or some high office, simply in order to display this superiority of will over reason. But I am sure at the least that an intelligent man would not do so. He would be presently aware that someone would nullify his sacrifice by pointing out to him that he had simply imitated Heliodorus, Bishop of Larissa. That man (so it is said) held his book on Theagenes and Chariclea dearer than his bishopric; and such a thing may easily happen when a man has resources enabling him to dispense with his office and when he is sensitive to reputation. Thus every day people are found ready to sacrifice their advantages to their caprices, that is to say, actual goods to the mere semblance of them.

26. If I wished to follow step by step the arguments of our gifted author, which often come back to matters previously considered in our inquiry, usually however with some elegant and well-phrased addition, I should be obliged to proceed too far; but I hope that I shall be able to avoid doing so, having, as I think, sufficiently met all his reasons. The best thing is that with him practice usually corrects and amends theory. After having advanced the hypothesis, in the second section of this fifth chapter,

that we approach God through the capacity to choose without reason, and that this power being of the noblest kind its exercise is the most capable of making one happy, things in the highest degree paradoxical, since it is reason which leads us to imitate God and our happiness lies in following reason: after that, I say, the author provides an excellent corrective, for he says rightly (§ 5) that in order to be happy we must adapt our choice to things, since things are scarcely prone to adapt themselves to us, and that this is in effect adapting oneself to the divine will. Doubtless that is well said, but it implies besides that our will must be guided as far as possible by the reality of the objects, and by true representations of good and evil. Consequently also the motives of good and evil are not opposed to freedom, and the power of choosing without cause, far from ministering to our happiness, will be useless and even highly prejudicial. Thus it is happily the case that this power nowhere exists, and that it is 'a being of reasoning reason', as some Schoolmen call the fictions that are not even possible. As for me, I should have preferred to call them 'beings of non-reasoning reason'. Also I think that the third section (on wrong elections) may pass, since it says that one must not choose things that are impossible, inconsistent, harmful, contrary to the divine will, or already taken by others. Moreover, the author remarks appositely that by prejudicing the happiness of others needlessly one offends the divine will, which desires that all be happy as far as it is possible. I will say as much of the fourth section, where there is mention of the source of wrong elections, which are error or ignorance, negligence, fickleness in changing too readily, stubbornness in not changing in time, and bad habits; finally there is the importunity of the appetites, which often drive us inopportunely towards external things. The fifth section is designed to reconcile evil elections or sins with the power and goodness of God; and this section, as it is diffuse, is divided into sub-sections. The author has cumbered himself needlessly with a great objection: for he asserts that without a power to choose that is altogether indifferent in the choice there would be no sin. Now it was very easy for God to refuse to creatures a power so irrational. It was sufficient for them to be actuated by the representations of goods and evils; it was therefore easy, according to the author's hypothesis, for God to prevent sin. To extricate himself from this difficulty, he has no other resource than to state that if this power were removed from things the world would be nothing but a purely passive machine. But that is the very thing which I have disproved. If this power were missing in the world (as in fact it is), one would hardly complain of the fact. Souls will be well content with the representations of goods and evils for the making of their choice, and the world will remain as beautiful as it is. The author comes back to what he had already put forward here, that without this power there would be no happiness. But I have given a sufficient answer to that, and there is not the slightest probability in this assertion and in certain other paradoxes he puts forward here to support his principal paradox.

27. He makes a small digression on prayer (sub-sect. 4), saying that those who pray to God hope for some change in the order of nature; but it seems as though, according to his opinion, they are mistaken. In reality, men will be content if their prayers are heard, without troubling themselves as to whether the course of nature is changed in their favour, or not. Indeed, if they receive succour from good angels there will be no change in the general order of things. Also this opinion of our author is a very reasonable one, that there is a system of spiritual substances, just as there is of corporeal substances, and that the spiritual have communication with one another, even as bodies do. God employs the ministry of angels in his rule of mankind, without any detriment to the order of nature. Nevertheless, it is easier to put forward theories on these matters than to explain them, unless one have recourse to my system of Harmony. But the author goes somewhat further. He believes that the mission of the Holy Spirit was a great miracle in the beginning, but that now his operations within us are natural. I leave it to him to explain his opinion, and to settle the matter with other theologians. Yet I observe that he finds the natural efficacy of prayer in the power it has of making the soul better, of overcoming the passions, and of winning for oneself a certain degree of new grace. I can say almost the same things on my hypothesis, which represents the will as acting only in accordance with motives; and I am immune from the difficulties in which the author has become involved over his power of choosing without cause. He is in great embarrassment also with regard to the foreknowledge of God. For if the soul is perfectly indifferent in its choice how is it possible to foresee this choice? and what sufficient reason will one be able to find for the knowledge of a

thing, if there is no reason for its existence? The author puts off to some other occasion the solution of this difficulty, which would require (according to him) an entire work. For the rest, he sometimes speaks pertinently, and in conformity with my principles, on the subject of moral evil. He says, for example (sub-sect. 6), that vices and crimes do not detract from the beauty of the universe, but rather add to it, just as certain dissonances would offend the ear by their harshness if they were heard quite alone, and yet in combination they render the harmony more pleasing. He also points out divers goods involved in evils, for instance, the usefulness of prodigality in the rich and avarice in the poor; indeed it serves to make the arts flourish. We must also bear in mind that we are not to judge the universe by the small size of our globe and of all that is known to us. For the stains and defects in it may be found as useful for enhancing the beauty of the rest as patches, which have nothing beautiful in themselves, are by the fair sex found adapted to embellish the whole face, although they disfigure the part they cover. Cotta, in Cicero's book, had compared providence, in its granting of reason to men, to a physician who allows wine to a patient, notwithstanding that he foresees the misuse which will be made thereof by the patient, at the expense of his life. The author replies that providence does what wisdom and goodness require, and that the good which accrues is greater than the evil. If God had not given reason to man there would have been no man at all, and God would be like a physician who killed someone in order to prevent his falling ill. One may add that it is not reason which is harmful in itself, but the absence of reason; and when reason is ill employed we reason well about means, but not adequately about an end, or about that bad end we have proposed to ourselves. Thus it is always for lack of reason that one does an evil deed. The author also puts forward the objection made by Epicurus in the book by Lactantius on the wrath of God. The terms of the objection are more or less as follows. Either God wishes to banish evils and cannot contrive to do so, in which case he would be weak; or he can abolish them, and will not, which would be a sign of malignity in him; or again he lacks power and also will, which would make him appear both weak and jealous; or finally he can and will, but in this case it will be asked why he then does not banish evil, if he exists? The author replies that God cannot banish evil, that he does not wish to either, and that notwithstanding he is neither malicious nor weak. I should have preferred to say that he can banish evil, but that he does not wish to do so absolutely, and rightly so, because he would then banish good at the same time, and he would banish more good than evil. Finally our author, having finished his learned work, adds an Appendix, in which he speaks of the Divine Laws. He fittingly divides these laws into natural and positive. He observes that the particular laws of the nature of animals must give way to the general laws of bodies, that God is not in reality angered when his laws are violated, but that order demanded that he who sins should bring an evil upon himself, and that he who does violence to others should suffer violence in his turn. But he believes that the positive laws of God rather indicate and forecast the evil than cause its infliction. And that gives him occasion to speak of the eternal damnation of the wicked, which no longer serves either for correction or example, and which nevertheless satisfies the retributive justice of God, although the wicked bring their unhappiness upon themselves. He suspects, however, that these punishments of the wicked bring some advantage to virtuous people. He is doubtful also whether it is not better to be damned than to be nothing: for it might be that the damned are fools, capable of clinging to their state of misery owing to a certain perversity of mind which, he maintains, makes them congratulate themselves on their false judgements in the midst of their misery, and take pleasure in finding fault with the will of God. For every day one sees peevish, malicious, envious people who enjoy the thought of their ills, and seek to bring affliction upon themselves. These ideas are not worthy of contempt, and I have sometimes had the like myself, but I am far from passing final judgement on them. I related, in § 271 of the essays written to oppose M. Bayle, the fable of the Devil's refusal of the pardon a hermit offers him on God's behalf. Baron André Taifel, an Austrian nobleman, Knight of the Court of Ferdinand Archduke of Austria who became the second emperor of that name, alluding to his name (which appears to mean Devil in German) assumed as his emblem a devil or satyr, with this Spanish motto, *Mas perdido, y menos arrepentido*, the more lost, the less repentant, which indicates a hopeless passion from which one cannot free oneself. This motto was afterwards repeated by the Spanish Count of Villamediana when he was said to be in love with the Queen. Coming to the question why evil often happens to the good and good to the wicked, our illustrious author thinks that it has been sufficiently answered, and that hardly any doubt remains on that point. He observes nevertheless that one may often doubt whether good people who endure affliction have not been made good by their very misfortune, and whether the fortunate wicked have not perhaps been spoilt by prosperity. He adds that we are often bad judges, when it is a question of recognizing not only a virtuous man, but also a happy man. One often honours a hypocrite, and one despises another whose solid virtue is without pretence. We are poor judges of happiness also, and often felicity is hidden from sight under the rags of a contented poor man, while it is sought in vain in the palaces of certain of the great. Finally the author observes, that the greatest felicity here on earth lies in the hope of future happiness, and thus it may be said that to the wicked nothing happens save what is of service for correction or chastisement, and to the good nothing save what ministers to their greater good. These conclusions entirely correspond to my opinion, and one can say nothing more appropriate for the conclusion of this work.

CAUSA DEI ASSERTA
PER JUSTITIAM EJUS

cum caeteris ejus perfectionibus cunctisque
actionibus conciliatam.

The original edition of the Theodicy contained a fourth appendix under this title. It presented in scholastic Latin a formal summary of the positive doctrine expressed by the French treatise. It satisfied the academic requirements of its day, but would not, presumably, be of interest to many modern readers, and is consequently omitted here.

INDEX

INDEX

INDEX